Understanding China's Urbanization

The Great Demographic, Spatial, Economic, and Social Transformation

Li ZHANG

Associate Professor, Department of Urban Planning, Tongji University, Shanghai, China

Richard LeGates

Emeritus Professor, Department of Urban Studies and Planning, San Francisco State University, USA

Min ZHAO

Professor, Department of Urban Planning, Tongji University, Shanghai, China

EE Edward Elgar PUBLISHING

Cheltenham, UK • Northampton, MA, USA

Published by
Edward Elgar Publishing Limited
The Lypiatts
15 Lansdown Road
Cheltenham
Glos GL50 2JA
UK

Edward Elgar Publishing, Inc.
William Pratt House
9 Dewey Court
Northampton
Massachusetts 01060
USA

A catalogue record for this book
is available from the British Library

Library of Congress Control Number: 2015950302

This book is available electronically in the **Elgar**online
Social and Political Science subject collection
DOI 10.4337/9781783474745

MIX
Paper from responsible sources
FSC® C013604

ISBN 978 1 78347 473 8 (cased)
ISBN 978 1 78347 474 5 (eBook)

Typeset by Servis Filmsetting Ltd, Stockport, Cheshire
Printed and bound by CPI Group (UK) Ltd, Croydon, CR0 4YY

Contents

Acknowledgments

Without the support and assistance of many people this book would never have been written. The editors and staff at Edward Elgar Publishing, our faculty colleagues and students at Tongji and San Francisco State Universities, our research assistants at Tongji, scholars we work with through the International Association for China Planning, Universities of Singapore and Melbourne, and the Urban Planning Society of China, China experts who critiqued drafts of our work and shared their own research at sites we visited while we were writing this book—the University of Hawaii and the Rockefeller Center in Bellagio, Italy—and our families.

Our Tongji graduate student assistants Lijuan Wang and Chuyang Lin deserve special thanks for their contributions to our field research, literature review, preparation of data graphics, figures and maps, proofreading and other help.

We are grateful for the support of the editors and staff at Edward Elgar Publishing who enthusiastically supported this project and helped see the manuscript through to completion. We are particularly indebted to Edward Elgar, the founder of Edward Elgar Publishing, Matt Pitman, who commissioned the book, Alexandra O'Connell Senior Supervising Editor, and Laura Mann who helped manage production. Other Edward Elgar Publishing staff at all levels performed their responsibilities with the professionalism and efficiency that is the hallmark of this remarkable publisher.

Our colleagues at Tongji University's Department of Urban Planning supported this project in many ways. Special thanks to Professors Zhenwei Peng, Guiqing Yang, Huizhi Geng and Jian Zhuo and Ph.D candidate Chen Chen and Jinwei Hao. Also thanks to the Scholarly Monograph (Nature Science) Publishing Foundation of Tongji University, TJAD grant, TJUPDI grant and Summit Plan Grant.

Professor Jieming Zhu from the National University of Singapore, Professor Sunsheng Han from the University of Melbourne, and Professor Gonghao Cui from Nanjing University and Nan Shi, vice-chairman of the Urban Planning Society of China helped shape our understanding of urbanization and urban planning and provided suggestions and feedback on our work.

Faculty at the University of Hawaii, Manoa's East-West Center and Department of Urban and Regional Planning (DURP) critiqued our preliminary findings and shared their own research during a three week visit and joint symposium in February, 2015. Special thanks to College of Social Science Dean Denise Konan, DURP chair Dolores Foley and Professor Ashok Das from the University of Hawaii and Nancy Lewis, Shabir Cheema at the East-West Center. We are especially grateful to Professor John Friedmann for his insightful comments on panels and the entire symposium.

We are indebted to the Rockefeller Foundation for awarding us writing residencies to finish writing our book at the Rockefeller Center in Bellagio, Italy in May and June 2015.

Our spouses, children, and grandchildren gave us their support and understanding and made time available for us to finish our work. Special thanks to Li's wife, Min Dai and Richard LeGates' wife, Joanne Fraser LeGates.

Introduction

The scale of China's urbanization since modernization began with reform and opening up after the Mao era is unprecedented in human history. It is one of the great earth-changing phenomena of the late twentieth and early twenty-first centuries. China's urbanization is now entering a critical phase with some 100 million additional urban residents projected by 2020. Understanding and responding to China's urbanization is of paramount importance to Chinese government officials, policymakers, and urban and regional planners at every level if China is to continue to modernize and create a livable and sustainable urban system. It is critical to developing countries that they learn from China's experience. As China assumes overwhelming dominance in Asia and a leading role in the global economy, understanding China's urbanization is of interest to scholars and practitioners throughout Asia and everywhere in the world.

The Chinese leadership sees China at a crossroads now—needing a "new style" of human-centered urbanization for a more efficient, equitable, environmentally sensitive and harmonious society. The way in which China urbanizes in the next few decades will have a critical impact on the world economy, global climate change, international relations and a host of other critical issues as well as for the lives of a fifth of the world's population.

WHY WE WROTE THIS BOOK

One main reason we chose to write this book is because China's urbanization is so important. Throughout we present current information on the scale of China's urban transformation and discuss the implications for China and the world.

A second reason we wrote this book is simply to tell the astonishing story of China's recent urbanization. While this book contains a great deal of detailed information, we have worked hard to make it a readable book that will tell the story of China's urbanization in a way that is suitable both to readers familiar with China and those who are not. Newcomers will find the literature review in Chapter 1 and the figures and tables particularly useful, as they give a good picture of China's urbanization. Seasoned

China hands will find much new information and original interpretations in this book as well as up-to-date statistics on all the critical aspects of China's urbanization. Illustrations from our field research through the book show readers concrete examples that illustrate the text. There is no reason why a scholarly book has to be dull—particularly when the subject is as fascinating as China.

A third reason we wrote this book is to draw together all the latest material on Chinese urbanization in one place—summarizing both the existing literature and the statistics. Chapter 1 provides an overview of the literature in English and Chinese, and the bibliography at the end of the book and citations throughout are a comprehensive reference to the literature in both languages. The many tables, figures, maps, line drawings, and appendices present the most up-to-date and comprehensive data about urbanization available at the time this book went to press (summer, 2015). China changes fast and the latest statistics we use are often quite different from data that are only a few years old. The descriptive information in the book represents much more than a collection of existing data. Many of the tables, figures, maps, and data graphics constitute our own synthesis of current data not available anywhere else. We devoted a great deal of time to presenting this information in as easy-to-understand form as possible without shying away from necessary complexity.

The fourth reason we wrote this book is to help clear away the great body of existing misinformation and half truths about Chinese urbanization now in print and available on the web. China is a huge, diverse and rapidly changing country. Policy implementation has been decentralized. Generalizing about issues like hukou status, what compensation farmers receive for land takings, or what social services urban residents receive compared with rural residents is dangerous. The answers to all these questions vary by province and local government within provinces. Statistics that are aggregated to the national or provincial level hide dramatic variations. The meaning of words, even as basic as the word "urban" is different from usage in other countries, and sometimes differs from place to place in China.

While telling a good story about an important topic, presenting accurate and up-to-date data, and dispelling errors are all worthy objectives, this book is intended to do more than that. Professors Zhang and Zhao have thought long and deeply about Chinese urbanization and conducted research on aspects of urbanization throughout China. LeGates has been studying and writing about urbanization for more than four decades. While we report the best mainstream research and conventional policy solutions proposed by government sources and scholars throughout the book, we have developed distinct alternative views about many issues related to Chinese urbanization. Contrary to the conventional wisdom, we do not think that hukou has blocked or driven urbanization nearly as much as most scholars assume and that it will be a much less important determinant of where migration occurs than structural change in the Chinese economy in the future. While we agree that China's dual urban/rural divide is a serious problem and that urban migrants need to be much better incorporated into the social welfare system, our field research found that many rural residents want to retain rural hukou and there are often good reasons for them to do so. As central and western China develop, the transportation infrastructure in peri-urban areas improves and more people can get from villages to urban work, there are more part-time and seasonal job opportunities in towns and villages, and as first generation migrants return to their villages of origin, we believe that great divisions between developed and developing regions of China will shrink and the dual urban/rural divide will begin to close. These and other thoughts and conclusions are presented throughout the book.

For us, writing this book together has been an experiment in how Chinese and Western scholars can collaborate, and is the fifth reason why we wrote the book. There is universal agreement that China can learn from the West, but must adapt ideas and policies to have "Chinese characteristics." This is a book about urbanization with Chinese characteristics. But what does this really mean? In writing this book we wrestled with two main issues: (1) how much detail to include on the distinctly Chinese characteristics of institutions in order to provide Western readers an in-depth understanding without overwhelming them with detail, and (2) how to describe analogies between Chinese institutions and practices of North American and European counterparts that will help Western readers understand distinctly Chinese reality without distracting them from the book's focus on China. The discussions of migration, hukou, and administrative divisions in China provide more detail that any existing English language book. But these are complex topics with great variation. We could have written much more. Our goal was to provide an in-depth description of each of these important topics and many more that are much better than existing dated and simplistic accounts, but at the same time any reader can understand with patience and careful reading. Throughout the book readers will find a few sentences or a paragraph describing how a current Chinese institution or practice is similar to or different from Western counterparts. These include topics as varied as sprawl, greenbelts, transit oriented development, transfer of development rights, bus rapid transit, urban villages, factory towns, immigration Green Cards, land takings jurisprudence, definitions of towns and cities, independent retirement accounts, and social security—all of which exist in China and all of which do, in fact, have Chinese characteristics that make them different from counterparts in the West. Sprawl in China is not the same as sprawl in Los Angeles. Guangzhou's bus rapid transit system (BRT) is not the same as in Curitiba, Brazil. Even the Orange County subdivision in Beijing—consisting of exact physical replicas of award winning Orange County, California single family detached homes—is not really like Orange County, California. It has distinctly Chinese economic, social, and spatial characteristics. Readers can judge for themselves how well we succeeded in striking the correct balance between readability and detail and whether or not the analogies we have drawn help readers understand Chinese institutions.

Most of the empirical work and analysis in this book was done by Zhang, Zhao and their students over the last ten years. Nearly all of the material in this book is new and has never been published in any form until now. With very few exceptions, it has been unavailable to English language readers or even Chinese language readers.

Our collaboration was a learning experience for us and we hope that other scholars can learn from our experience. We found that translations of draft book chapters written originally by Zhang in Chinese required substantial rewriting. Information that is common knowledge to Chinese readers required explanation. Institutions and policies could be misunderstood without Western context. The English translation needed work to meet our standards of both detail and readability. One of LeGates' main contributions to the book was to rewrite chapters at an appropriate level with explanations of differences and similarities between China and the West and to add examples and references to help a Western audience understand the material deeply. We hope this will inspire other collaborations to bring good Chinese scholarship to Western audiences.

A sixth reason for this book is to provide a theoretical explanation of Chinese urbanization with Chinese characteristics. Our book is informed by and refers to many theories developed by Western economists, planners, sociologists, anthropologists, and development experts and many new theories developed by other Chinese scholars adapting theory to the special situation in China or proposing entirely new ideas based on China's experience. An important aspect of this book is to bring together these two streams of theory and augment it with our own theoretical explanation of Chinese urbanization. In addition to helping Western scholars and practitioners better understand Chinese urbanization theory we believe other developing countries have much to learn from China. Many countries are borrowing or want to borrow from China's experience. But to do this they need a deep theoretical understanding that will help them determine which policies might apply to them and how they will need to adapt them.

Our final goal in writing this book was to provide useful information that can help improve Chinese urbanization. This book has a prescriptive component. We pride ourselves in doing applied policy-oriented research; not theoretical academic scholarship unconnected to policy choices. As Chinese government officials, policymakers, and urban planners at every level struggle to understand what a "new style" urbanization for China can be like and how to implement it, "scientific" planning based on data we present throughout this book will be necessary. Policymakers face normative choices. While it is not our place to tell policymakers with local knowledge how they should act, we trust that providing them useful and up-to-date information and describing the best available mainstream research and our own alternatives will help improve urbanization decisions throughout China at every level.

CHINA'S URBANIZATION AND DEVELOPMENT

In a little over thirty years China has transformed itself from an overwhelmingly poor rural society to a majority-urban society above the middle level of development for countries worldwide. Since 1978 the number of Chinese officially classified as living de facto in urban areas has grown by over 558 million people from 18 percent of the population to 55 percent in 2014 (NBSC-csy, 2013; NBSC, 2015). From a backward rural society comprised mostly of small-scale traditional farmers, China has modernized dramatically and become globally connected. Many aspects of Chinese society have caught up with or surpassed the most advanced developed societies. China has lifted more than half a billion people from abject poverty. By virtually every measure—growth in gross domestic product (GDP), increase in disposable income, foreign reserves, high school and college graduates, new housing units, railroads, highways, airports, bridges, ports, and other infrastructure—China has outstripped other countries in the world during the last thirty years. At the same time, China's development and urbanization have separated parts of migrating family members from parents and children, fouled China's air and water with industrial pollution, depleted resources, created social conflict over land conversion, allowed the income, infrastructure, and social service gap between urban and rural areas to widen, littered the landscape with some irrational development zones and enterprises, allowed development that is much too dense or not nearly dense enough, failed to create a sustainable system of local government revenue, and replicated on a vast scale many other urban problems that every country confronts. There is consensus that China must adopt a "new style" urbanization model from now on.

What exactly that should be and how to implement it are high on China's agenda.

WHO WE ARE

This book is the result of more than two years of collaboration among the three authors—two professors of Urban Planning from Tongji University (Zhang and Zhao) and one emeritus professor of Urban Studies and Planning from San Francisco State University (LeGates).

Li Zhang is an Associate Professor of Urban Planning at Tongji University, Shanghai. His research areas include urbanization in China and developing countries, countryside resilience and rural aging issues in China and East Asia, city regions, migration in China, and urban growth strategies. He received his PhD in urban planning in 2010, MA in 2005, and BA in 2002 from Tongji University. Professor Zhang was a visiting student at the University of Melbourne from March 2008 to March 2009. He is the co-editor of the book *New Style Urbanization: Transformation and Countermeasures* (Tongji University Press, Shanghai, 2014) and contributor to several academic books in Chinese and English. He has published more than twenty articles in *Urban Planning Review*, *Urban Planning Forum*, and other top Chinese urban planning journals. His research has also been published in English in *Population Mobility*, the *Journal of International Development*, *Planning Review, and Urban Planning and Management in China* (Springer, Berlin and London, 2015). In 2009 the Urban Planning Society of China awarded him first prize for the best article on urban planning by a young scholar for his article on "Transformation of Population Structure and the Second Transition of Urbanization in China." He has twice received Jin Jing-Chang Planning Foundation awards. In 2010 his dissertation was selected as the best PhD thesis in architecture and urban planning in China and nominated as one of the best 100 PhD theses in China that year. In 2014 he was selected as one of the ten best young urban planners in Shanghai.

Richard LeGates is an Emeritus Professor of Urban Studies and Planning at San Francisco State University (SFSU), where he taught from 1973 to 2010. He has been a Visiting Professor at Tongji University's Department of Urban Planning since 2008. Professor LeGates served for twelve years as director of the SFSU Urban Studies and Planning program and two years as director of SFSU's Masters of Public Administration program. He is the co-editor of *The City Reader 6th edition* (Routledge, London, 2015), co-series editor of the ten volume Routledge Urban Reader series, and co-editor of *The Chinese City Reader* (published in Chinese by

China Architectural and Building Press, 2013). Professor LeGates was the board secretary of the International Association for China Planning from 2009 to 2012. In 2012 he received the Urban Planning Society of China and Jin Jing-Chang Planning Foundation award for the best article in a Chinese urban planning journal for a co-authored article on "Urban Planning Theory in China after the Global Economic Crisis."

Min Zhao is a Professor of Urban Planning at Tongji University and the Executive Director of the Shanghai Urban Planning Society. He received BA and MA degrees in Urban Planning from Tongji in 1982 and 1986 and was a Research Fellow at the University of Melbourne's School of Environmental Planning in 1988–89. Since 2009 Professor Zhao has headed Tongji University's national teaching and research team. Previously he served as the head of Tongji's Department of Urban Planning from 1999 to 2006, and as assistant to the director of the Shanghai Urban Planning Bureau from 1995 to 1996. He is the author of many books, book chapters and journal articles on the theory and practice of Chinese urban planning, urban and regional economics, migration, urban community development planning, spatial administration, land use and rural development, property rights, and regional development. He has written articles in English in *Ekistics* and *Annals of the Regional Planning Society*. Since 2000 Professor Zhao has been awarded a number of prizes in the Shanghai Urban Planning and Design awards. In 2014 he won the Urban Planning Society of China and Jin Jing-Chang Planning Foundation award for the best article in a Chinese urban planning journal for a co-authored article on "Revisiting China's Urbanization in a Bottom-up Context and Assessing its Policy Implications."

WHO THIS BOOK IS FOR

Cities throughout the world can learn from the concepts and programs that China has developed as it has struggled with how to manage urbanization in the last three decades. China has a long track record with experiments in urban policies and programs and cities worldwide can learn from China's many successes and notable accomplishments and also from unsuccessful experiments.

This book should be of interest to academics—faculty, students, and researchers interested in urban studies, urban and regional planning, economics, geography, urban design, public administration, urban governance, development studies, China studies, Asian studies and other social sciences and applied public-policy programs. The accurate and up-to-date detail in the book and our original findings and interpretations should be of interest to China experts, government officials, staff of international development agencies and non-profits, and professionals involved in real estate, engineering, finance, and business management in the private sector. We have taken pains to make the book accessible to non-China experts and serious students and practitioners at every level. Chapter 1, which reviews the literature on urbanization in general and Chinese urbanization in particular, provides a good introduction to readers who are not very familiar with China or the urbanization, urban development, and urban planning literature. The bibliography contains references to the most important books, articles, and source material on Chinese urbanization in English and Chinese and citations throughout the book are keyed to the bibliography. We summarize conflicting opinions on the most important topics about urbanization in China and citations direct readers to source material by scholars who both agree and disagree with our conclusions.

HOW OUR BOOK IS DIFFERENT FROM OTHER BOOKS ABOUT CHINESE URBANIZATION

The academic literature on China's urbanization, economic development, and planning has exploded in recent years. The literature review chapter describes recent books and articles that summarize Chinese urbanization by Weiping Wu and Piper Glaubatz, Xuefei Ren, John Friedmann, Sunsheng Han, Fulong Wu, You-Tien Hsing, Yasheng Huang, Cindy Fan, Cam Wing Chan, Laurence Ma, Thomas Campanella, Tom Miller and others and the bibliography references hundreds of other books and journal articles of interest.

With all of this existing literature an important question is why do we need this book? Some of the reasons why our book is necessary have already been discussed above. It is unique in drawing together the most recent scholarship and data; grounding our findings in classic theory from economists, demographers, geographers and planners; providing cross-sectional and longitudinal analysis of data at scales ranging from the national to the village level; juxtaposing both macro-level structural analysis from secondary data and analysis on our own interviews and survey research; and articulating normative theory and making specific suggestions about how to apply our findings to the solution of urbanization problems.

Our book also reaches new conclusions. It is independent research. We were not accountable to any government body or funding source. While we cite mainstream research and views throughout and describe their conclusions and the reasons behind them objectively, we also express our own opinions and disagreements with mainstream views. In some cases our conclusions confirm other research, or generally confirm it, but add detail, qualifications, or exceptions. In other cases we reached conclusions that are different from the mainstream. Our conclusions are described in each chapter and summarized in the final chapter. Among the most important are: (1) migration is driven more by objective economic and social conditions than by hukou, (2) rural migrants' decisions are based more on social issues, such as taking care of their parents and a better rural environment than economic consideration when they make their settlement choices, (3) the distinction between urban and rural work no longer exists in many peri-urban areas where the workforce engages in both agricultural and non-agricultural work, (4) many aging early urban migrants are returning to rural areas because of necessity or choice, (5) urbanization of towns is an essential and promising part of China's urbanization, (6) towns and villages need more financial resources and decision-making authority to stimulate bottom-up rural urbanization, (7) structuring Chinese urbanization in polycentric networks within large urban agglomerations is a promising strategy—particularly in the most economically advanced regions of China, and (8) a planar pattern of towns and villages complements cities of different scales in an urban network.

OUR METHODOLOGY

Most books on China's development and urbanization are heavy on macro-level analysis of national level quantitative data from existing secondary sources. Chinese government entities at every level generate statistics. In the past these statistics were often self-serving and their validity questionable. This is still the case with some lower level statistics. But at the national and provincial level and in large cities many sophisticated demographers, economists, statisticians, and others are now working hard to develop good measures and gather and present valid and reliable data on urbanization. Chinese university research budgets have more than quintupled in the last decade and the number and educational level of Chinese faculty doing high quality urban research has increased rapidly. So has the number of qualified graduate students and recent graduates capable of doing good urban research. There has been rapid growth of high quality independent academic research on urbanization by scholars at Chinese universities and research centers and universities and research centers in other countries. Since so much of the best literature on Chinese urbanization is new, our up-to-date literature review and references to recent scholarship through the book make an important contribution.

One major approach in this book involves presentation of existing high quality secondary data—often simplified and reformatted for clarity—in tables, figures, data graphics, and maps. We present the most recent cross-sectional data available (summer, 2015) from the most reliable sources. Throughout the book there is re-analysis of secondary data. We frequently combined data from multiple sources or re-analyzed existing source data in original ways.

There is a difference between our research and most existing research on Chinese urbanization. Most analyses of Chinese urbanization suffer from overgeneralization. Because China is such a huge and populous country, national-level averages disguise great regional variation. We draw on data from provincial and local sources as well as national data. Our analysis is at multiple scales: national, the three great Chinese regions (east, central, and west), among provinces, within provinces, and sometimes at the city, county, town, township and even village level.

China is changing rapidly, and dated longitudinal data also leads to false conclusions and overgeneralization in much of the existing literature. In much of our longitudinal analysis we group findings into time periods. Over time new data will be necessary to update information in this book, but for the near-term our data should provide a good benchmark and our methodology a basis for updating.

Macro-level structural analysis is not enough. As China has moved more and more to a market economy and relaxed restrictions on individual mobility and other choices, understanding the reasons for individual choices is increasingly important. The Chinese often make decisions as a household, so *household* choices matter. The second prong of our research approach has been to gather information on individual and household choices through interviews and survey research at sites in eastern, central, and western China. Throughout this book we complement information from the existing literature, secondary data analysis, and interviews with evidence from households and individuals. We have found that even in the remotest areas of rural China even the least educated people are generally well-informed and make strategic choices that reflect their own values. In our approach, macroeconomic structural forces and micro-individual choice theory intersect.

THEORY

Good research is always grounded in theory. Our book draws upon the best available theory about urbanization from geographers, economists, political scientists, demographers and urban planners. Throughout the book we test classic theory against the reality we have found in our analysis of secondary data and our own fieldwork. Chapter 1 provides an overview of the main theories and references to the literature in which the theory can be found. Further elaboration of existing theory useful to understanding aspects of urbanization occurs in each of the chapters. Wherever we discuss existing theory we go on to describe whether or not our findings fit the theory and, to the extent that they do not, offer our own elaborations and new theory. Chapter 9 summarizes our overall theory of "urbanization with Chinese characteristics" building on pioneering work by scholars such as Arthur O. Lewis on the absorption of surplus rural labor into the modern urban sector of developing countries, Hollis Chenery and Moises Syrquin about the relationship between economic development and urbanization, Kingsley Davis and Ray Northam on the urbanization "S" curve, Ernest George Raventein, Donald J. Bogue, and Everett Lee about laws of migration, Indermit Gill and Homi Kharas about the "middle-income trap" facing countries at a middle level of development, Manuel Castells' theories of the network society, informational city and the space of flows, Peter Taylor's conceptualization of the world city network, Abraham Maslow's hierarchy of needs, Peter Hall's idea about polycentric urban networks and our own theory about how endogenous institutional reform and exogenous globalization affect China's urbanization.

Our hope is that the theory of double dual track urbanization with Chinese characteristics advanced in Chapter 9 and our synthesis and interpretation of other useful theory will be well received by western China scholars and practitioners and English-speaking scholars and practitioners in other countries who do not read Chinese as well as Chinese scholars and practitioners. It is a fascinating story. Enjoy!

Li Zhang, Richard LeGates, and Min Zhao
Bellagio, Italy, June 2015

1. Understanding China's urbanization

This book is intended to provide the most comprehensive and up-to-date description of Chinese urbanization since the beginning of the period of reform and opening up that began in 1978. It will draw together and summarize the complex and rapidly changing body of demographic and statistical information on Chinese urbanization. Beyond the numbers, it will present results of our extensive fieldwork in all parts of China and an original theory of the way in which political, economic, and social forces have shaped the vast transformation that has occurred as the urban population of China has grown from 17.9 percent in 1978 to over 54.8 percent in 2014.

China's society has undergone a series of radical institutional transformations since reform and opening up. Central governmental control has been reduced and partially decentralized and China now relies largely on market forces as it has changed from an agricultural society to an urban one. This is a true urban transformation with economic, social, spatial and demographic dimensions. Simple population counts or studies that only describe the relationship between economic growth and urbanization do not adequately describe the dynamics or nature of the change. Aggregate numbers tell us little about China's urban transformation. China is a vast and diverse country and the extent of urbanization varies enormously from region to region due to different development conditions (Li, 2008). Many of China's provinces have land areas and/or populations larger than entire countries. The historical, cultural, physical, resource, social, political, and economic features of different provinces and regions within provinces are as different from each other as individual countries. It is helpful to think of China as a "country of countries." Most studies, however, focus only on aggregate urbanization statistics or on the role of China's changing economic system in shaping Chinese urbanization and neglect other dimensions of China's urban transformation.

A basic hypothesis of this book is that China's urban transformation is related to many factors—not only differences in the regions and regional policies, but also governmental urban development and finance policies, administrative divisions, the household registration (hukou) system, globalization, and migration. These factors operate at the level of regional and provincial development and will affect future urbanization trends.

Based on this hypothesis, this book focuses on four key attributes of urbanization—demography, economics, space and society. It describes the whole process of urban transformation, including the impact of institutional transitions and the influence of globalization as an external force with the best available statistical data and supporting materials.

The book argues that China's urbanization process since reform and opening up has shifted from central government control of the planned economy to a new phase supervised by the government, but primarily driven by market forces. This deep social transformation and changes in the external environment due to globalization have jointly affected regional migration and have created regional disparities in urbanization that have produced a disconnect between the quantities and qualities of Chinese regional urbanization development.

We divide Chinese urbanization since the late 1970s into three phases: (1) the period of the planned economy from 1949 to 1977; (2) the period of reform and opening up from 1978 to 2013; and (3) a new phase beginning in 2014 characterized by a new style of urbanization. Of course the transitions were not immediate. We argue that the great ongoing transition from a planned to a market-based economy is beginning to have a parallel second transition from favoring the quantity of urbanization to improving the quality of urbanization. We argue that the second transition is necessary and indispensable for China's future.

Based on an analysis of the first transition and our examination of population structure and evolving social and economic development in different regions of China, our study concludes that overall the rate of increase in Chinese urbanization will continue, but is likely to slow down in the near future. Much of China's urbanization in the next 30 years will take place in central and western China. Rather than a problem, we argue that this slowing down in the rate of urbanization and the shift from eastern China to central and western China creates opportunities for China to focus on the quality of urbanization, rather than just focusing on the quantity of urbanization as in the past. But achieving the second transition of urbanization in China will require changing deeply embedded conservative ideas about development.

CHINA'S URBANIZATION

Stages of China's Recent Urbanization

For millennia, China was a traditional agricultural society. Some modern urbanization occurred in foreign-dominated treaty port cities as early as the mid-nineteenth century and between 1920 and the mid-1930s there was additional modest urbanization in a few areas of China. But a quarter-century of war with Japan and civil war disrupted normal development and urbanization in China between the late 1930s and the founding of the People's Republic of China in 1949. The years 1949, 1961 and 1978 are pivotal dividing lines between three periods in the urbanization of the People's Republic of China that we term the periods of "unrestrained urbanization," "counter urbanization," and "rapid urbanization."

The period of unrestrained urbanization (1949–1960)

The People's Republic of China was founded in 1949. Peace, greater stability, a strong central leadership that had not yet restricted urban–rural migration, and the need for post-war reconstruction resulted in a period of unrestrained urbanization when large-scale urban rebuilding and investment in basic industries and infrastructure (with aid from the Soviet Union) led to a great deal of urban construction and millions of rural residents poured into China's cities. China's planned economic system was not yet fully established at this stage. While a limited population registration system has existed in the PRC since its creation, the central government had not expanded this registration system countrywide and did not use it to limit rural–urban migration. The rural population could migrate freely between rural and urban regions. China institutionalized and greatly expanded its household registration (hukou) system in 1958 and began using it to manage the population's registration and social security. During this period China's urban population grew from 58 million in 1949 to 131 million in 1960. The urban population nearly doubled in 11 years, and the urbanization level increased by 9.2 percent from 10.6 percent to 19.8 percent (NBSC-ccs, 2005).

The period of counter-urbanization (1961–1977)

By 1963 a series of droughts and unrealistic projects brought the Great Leap Forward to an end. China's centralized economic planning and hukou systems were fully in place and the national government began to restrict urban migration, so the period of rapid urbanization effectively ended at that time. Urbanization experienced a sharp decrease between 1960 and 1963, deceasing by 2.91 percent. After a short period of fluctuation, China's Cultural Revolution (1966–1976) began a period of turmoil in China. Policy was driven by a desire to eliminate class distinctions and differences between urban and rural areas. In addition to the ideological motive to create a more egalitarian society, to relieve employment pressure in urban areas, over 43 million urban residents—particularly urban youth—were sent to work in rural regions (Liu, 2009: 532, 537). At the end of the Cultural Revolution in 1978 China's urbanization level was only 17.4 percent (NBSC-ccs, 2005), 2 percent less than the level 17 years earlier at the end of the Great Leap Forward.

As the Cultural Revolution ended, the Chinese Communist Party (CCP) under the leadership of Deng Xiaoping changed the course of national policy. We use 1978 as the dividing line ending the period of counter-urbanization and beginning the period of reform and opening up. That is the year in which the new direction was established and counter-urbanization ended. It took several years for new policies to be implemented and their impact to be felt. As described in subsequent chapters, China's real rapid urbanization was clearly evident by 1984.

The period of rapid growth (1978–present)

The household contract responsibility system (HCRS) introduced under Deng Xiaoping's leadership beginning in 1978 in rural China endowed peasants with autonomy in production and management. It remains the system in China governing land tenure and the sharing of agricultural produce between rural collectives and individual households. Rural land in China is owned by agricultural collectives. The initial practice was that the government specified quotas of agricultural production the collectives must sell to the state each year. Collectives in turn contracted arable land parcels to households and specified how much each household had to contribute to the required quota. Households could keep any surplus over the contracted amount for their own consumption or for sale on the private market. Establishment of the HCRS in the late 1970s succeeded in greatly increasing agricultural productivity in China. The HCRS represented not only liberation of rural productive forces, but also created favorable conditions for rapid urbanization.

At the same time as the HCRS was being implemented, the large population of educated youth (and others) who had been sent to work in the countryside during the Cultural Revolution was allowed to return to cities and towns. This resulted in huge employment pressure. The fragile recovering urban economy was not able to absorb all the new migrants returning from or migrating for the first time from the countryside. The new surplus labor force released in both rural and urban areas were preconditions for rapid growth and diversification of China's urban economy. The massive surplus labor force resulting from the liberation of rural productive forces and the original urban employment pressure encouraged individual and private entrepreneurship. In the countryside farmers rapidly increased agricultural production resulting in grain which could be used to feed a larger urban population. Freedom to start businesses and engage in market transactions spurred new enterprises in both cities and the countryside.

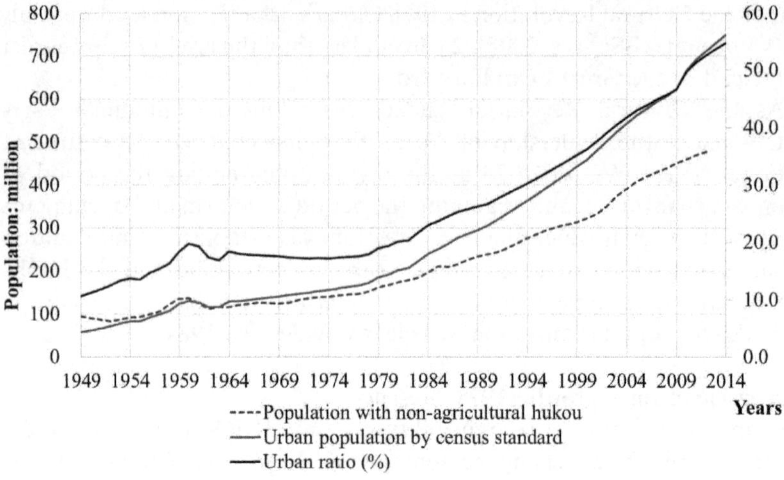

Source: NBSC, selected years.

Figure 1.1 Chinese population with non-agricultural hukou, urban population, and urban ratio, 1949–2014

These developments expedited China's economic restructuring and urbanization process. China emerged from stagnation during this stage.

By the end of 2014, China's urban population had reached 749 million, with a 54.8 percent urbanization level (NBSC, 2015b). During the 36 years from 1978 to 2014 China's urbanization level increased by 36.9 percent, at an annual average rate of increase reaching nearly 1 percent. Figure 1.1 illustrates changes in China's total urban population and urban population rate from 1949 to 2014.

How China's Recent Urbanization Compared With Global Patterns

The most common definition of urbanization and the one we employ throughout this book is the percentage of a country's population that lives in places classified as urban rather than rural. While increases in urbanization generally occur as a country's urban population is increasing, urbanization is not the same as urban population increase. It is a ratio, not an absolute number (Davis, 1965).

In most countries a national census or statistical offices produce a regularly updated number for the urban and non-urban population. In the essentially urbanized developed countries of North America, Europe and Australia census geographical unit definitions of urban and rural are relatively stable and census data inclusive—with the exception of illegal immigrants and some special hard-to-classify categories of people.

In China, because of China's hukou system there are two fundamentally different ways of describing the urban population: the *de facto* urban population who actually reside in places officially classified as urban for enough time to qualify as residents and the *de jure* urban population: residents of urban areas with official residence addresses there. How to classify China's urbanization has been the subject of extensive scholarly debate (Zhang and Zhao, 1998; Zhou and Ma, 2003; Shen, 2005, 2006; Chan, 2007) and the methodology used to define urban and rural areas has changed in different Chinese censuses, making longitudinal description difficult, as described in Chapter 3 on administrative divisions.

As this book goes to press the latest available official data shows that at the end of 2014 China's de facto urban population accounted for 54.8 percent of China's total population (NBSC, 2015b), but one-third of China's urban population does not have urban hukou (PRC-MHURD, 2014); this means they can't enjoy the full urban welfare benefits.

University of Washington geographer Kam Wing Chan has summarized different ways of classifying China's urban and rural population over time and provides detailed statistics through 2008 (Chan, 2010). Chapter 2 on hukou and hukou reform and Chapter 6 on large-scale population flows summarize the most important data and discusses this complex issue in depth.

For more than two centuries the world's urbanization level has been increasing, and this pattern has accelerated since 1950. A review of recent world patterns is helpful in understanding the context of China's urbanization and the importance of reform and opening up. It is useful to distinguish between two periods: 1950 to 1980 when urbanization in China rose and fell and 1980 to the present when rapid urbanization has been fully underway.

During the first period, from 1950 to 1980, medium-income countries and countries in Asia experienced the most significant growth. The United Nation's *World Urbanization Prospects: 2014* reports that in the 30 years from 1950 to 1980 the world's urbanization level increased by 9.7 percentage points from 29.6 percent to 39.3 percent (UN, 2014). The increases in high, medium, and low-income countries were 15.2 percent, 11.7 percent and 9.4 percent respectively. During this period the overall urbanization level of Asia increased by 9.6 percent. Urbanization was most rapid in high-income countries.

During the second period, from 1980 to 2015, the world's urbanization level increased more rapidly—by 14.3 percent compared with 9.7

percent between 1950 and 1980. Urbanization was most rapid in low and medium-income countries. The increases were 8.6 percent, 20.6 percent and 12.4 percent, respectively in high, medium and low-income countries. During this period Asia's overall urbanization level increased by 21.1 percent, which was driven mainly by the change in China from slow urbanization to rapid urbanization.

During the past three decades, the most rapid urbanization worldwide has occurred in medium-income countries, rather than high-income countries. This has occurred especially in Asian countries in what economist Walt Whitman Rostow (Rostow, 1956) call their periods of "takeoff." The world's urbanization level crossed the 50 percent threshold, which means that over half of the world's population lived in urban areas in 2007.

By 2014, the Chinese population had reached 1.37 billion (NSBC, 2015b)—the largest population of any countries'—and accounted for 20 percent of the world's total population. Hence China's urbanization is of global significance. China's urbanization level increased by 36.2 percent within 35 years from 1980 to 2015, by 15.1 percent more than the population increase of all other Asian countries combined, 15.6 percent more than medium-income countries as a group, and nearly 22 percent higher than the world average.

Between 1980 and 2014 China's urban population increased by 567 million—a quarter of the world's total urban population increase (UN, 2014). The United Nations estimates that China, India, and Nigeria will collectively contribute over 30 percent of the world's total urban population increase between 2014 and 2050, as illustrated in Figure 1.2.

Urbanization today is faster in developing countries than it was in the early stages of urbanization in countries which developed in the nineteenth and twentieth centuries, and are now at or above the 70 percent urban level.

"Catch-up" is often easier than "ground breaking." Developing countries are catching up fast with technology and capital provided by developed countries as described in Chapter 5 on the impact of globalization on China's urbanization. Unfortunately, this may lead to the "over-urbanization" phenomenon, which has occurred in some countries—particularly in Latin American and Africa—as a result of unsynchronized population growth and industrial and municipal development as described in Chapter 6 on large-scale population flows and Chapter 9 on China's double dual transformation. Urban slums and sprawl in countries which are urbanizing too rapidly without adequate control gives rise to a multiplicity of problems. In a re-interpretation of world urbanization data in Chapter 9 on China's double dual transformation, we conclude that China's urbanization development is nearly balanced with the rapid

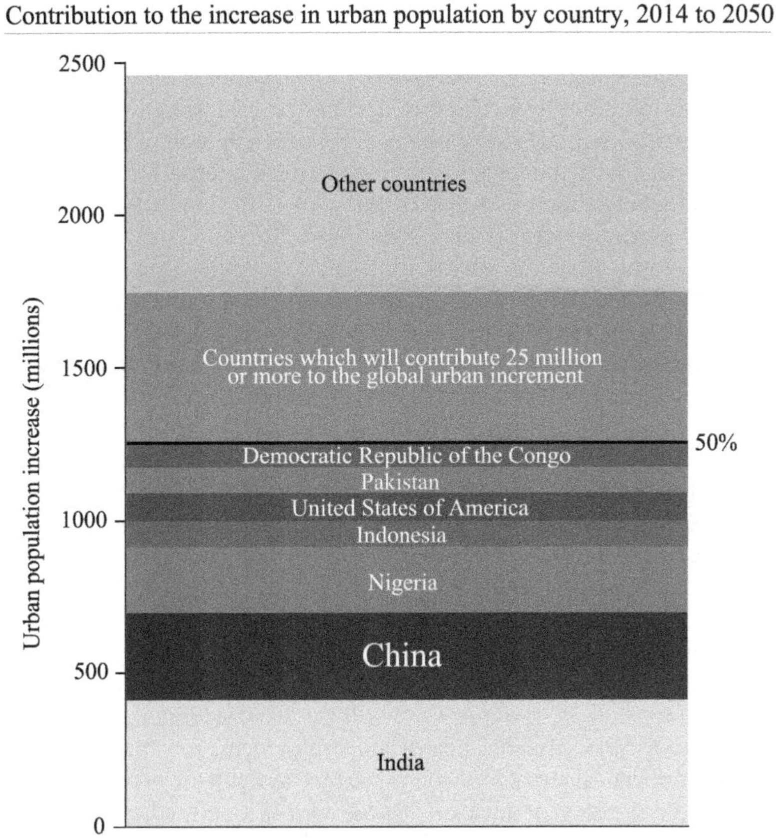

Note: The countries shown are projected to contribute 25 million or more to the global urban increment between 2014 and 2050. The category "Other countries" includes with urban increments of less than 25 million each.

Source: United Nations (2014: 12).

Figure 1.2 United Nations estimate of the contribution to the increase in urban population by country, 2014 to 2050

development of the economy and social progress: that China is not significantly under-urbanized as many other scholars claim.

China's GDP reached 63.6 trillion RMB (US$10.3 trillion) in 2014, ranking second after the US (NSBC, 2015b). China's per capita GDP estimated by purchasing power parity was US$9,800 in 2013—only 19 percent of US per capita GDP.

In terms of economic and social development China's experience is unprecedented in speed and scale in human history. In the space of three decades China has lifted more than half a billion people from abject poverty. In 1981 China's desperately poor population accounted for 39.5 percent of the world's total, but by 2011 it had declined to 1.32 percent (World Bank, 2014b). China's middle class, which was essentially non-existent in 1981, now numbers in the hundreds of millions. More international tourists are now from China than any other country. In 2014 more than 110 million Chinese traveled oversees (China News Web, 2015).

At the same time the distribution of wealth in China has become increasingly unequal. Gini coefficients are the most common measure of inequality, though we describe their limitations in Chapter 9. The higher the coefficient the more unequal the distribution of wealth. If estimates by academic researchers and China's National Statistics Bureau are correct, China's Gini coefficient may have increased from about 0.330 in the 1980s (Fan and Sun, 2008) to 0.469 in 2014 (NBSC, 2015a). This latest figure has exceeded the warning line—0.400 laid down by the United Nations—and is higher than the United States' Gini coefficient. Whatever China's true Gini coefficient is or how accurately it reflects true income disparity, China clearly faces growing income inequality.

China is rapidly building a nationwide social welfare/social security system. As described in Chapter 4 on regional policies and regional urbanization the process is being implemented on a decentralized basis. Coverage and the adequacy of programs are still far from adequate—particularly in rural areas. But pension, health, unemployment, job training, welfare and other social security and social welfare systems now cover the great majority of China's population. Rural cooperative medical service and pension security systems have been established, and coverage and the adequacy of benefits is increasing rapidly, as described in Chapter 4 on rural urbanization and rural policies.

More than 90 percent of China's rural areas can now be accessed by roads, although a large gap exists between urban and rural areas, different cities and even within the same city-region. China has not seen the emergence of extensive slums similar to what has occurred in many African, Asian and Latin American countries.

URBANIZATION STUDIES

Dual Structure of Urbanization in Developing Countries

Nobel Prize winning economist Arthur O. Lewis established the dual sector model of economic development in 1954. This model divides the economic structure of developing countries into industrial and agricultural sectors. Lewis assumes that a large surplus labor force exists in rural regions of developing countries and that the marginal productivity of the agricultural labor force is almost zero. Therefore, the agricultural labor force is impelled to migrate to cities. The Lewis model assumes that this process will continue until all the rural surplus labor force is absorbed by cities and salaries in rural regions and urban areas are comparable. At this point, the rural–urban gap will narrow and eventually disappear (Lewis, 1954).

Lewis' dual sector model has had a great impact on the formulation of economic policies in many developing countries and on the birth of developmental economics. The model serves as the theoretical basis for many studies of population urbanization (especially rural–urban migration). However, assumptions in the Lewis model do not fit with current phenomena in China such as limited surplus labors and the existence of unemployment in cities.

Addressing the defects in the basic assumptions in Lewis' dual sector model, Harvard economics professor Dale Jorgenson contended that the root cause of the migration of rural population to urban areas lies in changes of a country's consumption structure (Jorgenson, 1961). People have limited demand for agricultural products, but the demand for industrial products is unlimited. According to Jorgenson, once the supply of agricultural products can satisfy the demand the driving force for agricultural development will recede, leading to the transfer of rural population to the industrial sector. Both Jorgenson and Lewis emphasized the importance of facilitating rural–urban migration.

Yale economics professors John C.H. Fei and Gustav Ranis argue that the supply of rural labor force is not unlimited (Ranis, 2004). They believe that when the supply of agricultural labor has declined to the extent that total agricultural output begins to decline, the price of agricultural products will rise, and the profit of the industrial sector will decrease. As a consequence, the average salary of the rural labor force will become comparable with the average level in the industrial sector. As that happens, the unidirectional transfer of the rural labor force to the industrial sector will slow and eventually stop. The subsequent transfer of the labor force between the agricultural and industrial sectors will be determined by the market (Fei and Ranis, 1964). The Ranis–Fei model considers the increase of agricultural productivity. However, it assumes that unemployment does not exist in the industrial sector or cities. As long as the salary of workers in the industrial sector in the cities is higher than that of the agricultural sector, the hidden rural surplus labor force will continue migrating to cities and the industrial sector.

Jorgenson and Ranis and Fei improved Arthur O. Lewis' dual sector model. However, they still failed to account for the phenomenon of simultaneous growth of urban unemployment and the rural migration to cities in developing countries. Based on six years living and working Africa, New York University economist Michael Todaro recognized the prevalent unemployment problem in rural regions and urban areas of the developing countries, and thus he proposed another variation on the rural–urban migration model. Todaro believed that what actually influences migrants' decisions to migrate is not just income, but expected income (Todaro, 1969). The concept of expected income can better explain the coexistence of large-scale rural–urban migration and high urban unemployment rate in developing countries.

Although the dual sector economic model is not directly about urbanization, the model has become an important explanatory theory in urbanization. China's economy still has a dual sector structure and China is now facing an increasingly urgent contradiction between large population size and limited land resources. For China, the rural–urban dual structure is manifested in the level of economic development and in the gap in public services and administrative systems.

Desakotas

Canadian geographer Terry McGee conducted a large number of empirical studies on urbanization in Indonesia and elsewhere in Southeast Asia (McGee, 1991a, 1991b). McGee concluded that the Western model of urbanization does not adequately describe or explain the pattern of urbanization in agriculturally fertile urbanizing areas in Indonesia and elsewhere in Asia. As a result McGee proposed a model of mixed industrial and agricultural development and a unique Asia settlement form he named a desakota, combining the Bahasa Indonesian words *desa* (village) and *kota* (city).

Desakotas—very dense formerly rural areas that mix agriculture and industry—are arguably a distinct settlement pattern that is neither rural nor urban (McGee, 1991b). McGee argues that formerly high-density agricultural areas are becoming desakotas as their density increases and industry and other urban economic activities develop mixed in with agriculture. According to McGee, desakotas are most likely to develop along transportation corridors between major cities. They are most often found in wet rice agriculture areas because the high yield per unit of land can support dense rural populations. Desakotas are typically unplanned or poorly planned and take a variety of forms. Common features are: (1) average residential densities above the threshold that qualifies as urban, (2) mixing small-scale industry alongside agriculture, (3) water, electricity, transportation, sewage, and other infrastructure problems, and (4) serious air quality, water quality, and other pollution problems.

In China areas resembling Indonesian desakotas have arisen not only as urban centers have expanded, but even more often as industrializing villages are becoming more like towns (Abramson and Qi, 2011). Greg Guldin describes the processes he observed in southern China as former villages became mixtures of agriculture and industry as deagriculturalization, townization, and urbanization in place (Guldin, 1996).

McGee argued that the system in parts of Southeast Asia under which urbanization is combined with regional development is a complex system with the mixing of urban and rural elements. This situation is mainly due to industrialization and urban sprawl. McGee's concern focused on traditional agricultural areas in highly concentrated urban regions such as peri-urban areas around city centers and transportation corridors through agricultural land connecting major cities (McGee, 1988, 1991a, 1991b).

General Theories of Urbanization

In addition to research on the mechanism of migration and urban–rural spatial transformation, theories of urbanization are helpful as background for the chapters that follow. Demographers, geographers, and others who have studied the pattern of urbanization in different countries over time have concluded that urbanization—measured by the proportion of the population living in urban areas over time—tends to follow the shape of an attenuated S curve.

The earliest, and still the most complete and intellectually rigorous, description of the urbanization S curve was formulated by American sociologist and demographer Kingsley Davis [1908–1990] in a classic 1965 *Scientific American* article (Davis, 1965). Davis served as president of the Population Association of America and the American Sociological Association and was the first sociologist in the United States to be elected to the National Academy of Sciences. Davis and his students carefully assembled and analyzed data on 1,000 years of urbanization in Europe. Davis did not study China and his generalizations are Eurocentric.

Davis defined urbanization as an increase in the proportion (percentage) of the population in a given region, such as country, that lives in urban areas as opposed to the rural countryside or villages and towns that are too small to qualify as urban. Davis identified and clearly described core definitional and conceptual issues that plague all scholars attempting to demarcate urban and rural population: what population size or density of a settlement qualifies it as urban? Where is the boundary line between urban and rural areas on the urban fringe?

Davis argues that urbanization follows an attenuated S curve in which pre-industrial cities urbanize very slowly at the long bottom of the S, shoot up at the middle of the S as they industrialize, and then level off at the top of the S as they become fully urban. He observed that advanced industrialized countries had already reached the top part of the S curve by the mid-1960s, but that many rapidly urbanizing developing countries were in the steep middle of the S at that time. The pattern Davis described holds true today. Many developed countries in Europe, North America and Australia and some developing countries in Latin America have reached the flat top part of the S curve with urbanization levels higher than 75 percent. Many developing countries in Africa and Asia are in the steep part of the S curve. Some of the poorest countries in the world are still largely rural and are urbanizing only slowly. Davis' article was written shortly after the Great Leap Forward when only about 18 percent of China's population was urban. As described above, China's urbanization took off in the early 1980s after reform and opening and China's urbanization level reached 54.8 percent at the end of 2014 (NSBC, 2015b).

Six years before Davis' classic article was published, economist Walt Whitman Rostow developed a theory about the stages of economic growth in developing countries, as measured by indicators such as industrial output and per capita gross national product (Rostow, 1956). Rostow argued that when traditional economies reach a level of economic "take off", a limited group of sectors where modern industrial techniques are applied achieve rapid growth and this leads to diffusion of growth to other sectors. Eventually economic growth tends to level off as the country's economy matures (Rostow, 1956). While Rostow focused on economic growth others were quick to point out the connection between economic development and urbanization.

Geographer Ray Northam incorporated the concept of "take off" and maturity into the S curve. Northam argues that urbanization tends to proceed slowly during an initial state until a country is about 30 percent urban; shoot up much more rapidly during an acceleration stage; and then level off during a terminal stage when about 70 percent of the country's population is urban (Northam, 1979).

The Davis, Rostow, and Northam models are all simplifications of reality designed to reveal general truths. The reality of urbanization is more complex. Events such as epidemics, economic crises, political movements like the Cultural Revolution, and wars may disrupt the curve substantially. Economic historian Jan DeVries concluded that the bubonic plague epidemic of 1347–1351 which killed an estimated one-third of Europe's population, for example, reduced the urbanization rate in many countries because it hit urban areas particularly hard (DeVries, 1984). DeVries concluded virtually all cities of 10,000 or more in Europe had recovered their pre-plague populations by 1500.

Kingsley Davis describes a "family of S curves" on a horizontal x-axis representing time and a vertical y-axis representing the percentage of a country's population that is urban. England, which was only about 5 percent urban in 1500 and is now 80 percent urban, is at the top of the family of S curves in Figure 1.3. A long slowly rising left tail shows that England slowly urbanized during the middle ages. The steep part of England's S begins about 1750 with the start of the Industrial Revolution. A nearly level top to the S shows that England became nearly fully urbanized several decades ago. The long attenuated parts of the S curve for Germany and France follow a pattern similar to England's, but the time at which the S starts to rise rapidly occurs later in Germany and later still in France. In Japan the steep part of the S curve begins only after 1850 when Western colonial powers pushed the opening of Japan.

China is a special case. The long bottom part of China's S curve extends until about 1980 and only then begins to rise rapidly. The S curves for a few very poor African countries still have only the bottom part of the S because they have not yet begun to urbanize rapidly.

The developing countries of Asia, South America, and Africa already have many large and rapidly growing cities. As the twenty-first century progresses, it appears likely the human population will increasingly live in "megacities" of 10 million inhabitants and more, often flowing together in vast urban conurbations called mega-urban regions, megalopolis, or our preferred term "large city clusters" (LCCs) described in detail in Chapter 7 on large city clusters, megalopolises, and China's evolving city system.

Davis concludes that there will be an end to urbanization—but not necessarily to absolute population growth, the physical size of cities or the absolute number of people cities contain. He found that the rural population in developing countries today often continues to grow as these countries urbanize, unlike European cities in the nineteenth century where industrialization led to depopulation of rural areas. This occurred in China after reform and opening up, but is now changing direction and the rural population is declining as China continues to urbanize.

Research and scholarly debate continues on the nature and causes of world urbanization. The majority view, based on research and projections by the Population Division of the United Nations, holds that total world population will increase from about 7 billion today to about 9 billion in 2050, and that urbanization will continue virtually everywhere but especially in the developing world (UN, 2014).

The unique course of China's economic and social development has created a fundamental debate about whether China is urbanizing too slowly and whether its present urbanization level is appropriate given its current level of development. Most Western scholars believe that China's

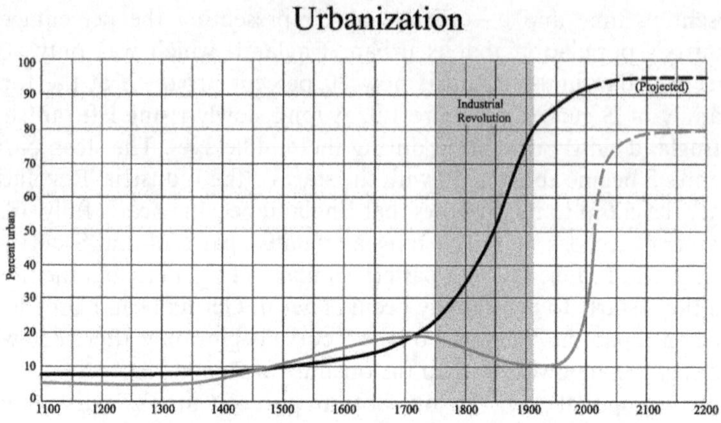

Percent of England and China urban 1100 ADE 2000 ADE

Urbanization refers to the percent of the population of a geographical area such as a nation state or region of the world that lives in urban as opposed to non-urban places such as farms and villages. Urbanization follows a pattern that historical urban demographer Kingsley Davis describes as an attenuated S curve, with a long left tail as the percentage of the population in a region slowly becomes more urban, a steep middle portion of the S as the region urbanizes rapidly, and then a nearly flat upper part of the S once the region is essentially fully urban. England (black curve) urbanized very slowly until the beginning of the industrial revolution in about 1750, then urbanized rapidly and today—with 92% of its population urban—is barely urbanizing if at all. For millennia China (gray curve) remained an overwhelmingly rural country. When the PRC was founded only 10% of China's population was urban. This increased to 18% under Mao, but since reform and opening began in the late 1970s has shot up to 55% in 2015. China's urbanization rate is expected to continue to increase rapidly to a level of 75% or higher in the next thirty years and then level off and gradually converge with fully urbanized countries.

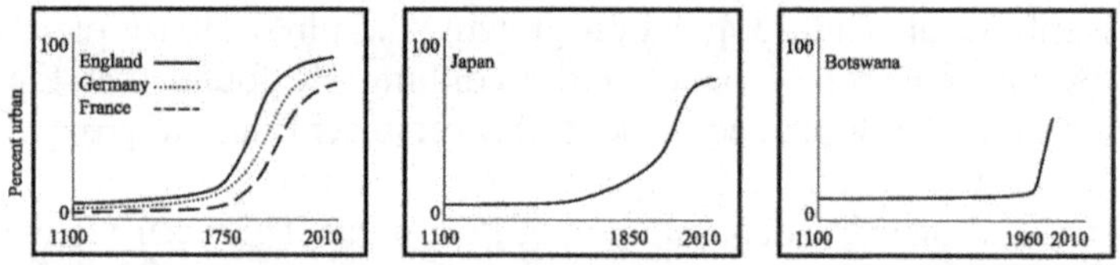

Davis argues that there are often "families" of similar S curves in a region. The s curves of Germany and France began increasing later and proceeded less rapidly than England's, but the overall shape is similar.

History, politics, economics, and culture affect urbanization. Japan's S curve began to increase rapidly only after 1850 when Japan opened up to the West politically and began to industrialize.

Some developing countries today are urbanizing very rapidly. Only about 2% of Botswana's population was urban as late as 1960, but today Botswana is more than 50% urban.

Data graphic by Michael Brestel based on Kingsley Davis, "The Urbanization of the Human Population," Scientific American (September 1965).

Source: Drawn by Michael Brestel based on Kingsley Davis' "The Urbanization of the Human Population" *Scientific American* (September, 1965). Chinese urbanization curve added by Lijuan Wang.

Figure 1.3 Kingsley Davis urbanization S curve

urbanization level is too low (Chan, 1992, 1994; Wang, X., 2002; Zhang, 2004; Perkins, 2013), but a few consider China as over-urbanized (Kirkby, 1985; Ran and Berry, 1989; Chang and Brada, 2006; Chen et al., 2013). This debate is complicated by China's hukou system and 220 million members of China's floating population who live and work somewhere other than their official residential address and are not true urban citizens and by the enormous differences in the level of development and urbanization in different parts of China. Aggregate data at the national, provincial, and even sub-provincial level is useful, but can also mask complexity. What is an appropriate level of urbanization is a normative question about which reasonable people can disagree. There is no "scientific" answer to this question.

Scholars who consider China to be under-urbanized base their argument on the fact that industrialization and urbanization are closely correlated and China's urbanization level is lower than it should be compared with other countries in the world (Wang, X., 2002). They rely on a methodology developed by economists Hollis Chenery and Moise Syrquin that compares urbanization and industrialization rates. A number of scholars have revisited this question using more recent data provided by the World Bank on countries' development and urbanization levels and refinements on the Chenery–Syrquin methodology (Zhao and Zhang, 2009).

Other scholars argue that China's urbanization rate is appropriate given its level of economic development (Li and Chen, 2001; Fan and Tian, 2003; Li, 2004; Ge et al., 2003; Zhao and Zhang, 2009). One argument is that the gap between China's urbanization level and industrialization level exists because industry—including small and medium-sized industries in towns and villages—is flourishing, that is, China is "over industrialized", not "under-urbanized" (Fan and Tian, 2003). Another argument is that measures of development that rely on per capita Gross Domestic Product (GDP) or income don't accurately reflect economic well-being where goods and services are less expensive. Comparing per capita Gross National Income (GNI) based on Purchasing Power Parity (PPP) and considering the extreme unbalance of China's regional development China's urbanization rate is arguably more appropriate (Ge et al., 2003; Li, 2004; Zhang and Zhao, 2003; Zhao and Zhang, 2009).

Chapter 9 reviews and presents the results of our own analysis of the most recent available data. We conclude that China's urbanization level is appropriate or only slightly lower than it should be.

Changing Motivations for Urbanization

Since the founding of the PRC, the national government in China has played a large role in urbanization and its motivations have changed dramatically over time. Both deliberate changes in policy and change as a result of decentralization and marketization have impacted the nature of China's urbanization since 1949.

American economist Allyn Abbott Young pioneered theory about the motivations for and mechanisms of urbanization. Young (1928) argued that, "the urbanization level is determined by the level of social division of labor, which is in turn determined by the magnitude of market; the realization of returns to scale relies on the division of labor." Given that the division of labor happens earlier in the industrial sector than in the agricultural sector, a large segment of the agricultural workforce migrates to cities as a result of market mechanisms. This accelerates the urbanization process.

Economists Masahisa Fujita and Paul Krugman build on Allyn's theory. They argue that urban economies provide returns to scale, which provide constant fuel for the urbanization process (Fujita and Krugman, 1995).

Weber and Gerth (1951) adopted a cultural perspective on development in China. They argue that Confucianism has hampered the development of China's capitalism and urbanization by promoting ruralism. In their view, China continued to be a rural society through the mid-twentieth century, and all social relations were based on rural connections.

Using the new classical urbanization model, Yang and Rice (1994) relate scale to the division of labor through the concept of transaction efficiency. They proposed that evolution of the division of labor, market expansion, and increases in transaction efficiency are the three pillars of urbanization development.

Yang and Zhang later developed the argument that external economic efficiency, rather than the internal economy of scale drives urbanization (Yang and Zhang, 2000). They suggested that, "the boundary of resources" and "surplus population" are the main factors restricting China's urbanization. The new classical urbanization model implies two development strategies for solving these problems: outward expansion or internal upgrading.

Outward expansion seeks to expand resources and markets through expansion of economic activities beyond a country itself through trade. In new classical economic theory internal upgrading seeks to promote development by knowledge accumulation and institutional innovation. This involves constant evolution of the division of labor within the system as well as overcoming resource boundaries. Under the new division of labor, the surplus population will be transformed into "utility population."

Although providing useful theoretical explanations for urbanization that can be adapted to understand China, Western classical theory fails to recognize and incorporate special features of China. China has a unique political and economic trajectory. Before 1978, the planned economy, withdrawal from the global economy, industrial location for defense purposes, and massive political struggles make much of Western theory about the division of labor, knowledge accumulation, expanding resource boundaries, and transaction efficiency irrelevant or require radical adaptation to Chinese circumstances. While Western theory is more relevant to understanding China's development and urbanization after 1978, the great changes that have taken place in economic, social, and institutional aspects since 1978 as China was experiencing transition towards a market economy and today's unique brand of market socialism require developing a new institutional economic theory with Chinese characteristics.

For a long time after the founding of the PRC, scientific research activities were suspended, and research on urbanization was stopped. Despite persisting doubts about the Soviet model, a highly centralized planned economy was established in China and development policy mainly bolstered the planned economy. Thereafter, and particularly during the Cultural Revolution, research and scholarly debate about the nature of Chinese urbanization and theorizing about alternative development and urbanization strategies were non-existent.

In 1979, after the Cultural Revolution, Youren Wu, a professor at Nanjing University, published an article titled "On the Topic of Urbanization in Socialist China" (Wu and Xia, 1979). This article is considered the first work on the history of urbanization research in New China (He, 2006).

The 1980s saw a return of economic growth and urbanization—particularly in small-sized cities. Academic research and theorizing about Chinese urbanization returned. Initially Chinese scholars focused on two questions: what propelled urbanization development and how the pulling force of jobs and higher wages was attracting urban migrants and impacting urbanization.

With industrial development in rural areas and urban expansion proceeding simultaneously, most Chinese scholars believed two types of urbanization were occurring in China (Shen, 2002): top-down urbanization and bottom-up urbanization. Top-down urbanization involves the central government investing in infrastructure, economic development zones, and urban construction—including the construction of new cities—according to plans. The motivation for this type of urbanization comes from industrialization initiated by the central government. Top-down urbanization was the dominant form of urbanization from 1949 to 1978 (Chan, 1992, 1994; Wang, X., 2002; Zhang, 2004), and is still important today (Dai et al., 2014).

Bottom-up urbanization, wherein rural collectives, firms, or individuals were the investors started in the late 1970s and was identifiable as a distinct form of urbanization with Chinese characteristics in the early 1980s (Gu, 1998; Ning, 1998; Cui and Ma, 1999; Zhu, 1999; Friedmann, 2005). Rural urbanization is realized through rural industrialization, and was motivated by reform of the rural economic system (Feng, 2004).

The motivations for urbanization become more complex with the deepening of the transition of China's economic system. As more studies are conducted over the motivation mechanism of urbanization, attention has shifted from internal factors to sources of capital. Yuemin Ning, a professor at East China Normal University, argues that the motivation mechanisms for urbanization in China have become diversified since the 1990s (Ning, 1998). On the one hand, remnants of the planned economy system still exists; on the other hand, as the market economy system is being constantly extended, diversified actors are involved in the economic and urbanization development, including government (fiscal decentralization, delegation of decision-making rights, loosening of institutional constraints), enterprises (state-owned and foreign-invested), and individuals (private sector, rural sector, and economic development zones). This body of scholarship describes and seeks to explain the diverse motivations that have come into play to replace the single- or dual-sector motivations of the past. The centralized urbanization model has now given way to a decentralized model of rural enterprise development (Ning, 1998).

In the context of global economic integration, foreign capital has had a great impact on the landscape, process, and mechanism of China's urbanization. Foreign capital constituted the third force besides the pulling force of urban development and the pushing force of rural development (Xue and Yang, 1997). Since China's rapid urbanization has occurred at the same time as greatly increased globalization of the world economy and an influx of a large amount of Foreign Direct Investment (FDI) in China an important question is to what extent have these exogenous forces driven Chinese urbanization. Sassen (1998, 2001) points out that globalization and informationalization are the main drivers of urbanization in the twenty-first century. Many Chinese and Western scholars uncritically assume this to be true. On the contrary, American urban planning professor John Friedmann takes the position in his pioneering book *China's Urban Transition* (Friedmann, 2005) that China's urbanization is predominantly fueled by endogenous, bottom-up, grassroots urbanization rather than the massive inflow of global capital as generally believed.

Liya Wu (2005) argues that the impact of globalization on China's urbanization consists of three parts: the construction of a production factor market, the industrial foundation created by both globalization and localization, and the boost international trade provides.

An anthology edited by professor Fulong Wu, Bartlett Professor of Planning at the Bartlett School of Planning, University College London titled *Globalization and the Chinese City* (Wu, 2006) provides the most scholarly and balanced review of this debate. Wu clarifies the close connections between China's urbanization and globalization. In the anthology and in a subsequent article co-authored with Laurence Ma, Wu concludes that spatial production, urban consumption, and the circulation of capital as well as population and technology have indeed had a considerable impact on China's urbanization (Ma and Wu, 2007). In Chapter 5 on globalization and urbanization we discuss these debates in detail and describe the conclusions we have reached based on our macro-level analysis and fieldwork.

China's Urbanization Path

There has been an ongoing debate about the relative importance of promoting small, medium, and large-sized cities in China and national and provincial policy with respect to this issue has changed from time to time since the founding of the PRC. Before 1978 most of the net growth of urban areas in China occurred because of rural migration to small and medium-sized cities, but not large cities (He, 2006). Since then China's urbanization is primarily a result of the movement of the rural population to towns and small and medium-sized cities (He, 2006). After reform and opening up, prioritizing development of small-sized cities and towns became scholars' and policymakers' predominant view of the best path for China's urbanization.

Based on his research on China's modernization, Princeton University sociologist Gilbert Rozman (1989) concluded that a network in China favorable for the development of small-sized cities had been formed after the implementation of urban development policies in the 1960s to 1970s. To the contrary, Nanjing University professor Gonghao Cui argues that prioritizing the development of small-sized cities fails to capitalize on scale effects (Cui, 1989). Arguably because of specialization and agglomeration economies, large cities have greater economies of scale than small-sized cities and the development of large cities is necessary for modernization, industrialization, and the development of tertiary industry. Cui draws on comparative research to conclude that the growth of large cities as development proceeds is an objective law. Western economists at the University of California, Berkeley (Quigley, 2009) and Brown University (Au and Henderson, 2006) reach similar conclusions.

Some academics have taken a middle ground arguing that development of medium-sized cities should be China's top priority (Wu and Xia, 1979; Liu, 1988; Shen, 1999; Jin et al., 2014). We explore these issues in Chapter 7 on "China's evolving city system and large city clusters" and Chapter 8 on "Towns and rural urbanization."

The idea of exploiting the scale effect of urbanization also has critics and some scholars question whether or not the entire debate about city size makes sense. Peking University professor Yixing Zhou has criticized the unreasonable use of scale as the criterion to determine whether a city should be developed or restrained (Zhou and Yu, 1988). He (2006) contended that no other country besides China has resorted to a certain model of urbanization. Rather, market forces determine the size and distribution of cities. In He's view, defining the optimum size of cities in China is in the same vein as favoring a planned economy system, and hinders reflection on what factors may make a city of one size or another preferable in a given place and time or utilizing the market mechanism to regulate the growth of cities (He, 2006). The urban system is composed of cities of varying sizes, and no uniform standard has been determined as to the optimal city size. The development of cities of any size may be reasonable depending on circumstances (Cui, 1989; Zhang, 2010).

Rather than debate the question of city size and a unified urbanization policy, a number of Chinese scholars have proposed regional urbanization as the best path for China's urbanization (Wang, 1988; Cui, 1989; Liu et al., 2003; Ma, 2005; Han, 2015). They argue that cities of all sizes are important and all should be considered and managed in a regional way. In a given region, all cities have connections and they influence each other.

On the legislative level, China's 2008 Town and Country Planning Act eliminates the stated policy of the previous (1988) Act of "strictly controlling the size of large cities and developing medium and small-sized cities." However other Chinese government policy documents—including the 2014 National New-style urbanization plan retain the policy of strictly controlling megacities with populations of more than 5 million and eliminate restrictions to migrants gaining hukou immediately when they migrate to small cities and towns.

In the debate over China's urbanization policy, we believe that the key is to enhance institutions to facilitate and humanize population migration and settlement. Urbanization is a social phenomenon that goes hand in hand with social and economic progress and structural transition. Urbanization has close connections with institutional arrangements and their evolution. So, policymaking and deep institution reform are key points for China's healthy urbanization in the near future, as described in the concluding chapter.

Research on Transitions in China's Urbanization

In the first two decades after the beginning of reform and opening up, Western scholars uniformly argued that China's urbanization has distinct socialist features that differentiate China's urbanization pattern from capitalist urbanization in the West (Kirkby, 1985; Chan, 1996; Fan, 1995; Chan and Zhang, 1999; Wei, 2000). More recent studies repeat this view for the early period and state that the legacy of the planned economy continues to influence more recent urbanization (Ma, 2002; Wu, 2002, 2015; Friedmann, 2005; Wu and Gaubatz, 2012; Zhang, F., 2014). Studies generally conclude that China's national policies continue to have a profound impact on urbanization processes.

Urbanization of a large and rapidly changing country such as China is complex and there is a rich literature seeking to explain China's unique urbanization path. Western scholars have attributed the historically low level of urbanization in China to a number of causes. Dwight H. Perkins, a professor at Harvard's Kennedy School of government and expert on the history of China's economic development, concluded that throughout history China's low agricultural productivity hindered the urbanization process (Perkins, 2013). William Kirkby a professor of China Studies at the Harvard Business School argues that China's emphasis on industrialization, especially on heavy industry, limited urbanization (Kirkby, 1985). Geographer Terry Cannon, currently a research fellow at the Institute for Development Studies in Brighton, UK, and Alan Jenkins a professor emeritus of geography at Oxford Brookes University attribute the low level of China's urbanization during the 1960s and 1970s primarily to China's heavy investment in defense-related industry in geographically remote areas of China under the so-called "third line" policy (Cannon and Jenkins, 1990) discussed in Chapter 4 on regional policies and regional urbanization.

Two leading experts on China's hukou system, University of Washington Geography professor Kam Wing Chan (Chan, 2013) and Fei-Ling Wang, a professor of International Affairs at Georgia Institute of Technology (Wang, 2005), consider hukou the principal drag on China's urbanization. Many other Chinese and Western scholars agree.

Chinese scholars have contributed additional possible explanations. Zhao, Bao and Hou (1998) argue that reform of China's land use system stimulated China's urban–rural development. Zhu (2002) feels that obscurely defined property rights have played an important role in slowing China's urbanization.

Some of the most recent literature as this book goes to press in 2015 provide an updated account of the status of urbanization in China and emphasize recent change and prospects for the future.

University of Michigan sociology professor Xuefei Ren (2013) summarizes recent developments in Chinese governance and migration and concludes that the urban–rural dichotomy that was constructed under socialism is rapidly disappearing and Chinese cities have become strategic sites for reassembling citizenship rights for both urban residents and rural migrants.

China at present is in the midst of two transitions. These are the transition from a rural agricultural society to an urban industrial society and from a planned economy towards a market socialist economy. A number of scholars describe China's unique form of urbanization in the context of these great economic and social transitions (Wu, 1995; Pannell, 2002; Wu, 2002; Friedmann, 2005; Wu and Gu, 2005; Wu and Gaubatz, 2012). Parts of some recent anthologies such as *Restructuring The Chinese City: Changing Society, Economy and Space* edited by Laurence Ma and Fulong Wu (2004) help illuminate aspects of Chinese urbanization. You-Tian Hsing, a professor of Geography at the University of California at Berkeley who studies changing land and property rights in China considers Chinese urbanization is the urbanization of the local state and that local government leaders are now pursuing urban modernity, rather than industrial modernity (Hsing, 2012: 6). Yumin Ye and Richard LeGates (2013) in their study of coordinated urban–rural development in Chengdu, the capital of Sichuan province in the west of China, describe Chengdu's ambitious pilot projects to regularize use rights in rural land, modernize agriculture, and do physical and social planning on a metropolitan basis. A new book by Fulong Wu, *Planning for Growth: Urban and Regional Planning in China* (Wu, 2015) argues that planning is not necessarily an "enemy of growth", but contributes much in Chinese urbanization and economic development.

Yasheng Huang (2008) argues that China is a balance of two Chinas—the entrepreneurial market-driven China and the state-led urban China. Fan Zhang (2014), a professor at Peking University, analyzes the relationship between urbanization and economic growth driven by the global economy and argues that urbanization is an engine of domestic demand for future economic growth of China. He argues that Chinese urbanization would speed up if existing institutional obstacles are removed.

Given the complexity of China's urban development, much of the existing scholarly literature in journal articles and anthologies provides fragmented descriptions of the history of China's urbanization, case studies, or detailed analysis of specific issues, but does not attempt systematic elaboration. Some overall descriptions of China's urbanization process have been published in recent years that describe the relationship between social and cultural evolution of Chinese cities and economic development and urban growth. In addition to providing up-to-date factual descriptions of aspects of China's urbanization Weiping Wu and Piper Gaubatz *The Chinese City* (2012), Xuefei Ren's *Urban China* (2013), and John Friedman's *China's Urban Transition* (2005) provide integrated syntheses of Chinese urbanization.

OUR RESEARCH METHODOLOGY

Research Background

Until 1978 China's national government dominated development and urbanization through a highly centralized planned economy. Today decision-making in China is much more decentralized to the provincial and sub-provincial level, much ownership is private or takes the form of public–private partnerships, and decisions are increasingly subject to market forces. But, in addition to the legacy from the planned economy, Chinese development and urbanization are still heavily influenced by government intervention and regulation. The Chinese government guides and places constraints on urbanization through national level infrastructure and economic zone decisions and a variety of laws, regulations, and policies implemented by ministries and bureaus at different levels (Gu and Gu, 2006).

Between 1949 and 1978 China's urbanization was a product of the planned economy. The central government controlled urban household registration (hukou), employment, and food supply. Major project-specific decisions were made in Beijing for all of China, and the national government provided direct funding for construction and virtually all enterprises were state-owned enterprises (SOEs).

The Third Plenary Session of the 11th Central Committee of the Chinese Communist Party held in 1978 marked the shift of focus from class struggle to the development of productivity, and explicitly declared China's main target to be economic construction. The long and hard reform towards a market economy began soon afterwards. In the late 1970s and early 1980s China's urbanization was still greatly influenced by national policies despite deep structural changes to institutions and public policies taking place. The impact of the changes on urbanization became much clearer after 1984. Ma and Wu (2007) conclude that multiple transitions occurred simultaneously, the most important of which were from a state-controlled economy to a state-regulated market economy, from top-down distribution of resources to resources more controlled by local governments, from national industrialization to industrialization largely driven by global market forces, from unprofitable land use to more profitable land use, and from free housing supplied by working units to commodity housing provided by private markets.

China's unique urbanization and transition are shaped both by its internal institutional structure and its place in the international environment. As institutions were adjusted, the changes impacted urbanization. The most important of these institutional changes included changes to the household registration system governing rural population migration, the fiscal and taxation system governing the distribution of finances to different levels of government, spatial policy governing regional development, urban development policy associated with the evolution of regional urban space structure, and changes in administrative divisions influencing the distribution of government power.

The changes in China's position in a rapidly globalizing international environment led to the emergence of a new economic order and international division of labor during the process of economic globalization. China made good use of opportunities and industrial restructuring mobilized its regional development potential. A useful metaphor is to envisage China's regional development like a ladder. Policy decisions prioritize more advanced development at the top rungs of a development ladder in the Eastern coastal provinces descending to more basic development moving west through central and western China. The influx of Foreign Direct Investment (FDI)—initially mainly from Hong Kong, and Macao—and the deepening of China's involvement in international trade altered the regional landscape of China's urbanization. International competition in the new era provided much of the impetus for China's urbanization and transition. As a consequence, regional urbanization patterns changed (discussed in Chapter 4) and large-scale regional population flows occurred (discussed in Chapter 6).

In addition to changes in institutions, laws, policy and planning, China has gone through tremendous economic and social changes during the 30-plus years of reform and opening up. The influence on China's urbanization by rational decision-making by individuals—or as we argue throughout the book more often by households—and market forces have greatly increased. Empirical studies have shown that the barriers created by the household registration (hukou) system and a problematic labor market partially account for some of the features of China's urbanization since reform and opening up, particularly in the early period. In addition to analyzing the macro-level structural factors that impact Chinese urbanization, the present study also advances the importance of individual and household choice. While the importance of choice is fundamental in many studies of behavior in the West it is less frequently included in studies of China. This is particularly relevant to the fundamental issues of population migration and regional disparities in development.

Data Sources and Levels of Analysis

In addition to our own field research this book relies on many different data sources and different levels of analysis at the national, three great regions, provincial, municipal, and county levels.

China is a large and diverse country and scholarship on the history of Chinese urbanization emphasizes regional differences that have existed for millennia (Skinner, 1977). Contemporary scholarship emphasize that in addition to an understanding of China's overall urbanization processes at the national level since 1978, understanding the large differences in regional urbanization is also essential (Ma, 2002; Zhang, 2004; Friedmann, 2005).

Two ways of dividing China's territory for sub-national analysis are useful: by provinces and according to the three great regions of eastern, central, and western China. The "three great regions" concept was first introduced in 1986 in China's seventh Five-Year Plan. Subsequent research has often classified China into the three great regions in order to illustrate differences within China (Fan, 1995, 2005; Chan, 2008; Fan et al., 2008).

China has 22 provinces, 5 autonomous regions, and 4 municipalities directly under the central government at the same rank as provinces, excluding Taiwan and the Special Administrative Regions (SARs) of Hong Kong and Macau. Figure 1.4 shows China's provinces and the three great regions. Western, central, and eastern China have 10, 9, and 12 provincial level districts, respectively. In order to avoid the cumbersome re-statement of these different types of administrative divisions we will refer to the 31 provinces, autonomous regions, and municipalities directly under the central government, excluding Taiwan, Hong Kong, and Macau as provinces or provincial level units for the purpose of the book unless specially noted.

Generally, unless otherwise noted, we limit our analysis to the People's Republic of China (PRC) excluding Taiwan, Hong Kong, and Macau. For consistency we include data on Hainan province (which was a part of Guangdong province until 1988 when it became separate) and Chongqing municipality (which was established in 1997) into Guangdong and Sichuan provinces respectively for data consistency in longitudinal analyses.

Accurate data are key to the research of China's urbanization. The Chinese government now devotes a great deal of time and attention to collecting data on urbanization, classifying it, and issuing reports.

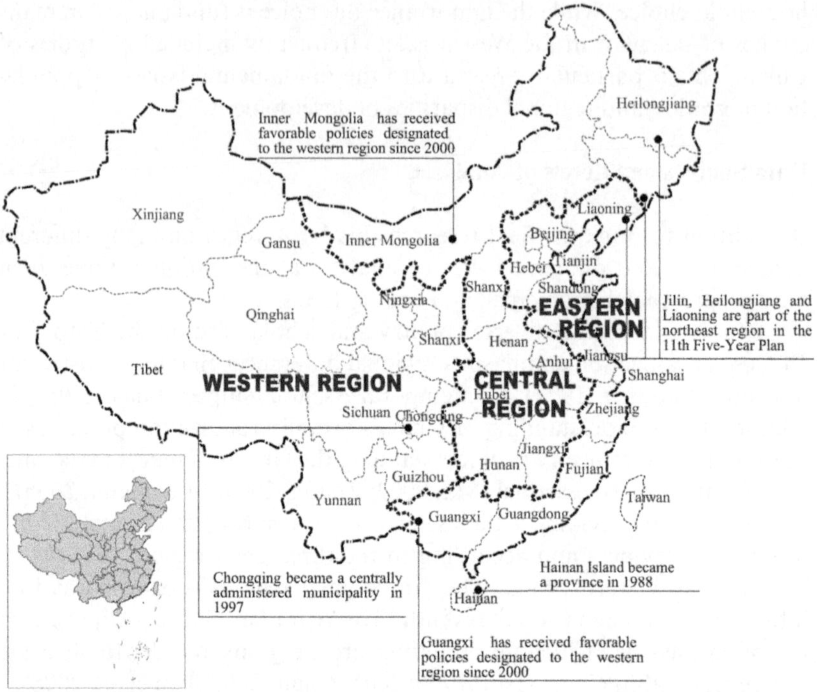

Note: The bottom left is the outline of China's boundary. Given space limits, the other figures showing China's great regions and provinces will only include the mainland of China.

Source: Drawn by Li Zhang.

Figure 1.4 China's three great regions

Nonetheless in China itself and to an even greater extent in the West, the nature of Chinese urbanization, is widely misunderstood.

Chinese urbanization is a complex moving target. While every Chinese citizen has a defined resident status (hukou) and is officially classified as an "urban" or "rural" resident and administrative boundaries are fixed and there is a large amount of data for different geographical areas in China, reality continues to outpace efforts to capture and describe it. Throughout this book we attempt to provide an accurate and up-to-date description of how different measures of urbanization were derived at different times, how they have been misunderstood, and what they really mean.

A key data source we use throughout this book is Chinese census data from the 1953, 1964, 1982, 1990, 2000, and 2010 population censuses and China's 1987, 1995, and 2005 1 percent population sample surveys. Other important data sources we use include China's annual *Statistical Yearbooks*, the *Urban Statistical Yearbook of China, Population and Employment Statistical Yearbooks, China Township Statistics* and annual reports and statistical data from the national ministries most directly concerned with land and resources, family planning, migration, and other activities that impact urbanization.

For provincial and sub-provincial level analysis since 2000 we rely primarily on City and County Statistical Yearbooks. The Chinese government began publishing provincial-level data on urbanization based on population surveys only after 2000. Before 2000, official sources of reliable continuous and comparable provincial data on urbanization do not exist. Yixing Zhou has reconstructed early data (Zhou and Tian, 2006) and we use his data in this book.

Where data were unavailable from official data sources we have drawn from media reports that we deem reliable and many reputable scholarly studies (in Chinese and English) reported in books, journal articles, conference papers, and unpublished sources. A major goal of this book is to make available to Western readers a great body of Chinese scholarship currently unavailable in English.

Data from different sources in China frequently differ for many reasons. Older data from the initial period after reform and opening is often less reliable than more recent data because institutions were less well equipped to collect it and they tended to present data in ways that were most favorable to them. High quality recent data often differs because of legitimate differences in definitions and methodology. Throughout we have attempted to use the most appropriate data source for Chinese data based on Professors Zhang and Zhao's longer professional experience. We provide caveats about the validity and reliability of different sources.

In order to place the Chinese experience in context we rely primarily on data from the two best international sources. The United Nations *World Urbanization Prospects: The 2014 Revision* (UN, 2014), and data from the Population Division of the United Nations contain much useful data on world urbanization that helps put China's urbanization in global perspective. The UN makes available more than fifty years of longitudinal data, current cross-sectional data, and a variety of projections. The World Bank's *World Development Indicators* (World Bank, 2014b) is another reliable source of longitudinal and cross-sectional data on world urbanization that we use throughout the book.

Aggregate population statistics describe what is actually happening only in the most general terms. People do not fall neatly into census categories that try to describe them. Two hundred and twenty million members of China's floating population (excluding the population relocated between their urban districts) do not live at their residential address for some or all of the time (NBSC-census, 2012). Many of these people are also members of China's amphibious population who move from one place to another depending on the time of year, life cycle, state of the economy, or for other reasons. Some people live in their village of origin during planting and harvest time, the New Year festival, or to take care of family members, but work in a town or city within the province or another province the rest of the year. Young people often move where there are abundant jobs and relatively high salaries even for people with limited education. Most of these jobs are in coastal China, provincial capitals, or large cities, but increasingly as we describe in Chapter 4 on regional policies and regional urbanization and Chapter 8 on towns, villages, and rural urbanization they are also in the core areas of small and medium-sized cities, towns, and the peri-urban areas surrounding them. More and more migrants, especially elders, are now returning home to rural areas to retire, work in new industries, marry, or start a business. When the economy is strong people tend to migrate to job centers and when China's economy weakens they may fall back on agricultural work in their rural areas of origin.

The rigid hukou classification of China's population between "urban" and "rural" no longer makes sense as many—perhaps the majority—of all employed people work in multiple jobs in both the rural and urban economy.

Administrative boundaries in China are constantly changed to try to keep pace with urbanization. This makes it extremely difficult to compare longitudinal data for administrative divisions over time. As a result of this great complexity, simple population statistics on the percentage of the population that is "urban" or "rural" don't capture reality. The more they are aggregated, the more deceptive they are. Urbanization varies from region to region and within regions.

Therefore, the official data is not enough to study China's urbanization. Data from field surveys in rural regions conducted by our research team in recent years provide a more nuanced view of China's urbanization. The integration of macro-level analysis based on quantitative "big data" and micro-level data on cities, counties, towns and individual behavior based on our surveys and interviews work together to provide the best possible explanation of urbanization. Following is an introduction to our field research. In the following chapters we refer frequently to these data by noting the site and time surveys were conducted.

Supplementing Macro-level Data With Field Data

This book is based on multiple quantitative and qualitative social science research methods, including the results of literature searches of Chinese and English books, articles, conference papers and other materials, secondary data analysis of data from the most reputable international and Chinese sources described above, analysis of difficult-to-find and unpublished local data, statistical and spatial modeling using SPSS and ArcGIS, observation, survey research, and interviews.

The core of our field research is studies in five areas of eastern, central, and western China conducted by Tongji University teams between 2010 and 2015. All of the investigations involved a combination of survey research, interviews, observation, and review of local secondary data, including unpublished local data. A description of the five field research projects follows. For the rest of the book we refer to this research using the location and year in which it was conducted. Detailed information on the fieldwork is in the Appendix at the end of the book.

Fifty-five towns in Hubei province, May 2010

The first field investigation was a study of Hubei's urbanization strategy conducted for the Hubei Provincial Government in May 2010. This research sheds light on the rationale for the urbanization policy of one of central China's most important provinces and empirical evidence of its impact on residents.

Yuelai and Zhengyu towns, Haimen city, Jiangsu province, March 2013

The second field investigation was conducted in Haimen city in Jiangsu province. The focus of this research was on the impact of industrialization on nearby rural areas.

Seventeen towns in Huaiyuan county, Anhui province, August 2013

Another field investigation was conducted in Huaiyuan county, Anhui province in August, 2013. Anhui is a relatively poor province in central China. Nearly one quarter of Huaiyuan county's population with local hukou have migrated. The main focus of this research was to understand the migrants' motivations for migrating.

Gaoming district, Foshan city, Guangdong province, March 2014

The fourth research site was in a district within Foshan city in Guangdong province in southeastern China. The main purpose of this research was to understand the impact of development on urban and rural areas near rapidly developing urban areas.

Quzhou city and nearby towns and villages

Between March 13 and 29 a Tongji research team investigated 27 towns and 5 urban streets in Quzhou city—a prefecture-level city in southwestern Zhejian province. In the first week the team visited each town and street and then selected 14 towns for in-depth investigations. Team members interviewed government leaders of the town and respected people in some selected villages. Four hundred and sixty-seven questionnaires were completed in this fieldwork, covering 14 selected towns. Between April 17 and 22, 2015 an international team including Professors Li Zhang, Min Zhao, Richard LeGates, Lee Inhee and Yoo Jaewoo from Busan University in South Korea, Yuka Himeno from Oita University in Japan and graduate students from Tongji, Busan and Oita Universities visited Quzhou. The team studied the relationship between villages, towns, peri-urban areas and urban development to gain a deeper understanding of Chinese urbanization by communicating with professors from other countries (see Figure 1.5).

In addition to the above field surveys, Tongji research teams investigated many additional cities and rural areas. Professors Min Zhao and Li Zhang obtained additional information from consulting projects over the past decade. Richard LeGates did field research in Chengdu in southwestern China during 2011 and 2012.

Source: Photos by Li Zhang.

Figure 1.5 Tongji team research methods

BOOK CONTENTS

This book is divided into ten chapters.

This first chapter is this introduction providing background on China and Chinese urbanization, a discussion of the most important topics and debates about urbanization, urban planning and policy in China, background on our research, background on the book's data sources and methodology, a description of our fieldwork in China, and an overview of the book contents.

The second chapter reviews the history of hukou and describes the dramatic changes in hukou that have occurred during successive waves of hukou reform. Chapter 2 argues that changes in hukou have not been able to keep pace with the rapid socio-economic development of China. Our analysis emphasizes the social structure hukou has helped create. We argue that even if hukou is entirely abolished its effects will continue to affect China, including Chinese urbanization for many years.

The third chapter reviews China's system of governance and administration at different levels and elaborates on the evolution of Chinese taxation, land use rights and other policies that affect urbanization. Administrative restructures have provided an essential institutional basis for changes in Chinese urbanization and economic and social development that has gone along with the rapid industrialization and urbanization processes. These changes have also affected statistics on China's urbanization level, including regional urbanization levels.

The fourth chapter reviews the evolution of regional urbanization policies and describes the characteristics of regional urbanization. We employ the Theil index to measure the change of regional urbanization disparities. Our research concludes that there is a close relationship between regional economic development and urbanization, but that market inertia often makes it impossible for policy transitions to keep pace, and sometimes policy transition does not occur at all.

The fifth chapter analyzes globalization and its influence on regional urbanization and regional migration. It describes growth of FDI and economic zones over time and the relationship between global and domestic capital flows and urbanization in different regions of China. While FDI and China's entry into the global economic system have had a large impact on urbanization, our analysis differs from most others. We emphasize different origins of FDI—mainly from Hong Kong, Macau, Taiwan and other countries of "Greater China" initially and only later from other parts of the world. Our quantitative study shows that the dependency theory does not explain China's fast urbanization and economic growth. Our analysis also describes the recent slowdown in FDI growth of and the growing importance of domestic capital and consumption and the implications of this trend for urbanization.

Chapter 6 established a framework to explain Chinese population flows from origins to destinations based both on macro-level institutional and economic forces and household choices. Using nationwide population census data and our own sample surveys we explore migration in different regions. Chapter 6 argues that economic considerations have become more important than social considerations as the main reason formal migrants migrate. Chapter 6 also discusses the new trends of migration redistribution and reverse migration.

Chapter 7 explores large city clusters, megalopolises, and China's evolving city system. While clearly the Beijing–Tianjin and Yangtze and Pearl River Delta regions are notable as the locations of the most advanced urbanization in China and make a disproportionate contribution to China's economy, we depart from most analyses that focus on megacities and megaregions to the exclusion of small, medium, and large-sized cities, towns, villages and rural urbanization. We depict China's urban system as a network of different-sized urban nodes connected by a variety of paths in the space of flows. We argue that large city clusters (LCCs) are already the main core of Chinese urbanization and will likely be even more important in the future. We review processes shaping Chinese urban systems and measure Chinese LCCs structure by analyzing population, cargo, information, and capital flows among regions, provinces, LCCs, and cities. Chapter 7 concludes that a diamond-shaped LCC system is developing China. We argue that LCCs are becoming the main units for China to strengthen global competition.

The eighth chapter describes the role of towns, villages, and urbanization in China's urbanization process. Towns perform an important function as service centers for rural areas, reservoirs for potential urban migrants, and the connectors of countryside and cities. A significant amount of China's urbanization is endogenous, bottom-up urbanization resulting from town and village residents. Town and village enterprise make a major contribution to China's economy.

The ninth chapter on China's double dual transformation discusses important topics related to Chinese modern urbanization such as the shrinking population dividend, Lewis turning point, and the middle-income trap. It argues that China's population dividend—a vast supply of cheap labor—has passed its peak and the unlimited supply of rural surplus labor is beginning to run out. While the turning point from an unlimited to a limited supply of surplus rural labor to a period of balance or shortage is coming, our macro-level analysis and field research suggests that labor surpluses and shortages in China are very uneven and a large additional pool of rural labor may be released as a result of agricultural modernization.

Many theorists believe that the most critical issue for countries such as China which have achieved a middle-level of development is how to break out of "the middle-income trap." We argue that a middle level urbanization trap may be coming and the central government should pay attention to it. We use Professor Li Zhang's double dual track theory, described in Chapter 9, as a framework to explain China's complex urban transition. The first dual track is state control and market orientation affected by indigenous institutional reforms and exogenous globalization. The second dual track is a change from simply increasing the quantity of cities, factories and urban population to the physical and social quality of cities to produce more livable, humane, equitable, ecological and sustainable cities to better serve the people of China and provide a model for other countries. This second transition is also affected by endogenous institutional reforms and exogenous global competition which are driving China's industry restructuring.

China's recent development is unparalleled in the history of world urbanization. China's cities and towns have absorbed several hundred million surplus rural laborers since the beginning of reform and opening up in 1978. But more than 200 million people who are considered urban in national population statistics are still floating between urban and rural areas. Their living standards and social welfare have lagged behind the urban population recognized as full citizens with rights stemming from hukou where they reside.

If we consider the urban transformation from government planning to market-oriented planning as the first great transition in China's urbanization, we argue that appropriate urbanization should be the second urban transition in China. Shifting the focus to the quality of urbanization should be the key objective in the coming urbanization process during the next great wave of Chinese urbanization as urban areas are projected to absorb another two hundred million migrants from rural China in the next decades.

In Chapter 10, the concluding chapter, we project that the pressure to increase urbanization levels will become less intense. This upcoming smooth period for Chinese urbanization presents policymakers with a strategic opportunity to re-orient Chinese urbanization from an emphasis on increasing quantity to an emphasis on improving the quality of urbanization. This period provides a window of opportunity during China's upcoming next urban transition. The conclusion offers some of our policy recommendations based on the findings in the book.

To sum up, one of this book's contributions is to fully outline the transitional process of Chinese urbanization since reform and opening up at the regional level by reviewing existing materials and analyzing available statistical data. It analyzes the effects of globalization on urbanization in different regions and the evolution of policies about Chinese urbanization, such as the household registration system, regional policies, and administrative regionalization. The book shows how China's urban processes have evolved from simple state-oriented guidance towards a combination of state-oriented and market-oriented guidance. There is a close relation between urban transformation and regional disparities. Urban transformation is restructuring the time and space arrangement of regional urbanization disparities.

Most importantly, this book divides Chinese urban transformation into two phases. The first transition (from state-oriented to market-oriented) has outstanding achievements, but to solve the social problems it has created requires grasping the opportunity now, during a narrow time window of opportunity, to direct China's next urbanization transition from a concern just with quantity to a concern with the quality of urban areas, economic, social and spatial equity, environmental quality, livability and integrated development of urban and rural China. This book's findings provide a basis for state policymaking to carry forward appropriate urbanization.

2. Evolution, status, and reform of hukou

INTRODUCTION

In China, the household registration (hukou) system has evolved for more than sixty years. After the founding of the People's Republic of China (hereafter, PRC) and the implementation of the planned economy, China's population management system had distinctive features highly integrated with social identity, social order, and economic policy. It remains a government tool for implementing social control by embedding population management within the political and economic system (Zhao, 2004). However, the functions of the population management system far exceed the domain of population migration control (Cheng and Selden, 1994; Chan and Zhang, 1999).

As a national policy, the hukou system originally played the role of allocating spatial resources and other welfare for urban and rural populations. Hukou management was relaxed after reform and opening up, but it has continued to be a major factor influencing population migration between urban and rural areas. The hukou system has been closely connected with the urbanization process, and discussions about China's urbanization typically involve the impact of the hukou system (Cheng, 1991; Chan, 1994; Mallee, 1995; Zhu, 1999; Zhang, 2004; Wang, 2005; PRC, 2014).

Kam Wing Chan (1994) calls Chinese cities "cities with invisible walls" because the hukou system creates stark divisions between the status and entitlements urban residents with urban hukou and an official residence address in a city or town and migrants with agricultural hukou status and an official residence in a rural area.

Currently all Chinese are assigned a hukou type: either agricultural hukou (nongye-hukou) or non-agricultural hukou (feinong-hukou) and a permanent residential address (see Figure 2.1). Most have their mother's hukou address and status, but China has permitted infants to be assigned their father's hukou status and address since 1998. Their entitlement to use agricultural land, a homestead, education, health, social welfare, pension and other services and benefits are based on the type of hukou they have and their registered permanent hukou address. To obtain hukou in a new

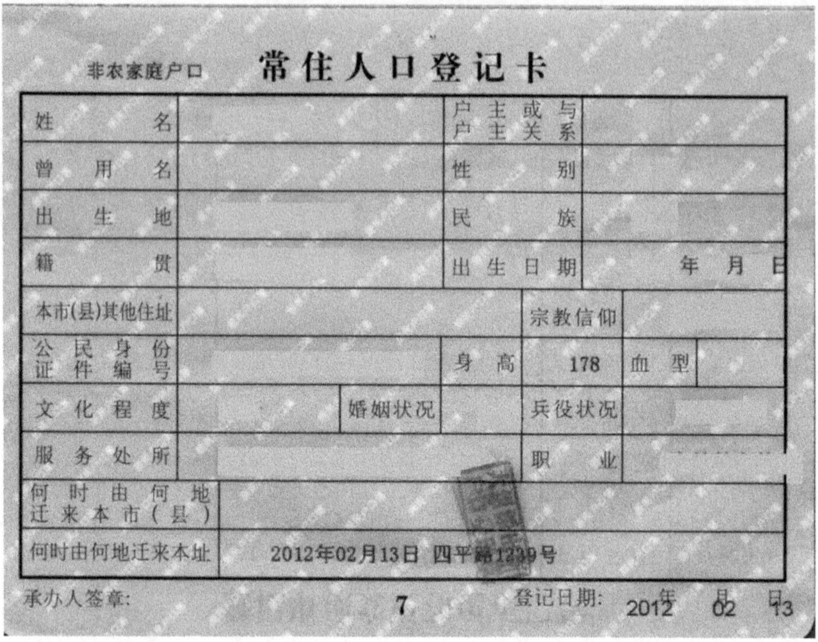

非农家庭户口 常住人口登记卡

姓名		户主或与户主关系			
曾用名		性别			
出生地		民族			
籍贯		出生日期	年 月 日		
本市(县)其他住址		宗教信仰			
公民身份证件编号		身高	178	血型	
文化程度		婚姻状况		兵役状况	
服务处所		职业			
何时由何地迁来本市(县)					
何时由何地迁来本址	2012年02月13日 四平路1239号				

承办人签章: 7 登记日期: 2012 年 02 月 13 日

Note: An individual's hukou document shows the name, birthplace, ethnic group, sex, ID, religion, occupation and other information.

Source: Supplied by Li Zhang.

Figure 2.1 Hukou content

location—such as a city to which a rural migrant has moved—requires approval by the local Security authority and a change of both hukou status and address.

In July 2014, the State Council issued a policy to abolish the functional divisions between agricultural hukou and urban hukou and set up a unified urban–rural residential registration system by 2020 (PRC-MSC, 2014).

Agricultural and non-agricultural hukou are statuses—not descriptors of the type of work a person actually does. Many people with agricultural hukou work in both agricultural and non-agricultural work and many no longer work in agriculture at all. Urban migrants with agricultural hukou are only entitled to some basic benefits that apply to agricultural households, not the often superior benefits that non-agricultural hukou holders have. In the countryside formal teachers in primary and secondary rural schools and formal officers in town or township government have non-agricultural hukou. There are also many informal teachers and informal officers in town and township government who do not have non-agricultural hukou. In this book we use the term urban hukou to refer to non-agricultural hukou and rural hukou to refer to agricultural hukou, although in a few rare cases people with non-agricultural hukou are not living in urban areas.

Most scholars are critical of hukou's unfair treatment of rural residents (Chan, 1994; Wang, 2005). However hukou confers some important benefits on rural residents, including entitlement to a use share of rural farmland, homestead land, a share of collective income from many different sources including profits from village-owned enterprises, and a share of compensation if collectively owned land is acquired by government. One of our key points throughout this book is that hukou has had a profound impact on the entire structure of rural social and economic relations. Reform or abolition of hukou alone will not bring about desirable changes critics of hukou advocate immediately.

Hukou statistics from different sources vary. The most reliable source is China's *National Statistical Yearbooks*. Unless otherwise indicated the hukou statistics in this chapter are from that source. According to the 2010 census 679 million Chinese live in cities and towns. Of the total, 460 million had urban hukou and 219 million had rural hukou (NBSC-census, 2012).

Despite fundamental social reforms in recent decades China's hukou system remains robust and continues to affect China's urbanization. Our macro-level structural analysis suggests that the "invisible walls" Chan (1994) described two decades ago have weakened and are likely to continue to diminish in the future.

This chapter reviews the history and current status of the hukou system in China and discusses its influence on regional urbanization. It describes the relationship between hukou and entitlements to health, education, social security, welfare, pension, housing, and other benefits. The chapter discusses how recent and proposed hukou reforms have impacted urbanization in the past and might impact it in the future. Finally, based on our macro structural analysis and field research on the behavior of individual households, we propose our own recommendations for hukou system reform.

EVOLUTION OF THE HUKOU SYSTEM

Founding of the Hukou System

Chinese household registration institutions can be traced back to about 2000 BCE (Zhu, 2003: 540). During the Zhou dynasty (1046–256 BCE)

China's population was divided by occupation (Wang, F., 2004; Fan, 2008: 43). Rural residents were organized into communities named jias which were in turn organized into communities named baos that reported to the local government—the bao-jia system. A more systematic bao-jia system for maintaining social order and collecting taxes was implemented throughout China during the Song dynasty (960–1279 ADE). The leader of each jia was responsible for preventing crime and collecting taxes for a small group of people. The bao-jia system influenced later social, administrative, and political organization in China. The nationalist government resurrected the bao-jia system in the 1930s when ten households formed one jia and ten jia one bao. Every jia had a leader and every bao also had a leader who was chosen from the ten jia leaders. The local government managed the leaders of the baos. Bao leaders managed the leaders of jia. Jia leaders were directly responsible for policing residents to prevent crime and had other oversight responsibilities.

Until the founding of the PRC in 1949, traditional household registration institutions based on the bao-jia system played an important social role, such as tax collection and land distribution, although the functions of household registration changed many times during 4,000 years (Fan, 2008: 43).

The rigorous hukou system was implemented in stages beginning soon after the founding of the PRC in 1949. The State Council issued *Regulation on Urban Household Management* in 1951 implementing a household registration system for urban residents to maintain security (PRC-MSC, 1951). Household registration for rural residents was established in 1953 in order to collect demographic data in rural areas for the First National Census in 1954 (PRC, 1953). The State Council issued *Directive for Establishing Permanent Hukou System* in 1955, formally extending household registration and migration management to rural areas (PRC-MSC, 1955).

The promulgation of *Hukou Regulations of the People's Republic of China* (PRC, 1958)—hereafter referred to as "Regulations"—in January 1958 is usually citied as the date on which China's full hukou system began. Though the core of the 1958 Regulations continued to be a demographic information system, hukou began to affect society in many ways. The Regulations specified the conditions under which the rural population could migrate to cities and towns. Since the mid-1960s they have restricted the flow of the rural population to cities or towns to a greater or lesser extent.

Establishment of Urban–Rural Segmentation

While the Regulations distinguish between the urban and rural nature of households, their effects on the differences in the welfare of the urban and rural populations prior to the early 1960s were limited. Economic conditions and household preferences rather than hukou restrictions exerted the greatest influence on migrant choices. The rural population retained the capacity to migrate to cities; this population joined the urban population through schooling, employment and marriage as well as by relying on friends and relatives in the cities.

In the early 1960s the Regulations began to curb rural migration to cities and towns. Tension between China and the Soviet Union, the failure of the Great Leap Forward campaign and drought disaster in the late 1950s and first years of the 1960s caused severe famine in various parts of China, which gravely affected both urban and rural societies. To maintain social stability, the Ministry of Public Security in 1963 made the distinction between rural and urban households the basis for food distribution. Urban households were privileged to obtain staple food (commodity grain) supplied by the government (Zhao, 2003). Households with agricultural (rural) hukou had to rely on food they produced by themselves. This further curbed rural migration because without food rations migrants could not survive in cities. During the 1960s and the early 1970s, the hukou system became the basis for distributing social benefits step by step. During the Cultural Revolution (1966–1976) more than 20 million educated youth moved from cities to rural areas (Liu, 2009). China's overall urbanization rate declined slightly from 17.86 percent in 1966 to 17.44 percent in 1976. China experienced a significant turning point in 1977. In the next few years millions of educated youths returned back to cities from rural areas.

As the population of cities and towns began to increase in the late 1970s they experienced growing pressure. The urban economy could provide only limited job opportunities due to long-term economic stagnation. Thus, in the early period of reform and opening up, as restrictions on movement into cities eased, the government continued to implement the policy that strictly controlled the conversion of rural hukou into urban hukou. The annual quota for conversions was initially limited to 1.5 percent of local residents (Wan, 1999). After 1980, the quota was increased to 2–5 percent of the local population (Wang, F., 2004). Most of the conversions were allocated to college graduates, cadres who had been deployed to the area, and resettlement of soldiers whose tour of duty was over, replacements for retired employees, and to reunite separated couples.

Contents of the Hukou System

In addition to hukou type (agricultural or urban) and official residence address, an individual's hukou includes other information such as age, occupation, marital status, migration history and the type of place where they are registered (village, town, small, medium, or large-sized city). It is generally easier for someone to migrate from a city or town to a city or town with a population no larger than the place they are migrating from. Together the difference between urban and rural status, differences among provinces, difference in the level of city, and the specific city where the household is registered create disparities in social welfare packages, such as grain supply (until the mid-1980s), job opportunities, education, housing, medical care and social security. Before reform and opening up in 1978, social welfare disparities in different level of cities and among provinces were not great and until the early 1990s the disparities among cities were only in the quality of welfare, not intrinsic difference like that between urban and rural resident status. Following market-oriented reforms and reform and privatization of state-owned factories, the disparities between cities began to increase.

Since the late 1970s hukou reform has evolved. Reforms were modest until the mid-1980s when increases in agricultural productivity made it possible for the government to abolish the grain ration system and allow food to be purchased as an ordinary commodity. More serious hukou reform began in the 1990s and 1997 is a particularly important year because it then became possible for couples to assign a baby the hukou address and status of either the father or mother. In the early 2000s many provinces and municipalities initiated bold hukou reforms, followed by a period of retrenchment when the problems with too much hukou reform too quickly created financial burdens on the cities where the reforms were implemented. At the time of this writing (spring, 2015) China appears to be embarking on a new round of serious hukou reforms. Table 2.1 summaries key changes in the hukou system.

Function of the Hukou System

Hukou is frequently cited as the indirect cause of urban–rural inequality (Ma, 2001; Liu, 2004), however most scholars agree that the hukou system contributes to China's rapid economic growth, providing massive cheap labor while maintaining social stability (Mallee, 2006). Despite the speed and scale of China's urbanization, many scholars point to hukou as a primary reason that China has not developed the large urban slums and high urban unemployment of cities like Sao Paolo, Brazil and Lagos, Nigeria which are arguably "over-urbanized" as described in Chapter 6 on large-scale population flows in China.

As a result of the rapid social and economic growth in China, the national government has been able to both abolish the agricultural tax and invest large amounts of money to improve the quality of life in rural areas.

Table 2.1 Evolution of the differences between rural and urban households

Contents	Period	Residents with non-agricultural hukou	Residents with agricultural hukou
Grain supply (food ration)	Before 1985	Government set grain and food ration standards, and urban residents bought at low price.	No grain supply from government. All grain food is from rural collectives' arable land.
	After 1985	The government canceled "central procurement of grain and food" and changed to contractual procurement. Grain and food prices were liberalized in 1993 and rural–urban differences in food rations were abolished completely in 1993.	
Employment	Before the mid-1980s	Local urban residents enjoyed priority over rural residents in employment. Restricted by the conversion quota of agricultural hukou to non-agricultural hukou, very few rural residents could find jobs in cities and towns unless through college enrollment or enlisting in the army.	Cultivation and other economic activities on collectively owned land.
	After 1985	Temporary residents were allowed to live in cities and towns. Thus, rural residents were given the rights to find jobs in cities. However, hukou status still affected getting formal jobs (by state-owned companies) in cities.	
Education	To the present	Urban residents enjoy higher education quality at primary and secondary schools. These urban schools generally reject the students from other jurisdictions including rural areas.	Rural areas have weaker basic education quality. Entering senior high school and college in China is by uniform national examinations, so rural students were disadvantaged in terms of access to higher education.
Housing	Employees at state-owned units may obtain welfare housing or rent public housing at a low price. After the 1980s, China began to implement the policy of commercialization of urban housing, and welfare housing was gradually phased out after 1998.		Rural households have use rights to residential homestead land. Rural houses are usually self-built and allowed to circulate only within the village (production brigade or production team).

Table 2.1 (continued)

Contents	Period	Residents with non-agricultural hukou	Residents with agricultural hukou
Social security	Currently urban residents typically have access to social insurance systems such as pensions, medical care, occupational injury and maternity insurance; social welfare for old age, assistance for children and the disabled; social relief programs such as low insurance, disaster relief, mutual assistance and relief for beggars; housing security systems such as participation in the housing accumulation fund and economically affordable low price housing.		For rural areas, the rural basic pension, new rural cooperative medical system and rural mutual aid systems are being constantly improved. But insurance for occupational injuries, and maternity housing subsidies are still rare.
Hukou at birth and hukou relocation	Before 1997	Children's hukou goes with that of their mother. Females with rural hukou are not allowed to adopt the husband's urban hukou.	
	After 1998	Children are allowed to choose whether to go with the hukou of father or mother. Husband and wife are allowed to adopt the hukou of either spouse. Restrictions imposed on relying on friends and relatives, obtaining hukou changes through investment and for old age are partly relaxed.	
Channels for rural residents to change to urban households	Before 2000	The quota of agricultural hukou changing to non-agricultural hukou was rigorously restricted. The only channels include college enrollment, enlistment, employment at state-owned enterprises, "back door" (Guanxi) and others.	
	2001	The uniform quota for changing agricultural Hukou to non-agricultural Hukou was canceled. Hukou at the county level and below continuously relaxed. Barriers for rural residents to settle in small towns (including most counties) were basically removed. But there were still limitations on changing Hukou to larger or higher level cities, economically developed cities and municipalities.	

Source: Li Zhang (2010).

As a result, advantages of rural hukou over urban hukou have increased; however, previous studies tend to dismiss this reality. Rural hukou guarantees the ownership of residential homestead land where a household can build its own house, use rights to a share of the collective's arable land which they and their heirs can farm (or rent), children's right to inherit residential parcel(s) and housing, the right to share the economic benefits of collectively owned Township and Village Enterprises (TVEs), health, education, and other social welfare benefits provided by the rural collective to which a household belongs, and a share of proceeds if the land is requisitioned for urban development. A final consideration is family planning policies. These often offer rural residents greater choice than urban residents. They are usually less stringent in areas that are classified as rural, including urban villages entirely engulfed by cities in which the land is no longer farmed. Together these entitlements provide both a social safety net and an asset. Our research found that in addition to making choices about where members of the household should live to maximize household income and utility, rural households carefully weigh the pros and cons of retaining rural hukou status, seeking urban hukou status, and particularly mixed household locational, work, and migration strategies. A common pattern in Hubei province, for example, is for most members of a household to retain rural hukou, but work at both farming and nearby jobs in industry, but with one or more household members (typically young and predominantly male) migrating to a town or city to work and send remittances home. While it is true that rural migrants to cities who do not obtain urban hukou face discrimination compared with their counterparts with urban hukou, overall urbanization and migration have greatly benefitted rural Chinese as well as urban residents with urban hukou. In recent years the relative status of rural residents has significantly improved.

Hukou System Reform

The current hukou system has been implemented in China for more than half a century. Prior to reform and opening up in 1978, this system impeded the progress of urbanization, and the speed of China's urbanization lagged behind the pace of industrialization. The institution of the Household Contract Responsibility System (hereafter, HCRS), which began in rural areas in 1981, liberated a huge surplus agricultural labor force at the same time that many educated youths were returning from the countryside to the cities (Liu, 2009). These factors fueled the rapid growth of the urban population beginning in the early 1980s. The number of migrant workers with informal jobs and without jobs in cities increased rapidly during this period. China's dual urban–rural structure was significantly affected. The effect of controlling population migration through hukou weakened, and hukou reform was inevitable.

Hukou Reform in Rural Towns

China began to relax hukou restrictions in the early 1980s. Initial reforms were concentrated in rural towns. To address the problem of the excessive labor force liberated from the rural areas, the Ministry of Public Security issued a policy in 1984 that established a new form of hukou, which permitted households to obtain staple food by themselves (not covered by food rations) in rural towns. This type of hukou was designed for migrant rural residents who possessed business skills or with technical expertise. Residents granted this form of hukou were regarded as part of the urban population, but without the right to buy low-priced grain supplied by the government. Given the rapid increase in agricultural production that occurred in the early 1980s as a result of the HCRS system and the emergence of a market in food beyond what was requisitioned by the state or consumed by rural households, more and more households were able to provide food they produced or purchased to family members who moved to rural towns. Nearly five million rural residents were granted this type of hukou between 1984 and 1990 (Wan, 1999).

The rapid growth of urban population exerted considerable pressure on urban infrastructure, particularly in rural towns. In some regions, a fee was charged for granting this type of hukou, roughly equivalent to exactions and user fees commonly charged in the United States to cover costs of infrastructure resulting from population increase. Illegal trading of hukou emerged. As a result, the Chinese government imposed restrictions on this kind conversion of rural hukou into urban hukou in 1989.

Another round of hukou system reform targeting rural towns was initiated in the mid-1990s. Initially the State Council developed new measures on an experimental basis. After a period of experimentation, in 1997 the State Council instructed rural towns to implement "Trial Measures for Reform of the Household Management System for Rural Towns" (PRC-MSC, 1997). The instruction focused on reforming the hukou system for rural towns while maintaining restrictions on rural migration to mid- and large-sized cities. In 2001, the State Council endorsed "Directions on Reform of the Household Management System for Rural Towns" (PRC-MSC, 2001). The new policy allowed rural people to apply for urban hukou in rural towns (urban districts of county-level cities, capital towns of a county, and other designated towns) only if they had a stable job either in a state-owned unit or private company and a dwelling place in the rural town. There was no quota on the number of hukou changes that could be granted in these places. As Chapter 3 on central and local governments, administrative divisions, and urban policies describes, most county-level cities have been upgraded from counties, so their urban districts are similar to key towns in counties. Accordingly the policy favoring rural towns also covers urban districts of county-level cities. Hukou reform for rural towns has been nearly completed. At least in theory, hukou in rural towns has been absolutely open since 2001.

Blue Stamp Hukou

The social welfare that accompanies urban hukou—particularly the promise of better education for their children—is important to some rural residents, which gives urban hukou economic value. Although any kind of trade or sale of hukou status violates the law, many people would be willing to pay for urban hukou if that were legally permitted. While many towns and cities fear that they will be overwhelmed by a large influx of unskilled migrant workers, they welcome migrants who will benefit the local economy. The most obvious way in which a migrant might benefit a city or town is to invest their own money in a new business they start there. Cities know that better educated workers—particularly with university degrees—and workers with special skills will also benefit the local economy. As a result a special category of hukou—blue stamp hukou—was initially implemented in some rural towns, special economic zones, designated economic development areas, and high-tech industry zones within cities. In China official documents are usually stamped with red ink using an official seal or chop. This is the case with conventional hukou documents. The term blue stamp hukou comes from the practice of using blue ink for the official stamp approving this special category of hukou. In the early 1990s several small and medium-sized cities likewise adopted blue stamp hukou, and later the practice spread to some large cities and even metropolitan regions, such as Shanghai, Tianjin, and Shenzhen. The purpose of blue stamp hukou was to attract domestic capital for local housing sales and local business development. Unless they made substantial investments in businesses or purchasing new housing, recipients paid a fee for blue stamp hukou. Their official hukou papers were stamped with an official blue chop seal rather than the conventional red seal.

Blue stamp hukou is different from conventional urban hukou. A quota for formal urban hukou conversions existed prior to 2001, and local governments had no authority to increase the number of urban hukou conversions beyond the quota limit. Excess new urban hukou approvals were disapproved by higher-level authorities, so applicants could not obtain a red stamp from the higher-level authorities. However as the central government decentralized hukou decision-making, local governments could use their discretionary rights to approve blue stamp hukou in excess of permitted red stamp quotas. Recipients of blue stamp hukou enjoyed the same health, education, pension, welfare, and other social welfare benefits as recipients of red stamp hukou. Nevertheless, significant differences remained. Blue stamp hukou was only acknowledged by the granting government. It still remained agricultural hukou beyond the jurisdiction. If recipients of blue stamp hukou migrated to other cities or provinces, their hukou status remained rural (Guo, 2010).

The experimental practice of granting blue stamp hukou has been gradually invalidated since the beginning of 2000. People who received blue stamp hukou were generally permitted to change it to normal urban hukou after a few years. Most blue stamp hukou has now been changed to urban hukou and no additional blue stamp hukou is being granted. Tianjin, which had been a long-time implementer of blue stamp hukou, was the last city to stop granting new blue stamp hukou approvals in May 2014.

Experiments with Uniform Household Registration in Mid- and Large-sized Cities

After completion of hukou system reform for rural towns in 2001, China's tenth Five-Year Plan (2001–2005) set targets for hukou reform in mid- and large-sized cities by the end of 2005. The Ministry of Public Security proposed to radically reform the dualistic urban–rural hukou system during the same period (Fan, 2008). Shortly after 2000 many cities embarked upon hukou reform. More than fifteen provinces declared their intention to abolish the distinction between urban and rural hukou for all people living within their jurisdictions, to create so-called unified hukou systems. This would apply only to people with local hukou, not to migrants from other areas living in the cities who do not have local hukou.

Several local governments experimented with uniform hukou systems. In 2001 Shijiazhuang city, the capital of Hebei province abolished the distinction between rural and urban hukou (Wang, 2003). Prior to 2001 migrants needed to satisfy many conditions related to their education level, marital status, local housing ownership or investments in order receive hukou. In 2001 the city began to permit people from other parts of China to migrate freely and immediately receive urban hukou in Shijiazhuang. But the reform was terminated in 2004. Shijiazhuang's experiment resulted in rapid growth of the urban population. Shijiazhuang's urban population in 2001 when the hukou reform began had increased by a little over 100,000 since the previous year. In 2002 the number more than tripled to 357,000, and in 2003 it reached 644,000—six times as many as in 2001. The dramatic increase of the urban population in Shijiazhuang shows the imprudence of radical hukou system reform. Many other Chinese towns and cities cite the Shijiazhuang case as a reason to proceed slowly with hukou reform.

Our research in central China illustrates the extent of the problem in provincial capital cities and other attractive destinations throughout China. Zhengzhou city, the capital of Henan province, is a case in point. In 2001 Zhengzhou city planned to increase its urban population from 2 million to 5 million in 2020. To achieve this goal, the city initiated a trial hukou system reform that abolished the differences among urban, agricultural and temporary hukou, to create a unified hukou system. The number of people granted urban hukou increased to 150,000 in 2003 alone (Zhu, 2006). Such a sharp increase in the urban population heavily burdened social services, transportation infrastructure, and other public goods. In the fall of 2003, the number of newly enrolled school children was one-third higher than in the year before the hukou reform. The number of students per class was as large as 90 in some schools—double the national standard maximum of 45. Such a large increase in the urban population caused difficulty in terms of public finance and service provision capacity. After the new hukou policy was implemented in 2001, the city's education expenditures increased to 1.12 billion RMB in 2003 and 1.34 billion in 2004. As the magnitude of these financial impacts became clear, the Zhengzhou government suspended the reform in 2004. However even after the reforms were suspended and the city stopped granting urban hukou in accordance with them, the costs associated with having granted so many people full hukou in the four years between 2001 and 2004 continued to rise. Once granted urban hukou household members became eligible for benefits at the time they were old enough to qualify. Young children who were not yet old enough to attend school at the time their families were granted hukou became eligible later—even after the reforms were discontinued and no new migrants were being granted urban hukou under the reform terms. In 2005, the year after the reforms were discontinued, as children who were two years old in 2001 reached school age, Zhengzhou's education expenditures increased to 1.83 billion RMB, and by 2006 as children who were one year old in 2001 reached school age education expenditures had grown to 2.43 billion RMB. A similar phenomenon has begun with respect to pensions and the cumulative effects will be felt far into the future. Elderly people become eligible for pensions at age 60. A 55-year-old who changed his rural hukou to Zhengzhou urban hukou in 2002, would start receiving a pension in 2007 when he reached age 60.

By 2014, rural hukou was partially revoked in 11 designated trial counties and cities in Zhejiang province. Guangzhou city abolished rural hukou in 2013.

Urban Residential Permit System Reform

After the radical trials of the hukou system reform and the problems they encountered, many local governments began to adopt a more cautious attitude toward hukou reform, particularly in large cities and metropolitan regions.

Shanghai, Beijing, Guangzhou, Shenzhen, Tianjian, Dongguan, and other large cities are disproportionately the cities of choice for rural migrants. These cities fear that they will be overwhelmed with migrants and fiscally challenged if barriers to hukou are lowered too much too fast, even though they have much higher per capita revenue than most other Chinese cities and are better equipped to manage fiscal strains. Because of their status in China's administrative hierarchy and also because many of China's top leaders are drawn from these cities, they have a large influence on national urbanization policy. As a result, the interests of very large cities that do not want to be forced to reform their hukou policies too quickly are very influential in national policymaking. This helps explain why China's National New Style National Urbanization Plan (2014–2020) (Hereafter, NNSUP) (PRC, 2014) proposes to relax hukou most rapidly the lower in China's administrative hierarchy one goes.

Cities with generous social service benefits and huge numbers of migrants seeking urban hukou whose contribution to costs will be much less than the benefits they will receive tend to be most resistant to hukou reform and set the highest standards to qualify for urban hukou. At one time Beijing made hukou available only to migrants investing at least 8 million RMB (US$1.29 million) or more in the city, university graduates with masters or PhD degrees, and spouses of residents with urban hukou only after a ten-year waiting period.

Jurisdictions that want a low-skilled migrant labor for their factories and assembly plants, construction work, and other low-skilled jobs are much more open to granting migrants hukou in order to compete for labor. Shijiazhuang, the capital of Hebei province, adopted hukou reforms in 2000 making it much easier for eight types of migrants to get hukou including teachers, businessmen, investors, university graduates, but also rural migrants who had lived and worked in city for two years (Wang, 2003). Guangdong province uses a 60-point point system in which migrants receive points based on their education, skills, social insurance contributions, and voluntary work. These are implemented mostly in smaller cities and towns; not Guangzhou, the large capital city of Guangdong province.

Shanghai looked to the Green Card system used in the United States and some other foreign countries in developing its urban residential permit system. US Green Cards are temporary work permits granted to non-citizens from other countries working in the United States. Holders of Green Cards are legal migrants, but are not entitled to many of the benefits of US citizens. Shanghai was among the earliest cities to implement such a system in 2002. The non-local population that obtained temporary residential permits in Shanghai exceeded 4.33 million by the end of 2007 (*Nanfang Daily*, 2008). In 2009, Shanghai published detailed regulations on residential permit management, and implemented a trial new policy for converting residential permits into local hukou, but only 175 people with residential permits successfully applied for local Shanghai hukou in six months due to the strict requirements for hukou conversion, such as educational qualifications and employment duration (Sina Web, 2009). Shanghai's conditions for hukou conversion were revised in 2014, but continue to emphasize high-end human resources. At the same time, Shanghai's residential permit policy was further revised to make it easier to get temporary residential permits. Regulations were standardized and conditions for converting residential permits into local hukou were clarified.

Apart from Shanghai, Shenyang (2006), Chengdu (2005), Kunming (2005), Shenzhen (2008), Guangdong (2010), and Jiangsu (2013) have adopted residential permit systems (see Figure 2.2). Some residential permits in one city may be used in other cities within the same province. The contents of the residential permit system vary from one province to another, but the common feature is the close connection with social welfare. Generally, more local public services are provided for the migrant population than was the case before, but less than residents with hukou receive.

Debates Over Hukou Reform

Conflicting opinions about hukou reform have emerged. Virtually all scholars and public officials are critical of the current hukou system and favor reform, but they hold differing views about what is most problematic about hukou, how to reform it, and how quickly to proceed. Very few people advocate a radical approach (abolition). Most suggest a progressive approach (incremental reform) more or less rapidly. Advocates of abolishing the hukou system altogether argue that hukou impedes the flow of market elements and hence economic development (Cheng, 1991; Hu, 2008; Hu and Yang, 2014). More pragmatic approaches acknowledge unequal benefit allocation in the hukou system, but take into account the practical difficulties encountered in the hukou reform experiments discussed above and adopt a more realistic view of the enormous cost and disruption that too radical hukou reform implemented too quickly

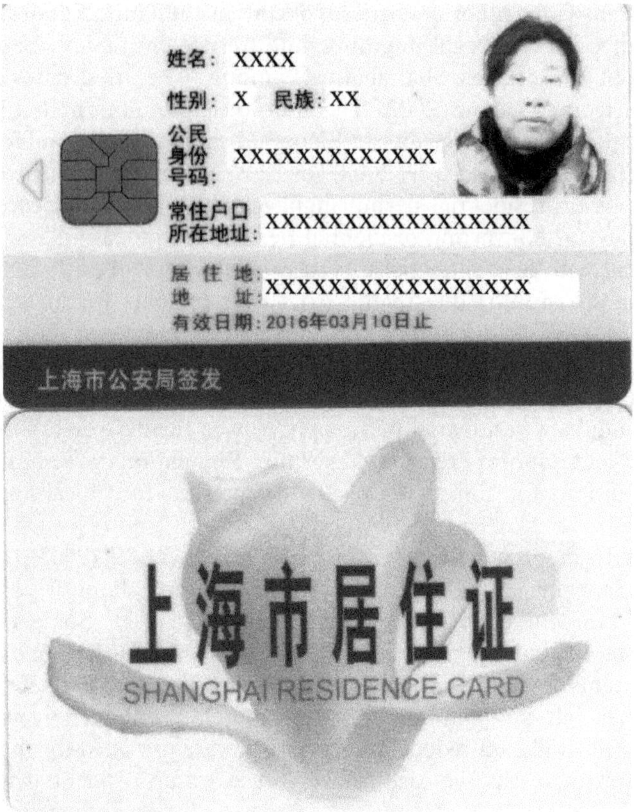

Note: This is a magcard with key information about the owner. The card shows the owner's name, sex, ethnic group, ID, hukou address, temporary living address and the date the card became valid.

Source: Supplied by Li Zhang.

Figure 2.2 Residence permit for a Shanghai resident

would have (Mackenzie, 2002; Zhao, 2003; Wang, F., 2004; Chan and Buckingham, 2008; DRC and WB, 2013).

The latest hukou system reform focuses on residential permits, and additional new conditions for granting urban hukou. The new conditions generally become more stringent as city scale and importance increase (Zhang, 2011). Hence, even after the differentiation between rural and urban households is completely abolished, new disparities based on city rank are likely to appear, and rural segmentation will persist. The new conditions for granting urban hukou typically require that rural migrants be economically well off, have purchased housing, and have a stable job. This means that to obtain urban hukou, the income level of migrant rural workers must be higher than that of most workers with rural hukou. Therefore, some scholars have pointed out that, with an increasing number of high-income rural migrants flooding into the cities, poverty in rural areas will be aggravated, and the urban–rural difference will increase (Lu and Chen, 2006).

The reform trials in Shijiazhuang and Zhengzhou demonstrate that opening hukou and implementing migration management are insufficient to fulfill the goals of hukou system reform. They show that well-intentioned hukou reforms are likely to create new social problems. So far, reforming the hukou system has failed to dispel and even reinforces households' awareness of the economic values. Therefore, eliminating the distinction between agricultural and non-agricultural households is only one aspect of hukou reform.

SOCIAL WELFARE SYSTEM REFORM

A Chinese resident who wants to move from the countryside or a village to a town or city that qualifies as urban may "become urban" by physically migrating and securing the local Bureau of Security Office's approval to change his or her permanent residence address to the city and hukou status from rural to urban. He is then a *de facto* member of the urban population and will be counted as such in the next census and a *de jure* resident of the urban area entitled to the benefits of other residents with urban hukou. A migrant already living in the city or town (a *de facto* member of the urban population) may "become urban" by obtaining the same approvals—simply a status change without moving. Like social welfare systems in other countries, entitlements and the level of benefits an individual receives once they are deemed eligible to receive social welfare are tied to age and prior contributions. A 50-year-old migrant who becomes eligible to receive a pension based on urban status, for example, but only makes contributions into the system starting at age 50 will not receive the same pension on retirement as a person with urban hukou in the same city who has been contributing to the system for many more years. In practice tens of millions of ex-rural hukou holders are not fully integrated into urban social security systems and receive fewer benefits than official urban residents.

This reality is not unique to China. The evolution of the primary US national social security and health programs suggest how China's system may evolve over time. The US Social Security System is the primary federal program to provide benefits to retired people over the age of 65, the disabled, widows, and dependent children. It was adopted in 1935 and the first modest payments were made in 1940. By 2013, Social Security expenditures had grown to $1.3 trillion (7.98 trillion RMB), 8.4 percent of total US GNP and the system provided benefits to 42 million people over the age of 65, 14 million people with disabilities, and 7 million others (US-SSA, 2014). The US federal Medicare system was adopted in 1966 and in 2010 provided health insurance to 48 million Americans. How far medical coverage should be extended and how it should be paid for has been one of the most controversial political debates in the United States for decades and is one of the major areas about which US political parties disagree today. In the United States a variety of other federal and state social welfare programs, public and private pension systems, and insurance paid by individuals and their employers provide additional security.

The close connection between the hukou system and urbanization can be largely explained by the difference in social welfare provided by hukou (Lu, 2008). That is why China's National New Style Urbanization Plan devotes a substantial amount of attention to hukou reform (PRC, 2014).

While past policies are being reformed and many decisions about migration and hukou have been decentralized, the current Chinese leadership is still committed to controlling the increase in the urban population in large cities. While China is making steady progress in incorporating rural migrants into urban society—a process generally translated as "citizenization" of rural migrants—and increasing social welfare benefits to migrants, the huge numbers of people involved and the enormous cost of adequate, uniform, universal social welfare requires policymakers to phase reforms and match them to the varied conditions in different parts of China.

Social Security

Prior to the early 1990s, insurance for medical care, old age, occupational injuries, and maternity was related to urban resident status and an individuals' relationship to a state-owned enterprise. Old age and medical insurance for urban employees in enterprises and public institutions were mainly the responsibility of enterprises or public institutions. Most migrant workers were excluded from these social welfare systems.

As the planned economy has given way to an increasingly market-oriented economy, China's social security system has undergone a series of reforms. The number of participants in the social security system has increased every year (PRC-NPFPC and ADMP, 2010, 2011, 2012).

A national social security system for urban residents that combines pooled and individual accounts was formally implemented in China in 1993. Since then, social welfare support for employees provided by enterprises has gradually diminished as coverage has shifted to the national system. Despite these changes, until 2003 social security was limited to rural residents. Reform of the social security system has been extended into rural areas after 2003.

China established a minimum life guarantee system (dibao) for urban residents in 1999. Dibao was later extended to rural residents. Before 2004 dibao covered rural people only in Beijing, Tianjin, Shanghai, Guangdong and Zhejaing. After 2004, Fujian, Liaoning and Jiangsu provinces set up dibao systems for rural residents and other provinces and cities followed at different times and with different benefit levels.

In summary, during the past 30 years, China's social security system reform focused on transforming people protected by state-owned enterprises into people protected by civil society. These social welfare reforms of the last twenty years have significantly promoted the migration of labor between regions and particularly between rural areas and urban regions. This is one of the most important reasons for the large increases in migration flows in the 1990s and the first decade of the twenty-first century shown in Figure 2.3.

The Chinese government has made social security for migrant workers a national-level legal imperative, but leaves a great deal of discretion about how to implement the policy to lower levels of government. Article 95 of

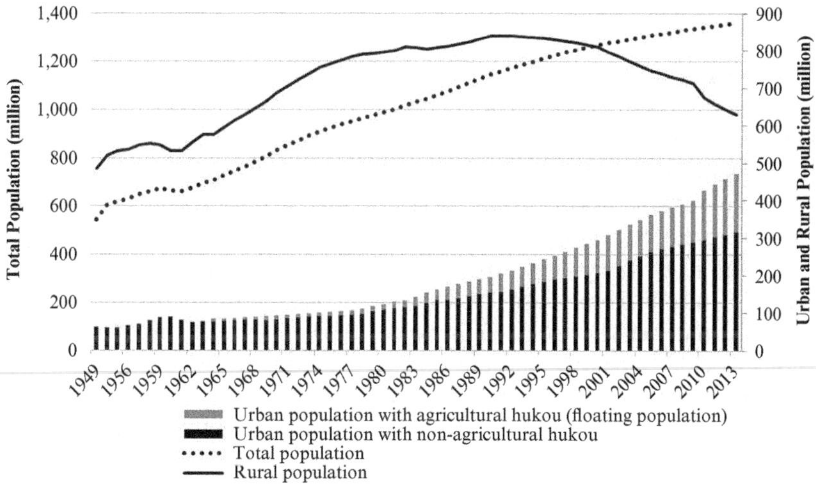

Source: Chinese *Statistical Yearbooks*, specified years. Data plotted by Li Zhang.

Figure 2.3 Growth of urban population with agricultural, non-agricultural, and rural hukou, 1949 to 2013

the 2011 Social Insurance Law of the People's Republic of China (hereafter "Social Insurance Law") states that the migrant rural population should participate in social insurance in accordance with the law (PRC-SSL, 2011). Data published by PRC's Ministry of Human Resources and Social Security (PRC-MHRSS, 2010, 2013) provides information on the current number of migrant workers covered by various social welfare programs and benefit levels and how they have changed in recent years, as reported in the following sections.

Medical Insurance

Experimental programs to provide medical insurance to the rural migrant population began in 2006 at the national level. By the end of 2013 50.18 million migrant workers were participating in the medical insurance system: double the number in 2006 (23.67 million). The percentage of rural migrants to cities covered by medical insurance and benefit levels varies depending on the province and municipality, so it is difficult to specify exactly how many migrants are covered by medical insurance and how adequate their coverage is. While there is still a long way to go before China's rural population and rural migrants to cities have uniform medical coverage identical to urban residents, China is making rapid progress in creating more uniform and adequate coverage—particularly for rural migrants and rural permanent residents.

Pension Plans

There are significant regional variations in the coverage and benefit levels of pension plans for migrant workers from one province to another and between jurisdictions within provinces. Local governments have been exploring more appropriate models of retirement pensions for the migrant population. By the end of 2013, 48.95 million rural migrant workers were participating in some form of basic retirement insurance system: triple with the number in 2006 (14.17 million). The practice of distributing pensions to elderly people who are not participating in the urban insurance system in rural areas is expanding. Before 2000, very few elderly people in rural areas received old age pensions with the exception of elderly residents in the peri-urban areas of Shanghai, Guangzhou, and some other affluent cities. Only a few people who had been employed by an urban unit (danwei) received a pension from their danwei. Despite significant progress, the adequacy of pensions for people with non-agricultural hukou depends on the economic situation of the rural collectives they belong to. Benefit levels that pensioners with agricultural hukou receive are much lower on average than pensioners with non-agricultural hukou receive—particularly compared with pensions of former employees of state-owned enterprises and civil servants—and many rural residents receive no pension at all. The average old-age pension payments for the rural population in 2012 was only about 859 RMB (US$140) a year compared with average payments to urban residents of 20,900 RMB (US$3,404) a year (Xinhua News, 2014). For retired enterprise employees and civil servants, some pensions are as high as 60,000 RMB (US$9,771) a year (TT News, 2014).

Our research found that many migrants now in their fifties and older return to their rural places of origin if they are unable to work in demanding jobs or for long hours because they cannot afford to live in cities. Over time incorporation of rural migrants into retirement systems that pay substantial benefits could increase the number of permanent migrants in cities because more would be able to afford to live there. Some older migrants might still choose to retire to lower cost rural areas where their pension income goes further as is frequently the case worldwide. These issues are discussed in greater detail in Chapters 4 and 5 on regional policies and regional urbanization and large-scale population flows.

Unemployment Insurance

Efforts to expand the coverage of unemployment insurance have been substantial in a number of provinces. Unemployment insurance is gradually covering the migrant rural population and non-local workers. Shandong (2002), Zhejiang (2004), Hebei (2005), Hubei (2011), Anhui (2011), and Jiangsu (2011) began to implement unemployment insurance for the migrant rural population and non-local workers as well as local urban residents. Other provinces are emulating this practice. The number of rural migrants covered by unemployment insurance reached 37.40 million by the end of 2013 (PRC-MHRSS, 2013).

Occupational Injury Insurance

Rural migrants to cities and towns disproportionately work in construction and less desirable factory jobs where they are more likely, on average, to sustain work-related injuries or contract work-related diseases than other participants in the urban workforce. As a result, rapid industrial development has increased the prevalence of occupational injuries and occupational diseases. Up to 90 percent of the victims of occupational injuries and diseases are migrant workers (ACFTU, 2011). Accordingly occupational injury insurance for migrant workers has attracted the attention of government. Under the guidance of relevant national laws and regulations, many provinces have issued local regulations governing occupational injury insurance. These regulations aim to extend occupational injury insurance from formal state-owned enterprise employees to other employees, including migrant workers. Nearly 72 million migrant workers had some form of occupational injury insurance by 2012 (Yang, 2014).

Since our research in central China shows that rural households are well informed and make rational choices about migration that include not only wages, but a calculus of all the likely costs and benefits of migration, better occupational injury insurance for migrant workers might encourage migration of able bodied workers contemplating work in construction and other demanding and dangerous jobs.

Maternity Insurance

Currently maternity insurance in China is only available to formal employees of urban enterprises and public institutions, with few exceptions. In 2013 163.92 million women were participating in some form of maternity insurance program (PRC-MHRSS, 2013). There have been trials of maternity insurance for migrant workers in Beijing (2011), Xiamen (2011), and some other cities, but compared with other forms of social insurance, few migrant women have any form of maternity insurance and discussions of maternity insurance remain at an exploratory stage in most parts of China. Significant extension of maternity insurance could accelerate migration of couples rather than the husband only or young unmarried workers as often occurs now, both increasing the urbanization rate and reducing problems of split families, leading to a healthier form of urbanization.

Minimum Wage Laws

Our research concludes that overall, notwithstanding significant labor shortages in some areas, the demand for labor in China has increased more than the labor force supply. Despite labor shortages and rapidly increasing wages in high-labor-demand areas, some enterprises still pay very low salaries. Since migrant laborers frequently work in the lowest paying jobs, the minimum wage standard particularly impacts them. The State Council's *Regulations on Lowest Salary for Low-income Workers* published in 2004 provides two minimum wage standards, one for monthly salaries and one for hourly wages (PRC-MSC, 2004). Local governments can set their own minimum wages, but not lower than what the national regulations require.

As China's population ages and the one child policy shrinks the working-age cohort, a trend of structural imbalance and demand exceeding supply has emerged in China's labor market. As a result, migrant rural workers' salaries have improved considerably in recent years. Between 2010 and 2013, a number of provinces facing the greatest labor shortages raised their wages dramatically, particularly for low-income workers. In 2013 the average minimum RMB/mo was 1,398 for Beijing, Shanghai, Tianjin, Zhejiang, Jiangsu, Shandong, Fujian, Guangzhou, and Shenzhen. It had increased an average of 40 percent in these nine provinces from 2011. In 2013 Guangzhou, Shenzhen, Shanghai, and Beijing the standard was 1,550, 1,500, 1,450, and 1,400 RMB/month respectively, up by 50 percent, 36 percent, 29 percent, and 46 percent from 2011 according to data from multiple provincial data sources.

HUKOU AND URBAN POPULATION GROWTH

Population Growth in China

There was very little difference in the growth rate between China's urban and rural population during the Mao era. What did occur was mostly the result of natural increase. With reform and opening up in the early 1980s, as restrictions on migration were relaxed and demand for factory labor in cities exploded, tens of millions of former peasants migrated from farms and villages to cities and towns. Very few of them received urban hukou. Rather they were classified as "temporary" workers or the "floating population" as described in Chapter 6. The 2010 census gives the total number of China's "floating population" who work somewhere other than where they have official residence status as 221 million (PRC-NPCO, 2012).

Figure 2.3 shows the growth of China's total population, urban population with urban hukou, urban population with agricultural hukou (the floating population), and the rural population from 1949 to 2013. After reform and opening up in late 1970s, the total population of China increased constantly until the 1990s, when the urban population (with and without urban hukou) grew rapidly,[1] and growth of the urban population also accelerated—particularly after 2000. However, the overall growth of the urban population with non-agricultural hukou was far smaller than that of the urban population with and without non-agricultural hukou. The difference between the urban population with non-agricultural hukou and those without non-agricultural hukou in 2010 was 178.45 million more than in 1982. Many rural people are now living in cities and being counted as members of the *de facto* urban population in the census, but they are still hold rural hukou. It is clear that the reform of the urban hukou system has lagged behind the growth of urban population, and the difference between the two has been increasing.

Table 2.2 Natural population increase (%)

	1982	1987	1990	1995	2000	2005	2010
Natural growth rate of total population[1]	15.68	16.61	14.39	10.55	7.58	5.89	4.79
Natural growth rate of urban population[2]	13.56	9.24	6.59	5.90	4.82	4.23	3.53
Natural growth rate of non-agricultural population[3]	12.96	10.4	11.5	5.90	5.48	4.04	4.71

Sources: (a) Natural growth rate of the total population from *China Statistical Yearbook 2011*; (b) Basic data from the 1% sampling censuses in 1987, 1995 and 2005 and 10% short tables of population census in 1982, 1990, 2000 and 2010; (c) Basic data are from *Urban Statistical Yearbooks of China* (NBSC-usy, 1988, 1991, 1996, 2001, 2006 and 2011).

Natural and Mechanical Growth

The population growth of a country or region consists of two parts: natural growth and what demographers call mechanical growth. Natural growth is the net result of births and deaths: mechanical growth the result of migration—both immigration and emigration.

Because international foreign immigration and emigration in China is a relatively small percentage of the total population, the mechanical growth of China's population is negligible. The mechanical growth rate of China's urban and rural population can be calculated by subtracting natural growth from the total growth rate. Table 2.2 presents full census and 1 percent Sample Population Counts and our calculation of the natural growth rate. It shows that the natural growth rates of China's urban population have always been lower than the growth rate of the total population.

Figure 2.4 shows how the policy liberalizing hukou for migration to rural towns adopted in the mid-1980s promoted rapid growth of the urban population. Hukou system reform in the mid- and late 1990s again fueled rapid growth of the urban population. The radical reform experiments in the early 2000s pushed the growth of non-agricultural population to its peak. The mechanical growth rate of the non-agricultural population exceeded that of the urban population for the first and only time in the three decades between 1982 and 2010. However, hukou policy was tightened during the late 2000s, which once again slowed down the growth of non-agricultural hukou. However, this did not slow the rapid increase of the urban populations in cities and towns. Overall, the difference between urban and non-urban population living in cities increased from 22.49 million in 1982 to 205.94 million in 2010.

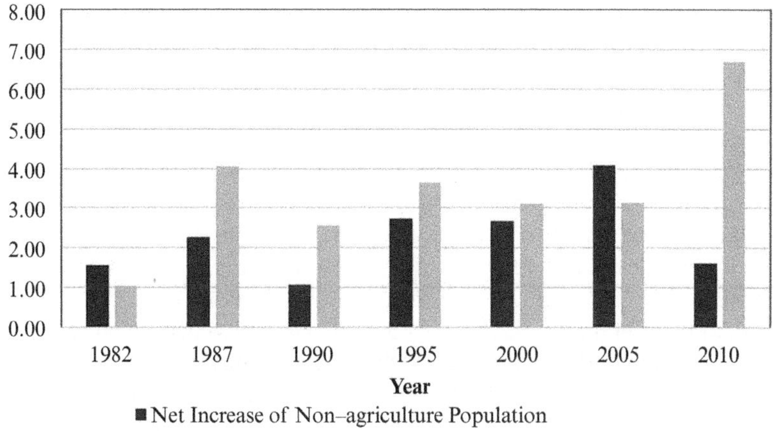

Source: Chinese *Statistical Yearbooks*, specified years. Data plotted by Li Zhang.

Figure 2.4 Net increase in China's agricultural and non-agricultural population after deducting natural growth (%)

Regional Urbanization and Hukou Reform

Hukou system reform has not been implemented uniformly throughout China; it differs from one province to another and among local governments within provinces. Given the enormous scale and number of separate jurisdictions in China, aggregate analysis does not disclose difference among or within provinces. In order to provide a more nuanced description of the relationship between urbanization and hukou, we disaggregated data and analyzed differences at the scale of China's three great regions (east, central, and west), among provinces, and within provinces. The variation in the difference between urban population with and without non-agricultural hukou is a powerful indicator of the contribution of migration to urbanization at different scales and the relationship between hukou reform and urbanization. For the balance of this chapter we refer to the difference between the non-agricultural and urban population as "difference."

Ideally the natural growth rate of both the urban population and the non-agricultural population would be deducted. However, data to do this are unavailable or incomplete. Our data are a good approximation of the magnitudes of rural-to-urban migration and differences in the extent to which migrants have been absorbed in different parts of China.

Urban Population Growth in China's Three Great Regions

Figure 2.5 shows the number of urban residents without urban hukou in the three great regions of China from 1987 to 2013. It shows that the differences among China's three great regions are always positive; that is, that growth of the urban population has been consistently higher than growth of urban population with urban hukou. There is great variation in the difference in the past two decades in different regions of China. The general trend is that the difference in the eastern region is higher than the difference in the central region, and the difference in the central region is higher than the difference in the western region. The differences in all three major regions increased rapidly after 2000. This indicates that the hukou reform has not kept pace with urban population growth at the scale of any of the three great regions of China. A particularly significant trend since 2010 is the rapidly increasing number of people without urban hukou living in urban areas in the central region. That means the central region is now facing greater pressure for hukou reform.

Comparing the differences between the eastern and inland (western and central) regions over time shows that prior to 2000, hukou reform targeting rural towns kept better pace with urbanization in the middle and western regions than in the east. This result is evident in the stability of the differences in these two regions before 2000. Hukou reform obviously lags behind in the eastern region, where much of the urban population consists of rural migrants without urban hukou. Despite the intensity of the radical hukou reform experiments initiated after 2000 their duration was short, and their long-term impacts modest. The reforms did not reduce the difference between the urban and non-agricultural populations. Hukou reform lagged behind urbanization progress. The abrupt suspension of the hukou reforms that were begun in 2000 has meant that urbanization has continued more rapidly than the shifting of population with rural hukou to urban hukou and a huge urbanized population with agricultural hukou has emerged and will continue to grow if hukou policy is not changed.

Hukou reform and urbanization progress in the eastern region

Between 1987 and 2013, with the exception of the narrowing of differences in Shandong province after 2000 and Guangdong province after 2010, differences in all of the other provinces increased. The increase was especially striking in Guangdong and Zhejiang provinces before 2010.

Hukou reform and urbanization in the central region

In contrast to persistent growth in the eastern region, the differences in all of the provinces in the central region decreased between 1995 and 2000,

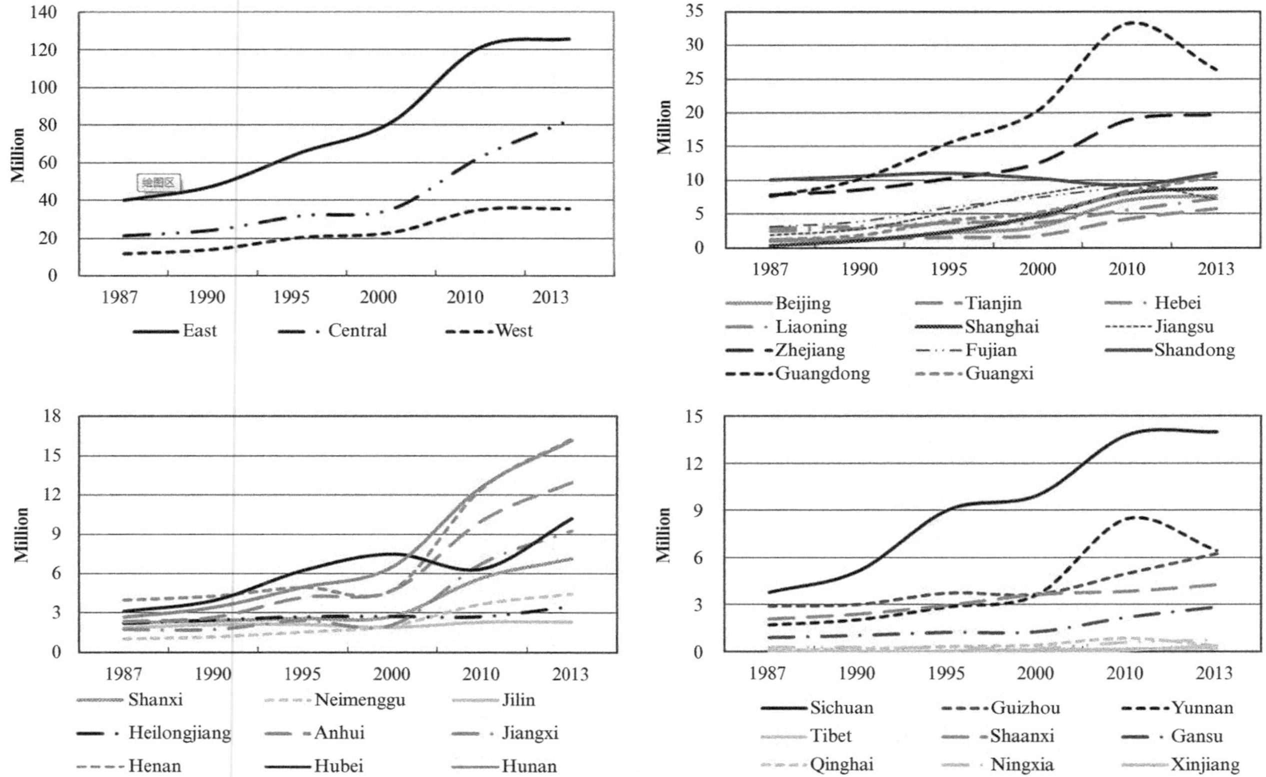

Source: NBSC-csy specified years and Ministry of Housing and Urban–Rural Development (2014). Data plotted by Li Zhang.

Figure 2.5 Number of urban residents without urban hukou in the three great regions and in Chinese provinces, 1987 to 2013 except in Hubei and Hunan. After 2000, however, the difference began to increase, with Hubei the only exception in 2000 to 2010.

Hukou reform and urbanization in the western region

With the exception of Sichuan provinces (including the adjacent provincial level city of Chongqing in the Sichuan total), until 2000 the differences for all of the provinces in the western region were relatively stable. After 2000, the differences in Sichuan and Yunnan increased rapidly, reflecting rapid urbanization in both provinces. Overall, pressure for hukou reform in the western region was not as high as that in the eastern and central regions. Yunnan is a special case. As Figure 2.5 shows, the urban population without urban hukou increased rapidly between 2000 and 2010 and then quickly decreased after 2010 as illustrated by the ascending and descending line in Figure 2.5. There are a number of reasons for this anomaly, including hukou reform.

Based on our analysis of the relationship between hukou system reform and urbanization progress in the three great regions and different provinces we concluded that:

(1) The implementation of hukou reform differs from one province to another.
(2) For each of the three great regions hukou reform is occurring, but at different paces.
(3) The continuing growth of differences in most provinces indicates that liberalizing hukou in rural towns has a very limited effect in promoting a healthy urbanization in which the rate at which migrants are granted urban hukou keep pace with migration.
(4) Hukou reform has not matched urbanization in most provinces.
(5) Hukou reform experiments begun shortly after 2000 did not significantly reduce urban–rural disparities. Sudden suspension of the reforms within a few years of the time they were begun caused the growth of the urban population in many provinces to continue to outstrip urbanization.

NEW DIRECTIONS IN HUKOU REFORM

Evolution of Local Government Hukou Reform Practices

The most important of the many changes in hukou policy the national government has made since the early 1980s has been the progressive decentralization of decision-making about hukou. While the national government still establishes standards and broad policy, most decisions about hukou implementation have been decentralized to provinces and local governments. National quotas on the number of hukou status changes that can be granted in a city or town per year have been abolished. Authority to change hukou status has been greatly decentralized to lower levels of government (provinces, cities, counties, and towns). While the central government continues to promote hukou reform, the pace and exact way in which hukou reform is proceeding now comes primarily from the bottom up. Different provinces, cities, and towns use hukou to encourage or discourage migration depending on their resources and their perception of their self-interest.

When started after the creation of the PRC, hukou was essential to maintain social order and for China's "big push" industrialization based on extracting the agricultural surplus from farmers for investment in heavy industry by setting agricultural prices low and granting industry monopoly prices (the so-called scissors effect). The relatively small number of urban workers and members of their households received a grain ration and other living essentials—the so-called "iron rice-bowl"—provided by the much more numerous rural population who were expected to be self-sufficient. Under Mao hukou decisions were highly centralized under the State Council and Ministry of Public Security. China was overwhelmingly rural and there was a sharp division between city and countryside. Most city-dwellers were expected to remain in the same urban work unit (*danwei*) and rural-dwellers in the same agricultural collective for life. Agricultural or non-agricultural status and residence address fit together logically.

Until the late 1990s the State Council and the Ministry of Public Security with involvement of other central government agencies have strictly regulated changes of hukou status. The overall number of changes was limited to within a range of 2 percent and 5 percent per year with some variation in different years and different provinces (Wu, 2013) and the central government decided how many changes could be made in different provinces and sub-provincial administrative divisions.

In 1964, the State Council approved the Regulation about hukou change and specified that population growth in large cities should be strictly controlled. This policy restrained more rural people flowing into cities, but did not set a specific quota (Wan 1999). Because many educated youth who had been sent to the countryside from cities during the Cultural Revolution wanted to return to cities, the pressure on nongzhuanfei—official change of hukou status—increased when the Cultural Revolution ended in 1976. As a result, in 1977 the Ministry of Public Security established new regulations about people migrating from lower level cities to higher level cities and from rural area to urban regions. De facto the increase in urban hukou was limited to 1.5 percent per year (Wang, F., 2004). After 1990, the quota was increased to 2–5 percent. In 2001, following hukou reform in small towns, nongzhuanfei quotas were abolished altogether.

Since the rise and fall of blue stamp hukou, discussed above, and the trial hukou reforms started after 2000 that have mostly been terminated now, provincial and local governments are continuing to reform hukou. In general, the smaller the population of the jurisdiction (and particularly in towns) and the smaller the migrant pressure the further the reforms have progressed, but there are many exceptions.

Local resistance to hukou reform is closely related to China's changing fiscal system. The proportion of revenue the central government retains has increased during the last 30 years, but their contribution to local social services has not increased proportionally. Today local governments provide most basic education, health, subsidized housing, pension, disability benefit, job training and other social service expenditures. The larger and more prosperous cities generally have higher social service benefit levels. Even though Beijing, Shanghai, Guangzhou, Shenzhen, Dongguan and other big cities with large numbers of migrants also have the most resources, they are the destinations of the largest migrant flows and fear that paying the costs associated with granting migrants hukou and giving them benefits would be an enormous financial drain.

There are a number of informed estimates of the cost of implementing hukou reform. The best recent studies are a joint study by the World Bank and the Development Research Center of China's State Council (DRC and WB, 2013) and University of Washington professor Kam Wing Chan (Chan, 2013). Both conclude that hukou reform will be costly and simply abolishing the hukou system altogether and extending all urban migrants the same benefits as the urban population with urban hukou is not financially possible. Both conclude that phasing in the reforms over time, while costly, would be financially possible.

At the current stage of China's economic and social development, making all migrant workers urbanized in their current working places by 2020 is a utopian dream. Population growth from migrants often outstrips cities forecasts. For example, by 2020 Shanghai's Comprehensive Plan for 1999 to 2020 forecast that Shanghai's population would be 16.8 million in 2020. Before the 2010 census data was published, the Shanghai government did not know how many people lived in Shanghai. The 2009 *Shanghai Statistical Yearbook* estimated Shanghai's population to be 19 million. But the 2010 census found Shanghai's population had reached 23.02 million in 2010. In theory Shanghai's entire transportation system and infrastructure was based on the long-term plan (Shanghai Comprehensive Plan from 1999 to 2020).

Early signs indicate Shanghai's infrastructure and public facilities are becoming overloaded. Residents are experiencing difficulties in accessing education, medical treatment, kindergarten access, and housing. Solving these problems is not easy. Since even Shanghai—China's most developed city—suffers from overloaded facilities, other cities in China are likely to face pressure on their infrastructure and service capacity as they grow in the future, particularly as migrants are offered greater access to social services.[2] In 2014 Shanghai started to prepare a new plan for 2040.

The DRC and WB study (2013) calculated that extending urban benefits and welfare to 300 million migrants spread out over 20 years would cost 1.5 trillion RMB per year (US$242 billion), 3.8 percent of 2010 GDP. Chan (2013) has calculated that to transfer the rural hukou of all the 230 million floating migrants to urban hukou in one year would cost an astronomical 23 trillion yuan, or 44 percent of China's 2012 GDP, which is clearly impossible. However, over a 15-year time frame, assuming that the migrant population will reach 300 million by 2030, Chan estimates that the cost of transferring hukou (and associated social welfare) of 20 million people per year would require an annual cost of 2 trillion yuan, or 3.8 percent of the 2012 GDP. However, Chan points out that the cost would not be incurred in a single year, but over the remaining lifetime of a migrant, so the annual cost would be 2,500 yuan a year per person. He concludes that offering urban hukou to 20 million people per year would cost 50 billion yuan, or 0.1 percent of China's GDP, a figure well within the country's affordability. While these are the best available estimates by respected authorities, we are skeptical of any attempt to simplify this complex social issue into numbers based on monetary payouts. Change of this magnitude would have economic side effects that are not captured even in the best economic research and positive and negative consequences on the lives of ordinary Chinese people that cannot be quantified. The best way to understand this complexity is by survey research and case studies of individual cities. The following section on coordinating hukou, health, pension and other reforms in Chengdu illustrates this point.

There is a political dimension to hukou reform. While at higher levels of government—provinces and especially the national government level—governmental officials generally favor rapid and comprehensive reform, local urban residents with urban hukou status understand that they have much to lose by granting large numbers of poor migrants urban hukou in their cities and often resist reform. Transfer payments from jurisdictions where migrants have hukou to cities that grant them urban hukou have been suggested as one way to ease the financial burden and gain local political support, but since the locations where migrants have hukou can almost never provide enough money, this policy has not been implemented.

Coordinating Hukou, Health, Pension and Other Reforms in Chengdu

Since hukou is so integral to every aspect of an individual's life, hukou reform and changes in other social service programs and other local policies are closely related. A major national initiative is coordination of urban and rural development. How coordinated urban and rural development can work and its relationship to hukou and other reforms was the subject of research by Ye Yumin, Richard LeGates, Qin Bo and Renmin University faculty in 2011 and 2012 (Ye and LeGates, 2013; Ye, LeGates, and Qin, 2013).

In 2007 the national government designated Chengdu a "National Comprehensive Reform Pilot Regions for Coordinated Urban–Rural Development."

Chengdu is the capital of Sichuan province in western China and is one of China's most productive agricultural regions. Chengdu's total population was 14.05 million in 2010, 9.20 million (65 percent) in urban areas and 4.84 million (35 percent) in rural areas (Chengdu Bureau of Statistics, 2015). Of Chengdu's residents, 11.42 million hold Chengdu hukou. Most of Chengdu's population is concentrated in the central area surrounded by a 198 square kilometer greenbelt. Chengdu covers 12,390 square kilometers. It consists of nineteen separate administrative units—nine districts, four county-level cities, and six counties.

Between 2003 and 2010 Chengdu made five large-scale adjustments to its hukou policy, significantly reforming hukou. The hukou reforms were integrated with improved regional planning, administration, and information systems, unified and extended health and pension systems, consolidation of farmland and villages, new housing, schools, and medical facilities and significant progress in equalizing infrastructure and social services between urban and rural areas of Chengdu. Chengdu created a citizens' information management system that unites housing, marriage, employment, tax, credit and other information for all Chengdu residents, both urban and rural. All Chengdu residents have been provided with an identification card keyed to all of this information. Chengdu is a special case, but their reforms provide one useful model of coordinated urban–rural development.

Hukou Reform in China's National New Style Urbanization Plan (2014–2020)

China's National New Style Urbanization Plan (2014–2020) sets out a number of big targets, including a goal of having 100 million additional people with rural hukou settle down in cities with urban hukou by 2020.

In addition to encouraging orderly rural–urban migration the NNSUP calls for an increase in "citizenization" by making change of hukou status easier. The NNSUP calls for the *gradual* resettlement of *qualified* rural migrant workers in cities and towns, leaving decision-making to local governments. Reform is supposed to be related to "the overall carrying capacity and growth potential of cities". The NNSUP provides little guidance to local governments about how to do this, but—in line with other recent policy and reflecting the political power of large cities opposed to rapid hukou reform—ties hukou reform to urban population as follows:

- Towns and small cities (under 500,000) "fully liberalized" for migrants with lawful and stable employment and residence (including leases)
- 500,000–1,000,000 "orderly"
- 1,000,000–3,000,000 "reasonable"
- 3,000,000–5,000,000 "reasonably determined"
- 5,000,000 or more: "strictly controlled."

The plan offers no definition of these terms or guidance as to how local governments are to accomplish the reform. The NNSUP does set a numerical target for the number of people whose status should be converted from rural to urban, but doesn't provide clear guidelines on how or where it should occur. It suggests a relationship between citizenization and scale—with hukou liberalization proceeding fastest in smaller jurisdictions. The NNSUP does not contain fundamentally new policy about hukou reform and will not drive reform itself. But it does signal the new leadership's commitment both to accelerating urbanization as the best path to China's economic development and pressing ahead with hukou reform to incorporate rural migrants into cities as quickly as possible.

Development Research Center (DRC) and World Bank (WB) Hukou Reform Proposals

The Development Reform Center of the PRC's State Council (hereafter, DRC) and the World Bank (WB) have jointly developed a detailed proposal about how to implement hukou reform (World Bank and DRC, 2014: 49–53). This is significant because the DRC reports directly to the State Council and is influential at the highest levels of the Chinese leadership. The World Bank devoted substantial support and expertise to the proposal and the DRC provided local expertise. Hereafter this proposal will be referred to as the DRC and WB proposal.

The DRC and WB proposal argues that reducing barriers to mobility and increasing migration will reduce China's rural labor surplus more rapidly, which would increase rural wages relative to urban wages and reduce urban–rural inequality. Integrating rural migrants will increase their wages and propensity to consume urban goods, stimulating domestic demand. They argue that equalizing access to basic social services would build a healthier, better educated, and more contented workforce which would in turn help make China more competitive in the global economy.

The DRC and WB proposal calls for gradual reform with progressively better standards rolled out over time in different ways in different parts of China. This is consistent with Kam Wing Chan's analysis that hukou reform will be costly, but if rolled out over time is financially possible (Chan, 2013).

The DRC and WB proposal calls for the national government to begin by defining the principles and a national framework for the residency-based system and funding a simple basic minimum package of fundamental services that would be offered to all citizens, with the fiscal system enabling every jurisdiction to meet the standard on an experimental basis. This is a significant departure from the shock therapy hukou reforms after 2000 where local governments bore the cost of immediate radical reform. More affluent provinces, cities, and towns and jurisdictions seeking to attract new residents or which feel their residents require additional services could raise service standards for residents in their jurisdictions above the national minimum, but would be responsible for providing additional funding. Consistent with the Chinese preference for experimentation, the DRC/World Bank report advocates experiments in which cities will seek an affordable balance that satisfies their residents and the needs of the local economy. Over time the system would be evaluated and adapted. While the DRC report envisages that it would become more comprehensive and the number of fundamental rights expanded, they do not expect reform following this approach to be completed by 2030.

The DRC and WB acknowledges that common eligibility criteria such as the number of years of residence or social insurance contributions may not be practical in the short to medium term, and that in the initial phases it would be too costly for all social entitlements of current local residents to accrue to new residents immediately upon obtaining a residency permit. They propose that local governments continue to be allowed to define the sequencing of access to benefits and the qualifying period to move step by step. Over time eligibility criteria would become more uniform as land reforms and pension reforms progress. The DRC proposal argues that a hukou system that provides the right to profit from land rights can operate in parallel with a residency-based system that provides access to specific services.

The proposed DRC and WB residency-based system would require additional resources and a rebalancing of central and local financing responsibilities—specifically subsidizing cities for the increased costs of providing services to migrants. Initially they propose a transitional subsidy to entire cities to entice them to participate and overcome resistance to expanding urban hukou by existing residents with urban hukou who fear that their entitlements will be threatened. Given urban citizens' interest-based resistance to hukou reform, this is an important principal. The DRC and WB argue that a new modern residency system should be closely linked to the fiscal system. Fiscal allocations would be based on residency counts. The DRC calculates that giving urban migrants rights to nine years of free compulsory education, access to basic public health care services, social security (medical and old-age pensions) for formal sector workers and residents, a social assistance program (dibao), and a welfare housing system identical to residents with urban hukou would require additional annual resources of about 1.5 percent of GDP—a large, but not impossible expenditure. The report describes education, health services, pensions, social assistance, and housing components of a basic program in detail with aggregate cost estimates.

The DRC and WB believe that the hukou system in China is the main reason for the low wages of migrant rural workers (DRC and WB, 2014: 49–53). On the contrary, our research based on analyses of the ratio of people to agricultural land, wage differentials, and employment flows described in Chapter 4 on regional policies and regional urbanization and Chapter 6 on globalization and large scale population flows suggests that such low wages are primarily decided by the market demand and the supply of labor. As the Lewis turning point appears in the demand–supply relationship of the labor force in some areas of China, the wages of migrant rural workers have already improved significantly, approaching the salary level of the local urban population or even exceeding it. Our research team conducted interviews in 2013 with construction workers from Haimen rural area in Jiangsu province now working in Shanghai. The monthly mean wages of the workers was above 5,000 RMB (US$806). For some skilled workers, the monthly wages reach 10,000 RMB (US$1,612). Even cashiers in supermarkets were earning up to 3,000 RMB (US$484) every month in Shanghai. However, the official lowest salary level formally declared by Shanghai government was 1,450 RMB (US$234) in 2013.

While rising wages gives cause for optimism that market forces will help to close the rural–urban gap and make hukou reform and ultimately the elimination of hukou possible, our research found that housing price increases pose a significant threat that runs in the opposite direction.

Housing prices in urban regions of China have been increasing in the past decade: often by double or even triple digit amounts in a single year.

This makes it difficult or impossible for migrant rural workers to settle down in cities long term even if they are receiving comparably better salaries and social service benefits.

Consistent with our approach of combining macro-level structural analysis with analysis of new primary data on individual choices, we administered a survey in 2014 to 112 migrant workers in Gaoming district, Foshan city of Guangdong province to determine their opinions about the principal barrier to settling down in Foshan city. Only 22 percent of the respondents said that lack of urban hukou was the major barrier for them to settle down in the city, compared with 65 percent who said that high housing price was the principal barrier.

The DRC and WB's *China 2030* analysis on China's developmental problems is objective and provides thoughtful recommendations. However, the situation in China varies enormously by region and is changing rapidly. Therefore, the DRC analysis and recommendations should be read with care. Throughout this book we provide new empirical information and sometimes describe different conclusions and the basis for them.

Smoothing of the Urban–Rural Welfare Gap

There are a number of promising experiments with social welfare reform for non-local residents. Since the main problem is cost, jurisdictions with a limited amount of money that want to improve urban migrants' conditions face a difficult choice to either provide: (1) only a small percentage of all urban migrants' benefits identical to urban residents or (2) benefits to all urban migrants at a lower level than the benefits urban residents receive, at least initially. In many western social welfare programs either approach is sometimes adopted as an acceptable compromise with the hope that over time either the pool of recipients can be increased or the benefit level of all of the newly incorporated recipients can be increased, eventually up to the level of the fully funded recipients. Chinese administrative units that establish barriers to obtaining urban hukou are essentially pursuing the first strategy. An alternative approach is to establish systems that allow most or all urban migrants to get a lower level of service than urban residents with some combination of government, employer, and personal contributions to cost. Zhejiang province allows migrants to make smaller contributions and receive more limited social welfare benefits. Shanghai has adopted a comprehensive insurance system designed for employees without local hukou allowing them to purchase different levels of insurance coverage tailored to what they can and choose to pay. Approaches like this permit the big gap in welfare between urban and rural population to be smoothed step by step. As wages in low-wage areas of China increase and the advantages of rural (agricultural) hukou improve, a combination of market reform and phased improvement of social welfare together will help close the dual rural-income divide and China's social welfare and opportunity gaps.

Some regions, such as the city of Shenyang in Liaoning province, and Foshan city in Guangdong province have adopted unified citizen status within their jurisdictions for years. This means that there is no difference between rural hukou and urban hukou and at the same time the rural collective economy and the rural welfare enjoyed by rural residents remain. In Foshan city's population registration information "farmer" remains an available selection for "occupation."

It has often been suggested that local governments grant rural residents urban hukou in exchange for giving up their use rights in collectively owned agricultural land, but so far official policy prohibits this. In China use rights of land are considered the rural population's safety net. While rural land is collectively owned, households receive the right to use agricultural land for farming (or renting for someone else to farm) and a homestead (house and related building). Farming their allotted parcels or renting them should provide at least enough food to survive. Compensation when the land is requisitioned can sometimes equal many times a household's annual income. While in some cases peasants give up their use rights in rural land voluntarily in many other cases there is a degree of coercion (O'Brien and Li, 2006; Lora-Wainwright, 2012; Miller, 2013).

By law every collective must receive compensation when collectively owned land is requisitioned. The adequacy of the compensation varies depending on individual negotiations. The way in which compensation is used for common benefits or distributed to individual households varies. While some people are adequately compensated—indeed some are unjustly enriched—many others are not. Survey research by a US based non-profit organization that studies land use, LANDESA, found that many former farmers feel that they received inadequate compensation for their land (Zhu and Prosterman, 2007, 2010; Zhu et al., 2011). It is not surprising that some survey respondents feel they received less compensation than they should have. There may be extreme cases where households received nothing, but these would be illegal and very rare. Whether or not people who lose agricultural hukou benefit in the long run compared with retaining their rural hukou depends on how successful the cities that grant them hukou are in in providing jobs for them and how well the local social welfare systems perform over time so that they received at least promised benefits and hopefully benefits improve weighed against the value of the use rights they would have had in rural land, which is in turn a function of location, quality, and—increasingly—market forces.

Our survey research provides further insights about the relationship between hukou and urbanization. Analysis of individual choices that migrants from central China have made or said they plan to make in a survey we conducted in Hubei province of 1,387 residents of 55 towns suggests that households make complex, rational choices based on their values and their perception of the benefits they will get from different strategies. They weigh probabilities of securing work, present and probable future income, the likelihood of economic downturns, their assessment of the quality of schools their children will attend if they stay or move, how highly they value agricultural land to which they will retain use rights if they keep rural hukou either for farming themselves, leasing, or for compensation if it is requisitioned, and how highly they value the quality of rural living compared with urban living. About 30 percent of our sample said they preferred to retain rural hukou in the countryside rather than live in towns where they could get urban hukou (Tongji University Research Team, 2014). The main motivation of those who said they would prefer to move from rural to urban areas was to reduce commuting time, followed by access to better education for their children (ibid).

We also obtained information from a survey of 112 rural migrant workers in Foshan city. Of the migrant workers surveyed, 54 percent (61 respondents) said that they would consider returning and settling down in their hometown (capital towns of counties, market towns or villages) in the future, and only 37 percent (40 respondents) said they wanted to settle down in Foshan city. Thirty of the 61 respondents who said they would consider returning to their hometown (49 percent) expressed a wish to return to rural life. Seventeen percent (10 respondents) said they would prefer to live in their rural towns and 34 percent (21 respondents) said they would prefer to live in the capital towns of their original counties (Tongji University Research Team, 2014). Based on these surveys the appeal of cities to migrant rural workers appears to be diminishing—at least in the areas we surveyed.

Urban–rural inequality is principally manifested as a difference in welfare, but it is not primarily the result of the urban–rural hukou division. In China today regional disparities are more pronounced than urban–rural difference. The differences in salary level, minimum life guarantee, and basic education quality among Shanghai, Jiangsu, Zhejiang, Gansu, and Ningxia are significant (Table 2.3).

SUMMARY

This chapter has reviewed the history and evolution of China's hukou system and discussed hukou reform from the 1980s to the present time.

Table 2.3 Comparison of social welfare between provinces in the eastern and western regions in 2010

	Shanghai	Jiangsu	Zhejiang	Gansu	Ningxia
Minimum salary level	1,120	670–960	800–1,100	630–760	605–710
Minimum living guarantee	450	382–478	377	204	200–230
Percentage of children entering senior high school	96.5%	96.0%	92.5%	79.2% (2009)	81.45% (2011)

Note: Shanghai, Jiangsu and Zhejiang are eastern provinces and Gansu and Ningxia are western provinces; 2009 data for Gansu province and 2011 data for Ningxia province.

Source: Provincial government websites.

It presents and analyzes data on population growth after reform and opening up. The results show that hukou reform lags far behind urban population growth, and the social gap between the two is increasing. The chapter compares mechanical growth rates of urban and non-agricultural populations. The results show that reform of the hukou system prior to 2000 only created transient effects of modestly increasing de facto urbanization, but did not substantially increase the *de jure* urban population. The major driving force behind China's urbanization has been industrial development, not hukou liberalization itself.

Our analysis of variations in the differences between the urbanized population with and without urban hukou in China's three great regions and different provinces over time shows that implementation of hukou reform has varied across the country, and *de jure* urbanization did not keep pace with accelerating urbanization in most provinces.

Hukou reform trials after 2000 created a differentiation among various hukou regimes, between cities and rural towns, large and small cities, central city districts and suburbs of megacities, and between developed and undeveloped regions. The reforms were often overly ambitious and had to be discontinued.

The hukou system plays a crucial role in China's economic and social development and urbanization, and is closely connected with rural residents' use rights in land. Although the system has been decentralized and liberalized during China's transition to a market economy, a deep-rooted rigid interest pattern remains. Respective advantages associated with urban and rural hukou persist and will likely continue to exist in at least the medium term. Reforming the hukou system fully cannot be accomplished within a short period, and hukou will continue to affect urbanization. Eventually when the urban–rural difference is sufficiently small and regional disparities have decreased, the hukou system will only serve its function as a means of recording population data and routine population management.

As of 2015, hukou reform has not yet fulfilled the national government's intended goals. The most recent national policy decision to implement the NNSUP is a policy guideline issued by the State Council titled "Instructions on furthering the hukou system reform" (PRC-MSC, 2014). This policy statement eliminates the distinction between agricultural, non-agricultural, blue stamp, and other types of hukou, unifies different types of hukou into one system that is only related to a person's living place, and establishes a residential (card) system for migrants. With a residential card, migrants can obtain basic public services. The State Council policy statement instructs the Ministry of Education to guarantee rights of children from households with a residential card to education equal to the education that children of residents with local hukou receive. It instructs local governments to allocate funds based on the number of children in school. According to the guideline, hukou in rural towns and small cities should be fully open, and in mid-sized cities it should be opened in an "orderly and progressive way," in large cities should be formulated "properly," and for very large cities the hukou population should be "strictly controlled." The specific policy will vary across different cities. For instance, Shanghai has indicated its intention to develop a system of hukou conversion based on a point system that permits people to change hukou when they have accumulated enough points based on a variety of factors. The flexibility and ambiguity in the NNSUP and State Council policy statements raise key questions: how quickly will the basic constitutional principles that individuals should be treated equally and ultimately be able to migrate freely be realized. Equity and choice are more important than meeting specified targets such as the goal of urbanization of some 100 million people, as specified in the NNSUP. Urbanization patterns should grow naturally from people's choices, exercised within a framework of principles to assure harmonious, healthy, urbanization that emphasizes quality over quantity with high standards for equity, efficiency, sustainability, livability, resilience, good designs, and preservation of tangible and intangible heritage. Returning hukou to its basic function as a recording system rather than a system of invisible walls is fundamental to these goals.

NOTES

1. The population fluctuation around 2010 can be principally attributed to the revision of data after the Sixth National Population Census. In the previous years, the statistical authorities tended to underestimate the urban population growth rate.
2. Recent policies allow children of migrant workers to attend local schools and permit migrants to transfer social insurance from one area to another to some extent.

3. Governments, administrative divisions, and urban policies

Every country needs to establish an administrative structure to both carry out national policies and make local decisions. The administrative structure itself has a large impact on urbanization. In large and rapidly changing countries like China, both the relationships among the central government, sub-national governments like provinces or provincial-level municipalities, and different levels of local government, and the boundaries and authority among different administrative divisions are complex and changing. Which level of government has authority to make key decisions and has access to revenue is highly political.

CENTRAL AND LOCAL GOVERNMENTS

The centralized top-down system of governance characteristic of China under Mao has evolved into a more decentralized system with a hierarchy of governments that is difficult to understand—especially for Westerners unfamiliar with reality on the ground. It is difficult even for scholars who understand the structure to do cross sectional or longitudinal analysis, because the structure permits great variation so that a category may mean quite different things in different places or from one year to the next. Higher levels of government often establish ambiguous policies that lower levels interpret in different ways, and some statistics are unavailable, unreliable, inconsistent, or collected in ways that make analysis difficult or impossible.

Because the units of government in China are so numerous and varied, a single term describing an administrative division may be describing quite different kinds of places. For example some county-level cities are dense, truly urban places, but others are mostly low density agricultural areas that were simply re-named county-level cities for reasons related to administration and political expediency rather than de facto urban attributes. As a result of these complexities, many macro-level analyses using units of analysis based on the terminology alone that assume consistency and stability are flawed. For example, when the number of administrative units named "cities" was greatly increased in the 1980s Chinese cities changed to be regional units, not only urban units and analyses that used the number of residents of cities as a proxy for urban population showed an apparent (but artificial) increase in urbanization.

Analyses of urban policy also age quickly and failure to understand the decentralization of power can lead to misunderstanding. China is no longer a monolithic centralized state with all significant decision-making made in Beijing, but a complex and rapidly changing system in which provinces and local governments have broad discretion to implement urban policy subject to central political control.

This chapter describes the current status of China's administrative divisions and urban policies and the ways in which they have evolved over time. Mindful of the complex and rapidly changing nature of Chinese government structure, it provides a nuanced description of change over time that acknowledges data limitations and steers clear of overgeneralizations.

Before the era of reform and opening up, China had a centrally planned economy, and, with the exception of some experiments to adjust central–local relationships, the central government dominated all major aspects of economic and social development. Planned goals and resource allocation set by the national government were realized through the hierarchy of provincial and local governments. Accordingly, governments below the national level had very limited power and authority about how to generate and spend revenue, particularly those at the municipal, county, and township levels. Local governments waited for guidance and appropriations from higher levels of government. They handed over the profits of state-owned enterprises and local tax revenues, but were not authorized to make fundamental decisions about plans and policies on how to spend revenue passed back to them from the national government. Thus, local governments during the Mao era were characterized by the absence of independent rights to plan their development. Under Mao decision-making was motivated by the desire to meet centrally set targets and demonstrate that cadres had complied with top-down orders rather than independent thinking about the best way in which to develop or pursue what appeared to be the most economically rational strategy from a local perspective.

China was unified during the reign of Emperor Qin Shi Huang (259BC–210BC). Over the next two and a half millennia a series of dynasties rose and fell, governed from capital cities in Xian, Kaifeng, Nanjing, Beijing and elsewhere—sometimes expanding China's borders far beyond their current size; sometimes contracting borders to control only parts of the present day People's Republic of China. Strong emperors exerted control over their territory; weak ones had only limited influence in the furthest reaches of their claimed land.

In contrast to the central governments, counties (xian) in China are basic administrative divisions that have remained remarkably stable. Counties have served as the basic administrative division for tax collection, defense, and administration of rural areas in China for more than two millennia (Skinner, 1977: 275–351; Friedman, 2005: 7–17). According to Skinner, the number of counties has remained between 1,200 and 1,500 for more than two thousand years. Because of the vast distances and travel and communication difficulties in China, Skinner concluded that imperial officials lacked effective means to direct local affairs. As a result much of the actual governance of China has historically taken place at the county level.

Imperial institutions for the administration of counties were located in settlements called Cheng-shi. To translate Cheng as "city" would be misleading. The word Cheng means a defensive unit with walls and accommodation for local officials and residents involved in non-agricultural work. Shi means a market serving local people. So for millennia the Chinese approximation of Western cities was walled places that served administrative, military, and market functions. The number, location, and size of Cheng changed during the two millennia that dynastic capitals rose, fell, and moved and county units remained relatively stable. Some eventually became more like Western metropolitan areas, consisting of a Cheng and a relatively dense hinterland functionally related to it. Still, at the beginning of the twentieth century China was an overwhelmingly rural society. Only about 6 percent of China's population lived in urban agglomerations of 50,000 or more. According to Friedmann (2005) until the beginning of the twentieth century Chinese cities did not have local governments in the Western sense. The exceptions were in the concession areas of treaty ports where European powers maintained public works, police, and other institutions and, after the creation of the Republic in 1912, modern public administration in Guangzhou, Shanghai, and Beijing. Civil society institutions were well developed in China and, with the exception of large imperial infrastructure projects, clan and kinship associations met basic needs.

Today counties in China are one rank from the bottom in China's hierarchical system (illustrated in Figure 3.1). Counties have local congresses, governments and party branches and are responsible for local community welfare, public security, public works, and other functions. Counties usually govern relatively sparsely settled rural land. They should be distinguished from county-level cities, which have the same rank as a county, but are usually more urban in character. There are usually towns and townships within a county and villages within towns and townships and other county land.

One of the salient features of reform and opening up is decentralization, in which the central government has conferred administrative authority to

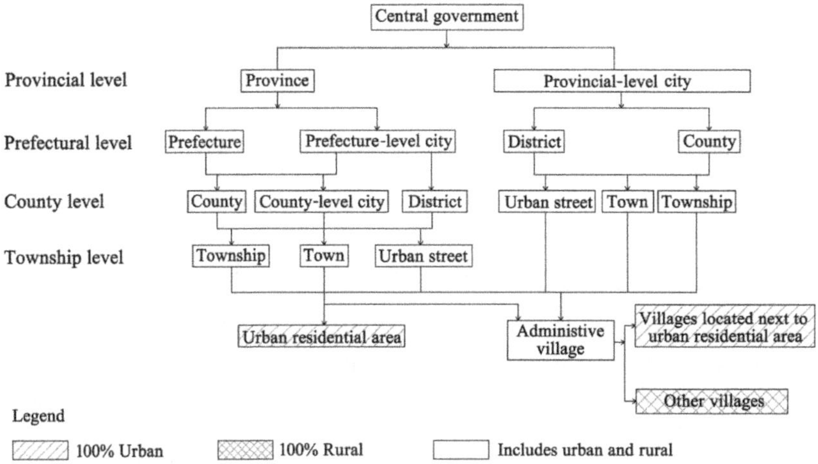

Notes:
Autonomous regions, autonomous prefectures and autonomous counties are not displayed. They are similar to provinces, prefectures and counties.
Sub-provincial cities are not displayed. In addition to provincial-level, prefectural-level and county-level cities there are 15 sub-provincial cities. They have greater power than prefectural-level, and county-level cities. Most sub-provincial cities are capital cities of provinces or comparably large cities.
Normally the districts of provincial-level cities are prefecture level, but for key targets of reform, some provincial-level cities or provinces established sub-provincial regions. These include the Pudong new region in Shanghai, Binhai new region in Tianjin, Liangjiang new region in Chongqing, the Xixian new region in Shaanxi and six other new regions. These regions have stronger powers than ordinary prefecture-level districts.
In some provinces, a few counties and county-level cities are directly under provincial administration, such as Jiyuan in Henan province and Xiantao, Qianjiang and Tianmen in Hubei province. These administrative reform experiments were promoted in 30 counties and county-level cities of eight provinces in China after 2010.

Source: Drawn by Li Zhang.

Figure 3.1 China's urban and rural system

provinces, cities, counties, rural towns and townships (Ma, 2002). Towns (zhen) and townships (xiang)—formally township-level divisions—are the lowest (fourth) level administrative unit in China's current political divisions hierarchy. They are similar to municipalities in the United States and communes in some other countries. Townships in turn may contain villages.

China's reform process since reform and opening up has been closely associated with the adjustment of administrative authority among local governments and between local and provincial governments and the central government. Lower levels of government have been granted much more authority over significant decisions including important decisions about industry, commerce, planning, and land development and much greater discretion about how to spend their own source revenue and intergovernmental transfers. Restructuring the rights of central and local governments has been accompanied by changes of administrative (jurisdiction) boundaries and adjustment of numerous urban policies.

China's Four-level Urban and Management System Hierarchy

Figure 3.1 shows the hierarchy of administrative divisions in the Chinese urban system. For purposes of visual clarity autonomous regions (provincial level), autonomous prefectures (prefectural level), autonomous counties (county level) and sub-provincial cities are described in the notes accompanying the figure, but are not displayed in the figure itself.

The figure shows four levels or ranks of administrative divisions below the central government. The higher the administrative division's level the higher its rank. Rank is critical. The higher the rank the greater an administrative division's authority to make decisions, the more financial resources are available to it, the greater cadres' prospects of career advancement, and the better the unit is positioned to interact with higher levels of government.

The first level—the provincial level—directly under the central government includes four designated provincial-level cities under central administration: Beijing, Shanghai, Tianjin, and Chonqing, as well as provinces and autonomous regions. The four provincial-level cities are very large megacities with land areas ranging from 6,340 square kilometers (Shanghai) to 82,402 square kilometers (Chongqing) and populations ranging from 15 million (Tianjin) to 30 million (Chongqing). They report directly to the national government and their status gives them greater autonomy over decision-making than cities lower in China's administrative hierarchy. They have much more formal and informal power to develop as they choose and greater access to resources than cities lower in the administrative hierarchy.

The second level—the prefectural level—includes prefectural-level cities and prefectures under provinces and districts and counties under provincial-level cities. For example the provincial-level city of Beijing has 14 districts and two counties under it and the provincial-level city of Chongqing has 23 districts, 11 counties and four autonomous counties. Districts (Shi-xia-qu) are administrative subdivisions of a municipality or a prefecture-level city. The rank of a district is based on the rank of its city. Districts of a municipality are prefecture level; districts of a sub-provincial city are sub-provincial level; and districts of a prefecture-level city are county level.

Under provinces at the second level in the hierarchy there are prefectural-level cities and prefectures. At the third level—the county level—there are also a number of different kinds of administrative divisions depending on whether they fall below provinces or provincial-level cities directly under central administration. Below prefectures there are two types of administrative divisions: counties and county-level cities. Below prefecture-level cities are districts, counties and county-level cities.

Because of their relative stability over time and importance to a rural society, counties (xian) are the most important administrative division in China. Counties usually govern relatively sparsely settled rural land, but some county-level cities—and even some counties—are quite dense and urban. At the county level below provincial-level cities are urban streets, towns, and townships.

While China's governmental structure formally ends at the township level there is an extensive system of villages and urban residential areas below them. Administrative villages are recognized administrative units, but not a level of government. Each administrative village has an elected village committee and a village head elected by all villagers. There is also a party branch and a village secretary of the Chinese Communist Party (CCP) elected by local CCP members in each village and verified by a higher-level party committee. In urban areas below the town, township, and urban street level may be urban residential areas with neighborhood committees. An administrative village may include two or more natural villages—organic villages consisting of clusters of houses geographically close to each other and often with household members related by kinship, but which are not officially recognized as separate administrative units.

Under districts there may be sub-districts called urban streets. Under streets are urban neighborhoods, each with an elected neighborhood committee.

In accordance with "Regulations on Statistical Urban–Rural Divisions" implemented in 2008, all the area covered by a neighborhood committee is considered an urban area (PRC-MSC, 2008). If an administrative village is adjacent to an urban neighborhood committee then for census purposes it is considered an urban area; otherwise, it is considered a rural area. The population living in an urban area for more than six months is considered an urban population; a population living in an urban area for less than six months is considered a rural population in official statistics regardless of the hukou status of the residents.

Two of the most important ways in which cities in China are different from cities in the West are that they are regional administrative units mixed with urban regions and rural areas and they are classified into levels of a hierarchy, each with a different status. The highest level in China's urban hierarchy is composed of four megacities (Beijing, Shanghai, Tianjin, and Chongqing) that are directly under the central government (Zhixia-shi). The second highest level in the hierarchy consists of 15 sub-provincial cities (also known as major cities or municipalities). These 15 cities have quite independent planning authority The third level in the hierarchy is composed of prefecture-level cities (xianji-shi) and the lowest level in the hierarchy consists of county-level cities (xianji-shi). Many county-level cities began as counties, but as they urbanized were reclassified to the status of a county-level city. As a county-level city they acquired certain new powers and status.

In general, the higher a city's ranking in the administrative hierarchy the more administrative power it has, the greater the scope of administrative decision-making it controls, and the greater its authority to make development decisions. Administative units at the higher levels of the hierarchy are generally favored locations for large projects. Administrative units higher in the hierarchy have a broader scope of economic and social administrative power, particularly in fiscal and economic matters (Figure 3.2). Normally, the economies of cities and rural towns are more developed than those of counties and townships within the same hierarchy, and the cities or towns look more urbanized.

The central governments' policy concerning changing the status of administrative units has evolved over time. During the 1980s and early 1990s many counties were converted to cities based on the national government's view that urban status would promote economic development and urbanization. Many counties sought to change their status because they would have more discretionary powers, cadres' benefits and prospects for career advancement would increase, and they would have greater access to favorable policies and approval of economic development zones.

In the late 1990s the Chinese leadership concluded that standards for converting counties to cities had been too lax and many counties had been converted to city status prematurely. After 1997, the policies for changing status from counties to cities were greatly restricted. As a result, there have been few additional conversions since that time. At present many counties that have become quite urban continue to have only county status.

Fiscal and Tax Relationships between the Central and Local Governments

The most important aspect of the relationship between the central and local governments in China's urban hierarchy is in the operations of fiscal and taxation systems (Figure 3.3). Taxes are the main source of local revenue. By adjusting the fiscal relationship between the central and local governments, responsibilities, rights and resources are reallocated.

Notes:
Top-left is a provincial-level city—Shanghai. Top-right is a sub-provincial-level city—Qingdao in Shandong province. Middle-left is a prefectual-level city—Tonghua in Jilin province. Middle right is a county-level city—Zhucheng in Shandong province. Bottom-left is a county—Huaiyuan in Anhui province. Bottom-right is Hunan town in Quzhou city, Zhejaing province.

Source: Photos by Li Zhang.

Figure 3.2 Different levels of administrative divisions

The following sections briefly review the history of China's fiscal and taxation system to provide for a better understanding of the evolution of central–local government relationships in China.

Before 1978: centralized unified revenue and expenditure system

Before 1978, most revenue came directly from the profits of state-owned enterprises. China's financial system relied on taxation only to a small extent. While the central government implemented several reforms to the

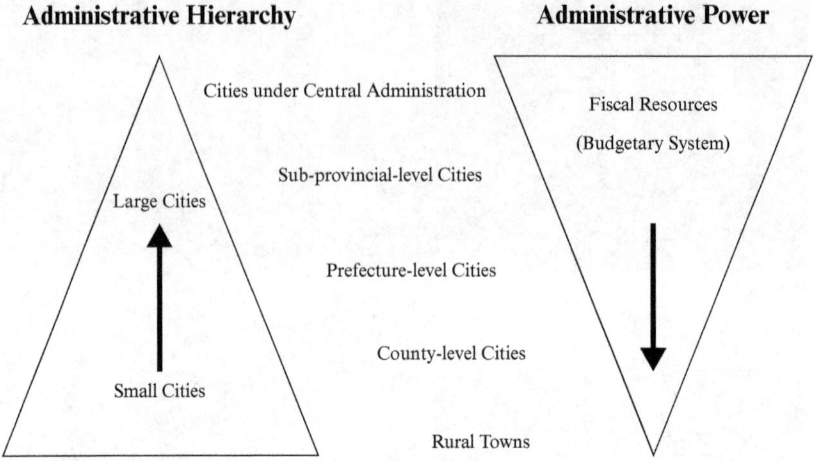

Source: Based on research by University of Washington professor Kam Wing Chan, 2009 adapted by Li Zhang.

Figure 3.3 Administrative hierarchy and administrative power system in China

taxation system, until 1978 the general fiscal structure remained a highly centralized unified revenue and expenditure system (Liu, 2000).

1980s: the local fiscal responsibility system

Changes to China's fiscal and taxation system that began in 1978 culminated in a radically different government finance system that greatly enhanced local government initiatives (Tao, 2007). After trial implementation between 1980 and 1984, "the local fiscal responsibility system" was introduced throughout China in 1985. The new system was strongly influenced by the success of the HCRS system in agriculture, which allowed farmers to keep excess crops beyond a contracted quota, which was delivered to the village collective. The new post-1985 financial system involved "dividing the source of revenues, checking revenue and expenditures, and popularizing the fiscal responsibility system by hierarchies." Popularizing means promoting the fiscal responsibility system by hierarchies; different levels of government have different fiscal responsibilities.

Most important, the quota of revenue local governments were required to hand over to the central government was specified, and the central and local governments shared any excess revenue. The proportions of revenues handed over and shared were maintained constantly for specified periods of time. After 1984, profits of state-owned enterprises were no longer directly handed over to the central government. Under the new policy, revenue was collected in the form of taxes on income, businesses, salt, products, and a value-added tax. Four draft administrative regulations were published: on products, value-added in manufacturing, business (retail sales and services) and salt. Subsequently, a complete taxation system covering more than 30 kinds of taxes was gradually established (Liu, 2000). Thus, a solid foundation was laid for the "tax-sharing system" reform that was established in 1993 (PRC-MSC, 1993a).

1990s: tax-sharing system reform

The fiscal responsibility system in the 1980s stimulated local governments to become more entrepreneurial and responsible. Local governments had more resources for economic development at their disposal. However, as reform and opening up proceeded, the fiscal responsibility system could no longer adapt to the rapid economic and social developments, and the drawbacks of the new system surfaced. For example, the regulatory function of taxation was weakened, which affected the formation of a unified market and the optimization of industrial structure. National finance had many distortions. Above all, the decline of central government revenue undermined the central government's own macro-level regulatory ability. It became clear that China's fiscal distribution modes were not properly standardized (Tao, 2007). The central government addressed these defects by launching a new round of fiscal and taxation system reforms in 1993. The core of this reform was to replace the "fiscal responsibility system" with a "tax-sharing system," beginning a transition from administrative sharing to economic sharing. The scopes of income of the central government and local governments were defined in the tax-sharing system on the basis of the division of authority between central and local governments described above. The new taxation system divides taxes into central, local, and shared taxes. Two sets of taxation offices (central and local) have been established. Under the new system, some of the tax collected from local sources is returned by the central government to local governments. This is similar to revenue sharing or intergovernmental transfers from higher to lower levels of government in the West. An institutional guarantee is provided for the collection and distribution of revenue between the central government and local governments. As shown in Figure 3.4, the central government's proportion of revenue increased from approximately 20 percent in 1993 to more than 50 percent since 1994. Thus, since the early 1990s the central government has greatly increased its fiscal regulatory control power. Because it has a large share of national revenue, it is in a position to affect development and urbanization by subsidizing infrastructure and economic development in locations deemed important

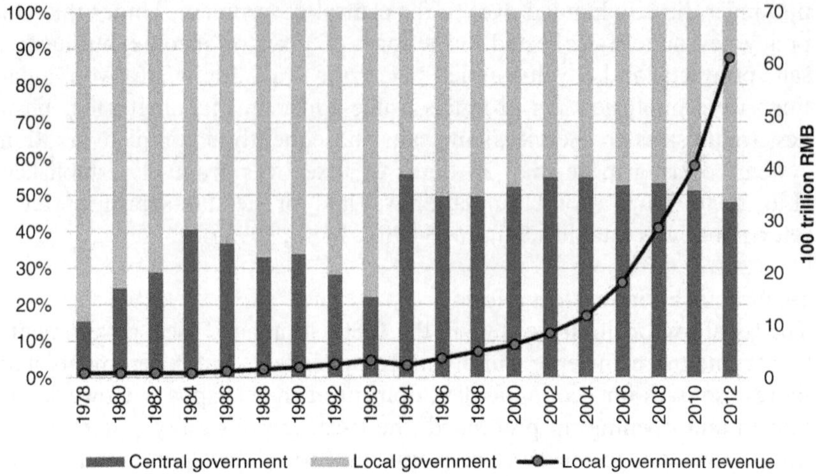

Source: NBSC-csy (2014).

Figure 3.4 Changing share of central and local government revenue and percentage of local government revenue increase, 1978–2012

from a national perspective. Massive high speed rail, highway, airport and other transportation projects; dams and hydroelectric power infrastructure, water diversion projects, social welfare, environmental remediation, funding for national economic development schemes and even funding of massive infrastructure projects in Pakistan, Indonesia, Angola, Kenya and other trading partner nations all help shape China's urbanization pattern.

Since the beginning of the twenty-first century, China has again implemented a series of taxation reforms mainly targeting individual types of taxes. However, the general relationship between the central and local governments in terms of the fiscal and taxation system still conforms to the framework laid down in 1993. After the implementation of the tax-sharing system, while the revenues of both the central and local governments have grown steadily, the increase in central government revenue has been much higher than the increase in revenue of lower levels of government.

In 1993, central government revenue accounted for 22 percent of total national revenue. In 1994, this proportion increased to 55.7 percent. Since then it has hovered around 50 percent (Figure 3.4). Therefore, since 1994 the central government has had proportionally much more revenue to spend on large-scale projects and more comprehensive social welfare, infrastructure, and environmental projects in less developed regions than sub-national governments. Because China is developing so rapidly the absolute amount of revenue at every level of government has continued to increase. The change in how revenue is divided between the national government and lower levels of government in 1993 led to lower revenues for local governments than they would have had if the percentage the central government took remained lower. This has engendered local government discontent. The relationship between provincial governments and subordinate levels of governments with respect to the fiscal and taxation system has not been standardized since 1993, and different provinces and local governments within provinces have their own fiscal and taxation arrangements. Generally the lower in the administrative ranking system shown in Figure 3.4 a jurisdiction is, the less funding it receives. At the lower levels of the hierarchy counties, county-level cities, districts, towns, townships, and urban streets often receive too little money to meet their service demands.

2000s: preliminary implementation of the fiscal and taxation system with counties directly under the provincial government

In absolute terms, the amount of local government revenue that appears in published budget statistics after 1994 has been comparable to that of the central government. However, as described above "local" refers to four hierarchies, namely, province level, prefecture level, county level, and town level which together have a large scope of responsibilities. When a local administrative unit is higher in the administrative hierarchy, it has greater power in the fiscal and taxation system (Figure 3.3). The constraints of the hierarchical administrative system as implemented in China have made it impossible for many governments at the lowest levels of the hierarchy—the county, town, township and urban street levels—to provide local residents with high quality public services because they simply lack the funds to do so.

In 2002, Zhejiang province in eastern China was selected for trial implementation of a reform of the fiscal and taxation system with the establishment of counties (including county-level cities) directly under the provincial government. Later, the reform was extended to Jiangxi, Jilin, Shandong, and Anhui provinces.

In 2009, a new round of fiscal and taxation system reform was initiated. The important feature of this recent reform was to promote the establishment of counties' and county-level cities' revenue directly under the provincial government. The policy was aimed at strengthening the authority of county government over local development decision-making. The central government originally planned to complete reform of the fiscal and taxation system with the establishment of county-level units' revenue directly under the provincial government before the end of 2012. However, the reform effort proved highly controversial and progress was not as rapid or smooth as expected (Li et al., 2014). In spite of the delay and criticism, the reform is continuing and is expected to energize many county-level governments.

China's regional spatial urbanization pattern may be altered if counties and county-level cities receive more solid fiscal support. Our analysis of the urban–rural distribution of China's population indicates that counties are now the largest source of new urban population. Therefore, enhancing the fiscal support for counties and county-level cities can have significant consequences. If counties and county-level cities are much better funded and greatly improve infrastructure and public services they should be more attractive to the population from villages and small towns within their administrative areas and potential returning migrants. By liberating the potential for quality urbanization at the county level, the spatial landscape of urbanization in China could be changed in a bottom-up manner.

ADMINISTRATIVE DIVISIONS

Every country has to create administrative divisions in order to govern. Relations between the central government and lower levels of government are often complex and changing everywhere in the world. Countries are often divided about how much central authority to retain over matters related to urbanization and development and how much to decentralize.

China's administrative division system reflects the changing relationship between the central and local governments and among the local governments themselves. China's system is both shaped by and in turn shapes differences in regional development and provides institutional guarantees for national economic and social development by offering important policy for regulating urban–rural rights and the distribution of interests (Luo, 2005; Wang, 2005; Cui et al., 2012). Following is a description and analysis of the evolution of administrative divisions in China since realignment and expansion in the 1980s that helps explain the history of China's urbanization.

The Evolution of Administrative Divisions

1981–1990: cities governing counties

One of China's most significant administrative division reforms is the system of "cities governing counties." Under this system counties (and county-level cities) adjacent to prefectural-level cities retain their own governments, but become subordinate to the city. Key decision-making authority is vested in the prefectural-level city. This has often succeeded in creating better-coordinated development, but has also bred conflict between cities and the counties they administer. This practice was inaugurated on a limited basis in the 1950s, but implemented on a large scale between 1981 and 1990. The power of the city to make planning and policy decisions for the region greatly increased. County-level governments provide input to decision-making, implement plans and policies the city makes for the combined city–county region, and retain some decision-making authority over local matters. During roughly the same time this reform occurred many county-level cities were created (Table 3.1). China has implemented a unique Chinese solution to a regional planning issue that many countries face: how to coordinate the development of a central city with surrounding areas that have their own governments. Many scholars are critical of the so-called Balkanization of metropolitan regions—the division into many competing political units—and favor consolidation, boundary changes, cooperation agreements and other solutions (Orfield, 2011). But no other country has implemented a solution similar to China's.

Two additional experiments underway in China involve different relationships between levels of government: (1) county-level cities directly under the jurisdiction of provinces, and (2) elevating the status of some strong towns to have power roughly comparable to counties (county-level cities)—de facto quasi-counties.

The first new development is experiments in which some county-level cities have been placed directly under the jurisdiction of a province (Wang, Y., 2004; Dai, 2004; He and Liu, 2009). This is generally either because a county-level city has become very strong and demands more authority or a less developed county-level city wants to be protected from being taken advantage of by the city above them. Many county-level cities began as counties, but as they urbanized were reclassified to the status of a county-level city.

The second new development gives some economically advanced towns most of the powers of a county. Some official towns in economically developed regions have attained populations of 200,000 or more, equivalent to some county-level or even prefecture-level cities and have large economies. However, their administrative authority does not match their development level, hampering the supply of social services and management of development. This may further incite conflicts between cities, counties (county-level cities), and towns. After the mid-2000s, the voice for expanding the scope of administrative powers and rights for strong counties and strong towns intensified. Pilot areas to address these concerns were set up in Zhejiang and Jiangsu provinces (Wang et al., 2010). The level of personnel and authority to make planning, policy, and development decisions for a town is similar to a county.

Table 3.1 *China's administrative divisions, 1982–2013*

		Prefecture level		County level			Town level	
		Prefectures	Prefecture-level cities	Counties	County-level cities	Number of urban districts	Rural towns (Zhen)	Townships (Xiang)
1982		210	109	2,133	133	527	2,660	54,352
1990		151	185	1,903	279	651	12,084	44,397
2000		74	259	1,674	400	787	20,312	23,199
2010		50	283	1,633	370	853	19,410	14,474
2013		47	286	1,613	368	872	20,117	12,802
Change	1982–1990	−59	76	−230	146	124	9,424	−9,955
	1990–2000	−77	74	−229	121	136	8,228	−21,198
	2000–2010	−24	24	−41	−30	66	−902	−8,725
	2010–2013	−3	3	−20	−2	19	707	−1,672
	1982–2013	−163	177	−516	345	335	17,457	−41,550

Note: "Township" in the 1982 data includes People's Communes, which were gradually transformed to townships in the early and mid-1980s.

Source: *China Statistical Yearbooks* in different years and website of Administrative Division www.xzqh.org.

Evolution of cities governing counties

Before the implementation of the city governing counties system, Chinese cities and counties rarely interacted except with respect to food supplies. The PRC's first constitution did not mention the concept of a city governing a county. The concept was tried first on an experimental basis with some prefectural-level cities beginning in the 1950s and then implemented nationally in the 1980s. The city organizational system was gradually transformed from being based on a municipal unit to a regional unit. This transition was accompanied by the restoration of townships from people's communes in rural parts of China. Today, except in some sparsely populated parts of western China, virtually all counties adjacent to prefectural-level cities are governed by the cities. Effectively many Chinese cities are managed as city-regions.

Continuing conflict, experiments and the debates

There are both advantages and disadvantages to the structural arrangements that have been adopted or are now the subject of experiments. Debates are continuing. Prefecture-level cities with significantly higher economic strength may offer economic help to adjacent counties and county-level cities with less strong economies. Often prefectural-level cities seek to concentrate economic activity within their borders. They may receive a disproportionate share of land use conversion quotas in the city proper or move successful businesses from adjacent counties and county-level cities they administer. In some cases this makes sense at the macro-level, but in others it does not. From the point of view of the counties it is almost always a source of conflict. Economically weak prefectural-level cities cannot effectively promote the development of adjacent counties or county-level cities.

Given the significant differences between provinces, relying on a model from one region may not be appropriate elsewhere. Too extreme reform of relationships too quickly may not work. Junliang Dai (2004), former vice president of the PRC's Ministry of Civil Affairs, and some other scholars have suggested that rationally re-dividing provinces—as actually occurred when Chongqing was separated from Sichuan province—would make it easier to carry out this kind of reform.

Evolution of the Administrative Hierarchy

Administration at the beginning of the PRC

China initially retained the four-hierarchy system after the regional adjustment in the beginning of 1950s, which is composed of (1) provinces, (2) prefectures (sub-provincial administrative regions), (3) cities and counties, and (4) townships and towns. Before reform and opening up towns were centers that provided services for daily life and production activities in rural areas.

Chinese cities during the period immediately after the founding of the PRC shared characteristics of their Western counterparts, in that they had a certain municipal service area. In the late 1950s, the central government aimed to drive the development of rural areas surrounding the cities by leadership from the central cities. The system of a "city leading the development of counties" was tried in some regions. By 1981 57 cities nationwide led 147 counties. More than two counties on average were placed under the jurisdiction of a (prefectural-level) city, and city administrative units effectively became city-regions. As described below this process has continued since reform and opening up and even though cities leading counties are still called cities in China, they may more accurately be viewed as city-regions.

During the 1980s reform of town administrative units was largely a remedial measure to recover from excesses of the Cultural Revolution. During the Cultural Revolution local government in rural areas was replaced by People's Revolutionary Committees, covering roughly the same area and population as township governments. People's communes were organized under the committees and these were in turn organized into work brigades. People's communes were both administrative and economic organizations. In the early 1980s the central government ordered the separation of administrative from economic functions. By 1984 almost all communes had become townships or towns. Work brigades became official villages and collective ownership bodies.

An important CCP Central Committee document in 1982 contained "Instructions on the Reform of Administrative Divisions and the Implementation of the System of Cities Leading the Counties" (CCP, 1982). This document promoted merging of prefectures and cities, and led to a rapid increase in the number of formally recognized cities. In 1983 alone, 32 new prefecture-level cities and 12 new county-level cities were formed.

In 1984, the State Council revised the standards for setting up official towns (PRC-MSC, 1984). This revision covered three areas:

- Lowering the population threshold for setting up towns from 3,000 permanent residents with non-agricultural hukou to 2,000;
- Changing a town's definition from urbanized built area of the town (referred to as "a municipal serviced block") to the whole surrounding administrative area, including much non-urban land. Therefore, in terms of administrative divisions, after 1984 a township and town are essentially the same; and

- Delegation of the power to approve the establishment of official towns to provincial level governments.

Lowering the standard for setting up official towns and the delegation of the power of approval led to a large increase in the number of official towns nationwide. From late 1982 to late 1990, the number of official towns increased nearly fivefold, from 2,660 to 12,084 (Table 3.1). Many books and articles in Chinese and English report urbanization statistics without noting that much of the increase in the so-called urban population since the mid-1980s was purely a result of these changes in administrative divisions.

In 1986, the State Council endorsed a Ministry of Civil Affairs' "Report on Standards for Setting up Cities and Conditions for Cities Leading Counties" (Zhang and Zhao, 1998). The new policy has greatly supported efforts to adjust administrative divisions since 1986. Between 1982 and 1990, the number of prefecture-level cities increased from 109 to 185, 146 new county-level cities were established, and the number of municipal districts under prefecture-level cities increased from 527 to 651. In contrast, the number of prefectures and counties were reduced by 59 and 230 respectively. During this period, the major directions of China's administrative division system reform included simplification of organization, merging of prefectures and cities, abolishing or consolidating counties, setting up cities and city districts, and establishing the system of "cities governing counties." County seats and some major urban settlements were granted town status.

1990–2000

Between 1990 and 2000 the number of cities and official towns continuously increased. Towns continued to change from municipal serviced blocks to regional administrative units.

By 2000 the system of "cities governing counties" was completely implemented in most of China except for Hainan province.

As market-oriented reform continued, local governments which aspired to economic development felt constrained by the small scope of their authority. Town, county, and county-level city governments are all motivated to move up the administrative hierarchy (Chan, 2010). Towns and counties aspire to be elevated to county-level cities or prefecture-level cities. If this occurs their governments enjoy a significantly broader scope of economic and social administrative powers.

During the 1990s eliminating counties and setting up cities or eliminating prefectures and setting up larger cities remained mainstream objectives of administrative division system reform. From 1990 to 2000, the number of county-level cities increased by 121, and the number of prefecture-level cities increased by 74. The number of prefectures decreased by 77 during this period (Table 3.1).

Parallel to the administrative structure reforms described above, market-oriented reform significantly liberated entrepreneurship and promoted the development of local economies. More and more rural people flowed into the cities and towns. As a result, an increased number of counties met the standards to become cities.[1] In response, the State Council set higher standards for setting up cities. They improved the standards for setting up county-level cities and specified standards for setting up prefecture-level cities in 1993 (PRC-MSC, 1993b). Even so, more and more cities or counties met these new standards. In some cases they stretched or even falsified data to meet the standards. As the central government became aware of these problems the State Council suspended nearly all creation of new cities in 1997 (Wang, Y., 2002; Chen, 2008).

Some county level cities were abolished, and city districts were set up in their place. Districts (Shi-xia-Qu) are sub-units of local government at the provincial, sub-provincial, and prefectural level. Districts have offices and staff, but report to the city government. These new districts were placed under direct control of prefecture-level cities. The new districts' scope of administrative authority was much narrower than the authority that the counties had possessed, which enhanced the resource pooling capacity of prefectural-level cities. In the 1990s, 40 counties were transformed to city districts, compared with 11 in the 1980s. During the 1990s, the number of counties decreased by 229, and the number of city districts increased by 136.

During the 1990s governmental restructuring at the town level was mainly driven by a desire for less redundant personnel and more efficient administration. Between 1991 and 2000, the total number of official towns and townships decreased from 56,481 to 43,511 while the number of towns increased from 12,084 to 20,312 (Table 3.1). The average population of people living in town centers of official towns in 2010 was 8,179 (NBSC-cts, 2012). The total number of residents within towns' jurisdictions increased to 44,000 in 2011 (NBSC-cts, 2013). Therefore towns were transformed from municipally serviced units in rural areas into geography-based administrative divisions similar to a city or city-region.

2000 to the present

Since 2000 the main objectives of administrative division reform have been to abolish counties (county-level cities) and set up districts. Between 2000 and 2013, the number of municipal districts increased by 85 (Table 3.1). Twenty-four counties were administratively transformed to districts between 2011 and 2013. The designation of districts also evolved from urban type districts to geography-based suburban administrative units. Those districts are an urban/rural mix.

Since 2000 more prefectures have been changed to prefecture-level cities, more counties and county-level cities to city districts, and more towns to sub-districts (urban streets). The merging of prefectures and cities and designation of cities leading counties continued. By the end of 2013, only 47 prefectures remained in China, most of which were ethnic autonomous prefectures with full governance authority located in remote regions. Prefecture-level cities had developed rapidly and their number had increased by 27 in 13 years. Counties or county-level cities retain an independent government and keep some constitutionally protected administrative powers even when they are subordinate to cities leading them. While establishment of county-level cities led by central cities often had the positive effect of stimulating better regional planning and policymaking it also led to competition and resentment between county-level cities and central cities.

After 2000, many major cities, including Guangzhou, Nanjing, Chengdu, Hangzhou, and Suzhou, achieved more integrated development by abolishing counties and setting up urban districts—rather than urban-level cities—in their place. While urban districts continue to have a local congress and elected government and have some bureaus and personnel in place to implement city policy, much of their authority is restricted, including the ability to make urban plans. Since they were to some extent subordinate to the central cities, overt conflict was minimized and the competence of major cities was enhanced (Luo, 2005).

Abolishing prefectures and setting up city-regions (prefectural-level cities) represents a delegation of government power by provincial governments. Abolishing counties (county-level cities) and setting up districts represents a ceding of government power to central cities. In this period, the delegation and withdrawal of power were concurrent, aimed at reducing institutional friction and promoting coordinated development in entire city-regions.

In 2002, the State Council suspended the old 1984 legal basis for setting up official towns and provincial governments were instructed to stop setting up additional official new towns. The new emphasis became improving conditions in existing towns rather than continuing the proliferations of additional towns. After 2002, governments at all levels intensified investments in infrastructure in rural areas—particularly transportation infrastructure. Infrastructure and public services in many townships and towns improved considerably. Governance at the town and township level was also emphasized and improved after 2002.

In order to simplify local government administrative structures, a new round of "revoking and merging" in town-level divisions has been underway since 2000. From 2000 to 2010, the number of official towns decreased by 902, and the number of townships decreased by 8,725. After 2010, the number of townships continued to decrease, whereas of the number of towns increased slightly. The general trend has been to reduce the total number of administrative divisions at the lowest levels of China's administrative division structure, reducing personnel and personnel costs, increasing their average population and land area, and integrating less developed fringe areas with urban core areas.

In the 30 plus years of China's reform and opening up, the adjustment of administrative divisions coincided with different stages of urbanization. The 1980s was the key period of restoring and improving China's economic and social systems from a chaotic past. The emergence of new cities and towns laid a solid foundation for the rapid development of urbanization that followed. The 1990s witnessed a large increase in the number of cities. Urban-only administrative units were continuously transformed into geography-based administrative units. The number of cities and towns reached its peak in the latter part of this period (Figure 3.5). Since 1990 the emphasis has been on reducing fragmentation, increasing the average size of the lowest-level administrative divisions, reducing personnel, increasing efficiency, and governing urban areas and adjacent rural areas together.

China became a member of the World Trade Organization (WTO)

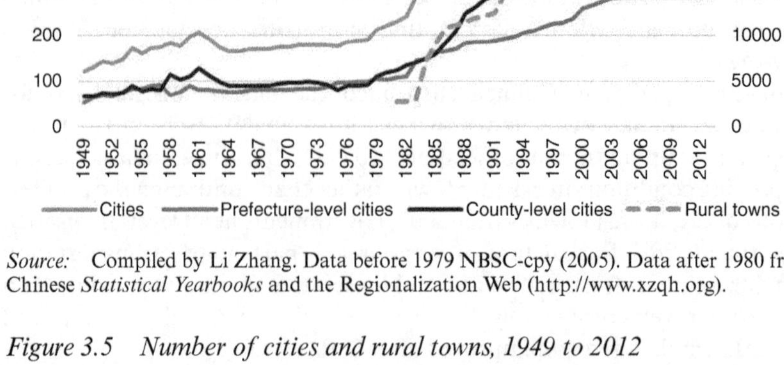

Source: Compiled by Li Zhang. Data before 1979 NBSC-cpy (2005). Data after 1980 from Chinese *Statistical Yearbooks* and the Regionalization Web (http://www.xzqh.org).

Figure 3.5 Number of cities and rural towns, 1949 to 2012

in 2001. As a result, globalization has intensively influenced China's development and urbanization and has created some conflict among jurisdictions seeking to control space for new development, reflecting China's greater integration into the global economy as described in Chapter 5. This created different kinds of conflict arising from administrative divisions particularly in large or prefecture-level cities as they competed to become integrated into the global economy. This helps explain the emphasis on fewer and larger administrative divisions described above. Overall, these changes have produced fewer and larger administrative units encompassing both urban and peri-urban land better equipped to compete in the national and global economy. However, changing administrative divisions in this way created new problems, including the dramatic expansion of the population and built-up areas in some cities, the existence of unproductive rural industries, the rural population and rural communities remaining in urban districts (especially in designated new districts), and the continuing urban–rural dual structure.

Significance of Administrative Division Reform

The practice of China's reform and opening up has shown that institutional innovation led by the government can be the major force driving economic and social development. An effective institutional design and innovation can promote the full utilization of social resources and accelerate capital accumulation and technological innovation. During the market-oriented transition period, reform of administrative divisions has become an important, but indirect device for governance. Rather than top-down micromanagement, the national government has focused on macro-level decisions and continuously modified the structure of lower levels of government in response to changing conditions in order to release the creative energy of local government and civil society.

Urban expansion and urban transformation in rapidly growing areas

Before reform and opening up, state policy divided urban and rural areas via the hukou system. In 1982, China had only 245 official cities and an urbanization level of 21 percent. After the implementation of new policy, the country experienced rapid economic development and social transition. The urbanized population increased from 207 million in 1982 to 667 million in 2010. The huge population increase in cities and towns, however, challenged the existing administrative division system. The 245 official cities experienced unprecedented urban expansion pressure. The spatial expansion of metropolitan areas, major cities, emerging small and medium-sized cities and a few market-oriented and rapidly growing rural towns intensified institutional friction between downtown and peri-urban areas and between large cities and adjacent counties and towns (Cui et al., 2012). Some rural areas in peri-urban and rural locations with relatively high development levels began to exhibit urban features. Both urban expansion and urban transformation in some rural areas demanded the reform of administrative divisions.

Transition from "regional segmentation" to "coordinated regional development"

In the course of the transition to an increasingly market-oriented society, economic and social relations in many parts of China exhibited an "economy of administrative divisions" (Liu, 2004). Conflicts of interest between counties and cities and the need for delegating rights to economic development challenged the existing administrative division system. Administrative borders were an invisible wall that restricted regional economic integration and the development of a market economy. Large regional differences in China require coordination and integration between urban-type and geography-based administrative divisions.

For remote regions, the system of geography-based administrative divisions fits local conditions better than in more developed urban regions. In regions with a higher level of social and economic development, cities and towns tend to be connected and the urban landscape is more integrated. In these areas de facto urban-type administrative units have basically replaced *de jure* geography-based administrative units (Wang et al., 2010).

One new approach—officially endorsed in China's National New Style Urbanization Plan—is to coordinate economic development within urban agglomerations. The United Nations terms a large economically interdependent region an urban agglomeration and has defined the boundaries of all urban agglomerations in the world with more than one million residents according to standards they have devised (UNPD, 2014). Chinese scholars such as Jiang Xu and Anthony Yeh (Xu and Yeh, 2010), and Chaolin Gu (Gu, 1998) and Western scholars such as Peter Taylor (2015), Peter Hall and Kathy Pain (Hall and Pain, 2006), Regional Plan Association (2015), Florida, Gulden, and Mellander (2007), and Sassen (2002) are exploring this approach using more user-friendly terms like "megacity region" and "polycentric urban network" in place of the word agglomeration.

Most agglomerations, as defined by the UN, consist of a single central city and its surrounding peri-urban region, including smaller cities and towns. The UN defines a few agglomerations as including two or more city centers and the urbanized land between them.

The Yangtze River Delta, Pearl River Delta, Beijing–Tianjin–Hebei region, greater Wuhan region, and some other regions in China are already developing prototype institutions and plans for the entire region. In these regions at the macro-level the traditional administrative division system that restricts the coordinated development of the regional economy is becoming more and more inadequate. The complex conflicts of interests between urban regions and rural areas in megalopolitan regions of this scale require the adjustment of administrative divisions to achieve inter-governmental cooperation (Wang, Y., 2002; Cui et al., 2012). The shift from an "economy of administrative divisions" to "coordinated regional development" should produce more innovation in China's administrative division system.

Changing motivations for urbanization

Before implementation of reform and opening up policies, China was shackled by the planned economy system and urbanization was carried out mainly in a top-down manner. The extent of regional urbanization was decided by top-down mandatory planning and development. After implementation of market-oriented economic reforms, the framework and goals of the socialist market economy changed, and the scope and intensity of market forces gradually increased. During the process of narrowing the scope covered by the planned economy system, planned urbanization and market-oriented urbanization coexisted (Han and Wong, 1994). During the last decades, however, the central government has ceased to act as the sole actor controlling the speed, scale, and spatial distribution of urbanization. Instead, state policy, capital (including foreign capital), enterprises, and regional initiatives have determined the direction and model of urbanization (Zhang, 2009). A "bottom-top" mechanism has evolved (Pannell, 2002; Cui and Ma, 1999; Ning, 1998). Adapting to globalization has become one of the new motives for China's urbanization (Pannell, 2002).

Since a new market environment has emerged, and the mechanisms driving urbanization in China have diversified, it appears likely that higher-level governments will continue to give local government more freedom to manage urbanization and those local governments will require more personnel with more specialized skills. This has been the pattern in recent reforms of administrative divisions. For example, after "abolishing counties and setting up cities," establishing a higher ceiling for foreign exchange, approval of major investments and large-area land use, establishing local banks and issuing local bonds, expanding urban construction and maintenance fees, and having more fiscal and taxation powers, local governments require more personnel, particularly skilled personnel with administrative specialties.

Administrative Divisions and Urbanization Statistics

One consequence of administrative system reform is that it complicates understanding of urbanization statistics. The third nationwide census in 1982 counted the total city and town population as the statistical urban population. Thus, administrative divisions were closely connected with urban–rural population distinctions (Wang et al., 2008).

Adjusting administrative divisions may include any of the following six types of modifications:

(1) Changing the local organizational system within an administrative unit;
(2) Changing the position of an administrative unit in the administrative hierarchy;
(3) Changing an administrative division's borders;
(4) Changing the location where administrative organs within an administrative division are located;
(5) Changing subordination relationships; and
(6) Naming or re-naming administrative divisions.

A direct consequence of urbanization in China has been changes to the entire local organizational system in many regions. This may involve (1) abolishing prefectures and setting up (prefectural-level) cities, (2) abolishing counties and setting up cities and/or districts, (3) abolishing townships and setting up official towns, (4) abolishing towns and setting up city sub-districts (urban streets), (5) changing the administrative hierarchy (elevating county-level cities to prefecture-level city status; or towns to county-level city status), (6) and merging administrative divisions (merging prefecture-level cities, merging counties and cities, and merging towns and townships).

A region, whether considered an urban area or not, is closely related to its administrative hierarchy and subordination relationships. With both population and space constant, the urbanization level of a region can be raised by adjusting administrative divisions within it. This, however, is meaningful only in a statistical sense. For example, based on the standards of the third nationwide census in 1982, a township could be "urbanized" simply by changing its status from a township to an official town. In the same way, using the standards of the fourth nationwide census in 1990, once a county or county-level city is transformed into a city district, the population either in urban streets or rural villages is defined as urbanized population. According to the standards of the fifth nationwide census in 2000, if a county is abolished and replaced with a new city or city district, the rural population, both of the adjacent villages and of the adjacent townships and towns is counted as urbanized population. All these forms of adjustment of administrative divisions do not immediately change the reality of urbanization and people's living standard in spite of the increased level of regional urbanization in the statistical sense. Over time, however, administrative changes matter. They can speed up or slow down urbanization or re-direct it from one area to another as favored areas grow more rapidly than less favored areas.

Census definitions of urban areas and urban population

A source of confusion in efforts to understand China's urbanization is the way in which definitions of urban areas and the urban population have changed over time. Many studies—particularly by Western scholars—present non-comparable statistics as if they were internally consistent. This can greatly under- or over-state the absolute size of China's urban population or rates of change. Following is a precise description of how urban areas and urban population in China have been defined since 1949.

China has carried out six nationwide censuses. Statistical definitions of the urban population are different in each of the six censuses (Figure 3.6).

Censuses of 1953, 1964, and 1982 Before reform and opening up China had a planned economic system with low population mobility, large urban–rural differences, and geographical separations between cities and the countryside. While the definitions of urban areas and the urban population in the three national censuses in 1953, 1964, and 1982 were not the same, their results were generally consistent with the actual degree of urbanization at the time they were administered.

Urban population in the third nationwide census in 1982 was defined as the sum of city population (excluding township population within a city jurisdiction) and town population. Based on this definition, the urbanization level of China in 1982 was 20.88 percent. At this stage, urban regions and rural areas were clearly divided. Cities and towns were set up according to social and economic indicators and their level of urban services, and the urban features of cities and towns were obvious and distinct. Almost no spatial mixture existed between urban and rural areas. Therefore, the statistical definition used in the 1982 census was a reasonably good indicator of the actual urbanization level.

Fourth nationwide census (1990) Administrative division reforms in the mid-1980s lowered the standards for setting up cities and towns as described above. This resulted in the emergence of many new cities and towns in official statistics. The original spot-like distribution of cities and

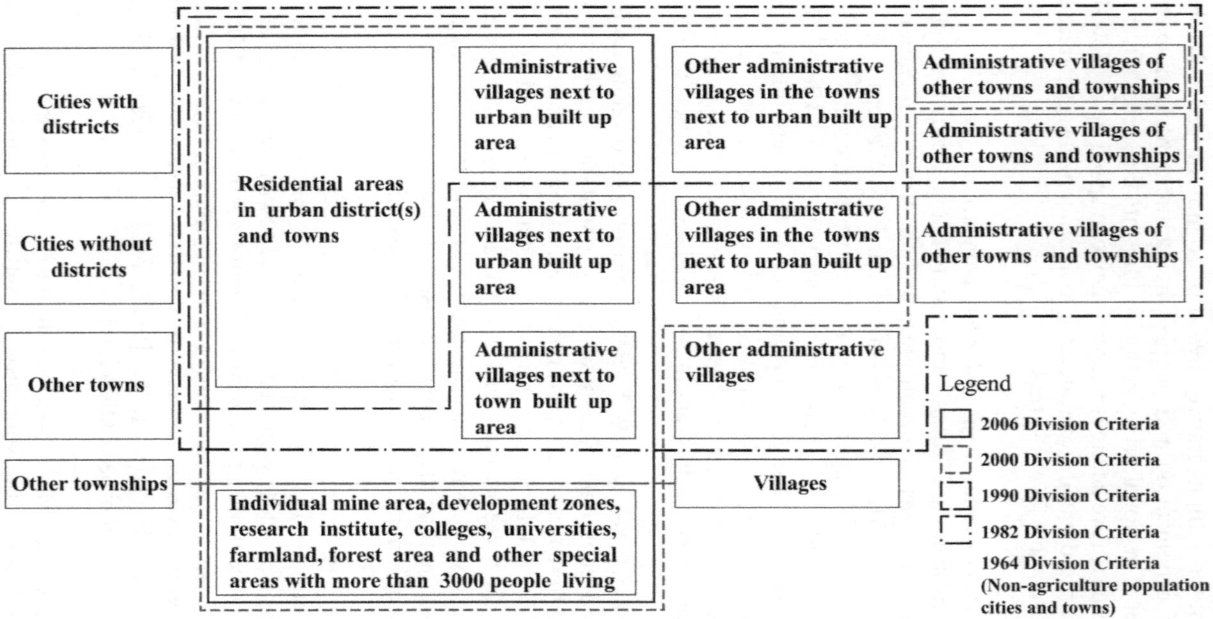

Source: Compiled by Li Zhang.

Figure 3.6 Urban–rural division criteria in different censuses towns was transformed into a planar distribution in which urban and rural areas became connected—a change from a pattern of detached cities and towns to connected urban–rural regions.

From 1982 to 1990, 233 counties were elevated to the status of cities or districts. Based on the statistical definition used in the third nationwide census, China's urbanization level would have been 53.19 percent in 1990 (Zhou and Ma, 2003). Even if the administrative divisions were not adjusted, using the statistical definition of urban population in the 1982 census the urbanization level in 1990 would have been 40.52 percent. Without a change in the census definition, the urbanization level would have been greatly overestimated (Ma and Cui, 1987; Zhou and Ma, 2003).

In order to produce urbanization statistics that better reflected reality, the fourth nationwide census in 1990 adopted new standards to define urban areas. For prefecture-level cities, 15 quasi-provincial-level cities, and China's four provincial-level cities the total population within their urban districts and built-up suburban areas was counted as urbanized population. For cities, only the population living in urban streets, town seats, and surrounding neighborhood communities was counted as urbanized population (Chan and Hu, 2003).

According to this new set of standards China's urbanization level in 1990 was 26.40 percent. If the influence of the change of the definition of urban population based only on Figure 3.6 is analyzed, the wrong conclusion might be drawn—that the new definition used in 1990 was responsible for an underestimation of urban population, compared with the 1982 census definitions. Careful estimation of the changes in the administrative divisions in this period leads to a different conclusion. Estimates by Zhang (2010) indicate that the increase of urban population due to administrative division adjustments between 1983 and 1990 was 58.19 million. Without the administrative division adjustments, the urbanization level would have been approximately 21.05 percent. In a statistical sense, adjusting the administrative divisions increased the urbanization level by approximately 5.35 percent.

Fifth nationwide census (2000) The practice of transforming counties to districts since the 1990s has blurred the definition of "district" which was originally an administrative unit with obvious urban features. Rapid urban growth has led to the development of suburbs and the original rural areas in some regions have become more urban. Professor Yixing Zhou of Peking University and Professor Laurence Ma of the University of Akron have concluded that China's urbanization level would be between 31.39 percent and 36.09 percent—lower than the reality—if the 1990 fourth nationwide census standards had been used in 2000 (Zhou and Ma, 2003).

The fifth nationwide census in 2000 downplayed the concept of "administrative region," while highlighting the urban features of space. The coverage in official districts was divided into two kinds of zones according to population density. The first type of zone is an area with population density higher than 1,500 persons per km^2. All the population in this type of zone is counted as urbanized population. The second type of zone is a zone with a population density lower than 1,500 persons per km^2. The population in this type of zone is counted as rural population except for the population living in urban streets. For county-level cities and a few prefecture-level cities which have no official districts, besides the population of the urban built-up area under city jurisdiction (urban streets), the population of towns and townships connected to the urban built-up area was also included in the 2000 urban population statistics.

The 2000 classification standard better fits the situation of rapid expansion of urban space. Based on this definition, China's urbanization level in 2000 was 36.09 percent (NBSC, 2001). Professor Zhang's estimates (Zhang, 2010) are that the increase in the city population due to the adjustment of administrative divisions from 1991 to 2000 was approximately 35.44 million. The adjustment of administrative divisions technically increased the urbanization level in 2000 by approximately 2.85 percent in a statistical sense. Though there was a possibility of overestimation, the urban population statistics in the fifth nationwide census conform reasonably well to China's de facto urbanization level at that time (Zhou and Ma, 2003).

Sixth nationwide census, 2010 Although the urban–rural division in the nationwide census in 2000 had considered the spatial characteristics of urban areas, and made some progress in refining the statistical standard, it was the most complex of all previous Chinese censuses. In the fifth nationwide census urban streets and towns were the basic accounting units. The actual situation, however, is that urban and rural areas overlap in towns, townships and a few urban streets. Numerous rural residents were included in the urban accounting, which resulted in an overestimation of the urbanization level.

In 2008, China's National Statistics Bureau released trial "Regulations on Statistical Urban–Rural Divisions" that establish the sixth standard of urban–rural division (Figure 3.6). In these trial regulations, the area covered by neighborhood committees and administrative villages are considered as the basic units in the urban–rural division. This enhances the accuracy of urban and rural accounting. From the national or provincial point of view, the new statistical standard is undoubtedly more advanced. In our opinion, the spatial features of urban regions and rural areas are highlighted, but the social features are still largely ignored. As of this writing in spring, 2015, the map data on the division of geographical units for the survey of urban population are not yet available, and the corresponding relation between population and space remains unknown.

Rethinking standards for urban–rural classifications

China's constantly changing national census standards and frequent adjustments to China's administrative divisions have resulted in changes in reported population statistics and urbanization levels (Ma and Cui, 1987). The scale of the changes in China is much greater than in Western countries that use more consistent standards for urban–rural divisions that change less over time. The complex urban–rural division system has made it difficult for scholars to do meaningful longitudinal analysis of urbanization and many scholars have criticized the complexity and changes (Holz, 2002; Shen, 2005, 2006; Zhou and Ma, 2003; Chan, 2007).

Chinese census population data are particularly difficult for Western scholars to interpret and have led to oversimplifications and errors in the Western literature on Chinese urbanization.

Although adjustment attempts in the standards for urban–rural division discussed above have been improvements, we believe there is one common defect: identifying urban features solely based on spatial characteristics. Urbanization has a wide range of connotations; thus, besides spatial factors, economic and social factors should be also considered. Censuses of other countries employ multiple criteria in defining urban areas. For example the US census considers commute and employment sheds in defining urban areas.

A new approach: the neighborhood committee as the basic unit to define urbanization

Based on a proposal by one of the authors of this book, Li Zhang (Zhang, 2011), we propose a new approach to measuring urban and non-urban population. Spatial factors are only one of the attributes of urbanization. In our opinion social and economic consequences of urbanization are as or more relevant factors that should also be considered in classifying an area as urban or rural.

Chinese cities have strict regulations on the setting up of districts in the case of prefectural-level cities or higher and urban streets in the case of county-level cities. Every district and urban street has a number of neighborhood committees. Neighborhood committees are autonomous administrative units in China. Rules for setting them up are regulated under China's Urban Neighborhood Committee Organization Law of 1989 (PRC, 1989a). The standards for establishing a neighborhood committee are related to urban features of land, population, infrastructure and basic public services. If a settlement is designated to have a Neighborhood Committee, that indicates that it is an urban settlement. Neighborhood committees could be used as the basic unit for defining urban–rural divisions. Generally each neighborhood services about 100 to 700 households.

In each of China's six censuses, the lowest unit is named a statistical unit—roughly equivalent to a "block" in the US census. Statistical units consist of about 50 households. The unit at the level above the statistical unit is either a neighborhood committee or an administrative village. Therefore, in each census the data at the neighborhood and village level for neighborhood committees already exists.

If neighborhood committees were used as a unit of analysis, city population would refer to the residents living in the areas under the jurisdiction of neighborhood committees. Using this definition, adjusting the coverage of urban–rural divisions would no longer be required. Instead, modifications could be made to standards for setting up of neighborhood committees or the standards and regulations for turning official villages or rural settlements to neighborhood committees particularly in peri-urban areas around cities and towns.

Another means of transforming administrative villages to neighborhood committees is listing "suburban population" separately in official population statistics to facilitate use by researchers and policymakers. The users can decide whether to include this portion of the community as part of the urban domain. If suburban population is broken out in this way, the task of specifying the urban–rural division will be simplified, and city population statistics can be determined more accurately and easily. Moreover, a statistics department can release comparable data on "urban population" in each past national census according to this division. Comparable data on urbanization levels from the six nationwide censuses would then exist. Such a division may result in underestimation in a few cities. In some larger cities, and even some small cities, urban villages (chengzhongcun) still exist because of the fast urban sprawl in recent decades. Those communities, named urban villages are in fact urban settlements. Those units should be changed to Neighborhood Committees after the villagers' land rights and people's welfare are assured. The new standards can help academic researchers and policymakers to estimate the urbanization level of China more accurately. A clearly defined standard for rural–urban division will help the formulation of urbanization policies (Chan, 2010).

URBAN POLICIES AND THEIR IMPACT ON ADMINISTRATIVE DIVISIONS AND CITY SIZE

Many of the urban policies at different stages in the recent development of China described in this book are related to administrative divisions and particularly city size. The issue of city size involves multiple dimensions related to economics, society, resources, and governance.

The Evolution of Urban Policies

Before reform and opening up: conflicting ideas on controlling the growth of large cities

In the period immediately after the founding of the PRC, China's leadership drew a sharp distinction between service-based cities whose main economic activities were commerce or tourism and industrial cities whose economic base was production of goods China needed. They considered the service-based cities to be parasitic and that they should be transformed from "places of consumption" into the "places of production" (MacFarquhar and Fairbank, 1990). The ideology and experience of the former Soviet Union deeply influenced China. Initial state policies favored construction of large industrial satellite towns in metropolitan suburbs. A typical example is Shanghai's satellite towns. In 1956, Minhang was the first satellite town to be set up. Shanghai's mechanical and power industry was concentrated there. In 1958, four other satellite towns—Wujing, Jiading, Anting, and Songjiang—followed and many heavy industries were located in these towns. In the early 1970s Jinshan satellite town was established for petrochemical industries and in the 1980s Baoshan satellite town was established to produce iron and steel. Following the transition of the state-planned economy to a more market-oriented economy, most of the satellite towns have changed from industrial towns to new towns with more diversified economies and relatively complete services and facilities.

In the 1950s, with the help of the Soviet Union, China placed particular emphasis on the development of Luoyang, Zhengzhou, Maanshan, Lanzhou, Baotou, and other major pre-existing industrial cities and some newly emerging industrial cities: Yinchuan in Ningxia province, Xinxiang in Henan province, and Yumen in Gansu province. Throughout the 1950s, policies generally favored urban development, but just of industrial cities, particularly of large industrial cities of 500,000 or more (Ma, 2002, 2005). Since the government imposed strict control on population migration in both urban and rural parts of China, urban policies only targeted industrialization. This is why urbanization prior to reform and opening up lagged behind the progress of industrialization (Chan, 1992).

The full scale implementation of the hukou system in the 1960s marked a transition in state policy regarding the growth of cities when city population growth was controlled through imposition of strict quotas limiting change of agriculture to non-agricultural hukou. Relocation of some specific urban population groups including moving vagrants out of cities, transferring technical staff to inland China, and sending urban youth to farm in rural areas further limited the growth of cities. Concerned about domestic and international threats—in particular the prospect of nuclear war with either the Soviet Union or the United States—state construction during this period was predominantly directed toward preparing for war. In the 1960s, state policy began to support the development of small and medium-sized cities in hinterlands and industrial bases in remote areas of central China, to build a so-called "third line of the country" (Chang, 1976).

At this stage, two kinds of urban development were hotly debated. One debate involved the merits of developing large cities versus small and medium-sized cities. The other debate involved developing coastal cities versus inland cities. The central government vacillated between these two development orientations until implementation of reform and opening up policy in the early 1980s.

1980s: controlling the size of large cities and rationally developing medium-sized and small cities

The Cultural Revolution (1966–1976) wrought havoc on the national economy. The scale of construction work in China shrank for a decade. After the end of the Cultural Revolution, urban residents demanded wage increases and improved living and housing conditions, and hundreds of thousands of youth returned to urban areas after doing farm work in rural areas for many years (Liu, 2009). All these events added to the burden on city governments.

In order to respond to these problems, the former National Construction Commission organized a working conference on urban planning in Beijing in October, 1980. During this conference, participants agreed on the general policy of "controlling the size of large cities, reasonably developing medium-sized cities, and proactively developing small-sized cities." In the mid-1980s the important policies regarding the standards for classifying towns and cities described above were implemented. In 1984, the State Council relaxed the standard for setting up official towns. The population threshold to qualify as an official town was lowered from 3,000 permanent residents to a population of more than 2,000 with non-agricultural hukou in the town proper (PRC-MSC, 1984). Two years later, in 1986, the standard for setting up official cities was also relaxed. Towns with an urban population with non-agricultural hukou higher than 60,000 and GDP of more than 200 million RMB (current price) were allowed to be elevated to the status of county-level cities. One of the immediate consequences of this regulation was the increase in the number of small-sized cities from 108 in 1980 to 291 in 1990 (Table 3.2). The three changes led to a proliferation of new towns, new cities, and new county-level cities.

China adopted its first City Planning Act in 1989 (PRC, 1989b). This law remained in effect until 2008, when it was replaced by China's Urban and Rural Planning Law. According to the original 1989 law, "the State puts into effect the principle of keeping strict control over the size of large cities and developing rationally medium-sized cities and small cities, so as to promote a rational structure of productivity and population."

As reform and opening up policy was first implemented in China's eastern coastal areas, many large coastal cities obtained strong support from the central government and received large amounts of domestic investment as well as FDI and grew rapidly.

1990s: promoting the development of small and medium-sized cities and small towns

While there was top-down State urban policy, bottom-up spontaneous urbanization was also evident (Cui and Ma, 1999; Friedmann, 2005). As described in Chapter 2, hukou policy for small towns was reformed in the 1980s before hukou reform was extended to cities. This invigorated the development of small towns. The development mode of rural industry in south Jiangsu province, in which much industrial development took place in towns and small cities, was very successful and was endorsed by the central government. Many small towns in the Pearl River Delta Region became locations for processing client-supplied materials for Hong Kong, Macau and Taiwan. Consequently, the entire Pearl River Delta region experienced rapid urbanization.

A well-known Chinese sociologist, Hsiao-Tung Fei, who had received his PhD from the London School of Economics and Political Science in 1938 and had published *Peasant Life in China* in 1939 (Fei, 1939), conducted extensive field surveys in small towns at the end of the 1980s. His study, "Small towns, large strategy" (Fei, [1984]2004), arguing in favor of town and village enterprises caught the attention of the central government and had nationwide influence (Fei, [1984]2004). In the 1990s, the bottom-up dynamics of industrial development and urbanization in rural towns and rural areas flourished even more, resulting in the emergence of a huge number of township enterprises. The central government continued to support township enterprises and encouraged new market-oriented policies to make property rights clearer (Tian, 2014).

Table 3.2 Number of cities at different scales and the percentage of the population residing in the city

Year	Total		Metropolises		Large cities		Medium cities		Small cities	
			Pop≥1 Million		1> Pop≥0.5 Million		0.5>Pop≥0.2 Million		Pop<0.2 Million	
	Number	Proportion of Population	Number	Proportion of Population	Number	Proportion of Population	Number	Proportion of Population	Number	Proportion of Population
1980	223	100%	15	39.0%	30	24.6%	70	23.5%	108	13.0%
1985	324	100%	21	39.4%	31	19.4%	94	24.5%	178	16.8%
1990	467	100%	31	41.6%	28	12.6%	117	24.2%	291	21.5%
1995	640	100%	32	34.9%	43	14.8%	191	28.8%	374	21.4%
2000	665	100%	35	36.9%	54	15.5%	220	28.9%	352	18.5%
2005	661	100%	54	29.0%	85	14.0%	226	30.0%	296	26.0%
2009	654	100%	60	32.0%	91	15.0%	238	31.0%	265	22.0%
2013	658	100%	69	35.0%	95	16.0%	242	30.0%	252	19.0%

Source: Data for 2005, 2009, and 2013 is from PRC-MHURD (2014). Data before 2005 is from Han and Wang (2013).

After 2000: coordinated development of large, medium, and small-sized cities and towns

In the late 1990s, negotiations on the admission of China to the World Trade Organization (WTO) entered their final stage. At this time, the Chinese leadership felt an urgent need to build a new industrial system to permit China to compete internationally on a much larger scale. Most small-sized cities and towns had weak infrastructure and poor quality development and were not in a position to compete in global markets. As a result, the national leadership was urgently looking for new models of town and small-sized city development.

In contrast, most large cities and metropolitan regions in China had better infrastructure and more solid economic foundations, which equipped them not only to compete, internationally, but also to lead the development of nearby small cities and towns so that they could also be competitive globally. In the context of globalization, the major cities in China were given the lead role in the urbanization process to gain global competitiveness.

Both the level at which policy statements in China appear and the wording of policy statements in the highest-level documents are extremely significant in China. China's Five-Year Plans are the most significant overarching policy documents of all. Both The Outline of China's tenth Five-Year Plan (2001–2006) and the plan itself identified urbanization as an outstanding issue. Urbanization had become an important part of China's national development strategy. The tenth Five-Year Plan changed the previous principle of "proactively developing rural towns" to "developing rural towns selectively and proactively developing small and medium-sized cities." In other words it reduced the emphasis on developing rural towns from developing them "proactively" (greater emphasis) to developing them "selectively" (implying that only some would be developed and/or that only certain aspects would be developed). Instead the tenth Five-Year Plan placed greater emphasis on developing small and medium-sized cities. It also proposed the idea of coordinated development of large, medium, and small-sized cities and towns for the first time. Therefore, the significance of large cities in the urbanization process was officially acknowledged and emphasis shifted from rural towns to also include small, medium, and large-sized cities.

In 2006, the outline of the eleventh Five-Year Plan continued the discussion of the issue of urbanization by devoting a separate chapter to urbanization. It suggested developing urban agglomerations as a major urbanization approach. The previous policy of "strictly controlling the population growth of large cities" was modified into "controlling overly rapid population growth through industrial restructuring." This modification indicates the central government's new thinking with regard to fast growth and prioritized development of large cities. It shifted the emphasis to the tempo of urbanization rather than city size per se, only discouraging development that was "too fast."

Strategy for urban agglomerations and key cities after 2011

As China's urbanization continued to transition from centralized national planning to more market-led planning, the national government devoted more attention to the quality of urbanization (Zhang, 2009). The eleventh Five-Year Plan (2006–2010) and twelfth Five-Year Plan (2011–2015) proposed "promoting healthy urbanization." This showed growing recognition of the fact that China's remarkable economic success had come at a cost to the quality of life in cities. Henceforth "livability" was to be a consideration in urban planning.

As China's urbanization level reached 50 percent and "passed the 50 percent Rubicon" in the words of University of Washington geographer Kam Wing Chan (Chan, 2009b), many new debates about the future course of urbanization in China have emerged. In March 2014, after a two-year preparation period the Chinese leadership released the first ever National New Style Urbanization Plan: 2014–2020 (PRC, 2014). The NNSUP is a long and complex strategic plan that describes a variety of policies at a high level of generality. It favors hierarchical urban development policies from towns to small, medium, and large cities and megacities. The NNSUP seems to place the focus of urbanization until 2020 on developing urban agglomerations and key cities.

The shifts in focus described above mark profound changes in China's city development orientation. Because of the pervasive reach of the Chinese Communist Party (CCP) at every level, these shifts in emphasis and wording have real consequences. Historically, the policy was changed from "favoring large cities" to "controlling the size of large cities," and finally to "preventing the excess increase of large cities." The policy of "proactively developing small-sized cities" was changed to "encouraging the rural population to settle down in small and medium-sized cities," and from "proactively promoting the development of rural towns" to "selectively developing rural towns." When viewed together, China's urban policies have shifted their focus from managing urban scale to "constructing a coordinated, healthy, and sustainable urban system with urban agglomeration as the main body and centering around the key cities" (PRC, 2014).

Investigating Urban Growth at Different Scales

The changes in China's urban policies described above have inevitably influenced the growth of cities at different scales at every level of China's urban hierarchy. The majority of studies of China's urbanization have focused on the national level (Zhou and Ma, 2003; Shen, 2005; Chan, 2007; Hsing, 2012; Miller, 2012; Chen et al., 2013; DRC and WB, 2014; Zhang, F., 2014) or the provincial or lower level (Shen, 2006; Zhang and Han, 2009; Hu, 2012; LeGates and Ye, 2012; Zhang, X., 2014). Much less research has focused on cities as the basic unit of analysis. The following sections of this chapter review the development of cities or towns of various scales and levels in China's urban hierarchy in order to promote a better understanding of changing urban policies and the actual trend of urban development.

Changes in the number of cities and their population proportions

The number of cities in China is constantly changing. In 2013, there were 658 official cities—nearly triple the number in 1980. In 33 years between 1980 and 2013, the number of metropolitan regions with populations of more than 1 million residents with non-agricultural hukou more than quadrupled from 15 to 69: the fastest growth at any level of China's city hierarchy. The number of large cities with populations of 0.5 million to 1.0 million and medium-sized cities with populations of 0.2 million to 0.5 million residents with non-agricultural hukou have tripled since 1980. In this period, the number of small-sized cities more than doubled from 108 to 252.

Table 3.2 shows the proportions of city residents with non-agricultural hukou at various scales to the total urban population between 1980 and 2013. While there were fluctuations, the overall trend has been for the population proportions of metropolitan areas to increase moderately, since 2005 the proportion of large cities with populations of more than 500,000 to increase slowly, the population proportions of cities with populations of 200,000 to 500,000 to remain stable, and the population of small cities with populations below 200,000 to decrease. The population data shown in Table 3.2 is for the non-agricultural hukou population only. The de facto urban population proportions of metropolitan areas, large cities, and some other cities would be higher if the resident migrant population with agricultural hukou is considered. Most of China's urban migrant population is located in either China's major cities or in capital towns. While some small and medium-sized cities and general towns have large numbers of migrants with rural hukou, their combined population and therefore their contribution to the overall proportion of urban residents are small. Table 3.2 is descriptive; it just shows population data at different scales over time. It does not answer the important question of why the trends it shows are occurring.

A number of scholars have analyzed the relationship between China's rate of urbanization and city size and the city's place in China's administrative division hierarchy.

Washington University Geography Professor Kam Wing Chan used data from the Fifth and Sixth National Chinese Censuses to analyze total population growth in districts under the jurisdiction of 414 Chinese cities (Chan, 2010). Chan found that population growth generally increased more rapidly the larger the city scale and the higher the city was in China's urban hierarchy. Chan concluded that the administrative division changes in the 1990s and the first decade of the twenty-first century profoundly affected *de jure* city population growth.

Zhou and his co-researchers analyzed population growth in cities of various scales from 1949 to 2010 (Zhou et al., 2013) looking at the ratio of the urban population to the total population of Chinese cities at various scales over time. Zhou and his colleagues concluded that cities with populations below 500,000 generally grew slowly after the 1990s.

Zhou's study ignored one influential factor: that some small-sized cities grew to large cities or became urban districts, and changed from one category to another. Urban population in cities of every size almost always grew rapidly during the stage of rapid urbanization As long as no new cities were set up, the number of small cities would naturally decrease or remain unchanged. This is the reason why most studies have concluded that the population of large cities has been rapidly growing. Professor Yixing Zhou criticized similar mistakes in analyzing the urban scale (Zhou, 1995b).

As a result of the research by Yixing Zhou, Kam Wing Chan, and others, most Chinese researchers are aware that ignoring the adjustment of administrative divisions, the elevation of towns and counties to city status, and other changes will result in mistaken conclusions. Less academic writers and Western researchers can benefit from their work and the work of other scholars who have worked out ways to overcome these changes.

The urban database for our research

In order to analyze the Chinese city system as it existed in 2013, the ideal dataset would include complete and longitudinally comparable data on the universe of 657 cities that existed at that time from the earliest year in which statistics are available. We chose 1984 as the starting year for our analysis because China's annual Urban Statistical Yearbooks (NBSC-usy, 1985–2013) began in that year. Because of changes of administrative divisions and accessibility of statistics, the dataset we chose for the analysis that follows consists of 287 prefecture-level, sub-provincial level, and provincial-level cities that existed in 2010. These cities have limited variations in terms of the administrative boundaries at the urban district level, except in Jiangsu, Zhejiang, Guangdong, Fujian and Shandong provinces. The adjustment of administrative divisions of cities from 1984 to 2010 were taken into account (Zhang, 2010). Cities with major administrative division changes were excluded from the research sample. The number of comparable cities between 1984 and 2010 are as follows: 227 from 1984 to 1990, 232 from 1990 to 2000, and 200 from 2000 to 2010, accounting for 79 percent, 81 percent, and 70 percent of the total number of cities in these three time periods. While this database is not perfect, it makes it possible to investigate the general trend of urban population increase and avoids the common error of failing to account for changes in city rank. Table 3.3 summarizes the data.

We classified cities at various time periods according to the non-agricultural population in the urban districts. Apart from informal migration, the growth of the non-agricultural population in cities of various scales sheds light on the extent to which the central government may or may not actually need to control urban population growth to achieve its objectives. We consider cities with populations of more than 1 million to be metropolitan regions, cities with populations between 500,000 and

Table 3.3 National non-agricultural population increase

Region	Time period	Metropolitan regions	Large cities	Medium cities	Small cities	Average
		Pop≥1 Million	1>Pop≥0.5 Million	0.5>Pop≥0.2 Million	Pop<0.2 Million	
East	1984–1990	2.24	3.22	3.82	6.32	4.66
	1990–2000	2.04	2.68	4.47	6.87	4.78
	2000–2010	2.19	3.64	5.46	6.89	4.93
Central	1984–1990	2.03	2.99	3.43	5.44	4.29
	1990–2000	2.22	2.03	3.22	7.33	4.71
	2000–2010	2.12	1.66	2.24	2.72	2.19
West	1984–1990	1.97	2.29	3.11	5.88	4.44
	1990–2000	2.79	2.55	2.83	5.01	3.99
	2000–2010	2.69	1.34	3.91	4.03	3.74
Nation	1984–1990	2.14	3.05	3.52	5.85	4.46
	1990–2000	2.25	2.36	3.68	6.66	4.61
	2000–2010	2.25	2.48	3.55	4.49	3.45

Source: Compiled by Li Zhang.

1 million residents as large cities, cities with populations between 200,000 and 500,000 as medium-sized cities, and cities with populations below 200,000 as small-sized cities. Our statistical analysis for each time period used the city group of the corresponding starting year. For example, the 90 cities in the east with no or only minor administrative division changes from 1984 to 1990 were taken as the basic database. We did the same for the other time periods.

Urban growth at the national scale

Table 3.3 shows that the growth of China's non-agricultural population since 1984 has been slower as city scale increases. This is consistent with the intended result of state policy of controlling population growth of larger cities. For metropolitan regions, the rate of non-agricultural population increase has been stable.

In contrast to non-agricultural population growth in metropolitan regions and large cities, the non-agricultural population of small cities has been increasing rapidly and has been less stable. Before 2000, the annual average population growth in small cities was approximately 6 percent, but after 2000, it dropped to 4.49 percent, as described in Chapter 2, and during this period the government relaxed control of hukou quotas in small cities. As a result small cities were unable to provide enough employment opportunities to accommodate as many migrants as the new relaxed policies hoped they could absorb. Generally the average increase rate declined after 2000 except for that of large cities.

Urban growth in China's three great regions

One stated goal of China's New Style National Urbanization Plan (2014–2020) is to achieve greater regional balance in urbanization. Our analysis is helpful in understanding differences in the rate of population growth of cities at different scales in China's three great regions.

The population of small cities has increased most rapidly in eastern China. From 2000 to 2010, the annual average population growth in small cities in eastern China was 6.89 percent. In metropolitan regions in eastern China the annual population growth from 2000 to 2010 averaged only 2.19 percent—just one-third as fast as in eastern small cities. Population growth in medium-sized cities in eastern China from 2000 to 2010 averaged 5.46 percent: faster than the metropolitan regions, but slower than the small cities (Table 3.3).

The pattern of urban growth in central China has been significantly different from the pattern of urban growth in eastern China. In central China small cities are also the fastest growing. But the growth of medium-sized and larger cities in central China has been significantly slower than in eastern China—with an annual average rate below 3.5 percent. After 2000, in central China, population growth of cities of all scales, including small-sized cities, has declined rapidly to an annual average of approximately 2 percent. The growth rate of large cities dropped to 1.66 percent.

In western China small cities have been growing rapidly: between 4 percent and 6 percent a year. The growth rate of medium-sized cities has been slower (3.11 percent to 3.91 percent) and also slower than the growth rate of medium-sized cities in eastern China (Table 3.3). After 2000, the growth rate of medium-sized cities in western China increased from 2.83 percent to 3.91 percent. While the growth rate of small cities in western China decreased from 5.01 percent to 4.03 percent between 2000 and 2010 it was still higher than larger cities in western China.

Our analysis of growth trends of cities in the three great regions of China confirms other evidence that small and medium-sized cities in eastern China are particularly attracting the migrating population. It provides precise and nuanced information about this phenomenon for planners and policymakers. Based on our field research and analysis of secondary data, this is largely due to abundant job opportunities and comparatively high wages, but also for social and cultural reasons because young migrants perceive them as exciting places to live. For central and western China, the growth of small cities slowed down after 2000. It is no longer driving the progress of regional urbanization to the extent that it did before 2000.

Based on these recent trends, small and medium-sized cities in eastern China are likely to continue to play an important role in China's overall urbanization. In central and western China, our analysis suggests that large cities and metropolitan regions may become the new drivers of further urbanization rather than further rapid growth of small cities.

SUMMARY

The relationship between the central and local governments and improvement of management in China's hierarchical urban system have been objects of administrative division reform that are very important to China's urbanization. Because the urban hierarchy is complex and there have been frequent changes, the impact of these changes on urbanization are poorly understood. The changes have made it exceedingly difficult to describe urbanization patterns over time accurately and have frequently led to oversimplifications and errors in published research. This is particularly true for outsiders unfamiliar with the Chinese administrative system and the precise meaning of Chinese population and economic statistics. Careful studies by Yixing Zhou and others have made it possible to describe the changes reasonably well and our analysis in this chapter provides an overview of urbanization that is as accurate as possible given data limitations and a nuanced description of changing ratios of urban population in different city sizes over time.

The transition to a tax-sharing system has increased local government revenue rapidly in absolute terms. It has both strengthened and invigorated local governments and at the same time increased the power of the central government. Financial resources have become more concentrated in the central government and the difference in revenue and expenditures between the central and local governments has expanded (Lou, 2006).

Since overall revenue has grown and the national government receives a much higher proportion than it did before the institution of the financial responsibility system, the national government is better positioned to make very large national-scale infrastructure and economic zone expenditures and promote national-level strategies through financial incentives. Local governments have been required to take more creative and entrepreneurial responsibilities for supplying public services. Even though their absolute revenue continued to increase, their percentage of total revenue has declined, leading to complaints that they are being required to make expenditures disproportionate to their tax shares.

Except for Beijing, Shanghai, Jiangsu, Zhejiang, and other economically developed regions, most Chinese provinces have been barely able to provide high quality public services because of their limited financial resources. This is the root cause of the increasing differences in public services offered in different provinces, counties, cities and towns. In the final chapter we recommend reform of China's administrative management system to adjust the central government's fiscal power and establish a responsibility-based distribution system that meets the needs of local governments, and an effective transfer payment system to increase transfer payments to less developed regions and those that promote ecological protection. This is important in the construction of an equalized and more environmentally sustainable public service system nationwide.

Reform of administrative divisions has been an important part of China's urbanization-centered transition. Reform of administrative divisions is primarily aimed at clarifying the relationships between different administrative units and on the simplification of administrative hierarchies. A series of adjustments of administrative divisions has helped provide institutional guarantees for the economic and social development of different regions and for the profound market-oriented transition during the urbanization process.

In past decades administrative divisions in China have been adjusted many times in parallel with reforms of China's fiscal and taxation systems. The Cultural Revolution caused the stagnation of the Chinese economy for 10 years. Consequently, the 1980s were a period of recovery and adjustment in many ways, including the implementation of new national development policies and changes in administrative divisions. The system of "cities governing counties" was widely implemented in the 1980s. The organizational system of cities was transformed from an urban-based system to a geography-based system. Many cities became city-regions, and the distribution of official towns was also changed from a spot-like urban pattern to a planar town-region pattern. By the end of the 1990s, the number of designated cities and towns reached its historical peak. Subsequently creation of new cities and towns was more closely controlled and became stable. Since 2000, the adjustment of administrative divisions has mainly involved replacing prefectures with cities, and—even more important—replacing counties and county-level cities with city districts and merging townships and towns.

Recently the Chinese government has promoted a system of counties directly under the jurisdiction of provinces. Some provincial and county-level governments hope that this will significantly invigorate the designated counties and county-level cities. It may influence the evolution of the urban spatial landscape of China.

The new Chinese leadership that took office in 2013 has shifted the emphasis of local government reform. Previously reforms were intended to improve operations of local government itself. The new leadership—particularly premier Li Keqiang—is now emphasizing changing relations between local government, the private market, and civil society to reduce bureaucracy and unnecessary regulations and delay. While we recognize the importance of this kind of reform, we emphasize the importance of stability and in the concluding chapter develop our ideas about not relying too much on boundary changes to resolve development conflicts.

Frequently adjusting administrative divisions affects the statistical analysis of urbanization. This chapter described and analyzed the changing coverage of urban–rural divisions in the four national censuses after the implementation of reform and opening up and the influence of changing census definitions on urbanization statistics. We propose that neighborhood and village committees be used as the accounting unit in specifying the urban–rural division. To make this work, we propose the establishment of a sound standard for defining resident committees. If this were done, the standard for urban–rural division would be improved and statistics on urbanization would more accurately reflect the real situation on the ground. Over time the standard for designating neighborhood committees could be revised to conform to the demands of urbanization. If this were done, urbanization statistics could be reconstructed for all six censuses so that they could be compared.

In addition to specifying the relationship between the central and local governments and administrative divisions, China's urban policy also provides guidance for developing cities at various scales. The review of the evolution of urban policies for controlling the scale of cities above describes how urban policy has changed from large city-oriented to medium and small-sized city-oriented and finally to rural town-oriented. The newly released NNSUP shifts the focus of policy to emphasize development of key cities and city clusters. The changes in China's urban policy correspond to stages in China's modernization and urbanization-oriented transition. China has passed the symbolically important 50 percent urbanization level. Now the quality and driving forces of urbanization are the two major issues of concern. If the NNSUP policy is implemented, key cities and city clusters will lead China's urbanization in the future. This will require more attention to the formation of urban clusters, coordination of industrial and labor divisions, and cooperation among city clusters. Regional variations, however, must be considered as new urban policies are developed and implemented.

This chapter reviewed the history of the administrative divisions of cities and describes our database of city population growth and the preliminary findings of an analysis of the longitudinal data. We analyzed the population growth of cities of different sizes at various times in different regions of China. The results reveal that small and medium-sized cities in eastern China are now growing rapidly. These cities are likely to play a more important role in regional urbanization in the future. In contrast, growth of small and medium-sized cities in central and western China has slowed recently. It appears that they are now attracting smaller numbers of migrants. In contrast large cities and metropolises in central and western China continue to grow. Therefore, for central and western China promotion of the development of metropolises and large cities may be a key to further development and modernization in these regions. To help this process, relevant urban policies must be formulated based on the kind of nuanced understanding of urbanization patterns in China described in this chapter.

NOTE

1. The lowest threshold for setting up a city in 1986 was a population more than 60,000 residents with non-agricultural hukou and GDP higher than 200 million RMB. After

1993, counties were divided into three categories by population density: (1) fewer than 100 residents per km^2, (2) 100 to 400 residents per km^2, and (3) more than 400 residents per km^2. The urban population with non-agricultural hukou necessary to quality as a city for these three categories had to reach 80,000, 100,000, and 120,000 respectively (Chen, 2008; Zhang and Zhao, 1998).

4. Regional policies and regional urbanization

China is a huge country with one-fifth of the world's population and a land area more than eight times as large as the UK, Germany, and France combined. As in other very large countries, China has wide regional disparities in economic development (Brandt and Rawski, 2008; Wu and Gaubatz, 2012; Scott and Storper, 2014), FDI (shown in Table 5.2), household incomes (Zhang, F., 2014), residents' consumption (Lee, 2000), infrastructure provision (Campanella, 2008), urban real estate development (Han, 1998) and economic structure (Hsing, 2012). To promote the overall development of China's national economy and to address disparities in the development of different regions, the central government has implemented various regional policies in different periods (Wu and Gaubatz, 2012; Ren, 2013).

In the transformation from a planned economy to a market economy, regional policies in China have experienced a number of important changes (Huang, 2008). The shift in policy from "favoring inland regions" to "reform and opening-up of coastal areas," and from "giving priority to the eastern region" to "coordinated regional development" reflect changing regional strategies. These policy shifts have profoundly influenced the spatial pattern of China's urbanization. This chapter reviews the changes in China's regional policies since reform and opening up and the influences of these policies on regional urbanization, then measures and analyzes urbanization disparities among China's three great regions (eastern, central, and western China), provinces, and geographical units smaller than provinces. The chapter ends with our analysis of the relationship between disparities in regional economic development and the level of regional urbanization.

CHANGES IN REGIONAL URBANIZATION OVER TIME

We analyzed spatial distribution of provincial urbanization using GIS. As described in Chapter 1 our unit of analysis is the provincial region which includes provinces (including provincial-level cities), and autonomous regions, but not Taiwan or the special administrative regions of Hong Kong and Macao. For data consistency Chongqing, which was created from part of Sichuan province in 1997, is grouped with Sichuan province. The four maps in Figure 4.1 display the results visually.

At the beginning of reform and opening up, urbanization rates of all provinces except three provincial level municipalities in China were low. This contrasted sharply with urbanization rates in the three municipalities directly under the central government—Beijing, Tianjin and Shanghai, all of which had urbanization rates higher than 50 percent at the time reform and opening began. The urbanization rates of the three northeastern provinces (Heilongjiang, Jilin, Liaoning) were higher than 35 percent in 1982.

The urbanization level in five of the eleven eastern provinces was among the top ten in China in 1982. Another six of the eastern provinces ranked below the top ten provinces and autonomous regions in China. The Ningxia and the Xinjiang Autonomous Regions in the west were among the top ten provinces and autonomous regions.

Our analysis in Chapter 3 dividing the country into three great regions showed that the urbanization level in the eastern, central and western regions developed slowly before 1978. At the time that the first national statistics after the Cultural Revolution became available in 1982, they had urbanization levels of 34.6 percent, 23.2 percent and 18.2 percent respectively (Table 4.1). Figures 4.2 and 4.3 illustrate national spatial policies before and after 1990. The following sections describe demographic, economic, and policy changes which led to the policies.

1982–1990

Between 1982 and 1990, the urbanization level in every province in China grew considerably. Disparities among the three great regions and between provinces within the eastern region began to emerge during this time. The overall urbanization rate of the eastern region increased by 9.9 percent. The urbanization levels of Guangdong, Zhejiang and Shandong provinces reached 37.5 percent, 36.5 percent and 31.1 percent respectively.

During this eight year period at the beginning of reform and opening up the urbanization rates in the central and western regions grew more slowly: by 8.3 percent and 6.1 percent respectively. With the exception of the northeastern provinces, the sharp division between the generally more urbanized eastern provinces and the less urbanized central and western provinces developed during the 1980s, 1990s, and first decade of the twenty-first century. Urbanization during this period was generally faster in the south than in the north.

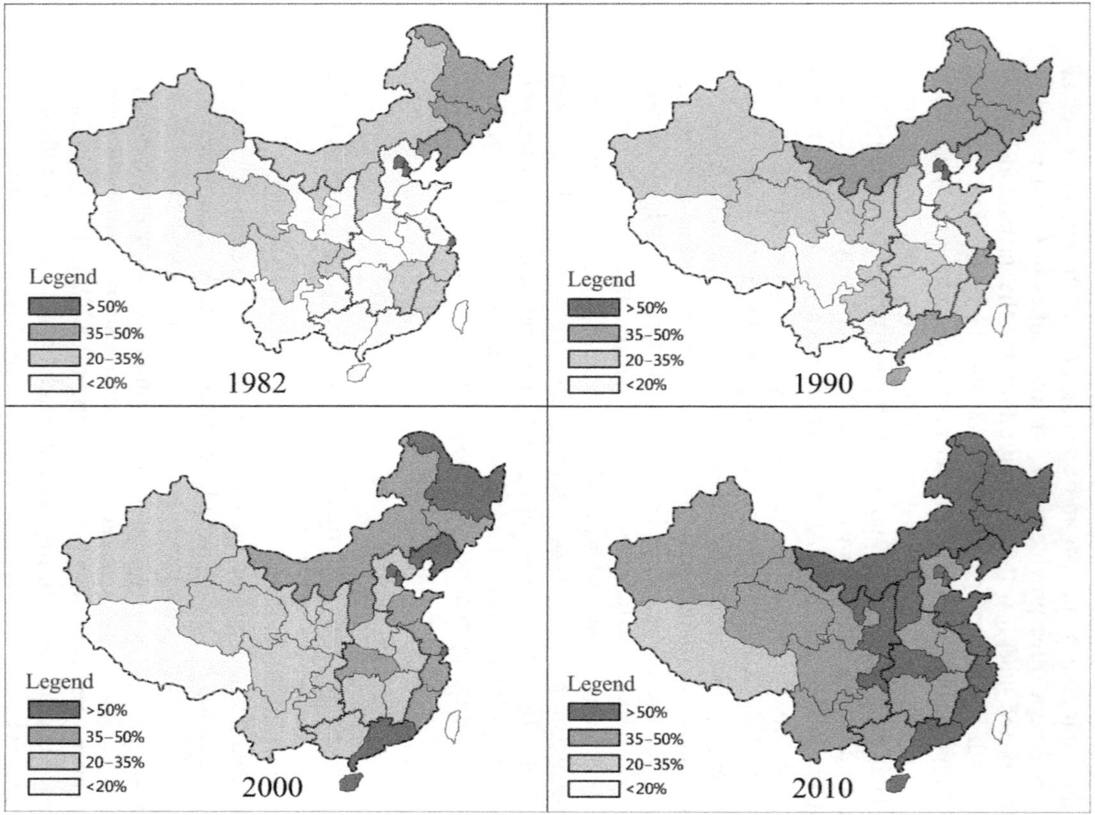

Source: NBSC-census (1984, 1992, 2002 and 2012). Maps drawn by Li Zhang.

Figure 4.1 China's provincial urbanization level: 1982 to 2010

Table 4.1 Urbanization level and growth of urbanization by province, 1982–2012

	Level (%)					Rank				Growth (%)	Average Annual Growth (%)		
	1982	1990	2000	2010	2012	1982	1992	2000	2012	1982–2012	1982–2012	1982–2000	2000–2012
Eastern	**34.6**	**44.5**	**53.3**	**58.4**	**60.7**					26.1	0.87	1.04	0.62
Beijing	65.1	70.6	77.6	86.0	86.2	2	3	2	2	21.1	0.70	0.69	0.72
Tianjin	68.8	70.8	72.0	79.6	81.6	1	2	3	3	12.8	0.43	0.18	0.80
Shanghai	59.9	74.2	88.5	89.3	89.3	3	1	1	1	29.4	0.98	1.59	0.07
Guangdong	19.4	37.5	53.8	64.9	66.2	17	7	5	4	46.8	1.56	1.91	1.04
Liaoning	42.7	49.8	54.4	62.2	65.6	4	4	4	5	23.0	0.77	0.65	0.94
Zhejiang	26.2	36.5	48.9	61.7	63.2	9	8	8	6	37.0	1.23	1.26	1.19
Jiangsu	16.3	24.8	41.8	60.2	63	20	18	11	7	46.7	1.56	1.42	1.77
Fujian	21.6	29.3	41.8	57.1	59.6	11	16	10	8	38.0	1.27	1.12	1.49
Shandong	19.5	31.1	38.2	49.8	52.4	16	12	13	13	33.0	1.10	1.04	1.19
Hebei	14.0	19.1	26.2	44.0	46.8	26	25	24	20	32.8	1.09	0.68	1.72
Guangxi	12.1	17.8	28.4	40.1	43.5	28	26	20	24	31.4	1.05	0.90	1.26
Central	**23.2**	**31.5**	**36.7**	**45.9**	**49.0**					25.8	0.86	0.75	1.03
Inner Mongolia	29.2	36.2	42.8	55.6	57.8	7	9	9	9	28.6	0.95	0.76	1.25
Heilongjiang	40.8	48.7	51.6	55.7	56.9	5	5	6	10	16.1	0.54	0.6	0.44
Jilin	39.9	46.9	49.8	53.4	54.7	6	6	7	11	14.8	0.49	0.55	0.41
Hubei	17.8	29.4	40.5	49.7	53.5	19	15	12	12	35.7	1.19	1.26	1.09
Shanxi	21.3	30.1	35.1	48.1	51.3	12	13	14	14	30.0	1.00	0.76	1.35
Jiangxi	19.6	23.2	27.8	43.8	47.5	15	19	23	18	27.9	0.93	0.45	1.65
Hunan	14.7	20.7	29.9	43.3	46.7	22	22	19	21	32.0	1.07	0.85	1.39
Anhui	14.5	19.6	28	43.1	46.5	24	23	22	22	32.0	1.07	0.75	1.54
Henan	14.3	17.8	23.3	38.5	42.4	25	26	28	25	28.1	0.94	0.5	1.59

Table 4.1 (continued)

	Level (%)					Rank				Growth (%)	Average Annual Growth (%)		
	1982	1990	2000	2010	2012	1982	1992	2000	2012	1982–2012	1982–2012	1982–2000	2000–2012
Western	**18.2**	**24.3**	**28.0**	**40.1**	**43.8**					25.6	0.85	0.54	1.32
Ningxia	22.7	29.7	32.5	48.2	50.7	10	14	17	15	28.0	0.93	0.54	1.51
Shaanxi	19.3	25.6	32.4	45.7	50.0	18	17	18	16	30.7	1.02	0.73	1.47
Qinghai	20.8	32.1	34.9	44.8	47.5	13	11	15	17	26.7	0.89	0.78	1.05
Sichuan	14.6	19.5	28.1	43.5	47.1	23	24	21	19	32.5	1.08	0.75	1.58
Xinjiang	28.5	32.8	33.9	42.9	44.0	8	10	16	23	15.4	0.51	0.3	0.84
Yunnan	13.1	17.6	23.5	34.8	39.3	27	28	27	26	26.2	0.87	0.58	1.32
Gansu	15.5	20.7	24.1	36.0	38.8	21	21	25	27	23.2	0.77	0.48	1.22
Guizhou	19.8	21.4	23.9	33.9	36.4	14	20	26	28	16.6	0.55	0.23	1.04
Tibet	9.7	12.1	19.0	22.7	22.7	29	29	29	29	13.0	0.43	0.52	0.37
National	**25.3**	**33.4**	**39.4**	**50.0**	**52.6**					27.3	0.91	0.78	1.10
						Discrepancy Measures							
Maximum	68.8	74.2	88.5	89.3	89.3					20.5	0.68	1.09	0.07
Minimum	9.7	12.1	19.0	22.7	22.7					13.0	0.43	0.52	0.31
Mean	25.6	33.8	39.7	51.0	53.5					27.9	0.93	0.78	1.15
SD	15.6	15.9	16.7	15.1	14.6					−1.0	−0.03	0.06	−0.18

Source: *China Statistical Yearbooks*, compiled by Li Zhang.

1990–2000

Between 1990 and 2000, the urbanization level of all provinces in China continued to increase rapidly. Urbanization disparities among the three great regions continued to widen and a gradient pattern in the spatial distribution of urbanization levels from coastal to inland regions became clearly discernible. However, there were some exceptions. Urbanization levels of eastern provinces were generally higher than 35 percent except for Hebei province. Urbanization levels of the central and western provinces were higher than 20 percent except for Tibet. A few provinces achieved urbanization levels above 50 percent: Liaoning (54.4 percent), Guangdong (53.8 percent), and Heilongjiang (51.6 percent). In this period, urbanization in the eastern region increased by 8.8 percent to 53.3 percent. In contrast urbanization rates in central and western China were much slower: only 5.2 percent and 3.7 percent, respectively.

2000–2012

From 2000 to 2012, the urbanization levels in all provinces continued to rise, but the urbanization growth rates in eastern China slowed and the urbanization growth rates in central and western China increased.

By 2012 the urbanization levels of all provinces were higher than 35 percent except for Tibet. Four provinces in the eastern region reached urbanization levels higher than 50 percent: Shandong (52.43 percent), Fujian (59.61 percent), Jiangsu (63.01 percent), and Zhejiang (63.19 percent) provinces. Five northern provinces in the central region reached urbanization levels higher than 50 percent. In 2012, the urbanization level of the whole eastern region reached 60.7 percent, which was 8.1 percent higher than the national average (52.6 percent). The level of the central region reached 49.0 percent, and the western region reached 43.8 percent, which was higher by 12.3 percent and 15.8 percent in this period, respectively. The pace of urbanization in the central and western regions has been accelerating, and the gap between the great regions has been decreasing since 2000.

From 2000 to 2012 the average annual urban population growth rate in the central region was 1.03 percent—significantly higher than the rate of 0.75 percent from 1982 to 2000. In the western region the growth rate from 2000 to 2012 was 1.32 percent—significantly higher than the 0.54 percent from 1982 to 2000. In contrast to these accelerating growth rates in central and western China, the overall growth rate in the eastern region from 2000 to 2012 was only 0.62 percent—significantly lower than the 1.04 percent growth rate from 1982 to 2000. However, the overall figure for eastern China is somewhat deceptive. If the three large, relatively slow-growing municipalities of Beijing, Tianjin, and Shanghai are excluded, the rate would be 1.17 percent—higher than the central region (1.03 percent) and slightly lower than the western region (1.32 percent).

Standard Deviation Analysis

Analysis of the standard deviation (SD) of the urbanization level of provinces provides evidence of how similar or dissimilar the situation of urbanization among provinces has been at different times. Table 4.1 shows that the SD of urbanization rates by province increased from 1982 to 2000. This indicates that at the provincial scale, the level of urbanization became more scattered or dissimilar. After 2000, the SD began to decrease, indicating that the urbanization level of provinces was becoming more similar.

Differences in urbanization levels by region

Table 4.1 shows the percentage of the population that was urban in each of China's three regions in 1982, 1990, 2000, 2010, and 2012, the percentage growth between 1982 and 2012, and annual average growth rates between 1982 and 2000 and 2010 and 2012. It shows dramatic differences in the pattern of urbanization in different regions of China and among provinces within the same region.

Provincial-level cities

Four large municipalities have the status of provincial-level cities in China. Beijing, Shanghai and Tianjin were provincial-level cities during the Mao era. All had relatively high levels of urbanization even before the beginning of reform and opening up.

The municipality of Chongqing was historically a part of Sichuan province until 1997 when it was designated a separate municipality directly under central government.

In this book we frequently classify and analyze the three original provincial-level cities together and break data on these outliers out from other regional data when analyzing trends in eastern China. We include data on Chongqing with Sichuan province for historical analysis consistency unless noted.

Table 4.1 shows that although Shanghai's urbanization level was the lowest of the three provincial-level cities at the beginning of reform and opening, Shanghai developed rapidly—particularly after the development of Pudong got underway in 1990. Though defining at what point a region is "fully urbanized" (at the top of the Davis S curve) is subjective and should vary depending on local circumstances, most analysts consider a country "fully urbanized" when its urbanization level reaches the 75–80 percent level (the US urbanization level is now 81 percent).

In 1995 Shanghai was the first of the provincial-level cities to reach an urbanization level higher than 80 percent. Shanghai reached the 88.5 percent urbanization level in 2000. Its urbanization level increased by less than 1 percent between 2000 and 2012. Shanghai has entered the stage of stable and slow urbanization growth.

Shanghai's population is continuing to grow and the distribution of population within Shanghai is continuing to change. Metropolitan Shanghai has a large land area that includes peri-urban and rural land. The population of the core districts of Shanghai, where most of the population is concentrated, is still growing, but the population in peri-urban and some suburban areas is growing much faster. Middle and high priced housing is being built in suburban Shanghai and much of the spatial restructuring is occurring as a response to industrial and demographic change. Since 2000 most new migrants to Shanghai have settled in peri-urban and rural areas of Shanghai where many factories are located and inexpensive housing is available in villages rather than in the urban core. Shanghai's rural population, for example, was 1.92 million in 2000 (NBSC-census, 2002), but grew to 2.46 million in 2010 (NBSC-census, 2012).

Did counter urbanization occur in Shanghai? The answer is "no." The statistic is caused by the rapid increase of the migrant population in the Shanghai metropolitan region. Between 2000 and 2010, the migrant population in Shanghai increased by 6 million, most of whom lived in peri-urban rural areas. By some criteria, a small part of this population is counted as rural population.

Beijing and Tianjin reached the 80 percent urbanization level in 2005 and 2011, respectively. Beijing's urbanization level has been generally stable, with fluctuations only in a few years. Recently Beijing has continued to urbanize at about 0.7 percent a year. Tianjin's urbanization level increased slowly in the 1980s, but rapidly after 2000. At the time of this writing in spring, 2015, Tianjin is the fastest growing provincial level city.

Eastern region

Urbanization levels in the eastern region were quite varied at the beginning of reform and opening up, and the growth rates of different provinces within the eastern region since that time have also been quite different from each other.

In 1982, the lowest urbanization level was of the Guangxi autonomous region—a mountainous frontier region in southern China bordering Vietnam with little industry (12.1 percent). The highest urbanization level in eastern China in 1982 was in Liaoning province (42.7 percent), a key

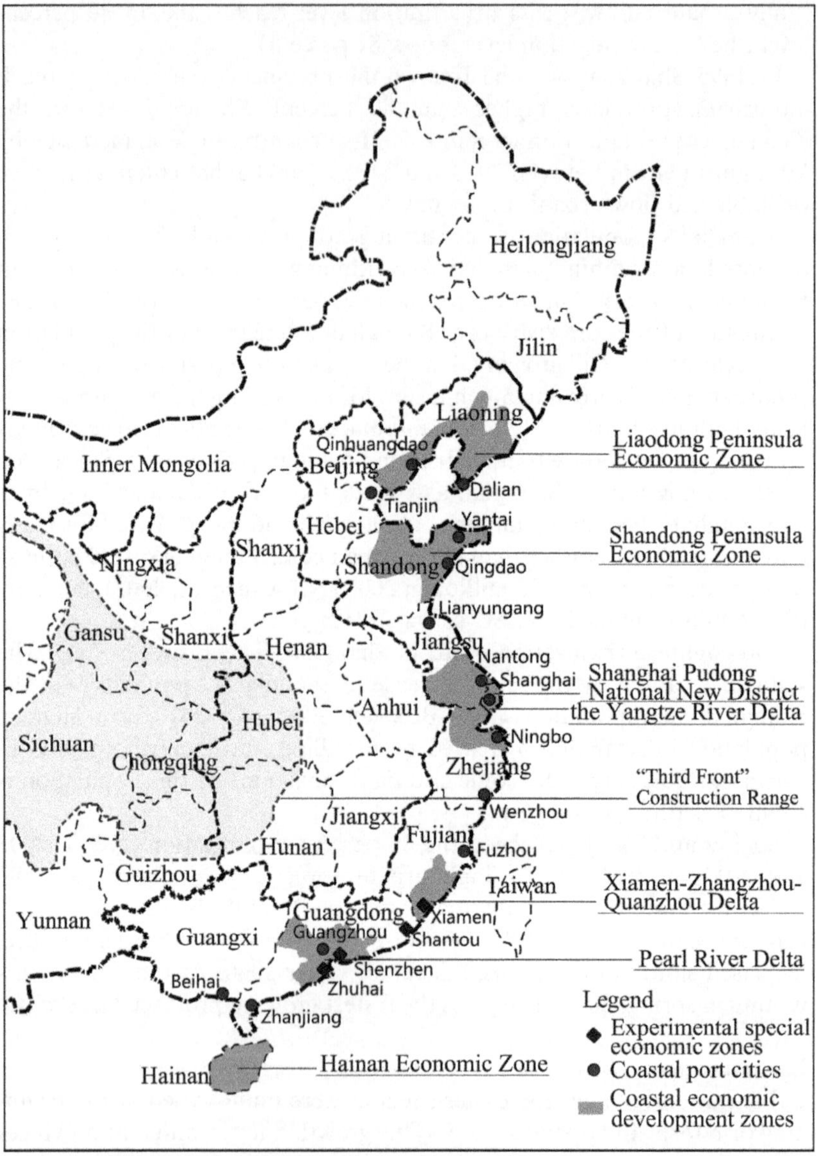

Source: Unpublished government files. Compiled and mapped by Li Zhang.

Figure 4.2 National spatial policies before 1990

industrial base since the founding of the People's Republic of China with rich deposits of coal and iron ore, smelting and steel production plants, and many state-owned factories producing machinery, construction and other industrial equipment, metal materials, and other products.

For the entire period 1982 to 2012, the urbanization levels of the coastal provinces adjacent to major command and control centers of the global economy—Guangdong province (adjacent to Hong Kong) and Jiangsu province (adjacent to Shanghai)—increased the fastest of all the eastern provinces, indeed of all provinces in China—by 46.8 percent and 46.7 percent in 30 years, respectively. The rapid growth of export-oriented manufacturing in the Shenzhen special economic zone, Dongguan and Guangzhou in Guangdong province, and Suzhou in Jiangsu province, were principal drivers of the rapid urbanization of these leading provinces. Even the province with the slowest growth rate—Liaoning province—experienced a 19.5 percent increase in the 18 years from 1982 to 2000 and it started from a high base rate (42.7 percent).

The fastest growth from 1982 to 2000 occurred in Guangdong province, with an average annual urbanization growth rate of 1.91 percent. Jiangsu province, with an average annual growth rate of 1.42 percent, was second. The lowest rates were in Liaoning and Hebei provinces in northern China, with growth rates of 0.65 percent and 0.68 percent, respectively.

Significant changes are now occurring in the urbanization of eastern China. Between 2000 and 2012 Jiangsu province continued to grow rapidly with an average annual growth rate of 1.77 percent. Hebei province came next, with an average annual growth rate of 1.72 percent. The growth of Guangdong province began to slow down notably, but its average annual growth remained above 1 percent. Although the growth of Guangdong and Liaoning slowed, they remained the provinces with the highest urbanization rates in the eastern region.

Central region

Compared with the eastern provinces, the urbanization levels of the nine provinces in the central region generally began lower and increased more gradually after reform and opening up, although this is changing today.

The central region has both a southern part and northern part with somewhat different urbanization patterns. The northern part of the central region includes Inner Mongolia, Heilongjiang, and Jilin provinces; the central south consists of Shanxi, Shaanxi, Henan, Anhui, Hubei and Hunan provinces.

The three provinces in the north started urbanizing earlier than most of the rest of China (except for the provincial-level cities of Beijing, Shanghai, and Tianjian). In 1982, the urbanization level of Jilin and Heilongjiang was already 40 percent, and Inner Mongolia 29.2 percent. Jilin and Heilongjiang province had been key industry bases since the founding of the PRC. Many state-owned factories were located there. In the Inner Mongolia autonomous region, most of the land is traditional grazing land with only a small, largely nomadic, population. Today only 24 million people inhabit more than a million square kilometers. The capital, Hohot, has 3 million residents, and there is only a scattering of other cities in Inner Mongolia.

The six provinces in south central China were much less urbanized at the beginning of reform and opening up. They had urbanization levels of 22 percent or less in 1982. Among the six, Henan province, with an urbanization level of 14.3 percent, had the lowest level. After 1982 the six provinces in the south central China urbanized rapidly. The fastest growth was in Hubei province, with an annual average growth rate of 1.19 percent. The urbanization level of Hubei increased by 35.7 percent in 30 years. Hubei had one metropolis, Wuhan, with more than 2 million people in 1982 and ten other small and medium-sized cities, so urbanization proceeded in many different areas of the province. During the 1990s and 2000s, the massive Three Gorges Dam project on the Yangtze River in Hubei province boosted the economy and helped drive urbanization.

Many of the more than a million people displaced by the dam construction settled in cities and towns. Hubei was followed by Hunan and Anhui provinces, both of which had average annual growth rates of 1.07 percent.

The slowest growth was in Jilin province, with an average annual growth rate of 0.49 percent. Jilin's population only increased by 14.8 percent between 1982 and 2012. Two factors largely account for the low increase. Jilin has a prosperous agricultural economy and an aging industrial base. Jilin province was a key industry base from the earliest days of the PRC, but as China has come to rely more on markets many poorly run state-owned factories were closed and many workers were laid off, so there were few jobs for newcomers. Farmers in Jilin province have relatively large amounts of arable and/or forest land per capita where they can earn a decent living, so they feel less pressure to move to urban areas than farmers with less good farmland.

Jiangxi had a slow growth rate until 2000, but from 2000 to 2012 Jiangxi became the fastest growing province in central China, with an average annual growth rate of 1.65 percent.

Although the growth of the three provinces in north central China was slow, they still had the highest urbanization levels in the central region in 2012 because of the high baseline in 1982.

After 30 years of development, urbanization disparities in the central region narrowed. The largest disparities among the provinces in the central region declined from 26.5 percent in 1982 to 15.4 percent in 2012.

Western region

Urbanization disparities among provinces in western China remain significant, but the gap has narrowed.

In 1982, the urbanization level in every western province was quite low. Even in Xinjiang, the provincial level autonomous region with the highest urbanization level, the urbanization rate was below 30 percent. The urbanization level of Tibet was only 9.7 percent, the lowest in all of China.

In terms of growth during different time periods, Qinghai province had the fastest growth from 1982 to 2000, with an average annual growth rate of 0.78 percent. Guizhou province had the slowest growth, with an average annual growth rate of 0.23 percent. In 1982 Qinghai had a small population base (3.90 million people) and only one large city, Xining, with 1.42 million people. This made it easier for Qinghai to increase its urbanization level than other provinces in the western region. In contrast, in 1982 Guizhou had a large population base of 28.55 million people, but only one large city (Guiyang) with 800,000 people and three small cities. The lack of cities made it difficult for Guizhou province to urbanize rapidly.

From 1982 to 2012, Sichuan province (including Chongqing) had the fastest growth rate of urbanization, with an increase of 32.5 percent.

In 2012, the urbanization levels of the western provinces were all below the national average. The evolution of regional policies China's national government is continuously re-evaluating national level regional policy. As China has developed there have been major shifts in national and regional policy and these have in turn affected regional urbanization.

REGIONAL URBANIZATION

An important issue for China's national urbanization policy is to understand the way in which urbanization is occurring in different regions. This is particularly important as the national government seeks to determine where to deploy resources to best develop this "country of countries."

Regional Policy Types and Regional Urbanization

Former University of Hong Kong Geography Professor Victor Sit (2001a) has classified the regional policies of nations into three types:

(1) General laissez-faire style, similar to the USA, where the government rarely intervenes in the market;

(2) Cohesion and equity style, mainly implemented in developed countries such as Canada and members of the European Union where government intervention is mainly executed through transfer payments and stimulation of growth of undeveloped regions; and
(3) Efficiency and zonal style, as exemplified by China's opening up and priority development policy for coastal areas after 1978 and Japan's urban regional policy after 1996.

Unbalanced development policy, which prioritizes economic efficiency, will inevitably cause differences in regional development. Scholars from different academic disciplines have offered discipline-specific explanations that help explain why these differences exist.

Terry Cannon (Cannon and Jenkins, 1990), a development studies expert at the University of Sussex's Institute of Development Studies, argues that regional disparities in China have been caused by a combination of geographical characteristics and the industrial development strategy after 1978 that has favored coastal regions.

David Goodman (2004), a Professor of Chinese Politics at the University of Sydney, argues that the Chinese central government always encourages local government to carry out the central government's policies in a flexible manner, which leads to regional differences.

To better understand regionalization in China, Chinese scholars have developed the concept of "regional urbanization" (Cui, 1989). "Regional urbanization" refers to the national population redistribution process between urban and rural areas and between agriculture and other industries and the diffusion process of urban space and lifestyles in a certain area or region (He, 2006: 57). Compared with national urbanization, regional urbanization emphasizes the independence and particularity of regions (Zhang and Han, 2009).

Region-balanced development policy dominated by politics and military concerns

After the founding of the PRC in 1949, the Chinese economy recovered gradually. In China's first Five-Year Plan (1953–1957), the government called for a strategy of "decreasing the unbalanced development across regions." The main way in which the central government initially sought to decrease unbalanced development across regions was through 156 Soviet aid projects—80 percent of which were allocated to inland areas and 694 local investment projects funded by the central government—68 percent of which were implemented in inland areas (Lu and Sit, 2001: 27). These projects established the PRC's basic industries around coal, power, steel, non-ferrous metals, aluminum, copper, chemicals, defense, shipbuilding, and other basic industries.

An industrial base initially formed in the northeastern region, which has coal and steel deposits and had comparatively good infrastructure established by the Japanese in the puppet state of Manchukuo before and during World War II. The geographical closeness of the northeast to the Soviet Union made it easier to receive aid and influence from China's main ally at that time than other parts of China. Since the northwest and southwest regions of China were less developed, the Chinese government believed that initially focusing development on this region was appropriate (MacFarquhar and Fairbank, 1990: 85).

In the mid-1960s, China remained hostile to the US and European former colonial powers, had broken with the Soviet Union, and had border tensions with India and Taiwan. These geopolitical realities affected China's regional development and urbanization policy. The central committee of the Communist Party of China (CPC) felt that a new world war was inevitable. Chairman Mao Zedong put forward the concept of "preparing for war, preparing against famine, and for people." A centerpiece of this program was "third-line construction" giving priority to development of war-related industries in inland areas that were geographically difficult to invade. China was divided into first-line, second-line, and third-line areas based on the strategic location of each region. The first-line areas refer to the strategic forefront, primarily the eastern coastal regions; third-line areas refer to the strategic rear areas, including parts of Sichuan, Guizhou, Yunnan, Shaanxi, and Gansu provinces, West Henan, West Hubei, West Hunan, South Shanxi, West Hebei, North Guangdong, Northeast Guanxin, and Eastern Qinghai province. The rest of China fell into second-line areas. The first- and second-line areas included some pockets within them called small third-line areas. Capital investment in "third-line construction" was mainly in military projects. It had limited influence on the development of local economies. It was not until the late 1970s that military-oriented enterprises in third-line areas gradually turned to civilian industry, and started to promote the development of local economies (Han and Wong, 1998).

From 1952 to 1975, 55 percent of China's national capital investment for basic construction was allocated to the inland region. Forty percent was invested in third-line areas. At the height of this period of investment in anticipation of world war during the third Five-Year Plan period from 1966 to 1970, capital investment in inland regions accounted for 66.8 percent of all national capital investment, and capital investment in third-line regions reached 52.7 percent (Lu and Sit, 2001: 28).

The mid-1970s was a period of national regional policy adjustment. During this period diplomatic relations between China and Western countries (particularly with the USA) improved. US President Richard Nixon visited China in 1972. China realized the high cost of third-line construction. As a result, the central government prioritized coastal areas instead of inland regions for economic development. This occurred well before the ascension of Xiaoping Deng and the beginning of reform and opening in the late 1970s and early 1980s.

The Cultural Revolution, begun in 1966, came to an end in 1976. After Mao's death and Deng's consolidation of power, the focus of political activity in China shifted rapidly from political movements, decisions based on ideology, and class struggle to pragmatic politics, "scientific" planning, and economic development. China's development path became more oriented toward economic efficiency and more subject to market forces. With China's reform and opening up beginning in 1978, regional policy favoring eastern China began to replace regional development policy characterized by investment of resources in inland regions to promote more balanced development, both for equity reasons and national defense.

As reform and opening up intensified during the decade from 1980 to 1990, the state implemented pragmatic approaches to attract foreign capital and implement an export processing strategy. During the implementation of the sixth Five-Year Plan (1981–1985), a regional development strategy that favored the eastern coastal region was implemented.

In 1984, based on the temporary success of four initial experimental special economic zones which were set up in Shenzhen, Zhuhai, Shantou, and Xiamen in 1979, China announced that 14 coastal port cities were to be opened: Dalian, Qinhuangdao, Tianjin, Yantai, Qingdao, Lianyungang, Nantong, Shanghai, Ningbo, Wenzhou, Fuzhou, Guangzhou, Zhanjiang, and Beihai.

In 1985, China approved the establishment of additional coastal economic development zones, in China's three great delta regions: the Yangtze River Delta, Pearl River Delta, and Xiamen–Zhangzhou–Quanzhou Delta.

The seventh Five-Year Plan (1986–1991) explicitly divided China into three major regions: the eastern, central, and western regions. Again priority was given to the coastal region as it had been in the previous five-year plan.

The Shandong Peninsula Economic Zone, Liaodong Peninsula Economic Zone, and Hainan Economic Zone were established in 1988.

The Shanghai Pudong New Area was announced in 1990, and a new and experimental package of development and open-door policy was implemented in Shanghai aimed at revitalizing the economy of Shanghai and promoting the overall development of the Yangtze River Delta.

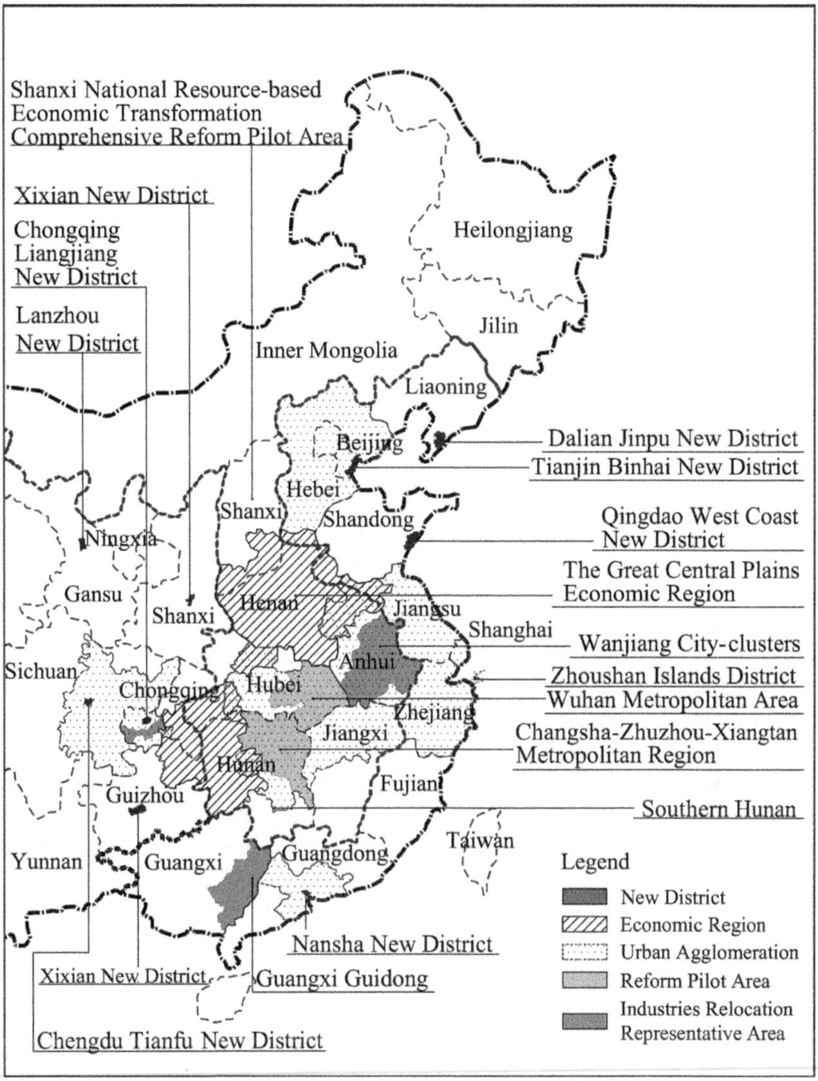

Source: Unpublished government files. Compiled by Li Zhang.

Figure 4.3 National spatial policies after 1990

Strategy Begins to Favor Central and Western China

In the eighth Five-Year Plan (1991–1995), China's national development strategy began to emphasize the orderly shift from special economic zones to development zones and from the coastal region to inland areas (Yang, 1990; Fan, 1995). A decade of reform and opening up had succeeded in attracting enormous amounts of FDI to Special Economic Zones and China's overall GDP had grown rapidly. But the rapidly widening differences in regional development had created political pressure from less developed inland provinces. As a result there is no mention of unbalanced regional development policy favoring eastern China in the eighth Five-Year Plan.

After ten years it was increasingly clear that the emphasis on economic development above all else was leading to environmental and sustainable development problems. As a result the central government made some important adjustment to regional policies to better protect the environment.

By 1992 the amount the central government invested in development had become smaller than the amount local governments were investing—just 79 percent as much due to the lower financial ability. The central government invested the majority in the northwestern region where the ratio of central to local investment was as high as 1.65:1. In 1995, the newly created China Development Bank provided 67 percent of its loans to the central and western regions (Lu and Sit, 2001).

The national government introduced the concept of "coordinated regional development" in 1992 and explicitly included it as policy in the ninth Five-Year Plan (1996–2000). Specific measures to implement coordinated regional development included increasing the amount of state loans to the central and western regions and encouraging FDI in the central and western regions. In 1996 of 109 projects which received state investment, 46 were in the eastern region, 41 in central China, and 22 in western China. Investment in fixed assets in the east increased to 42.6 percent, 48.8 percent and 55.6 percent in the sixth, seventh, and eighth Five-Year Plans respectively, and then decreased slightly to 54.4 percent and 52.5 percent in the tenth and eleventh Five-Year Plans (Yue et al., 2011).

Even though the national government directed more national investment and FDI to central and western China during the 1990s and there were many successful economic development projects funded with local revenue in these regions, regional disparities continued to increase. As a result, the Fourth Plenary Session of the 15th Central Committee of the CPC held in September 1999 explicitly requested a new grand strategy for the development of western China (Goodman, 2004).

Redevelopment and Regeneration in Northern and Central China

At the same time the central government began implementing the grand strategy for the development of western China in 2000, it initiated other regional development strategies directed at specific issues in different parts of China. Because the infrastructure and first generation factories developed in northeastern China with Soviet aid in the 1950s were often poorly constructed and aging, the national government announced a campaign to "revitalize the old industrial base in northeastern China" in 2003. Another strategy named "raising central China" was started in 2004. By the middle of 2004 a series of the overarching conceptual development strategies for China's major regions (considering the northeast a region) had evolved, based on a combination of theorizing, politics, and experimentation. Regional policies to implement the strategies were developed and implemented.

Changing Distribution of National Economic Development Zones

The transformation of state policies is illustrated by the timing when National-level Economic Development Zones (NEDZ) were approved. The Chinese central government accepts applications to set up NEDZs every year, but new zones are approved only in selected years. As Table 4.2 shows, the state approved 19 NEDZs (five of which were called economic parks) in the four years between 1984 and 1988. At this time national policy was focused on the east and all of the zones were located in eastern China. In the period 1992–2002, central government policy had shifted to focus more on central and western China. Of the 18 NEDZs approved in the two years between 1992 and 1994, six were located in the central and western regions. After 2000 national policy emphasized developing the west and

Table 4.2 Distribution of National Economic Development Zones, 1984–2013

	Certified 1984 to 1988	Certified 1992 to 1994	Certified 2000 to 2002	Certified 2009 to 2013	Total
Eastern	19	11	1	71	103
Central	0	4	5	51	60
Western	0	2	11	34	47
Total	19	18	17	156	210

Source: DZRCSCC (2014), *Research Report for China's National Economic Development Zones in 2013*.

north. Of the 17 NEDZs approved in the two years between 2000 and 2002, 11 are located in the west, 5 in central China, and only one in eastern China. Of the 156 NEDZs approved between 1984 and 2013, a little more than half (85) are located in the central and western regions. Thus the initial national policy favoring eastern China has been changed. While all the NEDZs approved in the 1980s were in eastern China, the number in central and western China increased in subsequent rounds of approval. By 2013 103 of China's 210 NEDZs were in eastern China and 107 in central and western China. The distribution of zones is nearly balanced between eastern China and the rest of the country.

Analysis of NEDZs tells only part of the story. The distribution of other important types of national level development zones intended to accelerate economic development which have been approved recently is reasonably balanced between eastern China and central and western China. In addition to NEDZs the national government authorizes other kinds of special zones. Of national-level "New Districts" approved in recent years, five are in eastern China and five in the central and western regions. Figure 4.4 illustrates Jiangdong new district in Nanjing city of Jiangsu province. Three "Reform Experimental Areas" (with specific themes such as environmentally friendly development) and "two Economic Cooperation Areas," designated by the State Council are all located in central China. Four newly approved demonstration regions for undertaking industrial transfer are all located in the central and western regions.

Source: Photo by Li Zhang.

Figure 4.4 Jiangdong new district, Nanjing city, Jiangsu province

Greater Focus on Key Developments and Strengthening Urban Agglomerations

The most recent expression of China's regional urbanization policies is contained in China's National New-style Urbanization Plan: 2014–2020 (PRC, 2014), a central policy document published by the State Council in March 2014. Spatial policies are one of the core contents of the plan. The NNSUP is a high-level strategic plan document that states many general principles. It restates many strategies and policies articulated in other policy documents. However, the NNSUP appears to represent a shift away from the "three major regions policy" to a "building a framework for China's urbanization" policy.

The NNSUP articulates an urbanization strategy with "two horizontal" and "three vertical" features. "Two horizontal" features refers to the Yangtze River Economic Belt from Shanghai in central coastal China to Chengdu in the southwest and the Longhai Economic Belt from Lianyungang, a prefecture-level city in northeastern Jiangsu province, to Urumqi in the Xinjiang Autonomous Region in the extreme northwest of China. "Three verticals" refers to three north–south corridors: a coastal corridor, the Beijing–Harbin/Beijing–Guangzhou corridor, and the Baotou–Kunming corridor (Figure 4.5).

In addition to the linear corridor structure, the central government is strongly encouraging the development of Large City Clusters (LCCs) to pool population and economic resources in order to create economies of scale and improve economic integration. They consider this essential in order to strengthen the international competitiveness of China's LCCs. In addition to promoting large high-tech agglomerations in east China, the NNSUP envisages LCCs in the central and western regions becoming important growth poles as part of the strategy of coordinated regional development. In Chapter 7 we describe China's LCCs and present our own views on how resources might best be targeted in such a strategy. In the NNSUP the state spatial policies no longer target balanced development of the three major regions, but the ability of LCCs to drive the economic development of their surrounding areas and form parts of an integrated nationwide horizontal and vertical polycentric urban network. As the nodes where resources are aggregated, urban clusters are seen as the vehicles for integrated development. This is similar to the recommendations the eminent British planner Sir Peter Hall has proposed for sustainable management of European Polycentric Mega-City Regions (Hall and Pain, 2006).

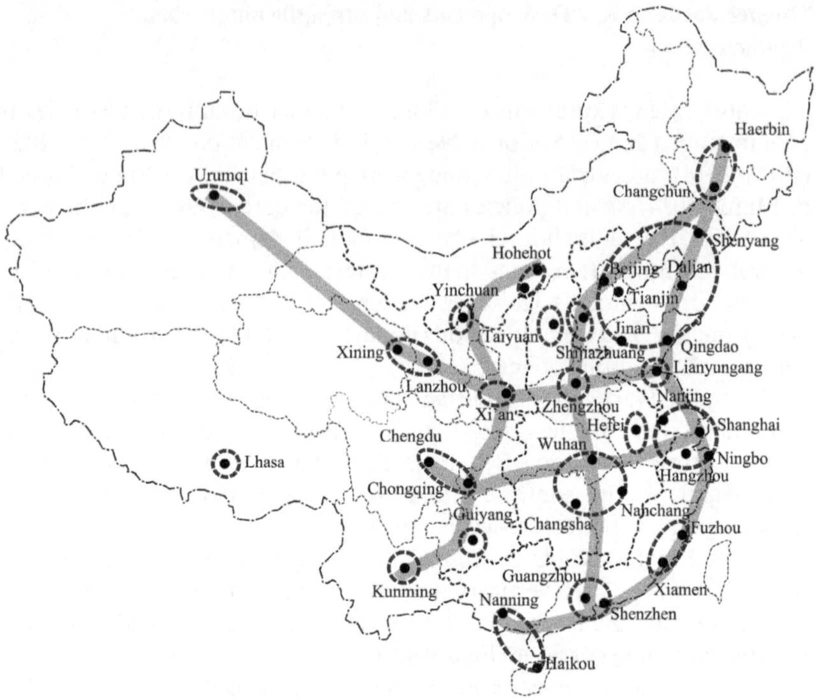

Source: PRC (2014). Redrawn by the Li Zhang.

Figure 4.5 China's NNSUP spatial strategy

ANALYSIS OF REGIONAL URBANIZATION DISPARITIES

The preceding sections have provided essential information on changes in China's regional urbanization by province and among China's three great regions and of changes in China's national urbanization policy. The two are reciprocal—national policy both responded to changes which were occurring and in turn affected urbanization. We move now to more systematic analysis of regional urbanization disparities. In the concluding parts of this chapter we advance some of our own thoughts about national urbanization policy for the future.

The Purpose of our Investigation

Despite more than three decades of policy experiments with national-level regional planning, abundant longitudinal statistical data at different scales, highly developed computational tools that permit analysis of the way in which regional development policies have affected China's urbanization in different ways among and within regions, and many post-2000 analyses of regional urbanization in Chinese, many English language studies do not adequately consider regional disparities in China in the process of urbanization (e.g., Ma, 2002; Fan, 2005; Zhang, 2008; Chan, 2012). Isolated case studies have often failed to consider correlations among the regions (e.g., Wu, 1995; Fan, 2001; Shen, 2002).

Currently China scholars disagree about the impact national policy has had on regional urbanization disparities. Several papers argue that the policies have decreased intra-regional disparities, but increased inter-regional disparities (Wang et al., 2006; Zheng and Lai, 2008). Others disagree, as their results show opposite results (Wang et al., 2005).

In 2009 one of the authors of this book (Li Zhang) and University of Melbourne urban planning professor Sunsheng Han completed a comprehensive analysis of China's regional urbanization disparities between 1982 and 2007 (Zhang and Han, 2009). In the following section we use the methodology of the 2009 study and new data from 2007 to 2012 to provide our own comprehensive and up-to-date analysis of the impact national policy has had on regional urbanization.

Measurement Method

Although provincial disparities have evolved over time as indicated by data on the growth of urbanization in each province, a full understanding of the evolution requires going beyond simple descriptive analysis. Therefore, we resorted to mathematical tools to compute the evolution of regional disparities in the process of urbanization. There are many ways to calculate regional disparities: using an index of urbanization imbalance, location quotients of differing urbanization levels, Gini coefficients, standard deviation (σ), coefficients of variation (CV), a standard deviation index (S), a geographic concentration index (G), coefficients of regional distribution disparity (D), and the extreme coefficient (E).

One of the best methods, and the one we chose to use, is a Theil index. The Theil index is a statistic used to measure inequality. It was invented by Henri Theil (1924–2000) a Dutch econometrician at the Netherland School of Economics. The Theil index measures the maximum possible entropy of a dataset minus the observed entropy. It has been widely used to study income inequality, racial and sexual inequality, and lack of diversity among individuals and other units of analysis. It is well suited to analyze disparities among Chinese provinces and regions. The Theil index can be decomposed; thus we used it to measure the evolutionary trend of regional disparities in terms of the urbanization of 29 Chinese provincial regions from 1982 to 2012. We decomposed regional urbanization disparities into disparities among the three great regions (eastern, central, and western) and disparities within each region.

Evolution of Regional Urbanization Disparities

Two types of disparities—inter-regional and intra-regional disparities—jointly determine national urbanization disparities. While inter-regional disparities may be analyzed based on the three great regions (east, west, and central), four (separating out the northeast), or any other schema, we chose to analyze inter-regional disparities between the three great regions. Similarly intra-regional disparities could be analyzed using any sub-grouping of regions. Using provinces as the unit of analysis is straightforward and that is what we chose to do.

As Figure 4.6 shows, provincial urbanization disparities continuously decreased between 1982 and 2012 except for slight fluctuations in some individual years around 1990 and 2000. The evolution of urbanization disparities within each of the three great regions (intra-regional disparities) basically follows the same pattern as provincial disparities. From 1982 to 2002 the disparities among China's three great regions were less significant than those within each of the three great regions.

As Figure 4.7 shows, inter-regional urbanization disparities were only 25 percent of the provincial disparities in 1982. In 2003, this proportion exceeded 50 percent—higher than the disparities within each of the three great regions. The proportion of inter-regional disparities to provincial disparities peaked in 2009 at 54.1 percent. After 2009 the proportion stayed essentially constant at approximately 53 percent.

Analyzing the trend of urbanization disparities within each of China's three great regions over time reveals a general reduction in each of the regions (Figure 4.8). The disparity within the western region is the highest, followed by the eastern and central regions after 2008. Provincial disparities in the western region have increased significantly in recent years. Although the disparities within the eastern and central regions are generally declining, the decrease in disparities in the central region after 2004 has been lower than in the east region.

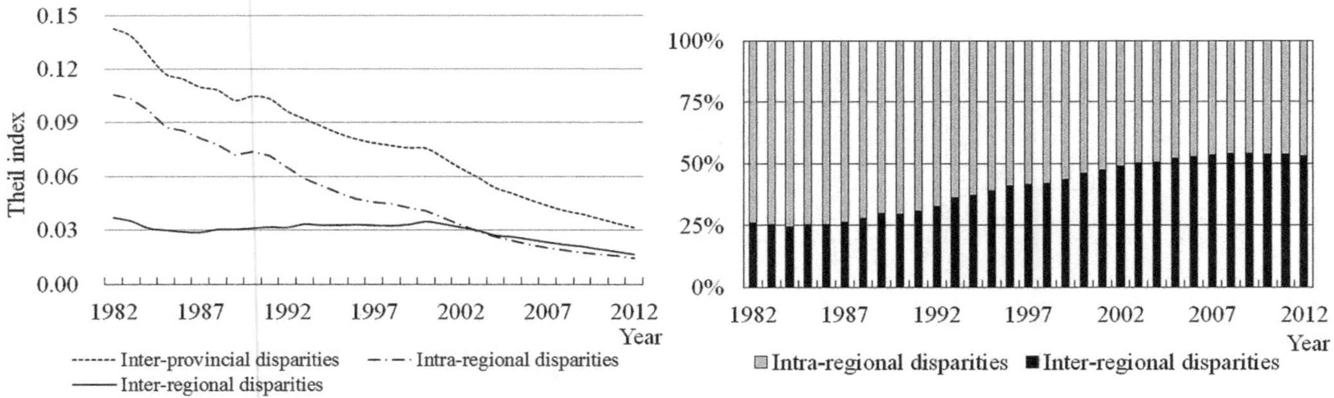

Source: NBSC-csy (1984–2014). Plotted by Li Zhang.

Figure 4.6 Inter- and intra-regional urbanization disparities in China, 1982 to 2012

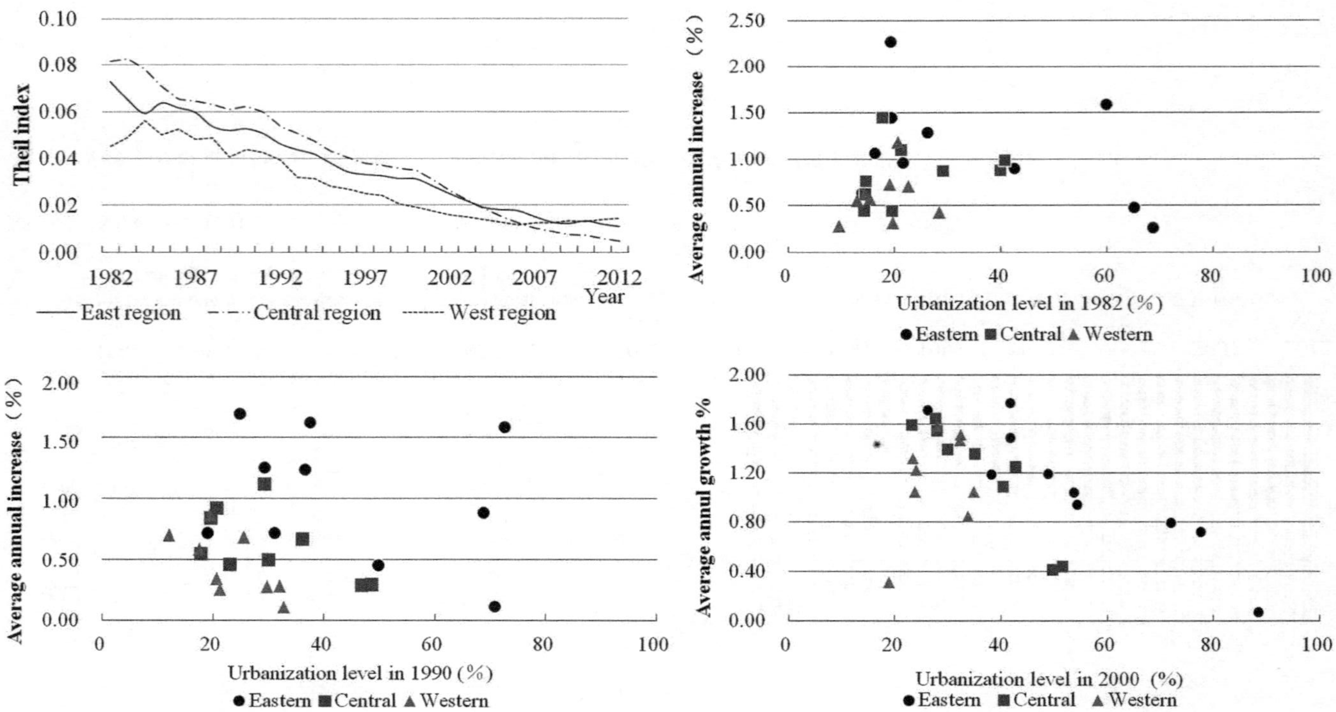

Source: NBSC-census (1984, 1992, 2002, and 2012). Plotted by Li Zhang.

Figure 4.7 Inter-provincial urbanization disparities in China's three great regions, 1982 to 2012

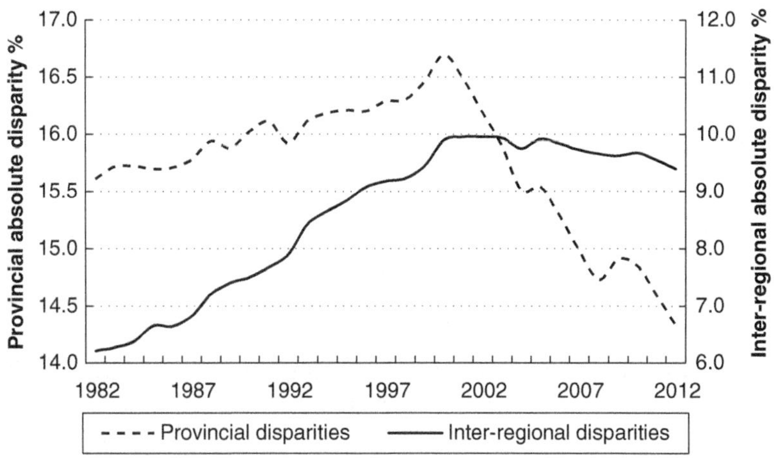

Source: NBSC-csy (1984–2014).

Figure 4.8 Absolute urbanization disparities among China's three great regions and 29 provincial regions by ST index, 1982 to 2012

Absolute and Relative Disparity

Although the Theil index explains disparities among provinces and great regions, its result is relative disparity, which is composed of the ratio of absolute disparity to its mean. Figure 4.7 shows that absolute disparity among provincial urbanization levels throughout China, unlike relative disparity, increased between 1982 and 2000 with only a few fluctuations, but has been falling sharply after its peak in 2000. By 2012, absolute provincial disparity was lower than it was in early 1982. The evolutionary path of absolute disparity among the three great regions is slightly different from that of the country. Since 2002, it has remained stable with only a little decrease.

Absolute disparity is easier to observe than relative disparity. This is the reason why ordinary Chinese feel increases in the regional disparity of urbanization. This is also the reason why some studies (especially those that utilize only descriptive analysis) have concluded that Chinese regional disparities continue to increase (Ren and Yang, 2010). It is notable that absolute disparity of provincial urbanization levels in all of China peaked in 2000 (Figure 4.8). That was the year the central government started a round of hukou reform, revised urban development guidelines, implemented a regional development policy favoring the central and western regions, and slowed down the adjustment of administrative divisions. These reforms addressed key institutional factors that had affected the direction of provincial urbanization development and caused the urbanization disparities among provinces and great regions.

Provincial Urbanization and Regional Urbanization Disparities

Since most provinces began with low urbanization rates in the early 1980s, the variation in regional urbanization levels that emerged in the 1980s and 1990s are primarily due to differences in the rate at which different provinces have urbanized.

Provinces' average annual urbanization level growth rates from 1982 to 2012 were within 2.0 percent except for Guangdong for the period 1982 to 1990 (2.27 percent). From 1982 to 1990, two eastern provinces (Guangdong and Shanghai) had an annual growth rate higher than 1.5 percent. Of the six provincial units whose growth rates were lower than 0.5 percent, three (Guizhou, Tibet, and Xinjiang) are in the western region, two (Jiangxi and Henan) are in the central region, and one (Tianjin) is in the eastern region.

From 1990 to 2000 average annual urbanization growth rates were less uniform. Provinces in the eastern region developed at a fast rate, whereas the provincial regions in the central and the western regions developed at a slow rate. The three provincial units whose average annual growth rates were higher than 1.5 percent (Guangdong, Shanghai, and Jiangsu) are in the eastern region. Of the eleven provincial units whose growth rates were lower than 0.5 percent, five (Guizhou, Gansu, Qinghai, Ningxia, and Xinjiang) are in the western region, four (Shanxi, Jilin, Heilongjiang and Jiangxi) in the central region, and only two (Tianjin and Liaoning) are in the eastern region.

Since 2000, urbanization growth rates have been more evenly distributed. Except for three of the four provincial-level cities (Beijing, Tianjin, and Shanghai) and the three northeastern provinces, Xinjiang, and Tibet, all the other provinces have maintained an average annual growth rate higher than 1 percent. Eight provinces have had average annual growth rates higher than 1.5 percent. Only two of these fast-growing provinces (Hebei and Jiangsu) are in the eastern region, three are in the central region (Anhui, Jiangxi, and Henan), and two are in the western region (Sichuan and Ningxia). A new feature in the period since 2000 is that each province in the three great regions continued to experience rapid urbanization. In general the lower the level of urbanization of a province, the higher the growth rate since 2000. This has reduced urbanization disparity within the regions. Figure 4.9 illustrates how large and modern formerly small and relatively undeveloped cities in the West have become in the last 15 years.

Source: Photo by Su XU.

Figure 4.9 Night view of Xining city, Qinghai province, western China

REGIONAL ECONOMIC GROWTH AND REGIONAL URBANIZATION

We also examined the relationship between regional economic growth and urbanization. The results of our investigation are described below.

A Theoretical Model of the Relationship between Regional Economic Growth and Urbanization

We carried out cross-sectional correlation analysis of data on economic development (measured by per capita GDP) and the urbanization level of each province from 1982 to 2012 from data in Table 4.1. We computed Pearson's product moment correlation coefficients (R^2)—the most widely used measure of association between two ratio level variables. We determined how close the association was for each year and whether there was a discernible trend over time.

The results show a statistically significant correlation between economic development and urbanization at the .01 level in every year from 1982 to 2012. The correlation coefficients gradually increase, showing that the correlation between China's economic development and urbanization level has become closer over time. The fitted cross-sectional curve resembles an exponential index curve more before 1994, and is closer to a straight line after 1994. For consistency with the Chenery–Syrqin model (see Chapter 9), we first calculated an exponential curve. After we discovered that there is a close fit between the exponential curve and a linear function we did ordinary least squares (OLS) analysis and, for simplicity, discuss the relationship and show results below for three time periods using linear curves where: *Urbanization level = b * ln (GDP per capita) + a where b represents the slope of the curve and a represents a constant.*

In the formula, *b* denotes the number of units of growth in the urbanization level produced by one unit of economic growth. Figure 4.10 shows that the slope of the curve decreases after 1990. The implication of the decrease is that increasing urbanization levels demand higher and higher economic growth, that is, a certain amount of economic growth brings smaller and smaller increases in the level of urbanization. The policy implication is that additional urbanization of China's provinces must be based on higher economic growth. A certain amount of economic growth is necessary to support a corresponding urbanization level. If economic growth

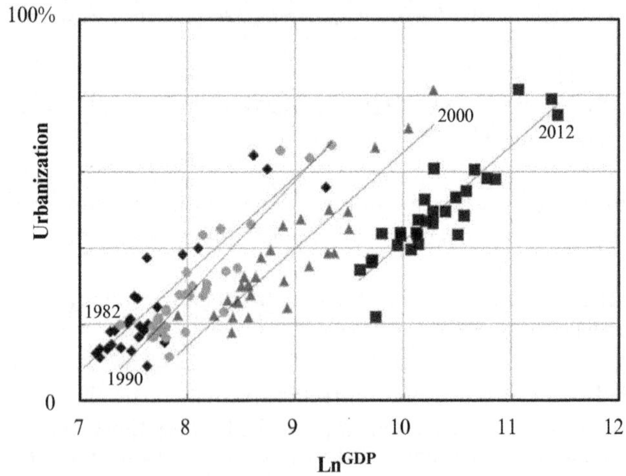

Note: GDP is in based on 2000 RMB.

Source: 29 provincial regions by ST index, 1982 to 2012. NBSC-csy (1984–2014). Compiled by Li Zhang.

Figure 4.10 Relationship between provincial per capita GDP and urbanization levels

cannot sustain the threshold value needed for an increase in the urbanization level, then either the urbanization will not happen or the quality of urbanization development will decrease, and over-urbanization may occur.

Changes in the Relationship between Economic Development and Urbanization

We used the same provincial data on the relationship between provincial level economic development and urbanization levels to explore changes in the relationship over time. The correlation of these variables for all the provinces is significant at the .01 level. The diachronic-fitted curve, variance (R^2) for each province resembles a straight line. For the convenience of descriptive analysis we show change in the slope of the straight line (b_Linear) in Figure 4.11. There is no obvious relationship between provincial economic development levels and per capita GDP, only small marginal variations. More developed economies tend to result in a slightly flatter curve slope (b1). In other words, the increase in the level of urbanization

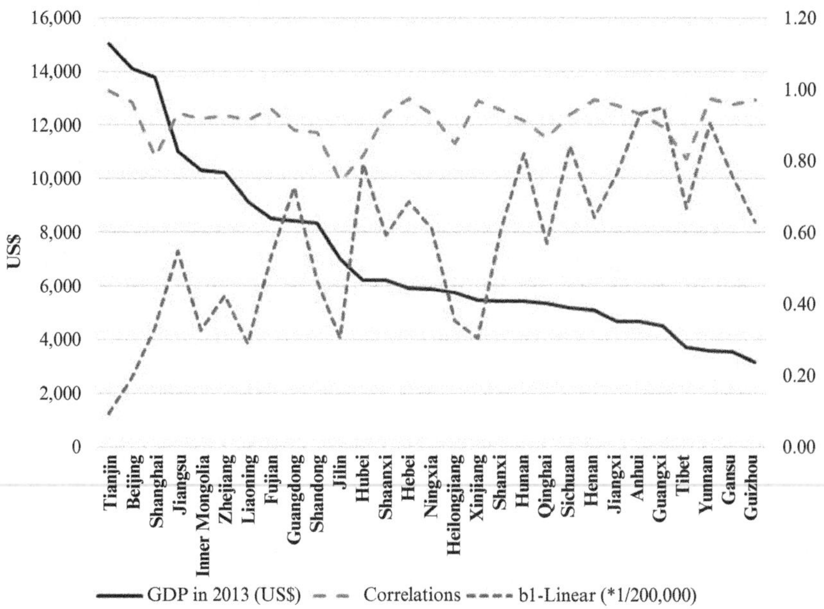

Source: NBSC-csy (1984–2014). Compiled by Li Zhang.

Figure 4.11 Relationship between GDP and b1-linear correlation by provinces: 1982 to 2012

brought about by increases in per capita GDP will be somewhat greater in economically backward provinces than in more developed provinces—which makes sense intuitively. However, fluctuations in the curve indicate that the relationship is not strong or uniform. The policy implication is that the economic growth of a province is not always accompanied by a corresponding increase in its urbanization level, as in the case of Xinjiang, Tibet, Heilongjiang, Jilin, Liaoning, Tianjin, and other provincial regions (Figure 4.11). A full understanding of the relationship between economic growth and urbanization requires an understanding of historical, geographic, social, political and other factors as well as the underlying quantitative data.

Regional Economic Disparities and Regional Urbanization Disparities

Regional economic development disparities have always been a topic of interest in China (Démurger et al., 2002; Chan and Wang, 2008; Fan and Sun, 2008). Like many countries, China has struggled to both reduce regional disparities and promote an efficient national economic structure that will enhance its competitiveness in the global economy. Applying the method in this chapter, the regional disparity coefficient of economic development (Theil index) and data on how it has changed over time can be obtained by replacing the urbanization rate index with per capita GDP. As shown in Figure 4.12, disparities in provincial economic development dropped in the 1980s, but rose rapidly in the 1990s. After a short fluctuation in 1995, the disparities continued to increase slowly, peaked in 2003, and have subsequently declined.

By 2012, the disparity in provincial economic development had fallen far below the level in 1982. The economic development disparities of the three great regions stabilized in the 1980s. After a short fluctuation, the level began to soar in 1990. After 1995, growth slowed down. It peaked in 2003 and has subsequently decreased: first slowly and then more quickly. Net, the disparity level in 2012 had fallen below the level in 1982.

In 1982 40 percent of China's total economic development disparities were among the three great regions (Figure 4.12). By 1989 this proportion reached more than 50 percent. It exceeded 60 percent in 1994. In 2007, 63 percent of the provincial economic development disparities were those among the three great regions. Although the proportion slowly declined, it remained higher than 50 percent in 2012. In short, the intra-regional disparities in the 1980s contributed much to provincial disparities. However, after the 1990s, development disparities among the three great regions predominated, which is closely related to the gradual deepening of the unbalanced regional development policy.

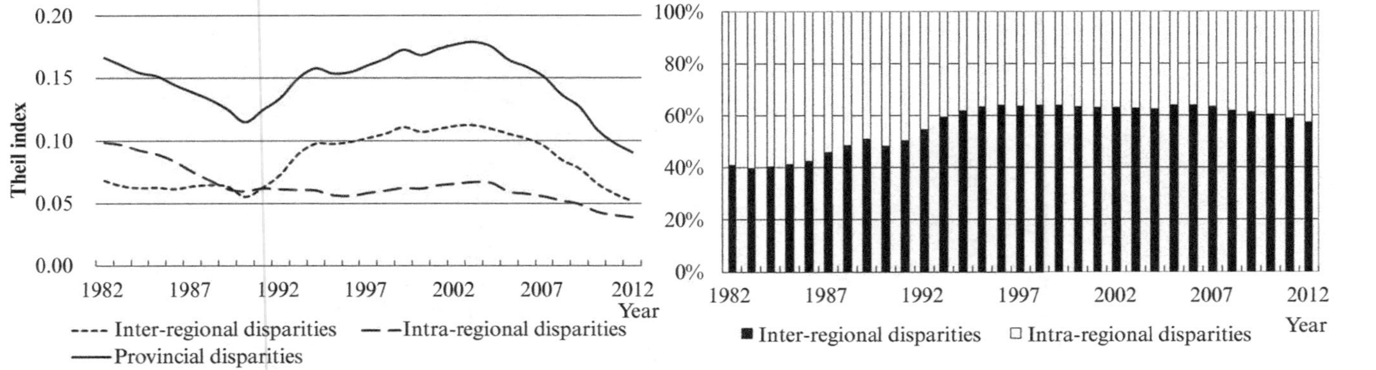

Source: NBSC-csy (1984–2014). Compiled by Li Zhang.

Figure 4.12 Composition and structure of regional economic disparities based on Theil index 1982 to 2012

Figures 4.6 and 4.11 show that in the 1980s provincial economic development disparities and urbanization decreased roughly in parallel. Provincial development disparities decreased during this period as state investments were shifted to support developing and opening up east coast regions rather than favoring inland China as in the previous decade. Eastern China caught up with the interior.

In 1990 the relationship between regional and provincial economic development and urbanization began to diverge. As a result of overall economic development, readjustment of administrative divisions, and inter-provincial migration, regional disparities in urbanization levels continued to decrease each year during the 1990s and beyond. Beginning about 1990, the opening up policy and a series of reform measures achieved spectacular further rapid economic growth of the coastal areas. Bottom-up driving forces inevitably led to greater economic development in some regions more than others, and as economic growth in the eastern provinces greatly outstripped growth in the interior, both inter-regional economic development disparities and economic development disparities among provinces increased until 2003. The gradient of economic development from the more developed east to less developed central and western China grew stronger year by year.

After 2000, the state policy that favored inland areas—the "Develop the West" and related campaigns discussed above—helped to reduce

Source: Photo by Li Zhang.

Figure 4.13 Modern industry in Zhucheng city, Shandong province

provincial economic development disparities. Inter-regional urbanization and economic disparities decreased simultaneously again, as they had in the 1980s.

During the entire period 1982–2012, despite several shifts of direction, economic and urbanization disparities both decreased significantly. The main difference between the two was a considerably smaller variation in the urbanization disparities, and the earlier appearance of increases or decreases in urbanization disparities than economic development disparities. This suggests that the national government was able to recognize emerging problems and take timely action to keep both types of disparities decreasing over the long run. A wealthier, globally connected China is now poised to further reduce these disparities at the same time that it improves the quality of urbanization. We return to these important issues in the concluding chapters of this book.

CONCLUSION

Regional policy has profoundly shaped China's spatial pattern of urbanization. Since the beginning of reform and opening up at the end of the 1970s, regional development policy has gone through four major phases.

First was the pragmatic "East takes the lead in development" policy of the early 1980s and the ideological breakthrough of "Allow some people to become rich first." The establishment of special economic zones (1979), coastal open port-cities (1984), economic open zones (1985, 1988), and the Pudong New Area in Shanghai (1990) were notable milestones during this period. These policies prioritized the development of the eastern region. They led to rapid economic growth and a reduction in both economic and urbanization disparities among provinces.

The second phase called for "balanced development between great regions." This was largely in response to bottom-up pressure from less developed regions. This shift gradually transformed regional policy that favored coastal areas into a policy that addressed the major regional economic development disparities that had developed during the 1990s.

The third phase, after 2000, emphasized coordinated development between coastal and inland provinces. This phase also involved an emphasis on coordinating urban and rural development, as discussed in Chapter 8 on the role of towns. It involved a number of related campaigns for the grand development of west China (2000), the revitalization of the northeast (2003), and the rise of central China (2004).

The fourth phase has just begun. It is best summarized in China's New Style National Urbanization Plan: 2014–2020. The NNSUP is a long and complex strategic document that provides a general framework and new norms, but has internal contradictions and ambiguity. It leaves implementation strategies largely to be worked out by relevant ministries and at the provincial level and below. Key aspects of the NNSUP are to convert national spatial policy from a grand regional policy to one that places much more emphasis on the main functional areas and seeks to promote the growth of polycentric networks and urban agglomerations. In addition to emphasizing sustainability and environmental quality, the NNSUP focuses on more human-oriented urban development that will provide better infrastructure and social services, promote equity, and improve livability. How successful the NNSUP vision proves to be will depend on implementation strategies tailored to the diverse conditions in China at every scale—a topic to which we return in the final chapters of this book.

The different phases of China's regional policy have been accompanied by changes in the spatial pattern of urbanization. From the initial urbanization distribution pattern, which featured "higher in the north than in the south" in 1982, a gradient model of "coastal to inland regions" was initiated from 1990 to 2000. By 2012, China's "eastern–central–western" spatial pattern was basically formed. During this period, most eastern provinces experienced fast and steady growth, whereas growth in central and western provinces was slow at first, accelerated, and at the time of this writing in spring, 2015 appear to be accelerating even more rapidly.

The results we derived from the analysis of regional urbanization disparities using the Theil index show that the relative disparity of provincial urbanization levels has been decreasing since the 1980s. After 2000 not only were national provincial disparities decreasing rapidly, but disparities among the three great regions were also decreasing. Further analysis of absolute urbanization disparities among the provinces compared with disparities among the three great regions show that both have experienced increases and decreases roughly in parallel, with peaks followed by declines. Absolute disparities have remained greater among the three great regions than within provinces.

According to our analysis there is a close correlation between economic development disparities and urbanization disparities. This was particularly true when the pace of urbanization was relatively slow in the 1980s and the 2000s. The pattern changed in the 1990s when the nature, location, and speed of urbanization and economic development were changing rapidly. Though economic development disparities and urbanization disparities had different paths at some points, in general terms there has been a close connection between the two types of disparities and over the long term the outcomes are reasonably similar.

We used economic and urbanization development data to compare the paths of both economic development and urbanization, represented by regression curves. The results show that the fit between the logarithmic curve and a straight line is reasonably good. Urbanization and economic growth in China have been strongly and positively correlated. Urbanization and economic development show a clear positive correlation for each province. Provinces with higher economic development levels tend to have higher urbanization levels. In a diachronic fitting, the two variables show a less clear positive correlation. The policy implication we draw from this is that the economic growth of some provinces has not always been accompanied by matching increases in urbanization. Economic development and urbanization have not been as strongly correlated in Xinjiang, Tibet, Heilongjiang, Jilin, Liaoning, and Tianjin, as in other provinces and provincial regions. Our analysis of the relationship between economic growth and regional urbanization shows that urbanization growth in provinces is closely related to, but not entirely a function of, economic development. The level of economic development and industrial structure jointly determine the level of urbanization.

The adjustment and transformation of the central government's regional policy has had a significant effect on regional development and urbanization. The rapid growth of urbanization has decreased the urban–rural gap to some extent (Lu and Chen, 2006). National development policy over the years has led to an eastward population shift. The inertia of market development has sometimes caused the effects of the policy to lag or even to neutralize policy. For example, considering their good infrastructure and industry base, the Yangtze River and Pearl River Deltas would naturally attract more people to migrate from undeveloped regions, especially central and western China. Although China in the new age has tended to adjust the development of the central and western regions through a variety of financial and spatial policies, major disparities in terms of economics, society, and urbanization between the eastern, central, and western regions still exist and will continue to exist for some time, because of the reality of very different natural conditions, market forces and the sluggishness of past development.

Balanced development does not mean that every region can and will have a comparable level of development. It can increase equity and provide more uniform social welfare and security through China. To accomplish these goals, more efficient, specific and appropriate regional urbanization policy is needed. We return to this issue and make recommendations in the final chapter.

5. Globalization, foreign direct investment, and China's urbanization

This chapter provides an overview of current scholarship about globalization and how it has affected China's urbanization and essential information on the volume and spatial distribution of foreign direct investment (FDI) in China over time. The following chapter discusses the closely related topics of how engagement with the world economy has contributed to the vast migration of China's rural workforce to urban areas. Unlike most other studies of FDI, this chapter provides information on how much of China's FDI has come from Hong Kong, Taiwan, Macao and other parts of "Greater China" and how much from more remote global sources over time. This is essential information for understanding the spatial pattern of China's urbanization since reform and opening up and projecting the future volume and distribution of urbanization in China.

GLOBAL ECONOMIC INTEGRATION AND CHINA'S INDUSTRIAL LOCATION GRADIENT

Since the second half of the twentieth century, the global economy has become more and more integrated. The revolution in digital information technology and freer trade among nations are principal drivers of this change (Sassen, 1998, 2001, 2002; Brenner et al., 2015; Taylor, 2015). The rapid development of computer technology, the Internet, bullet trains, wide-bodied jet planes and airports, and businesses clustered around some airports (aerotropoli[1]) have made the world smaller than before. Cities around the world have become connected by air, sea, and land as well as by the web. Increasingly urban theorists perceive the world city system as a "network" composed of a hierarchy of hundreds or even thousands of world city nodes bound together by complex transportation and communication linkages (Castells, 1996, 2005; Taylor and DeRudder, 2015; Brenner et al., 2015).

Global Economic Restructuring

Given the global economic growth-driven international capital and trade flows, transnational companies and FDI have exerted a profound effect on almost every aspect of the world economy, particularly in China and other developing countries (Dollar and Kraay, 2002; Huang, 2005; Brandt and Rawski, 2008; Gilpin, 2011; Gregory and Stuart, 2013).

Significant features of globalization are the widening division of labor cost differentials and relocation of industries by transnational corporations throughout the world: "the spatial division of labor" (Massey, 1995). The economies of developed countries are increasingly built on finance, advanced producer services, information, research and development, and high-end manufacturing. Many multinational corporations initially transfer their labor-intensive assembly and low-end, low value added basic manufacturing operations such as textiles and shoes to emerging industrialized countries where labor costs are lower and regulations most lax. Over time they tend to move more complex capital- and technology-intensive operations to these countries as the countries reach a mid-level of development. China, and a few other large developing countries such as India and Brazil replicate this pattern internally. Currently in the more developed parts of China such as the Beijing–Tianjin corridor and the Yangtze and Pearl River deltas where FDI, expertise, and domestic capital are concentrated and land and labor costs are comparatively high, low-end, low value added industries are being moved to less developed parts of central and western China, as described in Chapter 4 on regional policies and regional integration, and other less developed countries such as Vietnam, Indonesia, Bangladesh, and Myanmar. In their place there is a growth of more complex manufacturing of products such as automobiles, pharmaceuticals, alternative energy technology, and consumer electronics that require large amounts of capital and a skilled workforce, financial and consumer services, and research and development (R&D). Since development in China has been so rapid, phases of this pattern have occurred very quickly and because China is a "country of countries" different parts of China have reached different levels of development at different times. Shanghai, Beijing, and Guangzhou are economically more like London and New York than they are like the least developed cities in central and western China (see Figure 5.1).

The most advanced regions in China are increasingly restructuring their manufacturing to sophisticated, large-scale, automated, and innovative industries that require a smaller and more skilled workforce. A key question in development economics is whether countries at about China's level of development can break out of "the middle-income trap"

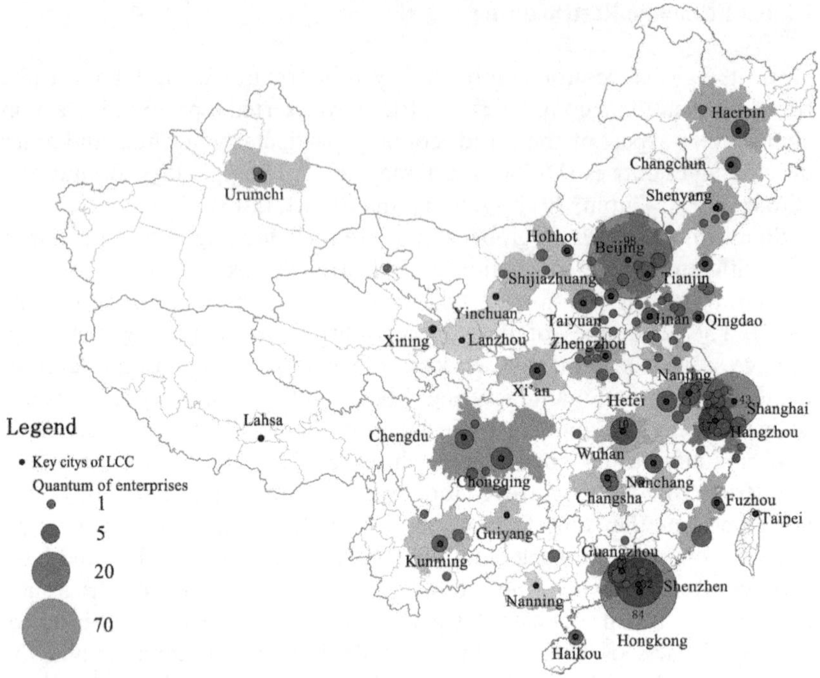

Source: Fortune China Web (2014). Drawn by Lijuan Wang.

Figure 5.1 Fortune 500 companies in China, 2014

(Gill et al., 2007) where they succeed with complex, but not very innovative economic activities, but are unable to become sufficiently innovative and nimble to join the ranks of the most developed countries: a question to which we return in Chapter 9 on China's "double dual transformation."

As early as the 1950s the United States began to focus on expanding semiconductor, communication, aerospace, and other sophisticated and rapidly evolving technology-intensive industries and transferred their steel, textiles, and other traditional industries to countries such as Japan and the former West Germany. In turn Japan and West Germany experienced industrial restructuring and upgrading in the 1960s and 1970s and started to move labor-intensive industries to other developing countries and regions in East and Southeast Asia: particularly the so-called "Asian Tigers" (Singapore, Korea, Taiwan and Hong Kong).

Developed countries in North America and Europe are now devoting a great deal of their efforts to promoting alternative energy,

Source: Photo by Li Zhang.

Figure 5.2 China's domestic auto industry in Zhucheng city, Shandong province

material-conserving and high value added industries such as integrated circuits, precision machinery, fine chemicals, and bio-medical and alternative energy and alternative automobile industries (Figure 5.2).

China's niche in the global economy: the world's factory

The international division of labor is created by extremely uneven world economic growth, different development stages of nations, and increasing cooperation among countries (Massey, 1995). Transnational economic activities are growing rapidly as markets for middle- and upper-class goods and services in Asia, South America, and Africa expand. This motivates large multinational corporations to pursue higher profits by building multinational industrial production and distribution chains.

As described in the preceding chapters, China has progressively restructured what was once a stagnant, closed and centrally planned economy into a robust, increasingly open, market-oriented, globally connected economy. China has emerged as an economic power and integrated itself into the world economy at an impressive speed.

In order to understand the role of FDI in China's economy it is useful to analyze it in relationship to China's overall assets over time. Gross Fixed Capital Formation (GFCF) is a macroeconomic concept used by the United Nations and others to show a country's assets and how

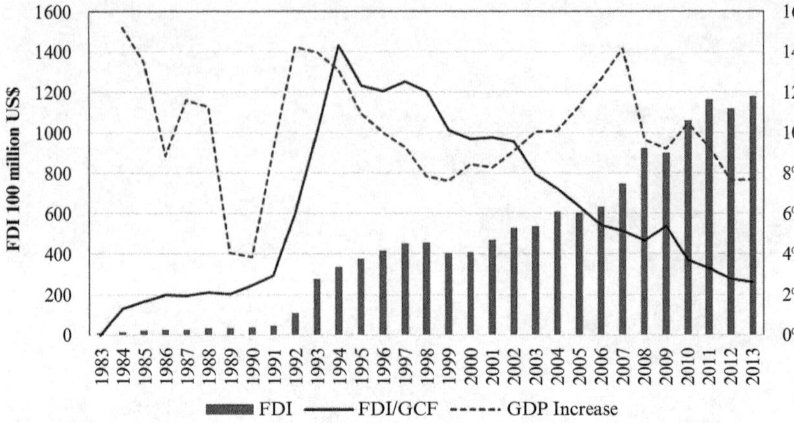

Source: NBSC-csy (2013). Compiled by Li Zhang.

Figure 5.3 China's foreign direct investment (FDI), gross domestic product (GDP) increase, and FDI/GCF ratio, 1983–2013

much new value is invested or consumed. At the beginning of reform and opening up China's Gross Fixed Capital was very low and as FDI flowed in it represented a significant percent of GFCF. The proportion of FDI in Chinese GFC rose rapidly during the late 1980s and early 1990s and then gradually fell. FDI's contribution to China's GFCF reached its peak—more than 14 percent—in 1994. Since then the contribution as a percentage of total GFCF has declined year by year. In 2013 it was only 2.6 percent. Nevertheless, given the enormous expansion of the Chinese economy, the *absolute* volume of FDI was nearly $120 billion at the end of 2013—80 times what it was in 1984 (Figure 5.3).

Initially China relied largely on labor-intensive industries and low-end manufacturing characterized by low wages, high energy consumption, and high levels of pollution. More recently as China's Gross Fixed Capital and sophistication in manufacturing have grown it is increasingly shifting to higher-end, cleaner, more capital intensive, high-tech, high value added activities.

China has become the top exporter in the world since joining the WTO in 2001. Chinese exports exceeded $2 trillion in 2012—almost 100 times the value of China's exports in 1982. China's export trade accounted for 11.18 percent of all the world's exports in 2012 compared with just 1.21 percent in 1982 (NBSC, 2014). China has become an important part of the world economy and has evolved into a genuine "world factory" (Table 5.1).

Table 5.1 Chinese exports and imports, 1982–2012

	1982		1990		2000		2010		2012	
	Export	Import	Export	Import	Export	Import	Export	Import	Export	Import
World	$1,853	$1,920	$3,365	$3,511	$6,220	$5,742	$13,898	$14,211	$18,323	$18,567
China	$22	$19	$62	$53	$249	$206	$1,578	$1,395	$2,049	$1,818
Share of China	1.21%	0.99%	1.85%	1.52%	4.01%	3.59%	8.76%	6.73%	11.18%	9.79%

Note: Billion US$ current price in years listed.

Source: *China Statistical Yearbooks* 1984, 1991, 2001, 2011, 2013 (NBSC-csy, 1984–2014).

Owing to a combination of FDI and rapidly growing domestic investment, China has been able to maintain an unprecedented level of economic growth. China's annual GDP growth rate between 1991 and 2010 exceeded 8 percent except in 1997 and 1998 when state-owned enterprises were being reformed (NBSC-csy, 2011) and at the beginning of the global financial crisis in 2008. Although China's export-oriented economy was hit hard during the early stage of the global economic crisis in 2008, the Chinese government moved quickly with a large stimulus package and restructuring and the unemployment rate quickly dropped and economic growth bounced back (Giles et al., 2012). In recent years China's GDP has continued to increase by more than 7 percent per year as indicated in Figure 5.3.

China's FDI and Urbanization

Studies in the 1990s generally concluded that that FDI was the new engine driving urbanization in China. Some scholars term the process "export-oriented urbanization" (Sit and Yang, 1997; Ning, 1998; Ma, 2002). Studies conducted after 2000 have also shown that FDI stimulates the spatial evolution of urbanization (Zhang, 2001), but describe a more complex relationship between FDI and urbanization in China. The most recent scholarship argues that endogenous domestic investment played a large role in China's rapid economic growth even during the early phases of reform and opening up and has been increasingly important as China has accumulated domestic capital to invest.

FDI, Global Restructuring, and the Changing International Division of Labor

As the international division of labor continues to increase, cheaper labor costs in Southeast Asian nations like Vietnam, Myanmar, Indonesia, and Cambodia, the Indian subcontinent including Pakistan and Bangladesh, and some African countries is impacting labor-intensive industries in China where a substantial rise in wages has already occurred and further increases are inevitable. Developed regions of China, such as the Pearl and Yangtze River Deltas and the Beijing–Tianjin corridor, are under increasing pressure to transform and upgrade their industrial structures. For labor-intensive industries to survive in the face of fierce global competition, they have to maintain low production costs. Transferring labor-intensive industries from the developed parts of eastern China to less developed parts of the eastern region and the central and western regions has become a potential choice—sometimes a necessity—for enterprises because of China's large regional economic development disparities.

The central and western regions of China are further accelerating their pace of inward industrial transfer by relying on advantages such as minerals, power, and water, and their abundant labor forces. This has been especially the case since 2010, when the State Council introduced important policies to support central and western regions in undertaking industrial transfer. Development of the world's largest original equipment manufacturing (OEM) enterprise is an example. After 2008, Foxconn—an enormous Taiwanese-based conglomerate, notable for managing big electronics assembly plants, established factories in the inland provinces of Henan, Hunan, Chongqing, and Sichuan. These locations are attractive to companies like Foxconn because of their abundant and relatively cheap labor and land costs.

Some scholars point out that overall FDI is not a true indicator of globalization, because much of China's FDI comes from so-called greater Chinese economic entities such as Hong Kong, Macau, and Taiwan. In order to shed light on this insight, Table 5.2 shows total FDI in China and FDI excluding FDI from Hong Kong, Macau, and Taiwan—what we term "pure FDI"—from 2007 to 2012. Pure FDI is arguably a better indicator of true "global" FDI than the aggregate figure that lumps together FDI from greater Chinese economic entities and other sources. The table shows that pure FDI from sources other than greater Chinese economic entities has slightly declined since 2007. Pure FDI as a percentage of total FDI in China has declined from a high of 59.7 percent to 38.3 percent at the time the most recent data became available.

Table 5.2 Chinese FDI sources: 2007 to 2012

	2007	2008	2009	2010	2011	2012
Total FDI	74.8	92.4	90.0	105.7	116.0	111.7
Hong Kong, Macao, Taiwan	30.1	43.5	48.8	637	73.4	68.9
Pure FDI	44.7	48.9	41.3	42.0	42.7	42.8
Pure FDI / Total FDI	59.7%	52.9%	45.8%	39.7%	36.8%	38.3%

Note: Billion US$ current price in years listed.

Source: *China Statistical Yearbooks* from 2008 to 2013 (NBSC-csy, 1984–2014).

The decline in the percentage of pure FDI in China does not mean that significant problems exist in economic relations between China and the world or that China will no longer be able to rely on FDI to the same extent as in the past. FDI is still stable in absolute terms. Domestic investment is increasing even more rapidly than FDI, so the proportion of FDI to total investment is decreasing. It is difficult to describe the change precisely, because of interactions of foreign corporations, greater China economic entities, and the PRC. For capital investment and global value-chain integration, some transnational corporations choose to use Hong Kong, Macau, and Taiwan as intermediaries to link with mainland China, because they perceive their financial and management capabilities to be more advanced than counterparts in China. As Shanghai continues to grow as a financial center it may supersede Hong Kong in this role. This blurs the distinction between greater China FDI and pure FDI. Apple Incorporated, for example, relies on the Foxconn Group in China whose mother company is Hon Hai Precision Industry in Taiwan as a principal intermediary for assembling iPhones and iPads. Taiwanese companies invest heavily in the construction of industry complexes in the PRC to serve Apple Inc. Formosa Petrochemical Corporation and ASUS from Taiwan, as well as Noble Group, Jardine Matheson, and Hutchison Whampoa from Hong Kong, are all global multinational companies that perform similar roles as intermediaries between foreign-based multinational corporations and the PRC.

The history and structure of these multinational entities that do business in China is complex. Jardine Matheson, for example, was an Anglo-Scottish company that began trading opium, cotton, tea, silk and other goods in 1844. After the founding of the PRC Jardine Matheson moved its offices to Hong Kong. It is now legally incorporated in Bermuda and trades throughout Asia and beyond. The distinction between greater China FDI and domestic investment is also becoming blurred as Shanghai's role as a global financial center grows and as the new Asia Infrastructure Investment Bank, located in Beijing, promises to strengthen the role of Beijing as a financial center.

Debates over how Globalization Impacts China's Urbanization

While scholars agree that globalization has had an enormous influence on China's economy, how much of an impact it has had on China's urbanization remains a subject of debate. In 1991 Columbia University sociology professor Saskia Sassen (2001) argued that a global urban system had already emerged because of globalization. She placed a small number of global cities—led by New York and London (NYLON)—at the top of a global city system hierarchy that cascades down to "national key cities, regional cities, local cities, and towns" to integrate economic activities across the world into a single framework. At that time (1991) Hong Kong and Shanghai had not yet emerged as top-tier global cities, but that has changed. A recent study of global network connectivity by British economic geographer Peter Taylor concluded that by 2012 Hong Kong had become the third most "connected" global city after London and New York. In 2012 Shanghai was the sixth most connected global city (Taylor, 2015). According to Taylor between 2000 and 2012 Shanghai's global connectivity rank jumped from thirty-first to sixth.

Sassen argues that the formation and development of the world city system and the emergence of global cities greatly affects the urbanization process in all countries (Sassen, 1998, 2001, 2002). Functional specializations and economic activities of cities of different sizes at different stages of development inevitably lead to differing degrees of urbanization. Similarly, many scholars argue that economic integration has dramatically affected the spatial distribution of urbanization in China. Recent English language books on Chinese urbanization all point out the difference between generally more urbanized coastal regions and generally less urbanized inland areas of China (Wu, 2015; Zhang, F., 2015; Wu and Glaubatz, 2012; Ren, 2013; Bracken, 2012; Brandt and Rawski, 2008; Fan, 2008; McGee et al., 2007; Friedmann, 2005).

Professor John Friedmann, a leading international urban planning scholar, has advanced an interesting argument—that China's urbanization, although entwined with globalization processes, is best understood chiefly as an endogenous process leading to a specifically Chinese form of modernity (2005). Friedman traces the long history of Chinese cities and discusses endogenous political and administrative reforms during reform and opening up and the growth of town and village industry that promoted "urbanization from below" in support of this view. The differences between Friedmann's and Sassen's views can be attributed largely to the fact that Sassen focused on the global urban system and functional economic divisions and differences in labor costs. By contrast, Friedmann's analysis draws on historical and cultural information and emphasizes private and township enterprises in China that emerged in the 1980s and 1990s. While he acknowledges that China's urbanization is linked to globalization, he makes a compelling case that core activities are endogenous or spontaneous. Based on our research we concluded that both endogenous forces and globalization have impacted and will continue to impact urbanization in China. Chapter 8 on towns, villages, and rural urbanization explores these issues in depth.

FDI AND CHINA'S URBANIZATION

Many scholars assert that FDI has affected China's urbanization. This makes sense intuitively. In order to explore this hypothesis we analyzed changes in FDI and urbanization in China over time.

The Growth of FDI in China

A look at the way in which FDI has grown and the way in which the spatial distribution of FDI in China has changed over time is helpful in understanding FDI's contribution to China's urbanization.

FDI in China grew rapidly in the 1980s, 1990s, and after 2000. FDI in China increased from $916 million in 1983 to $3.49 billion in 1990, $40.7 million in 2000, $105.7 billion in 2010, and $119.6 billion in 2014 (NBSC, 2015).

In terms of FDI distribution in the three great regions of China, the eastern region accounted for more than three-quarters of the total FDI between 1983 and 2013. The central and western regions together accounted for less than one-quarter of the total FDI in the same period. However, the regional location of FDI in China is now changing rapidly. The eastern region's share of FDI has declined annually since 2003: from 87.19 percent in 2003 to 67.50 percent in 2013—a 19.26 percent decrease. In contrast, the central region's share of FDI doubled from 10.18 percent in 2003 to 21.26 percent in 2013 and the western region's tripled from 2.61 percent in 2003 to 11.24 percent in 2013.

Regional Difference in FDI

The spatial distribution of FDI in China is unbalanced (Table 5.3). In the 1980s, Guangdong province—close to Hong Kong and where the enormously successful Shenzhen special economic development zone is located—received 41 percent of China's total FDI. This is a major reason for the rapid early urbanization in the cities of Guangzhou, Shenzhen, Dongguan, and Zhongshan in Guangdong province. In the same period, the 14 provinces that received the least money collectively received only 4.47 percent of China's total FDI.

In the 1990s, the amount of FDI increased in Fujian, Jiangsu and Shandong provinces. Even though Guangdong province's share of FDI declined to 28.32 percent during that period, it still received the largest share of total FDI of any province in China in 2000. Between 2001 and 2010 Guangdong province's share of FDI continued to decline to 15.30 percent.

Jiangsu province is in the Yangtze River Delta adjacent to Shanghai and benefits from Shanghai's economic growth. It has also captured a large percentage of China's total FDI. Jiangsu province's rural industry was developed earlier than other provinces and the first cross-province expressway within China was built in the south of Jiangsu and Shanghai, along with many industrial parks in smaller cities. Between 1991 and 2000

Table 5.3 Distribution of FDI from 1983 to 2013

		1983–1990	1991–2000	2001–2010	2013
Regional share	Nation	100%	100%	100%	100%
	East	82.02%	85.17%	79.30%	67.50%
	Middle	12.55%	11.21%	15.49%	21.26%
	West	5.43%	3.62%	5.20%	11.24%
Provincial share	Nation	100%	100%	100%	100%
	Guangdong	40.94%	28.32%	15.30%	9.82%
	Beijing	11.54%	4.01%	3.80%	3.15%
	Shanghai	8.70%	8.47%	7.70%	6.21%
	Fujian	6.60%	9.44%	6.60%	4.75%
	Hubei	5.35%	2.82%	2.31%	2.55%
	Heilongjiang	3.69%	1.73%	1.58%	1.71%
	Liaoning	3.59%	4.44%	7.96%	10.74%
	Jiangsu	2.68%	12.57%	16.59	12.30%
	Shaanxi	2.61%	0.77%	0.86%	1.36%
	Shandong	2.46%	5.98%	7.54%	5.20%
	Tianjin	2.17%	4.44%	4.80%	6.22%
	Jilin	1.45%	1.69	0.74%	0.67%
	Guangxi	1.40%	1.77%	0.56%	0.26%
	Zhejiang	1.27%	3.24%	7.08%	5.24%
	Sichuan	1.10%	1.68%	3.32%	7.83%
	Other 14 provinces	4.47%	8.65%	13.90%	21.99%

Source: *China Statistical Yearbooks* from 1984 to 2013 (NBSC-csy, 1984–2014), Provinces' statistical yearbooks from 1984 to 2014, calculated by Li Zhang.

Jiangsu had 12.57 percent of China's total FDI second only to Guandong province. Between 2001 and 2010 Jiangsu's FDI continued to increase to 16.59 percent. Thus, Jiangsu replaced Guangdong as the province with the highest FDI.

Fujian province on China's southeast coast across from Taiwan, which receives a substantial amount of Taiwanese investment, moved from fourth to third with 9.44 percent, and Shandong province—a coastal province with historic ties to Japan and Korea, which was tenth in the 1980s, became fourth in the 1990s with 5.98 percent of China's total FDI.

While the extreme disparities in the spatial distribution of FDI eased in the 1990s, more than half of China's FDI remained concentrated in Guangdong, Jiangsu, and Fujian provinces in 2000. The most recent data for 2013 show that Liaoning province's share of China's total FDI has increased to 10.74 percent and the share of Jiangsu and Guangdong fell further to 12.30 percent and 9.82 percent, respectively. In contrast, the share of Sichuan province (including Chongqing) increased to 7.83 percent, the province with the fourth largest FDI in China. The share of the other 14 provinces increased to 21.99 percent in 2013. FDI in central and western China, and in part of the northeast region, is now surging.

FDI and Regional Urbanization

There is scholarship and lively debate about the relationship between FDI and urbanization in China and antecedent questions of how FDI has affected economic development. Much of this literature is dated and we question the methodology used in some studies. Following is a discussion of prior studies. The next section discusses our own methodology and our conclusions about how FDI has affected urbanization in different parts of China.

THEORY ABOUT FDI AND URBANIZATION

Dependency Theory and Studies Critical of the Role of FDI

In the 1980s a number of scholars argued that FDI-induced growth, migration, and urbanization in developing countries created dependency (Kentor, 1981; Friedmann, 1986; Timberlake and Kentor, 1983). In their opinion FDI was negative for developing countries as the more FDI the greater the dependency. These theorists argued that the negative effects of FDI may not be immediately apparent, but hurt developing countries in the long run. A possible negative consequence they highlighted is over-urbanization—a greater concentration of population in urban areas than the urban economy can absorb leading to un- and under-employment and creation of slums (Kentor, 1981; Myers, 1997). We will return to the question of what China's experience contributes to the dependency theory debate later in this chapter.

Quantitative studies that have analyzed the relationship between FDI, development, migration and urbanization in China, have produced contradictory and sometimes counter-intuitive results.

Zhou (2006) using a conditional logistic model and data from the fifth national census (2000), concluded that national and private capital had a statistically significant positive impact on provincial migration, but FDI had a negative impact on provincial migration. Wu (2005: 57) affirmed the important effect of foreign capital on overall urbanization in China, but concluded that there was no statistically significant correlation between

FDI and regional development. There are three problems with these studies.

First, the analyses are both based on the assumption that the development and urbanization level of different regions (such as province-level administrative regions) may be considered equal before FDI occurred, and test the hypothesis that the more FDI in a given region, the higher their level of urbanization will be. In fact, the urbanization level in different regions of China was significantly different during the early stage of reform and opening up.

Second, there is usually a lag between the time an investment is made and the impact is measurable. The relationship between FDI and urbanization in a given year should not be judged based only on data for that year.

Third, evaluating the influence of FDI on urbanization by urbanization level ignores the fact that the distribution of FDI and the size of provinces are not necessarily correlated. Sichuan province has a little over 100 million people and its FDI has been relatively low for a long time—less than 4 percent of China's total before 2010, which means that FDI played only a limited role in Sichuan's urbanization. However, if the same amount of FDI was invested at Ningxia autonomous region where less than 7 million people live, we can imagine how fast urbanization would increase at Ningxia. Conclusions reached based on comparing FDI and the proportion of the population that is urban is not valid.

Studies Arguing that FDI is Positive for Developing Countries

Recently most scholars question dependency theory. They argue that while FDI can have negative consequences, on balance FDI is positive for developing countries (Kasarda and Crenshaw, 1991; Lin, 2007; Fujita and Hu, 2001).

Most recent studies have concluded that developing countries cannot develop alone without participating in the global economy and while reliance on FDI has some negative consequences the net benefits outweigh the negatives for developing countries including China (Wang, 2010). University of Hong Kong geography professor Victor Fung-shuen Sit's research on the Pearl River Delta (Sit, 2001b) and Weiping Wu and Chaolin Gu's study of the Yangtze River Delta (Wu and Gu, 2005) document the positive influence of FDI on local urbanization.

Analysis of FDI and Urbanization

To explore the relationship between FDI and urbanization, it is necessary to analyze the relationship between FDI over a period long enough to smooth out short-term variation, consider the lag between the time FDI is made and its impacts occur, and factor in the total urban population growth (UPG) in a given region. When analyzing the correlation with the Statistical Package for the Social Sciences (SPSS), a computerized statistical package with strong mathematical analysis functions, it is important to control the regional population scale and explore partial correlations.

We analyzed FDI and UPG for all of China and in the three major regions of China in three periods that were long enough to smooth out short-term anomalies in the data, from 1983 to 1990, 1991 to 2000, and 2001 to 2010. Table 5.4 shows Pearson product moment correlation coefficients between FDI and UPG during the three periods. The correlations are clear—statistically significant at the 0.00 or 0.01 levels. However, variations in the regional population among the three regions influenced UPG. We performed partial correlation analysis comparing FDI and UPG using regional population size as a control variable. We found that the correlation between FDI and UPG after excluding the influence of total population size was strong and statistically significant from 1983 to 1990 and from 1991 to 2000. The relationship from 2001 to 2010 was slightly weaker, but still highly statistically significant. Thus, we conclude that FDI has had a strong and statistically significant impact on China's urbanization.

Table 5.4 Correlation analysis and partial correlation analysis of FDI with regional urban population increase: nation and by major Chinese regions, 1983–2010

		Correlation analysis	Partial correlation analysis controlling the effect of total population			
			Nation	East	Middle	West
1983–1990	Correlation	0.632	0.792	0.571	0.840	0.652
	Sig(2-Tailed)	0.000	0.000	0.001	0.009	0.080
1991–2000	Correlation	0.781	0.904	0.849	0.499	0.661
	Sig(2-Tailed)	0.000	0.000	0.000	0.209	0.074
2001–2010	Correlation	0.602	0.586	0.421	−0.249	0.837
	Sig(2-Tailed)	0.001	0.001	0.225	0.552	0.010

Source: Provinces' statistical yearbooks from 1984 to 2011. Calculated by Li Zhang.

In order to better understand changing relationships between FDI and urbanization we grouped China's 29 province-level units into eastern, central, and western regions and did partial correlation analysis of the relationship between FDI and UPG at the regional level.

The correlation between FDI and UPG was statistically significant and relatively strong in the eastern region during all three time periods. The correlation was strong in the central region in the 1980s, became moderate in the 1990s and non-existent by the 2000–2010 period. The relationship between FDI and UPG in the western region was weak and not statistically significant at the .05 level in the 1980s and 1990s, but it became statistically significant at the .01 level in the 2000–2010 period.

Based on our alternative methodology analyzing the relations between the total amount of FDI in a period long enough to smooth out short-term variation and the lag between the time FDI occurs and its impacts are discernable and the total urban population growth in China's three great regions, we conclude that there has been a significant relationship between FDI and urbanization in China.

Our analysis shows that there are close connections between FDI and UPG, but the driving effect of FDI in urbanization is non-linear. Therefore, other factors need to be considered to fully understand the role of FDI in urbanization. One important consideration is synergistic effects as economic clusters develop. Successful clusters may develop the ability to attract still further FDI and population. Shanghai is a case in point. In 2013, investments of the top 100 foreign companies contributed 21 percent of Shanghai's GDP growth (Jiefang Daily, 2014). The population of Shanghai increased by over 7 million between 2000 and 2013. Foreign capital stimulated UPG while promoting local economic development. FDI in Guangdong, Zhejiang, Jiangsu, Shandong, and other eastern provinces has also developed to a scale that can give these regions an advantage in attracting still more FDI and urban population.

China's experience with FDI sheds important light on the dependency theory debate. The amount of FDI entering China has grown continuously since the early 1980s, expanding eightyfold to $120 billion at the end of 2013. In contrast the percentage of Gross Fixed Capital Formation (GFCF) that FDI constitutes grew during the 1980s and early 1990s to a peak of 14 percent and then declined to just 2.6 percent in 2013. FDI allowed the Chinese economy to "take off." Now China's economy is large enough that domestic investment largely meets China's finance needs and the Chinese government and private Chinese corporations' investments in other countries exceed FDI coming to China. Initial infusions of FDI stimulated endogenous growth and helped China move from a labor dependent, low value added economy producing simple products like textiles, shoes, and toys to an increasingly advanced economy engaged in research and development, advanced producer services, finance, and capital intensive manufacturing. FDI is still important to China—particularly for developing the high-tech tertiary sector and in partnerships that help China further develop its technology and management. Dependency theory does not explain what happened in China. Rather, the lesson appears to be that with appropriate policies some countries can use FDI to stimulate their economies and over time wean themselves from FDI. Because of its size and long history of endogenous entrepreneurship China may be a special case. But the general lesson is of universal interest.

The import–export volume of commodities is as important as FDI as an indicator of globalization. The regional amounts of both FDI and import–export volumes reflect the distribution of foreign capital and its influence on China compared with endogenous economic development and urbanization. This sheds light on the debate between John Friedmann—who stresses endogenous forces in China's development and urbanization—and scholars like Saskia Sassen who emphasize the impact of exogenous global forces.

We obtained results consistent with the correlation results in Table 5.4 when we replaced FDI with the import–export volume of commodities. Both measures confirm that exogenous forces have had a significant impact on China's urbanization. This does not mean that endogenous forces are unimportant. In Chapter 8 we document the importance of Town and Village Enterprises (TVEs) as important drivers of China's economy today that make a major contribution to China's import–export volume. This is the basis of our conclusion that both China's economy and urbanization are affected by both endogenous and exogenous forces.

China's Outward Investment

An important new trend is China's investment in other countries. From its position at the beginning of reform and opening up where China's foreign investment flowed only one way—inward, into China, increasingly money from China is flowing outward as it is invested in other countries.

Descriptive analysis of the sources and destinations of these capital flows and normative analysis of whether this is good or bad is beyond the scope of this book, but it is important to understand the scale of outward investment. The most recent data from China's national Ministry of Commerce shows that outward investment has reached to US$116 billion. If reinvestment of the capital from third parties is included, outward investment would be more than US$140 billion—more than the US$119 billion in FDI that flowed into China in 2014 (*People Daily Web*, 2015). This has implications for China's urbanization. Some low-end manufacturing will likely shift overseas. Labor-intensive industries are likely to shrink. China's urban structure will be increasingly based on domestic production and consumption.

CONCLUSION: GLOBALIZATION, FDI, OUTWARD INVESTMENT AND URBANIZATION

Globalization stimulates the formation of international production networks via capital flows, giving rise to unprecedented changes in the regional division of labor. The newly formed pattern of the regional division of labor shows the following primary features: an expansion from national to international scale, extension from inter-industrial divisions and intra-industrial division to division of labor based on value chains. The new pattern of the regional division of labor and other factors profoundly affects the landscape of urbanization.

The impact of globalization has never been confined to the difference in UPG in various regions. It also affects the clustering morphology of the urban population, relations among cities and hierarchical structures and polycentric networks of cities, and upgrading and sometimes revolutionary changes in urban industrial structures. These relationships are discussed further in an article by Li, Yan and Jiang (2010).

Our analysis has demonstrated the impact of global capital on China's urbanization and provides up-to-date regionally disaggregated data on sources and destinations of flows of FDI. It relates these macro-level forces to differential urbanization in different regions and provinces within China.

Largely as a consequence of China's rapid globalization process, in addition to internal migration, there is now a substantial amount of international migration to Chinese cities. Beijing, Shanghai, Guangzhou and other financial and technical centers have large numbers of foreign nationals from all parts of the world. Many migrants from African countries are now coming to China—particularly cities in southern China—to build networks of connection to do business with their home countries. International migration is further contributing to China's globalization.

This chapter sets the stage for a clearer understanding of the great population flows that have occurred in China and have been closely related to FDI and the course of globalization. We turn now to our analysis of the greatest migration in human history.

NOTE

1. The term aerotropolis (plural aerotropoli) was invented by University of North Carolina geography professor John Kasarda to describe cities built around airports whose economies depend almost entirely on managing flows of people and goods through activities such as serving as departure and arrival points for passengers, logistics, warehousing, and hosting conferences.

6. Population flows and semi-urbanization

Chapter 5 described the impact of globalization, FDI, and China's engagement with the world economy. A massive influx of FDI, the flourishing of export-oriented industry, growth of domestic capital, maturation of industry in the best-developed parts of China, the shift of less sophisticated manufacturing and assembly operations to central and western China and other macro-level forces have had a huge impact on China's population. Development and urbanization are closely linked. This chapter builds on Chapter 2 on China's hukou system and Chapter 5 on globalization to describe large-scale population flows which have occurred in China since reform and opening up and further elucidate the complex nature of China's urbanization.

China has had a dual society for millennia with large differences between the income and quality of life in urban areas compared with rural and peri-urban areas and among regions in China. As restrictions on migration have been relaxed and China's rural population has become more aware of differences between rural and urban areas and their expectations have increased, population flows between rural and urban areas have occurred at a scale unprecedented in human history. How to incorporate urban migrants as full citizens with the same health, education, pension, and other social benefits as residents with urban hukou is one of the great challenges facing China during the next phases of urbanization.

CHINA'S POPULATION PROFILE

With more than 1.37 billion people as of this writing in May, 2015 China has a fifth of the world's population (NBSC, 2015). China's population structure and migration patterns are experiencing enormous change. National Census data shows that between 1980 and 1990 China's population grew by 14.4 percent. Between 1990 and 2000 it decreased by 11 percent and by 5.7 percent from 2000 to 2010 (NBSC-census, 2012).

China's population is aging. In 2013, the proportion of people aged over 65 rose to 9.7 percent of the total population (NBSC-csy, 2014)—well over 7 percent, which the United Nations has established to define "aging societies." Life expectancy in China increased from 67 in 1980 to 75 in 2013 (World Bank, 2015).

The way in which birth rates are measured is complex, but most demographers consider the Total Fertility Rate (TFR) to be the most useful indicator. China's average TFR has held steady at a low level. There is scholarly debate about the way in which the Chinese government calculates TFR and their official statistics. One recent analysis has concluded that it is currently no more than 1.5 percent (Zhu, 2012).

Regional differences in population change in China are increasingly significant. For example, the population living in Shanghai and Beijing—including people without local hukou—increased by more than 30 percent in 10 years from 2000 to 2010, but the population in inland provinces, such as Anhui, Hubei, Sichuan, and Chongqing, substantially declined during the same period (Figure 6.1).

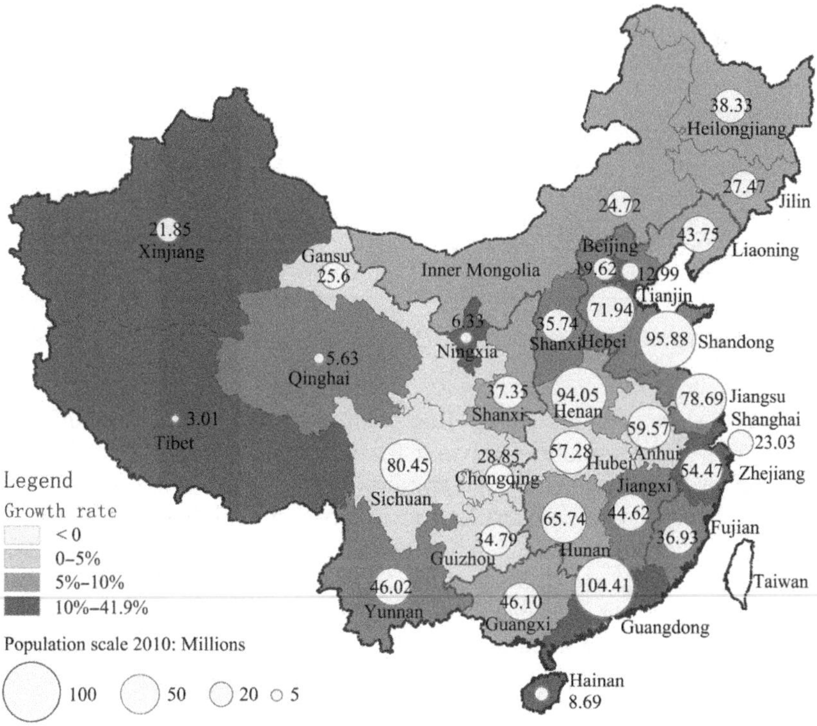

Source: Calculated from population by province in 2000 and 2010 censuses. Drawn by Li Zhang.

Figure 6.1 Average annual population growth by province, 2000–2010

Table 6.1 Population change in China's eight fastest growing province-level administrative units and six provinces that lost population 2000–2010

	Population (millions) 2000	Population (millions) 2010	Population change (millions)	Average annual increase rate (%)	Natural increase (millions)	Net migration (millions)	Migration's share of change (%)
Fastest growing			A+B		A	B	B/(A+B)
Beijing	13.82	19.61	5.79	3.5	0.29	5.50	95
Shanghai	16.74	23.02	6.28	3.2	0.20	6.08	97
Tianjin	10.01	12.94	2.93	2.6	0.19	2.73	93
Guangdong	86.42	104.30	17.88	1.9	6.74	11.15	62
Zhejiang	46.77	54.43	7.66	1.5	2.16	5.50	72
Xizang (Tibet)	2.62	3.00	0.38	1.4	0.31	0.07	19
Xinjiang	19.25	21.81	2.56	1.3	2.2	0.35	14
Ningxia	5.62	6.30	0.68	1.1	0.63	0.05	8
Losing population							
Gansu	25.6	25.6	−0.04	−0.2	1.7	−1.7	–
Anhui	59.9	59.5	−0.36	−0.6	3.9	−4.3	–
Guizhou	35.3	34.8	−0.50	−1.4	3.1	−3.6	–
Sichuan	83.3	80.4	−2.87	−3.4	2.6	−5.5	–
Hubei	60.8	57.2	−3.04	−5.0	1.7	−4.7	–
Chongqing	30.9	28.9	−2.05	−6.6	1.0	−3.0	–

Sources: NBSC-census (2002, 2012); Cai (2013); NBSC-csy (2001–2011).

Table 6.1 shows that the causes of population growth or decline in different provinces vary. Population growth in the eastern provinces has mainly been caused by inter-provincial immigration, whereas population growth and decline in central and western provinces has been mainly due to a natural growth and emigration.

All the provinces with net population decline are located in central and western China. The decline is attributable to large flows of emigrants, rather than a decline in natural population growth. This decline is directly related to the regional industrialization process and FDI described in Chapter 5.

POPULATION FLOWS

Defining Population Flows

The International Union for the Scientific Study of Population (IUSSP, 1982) defines a population flow as "a form of regional movement or spatial movement between one regional unit and another regional unit, which usually includes movement from the source region to a destination or a permanent change in settlement area." We follow the IUSSP definition and use the terms "source" and "destination" to refer to the administrative divisions from which migrants move and the units to which they move at different scales. A study of population migration flows must focus on two basic dimensions: time and space.

The time dimension involves how long a migrant must have resided at a destination in order to qualify as living there. This standard has changed in China's statistics. China's fourth national census (1990) considered a person who had resided in a place for over a year a local resident. A respondent who said that their hukou address was different from the address where they currently lived and that they had resided where they were living at the time of the census for a year or more would be classified as a migrant. In contrast the fifth and sixth censuses in 2000 and 2010 reduced the time necessary to be classified as a resident to half a year. The increase in the number of migrants enumerated in 2000 reflected both an increase in actual migration and a statistical paper increase as a result of the lower standard.

The spatial dimension of population flows involve specification of how far a person must have moved to qualify as a migrant. In 1990 a person was defined as a migrant only if the address where he was living on census day was in a *county* different from his original county and he had lived there for more than one year. In the 2000 and 2010 censuses, a person is defined as a migrant if the address where he was living on census day was different from his original *town* or *township* even if he is living in the same county. The required length to live in the current address was reduced to six months instead of one year.

We analyzed migration flows at multiple scales. Most of the analysis that follows describes migration either between China's three great regions (eastern, central, and western): which we term inter-regional population flows or migration within provinces (including provincial-level cities and autonomous regions), which we term intra-regional population flows. We also include some information on population flows of particular interest—such as flows among provinces in eastern China (which are the destinations of most of China's migrants), and among smaller administrative units such as cities, counties, towns and the peri-urban areas around the urbanized core of cities and towns and the core areas. We treat population activity that involves a change in an individual's registered permanent residence (hukou address) as permanent migration. We follow the latest census definition and include people who lived in an area for half a year or more as de facto residents. We treat changes in residence area only rather than in the registered permanent residence, as population flows or migration. This multi-scalar analysis gives a nuanced understanding of how migration has affected China's urbanization.

Population Flow Statistics

Large-scale collection of population flow data in China started with the 1987 1 percent population sample survey. Scholars have only acquired data on pre-1987 population indirectly by inference from other data. At the time of this writing in spring, 2015, nationwide surveys of population flows have been conducted six times, in censuses in 1990, 2000, and 2010 and 1 percent population surveys in 1987, 1995, and 2005. The standards of both time and space defining population flows in these censuses and surveys have changed several times.

The fourth census in 1990 defined the time necessary to consider that migration had occurred as departure from the individual's registered permanent residence (place of origin) for over one year. The 2000 and 2010 censuses define migration to have occurred if more than half a year has passed between an individual's departure and the census date. Thus part of the increase in migration between the 1990 and later censuses is attributable to the more permissive definition.

In terms of space, before 1990 departure from a resident's county (including a county-level city) was regarded as migration. After 1990 a resident's departure from their town, township or urban street (sub-district) is also regarded as migration (Table 6.2). This re-definition also accounts for part of the increase in people defined as migrants after 1990.

Since changes in the standards used to calculate population flow statistics in the censuses have changed several times, it is not possible to directly compare the total flowing population over time. But it is possible to compare the changing structure of population flows over time (Chan, 2003; Duan and Sun, 2006).

Nationwide Population Flows

China's total population increased by more than 300 million from 1982 to 2012. During the same period, the size of China's floating population grew

Table 6.2 Census migration statistics 1982–2010

		3rd census: 1982	1% census: 1987	4th census in 1990	1% census: 1995	5th census: 1990	1% census: 2005	6th census 2010
Investigation time		6.30	6.30	9.30	10.30	10.30	10.30	10.30
Total population (millions)		1,008	1,072	1,131	1,208	1,266	1,306	1,340
Sample ratio		100%	0.999%	100%	1.027%	100%	1.325%	100%
Definition of migration	Time (living for)	One year	Half year	One year	Half year			
	Space (leaving from)	County	City, town or county	County	Town, township and urban street			
Migration (1 million)		6.6	15	22	48	144	147	261

Note: Does not include serviceman and the population living in Macau, Hong Kong and Taiwan.

Source: Compiled by Li Zhang from the 1982, 1987, 1990, 2005 and 2010 censuses (NBSC-census, 1984, 1992, 2002, 2012; NBSC-1% census, 1988, 1996, 2006).

to 220 million people. It increased as a percentage of the total population from 0.65 percent in 1982 to 16.58 percent in 2010: one-fifth of China's population.[1]

A number of different standards for measuring migrants are used in China.[2] The following pages are based on the pre-2000 standard classifying someone who had lived away from their official residence address for more than one year on the census enumeration day as a migrant for migration up to 2000, and reducing the time to half a year for the post-2000 period.

There are a number of other sources of data on migration for different time periods, at different scales, and using different time periods to define a migrant. China's Ministry of Public Security has summarized data on temporary population and migration with hukou change in various places. University of Washington professor Kam Wing Chan has summarized findings of these and other sources (Chan, 2008).

Inter-provincial migrating population (migrant labor) has become an irreplaceable factor for economic development in migrant destination areas in eastern China (Wang and Huang, 2005). In contrast, the total labor force in central and western China has decreased because of the large number of emigrants for these regions.

The migrating population as measured by people who had left their official residence addresses for over half a year, was 109 million in 2000 and grew to 221 million in 2010 (NBSC-census, 1992, 2012). By this measure, the share of the migrating population in the total population nearly doubled, from 8.77 percent to 16.58 percent. During this period there were enormous population flows in each of the three great regions of China (Figure 6.2).

The provinces that are the main population flow destinations are Guangdong, Zhejiang, Jiangsu and Fujian provinces and the provincial-level cities of Shanghai, Tianjin and Beijing. The population immigrating to these administrative units accounted for over 25 percent of the total population of these areas.

Inter-provincial Population Flows

Inter-provincial population flows accounted for approximately a third of China's total population flow. The censuses of 1990, 2000, and 2010 provide comparable data on inter-provincial migrants who had been at a location other than their official residence for five years. Hence, they can be used to analyze changing patterns of inter-provincial population flows over time. Figure 6.3 summarizes nine population flows within and between the three great regions of China during four five-year time periods from 1990 to 2010.

The following patterns can be identified by comparing the population migration flows during these four time periods.

There was little inter-provincial population migration between 1985 and 1990. Eastern China was the main destination.

After 1990 the flow of migrants from central and western China to eastern China has grown exponentially. Between 1990 and 1995 the inter-provincial migrating population from central and western China to eastern China totaled 4.72 million: 42.64 percent of the total population migrating among provinces. Between 1995 and 2000 it was 20.17 million (59.32 percent of total inter-provincial migration). Between 2000 and 2005 it was 23.85 million (62.66 percent of total inter-provincial migration), and between 2005 and 2010 it further increased to 33.41 million (60.85 percent of total inter-provincial migration).

Between 1995 and 2000, the population migrating across the eastern provinces reached 6.16 million, in 2000–2005 7.41 million, and in 2010 10.76 million. Among eastern provinces, Beijing, Shanghai, Jiangsu, Zhejiang and Guangdong accounted for most of the total inter-provincial migrants.

Most migrants continue to flow from places of origin in central and western China to destinations in eastern China. In 2010, migrants from central China accounted for 45 percent of total migrants across

Source: Photo by Li Zhang.

Figure 6.2 Floating population in Shanghai station

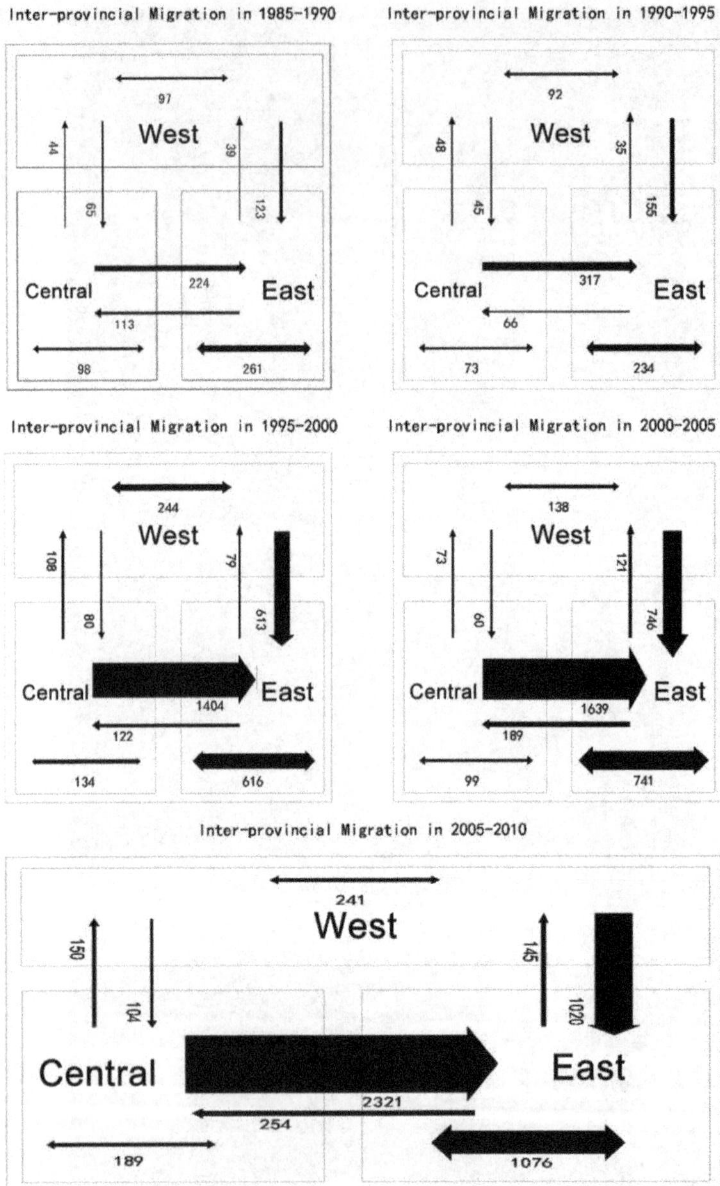

Source: Compiled by Li Zhang from 1990, 2000 and 2010 population censuses.

Figure 6.3 Migration among eastern, central and western China 1985–2010 (10,000s)

*Table 6.3 Immigration and emigration between provinces 1990 to 2010 (*10000)*

Years		1990	2000	2010
Total migrating population between provinces for more than five years		1,107	3,400	5,813
The five provinces with the largest immigrating population	Population	415	2,148	3,787
	Share	37.47%	63.18%	65.14%
The ten provinces with the largest immigrating population	Population	659	2,696	4,586
	Share	59.53%	79.29%	78.89%
The five provinces with the largest origin population	Population	382	1,752	2,562
	Share	34.54%	51.55%	44.07%
The ten provinces with the largest origin population	Population	660	2,540	3,932
	Share	59.62%	74.76%	67.64%

Source: Census data in 1990, 2000 and 2010, compiled by Li Zhang.

the provinces. The central region has had more emigrants than the western region in each of the five-year periods from 1985, as illustrated in Figure 6.3. In the most recent period, from 2005 to 2010, more than twice as many people migrated from central China to eastern China as from western China to eastern China; 23.21 million compared with 10.20 million.

Two patterns stand out. First, five provinces receive a disproportionate share of all immigration in China. Second, the share of all migration the top destination provinces received increased significantly before 2000, but has since been relatively stable (Table 6.3).

The five provinces with the largest inter-provincial immigration accounted for 63.18 percent of the total flowing population in 2000: 25 percent higher than in 1990. The flowing population of the 10 provinces with the largest inter-provincial flowing population accounted for 79.29 percent of the total, almost 20 percent higher than in 1990. The immigrating areas in 2000 were more concentrated than before. However, they have been relatively stable since 2000 without further concentration.

From the perspective of emigration, the population flowing from the five provinces with the largest population outflows accounted for 51.55 percent of total emigration in 2000—an increase of 17 percent from 1990. The population flowing from the 10 provinces with the largest outflows in 2000 accounted for 74.76 percent of total emigration—an increase of 15 percent from 1990. In this period, the origin provinces were mainly in central China. The proportion of migrants from the five provinces with the largest number of immigrants decreased to 44.07 percent in 2010—a reduction of 7 percent from 2000. The proportion of migrants from the 10 provinces with the largest number of migrants also decreased by 7 percent. The origin areas now tend to be scattered. To simplify visualization we selected the 30 largest migration flows to illustrate the main inter-provincial migration flows in China; Figures 6.4 illustrates these flows.

In order to better understand inter-provincial population flows we developed a matrix using 31 provincial level units and analyzed the provinces of origin and destination of people migrating across the provinces for over five years at the census time.[3] To simplify visualization we selected the 30 largest migration flows to illustrate the main inter-provincial migration flows in China (Figure 6.4).

The total inter-provincial migrating population in 1990 was 11.07 million. The population of the 30 largest migration flows was 3.51 million, which accounted for 31.75 percent of total inter-provincial migration. Inter-provincial population migration in this period mainly occurred among the northern provinces: Heilongjiang, Jilin, Liaoning, Hebei, and Shandong. Large migration flows also occurred between Sichuan as the origin area and Xinjiang and Guangdong as the destinations. Overall inter-provincial population flows were scattered.

The total inter-provincial migrating population in 2000 was 34 million. The main areas from which migration originated were Sichuan, Jiangxi, Anhui, Henan, Hubei, and Hunan provinces. The population of the 30 largest migration flows was 17.79 million, 52.33 percent of total inter-provincial migration. Not only did the scale of migration increase significantly in this period, but the destinations became more concentrated. Eleven of the 30 migration flows chose Guangdong as the destination. Other important migration destinations in 2000 were Jiangsu, Shanghai, Zhejiang, Fujian, Beijing, and Xinjiang.

In 2010, the total inter-provincial migrating population was 58.13 million. The main areas where these flows originated were Heilongjiang in the north, Hebei, Henan, Hubei, Jiangxi and Anhui provinces in central China, and Sichuan and Guizhou provinces in western China. The population of the 30 largest migration flows was 28.69 million: 49.36 percent of total inter-provincial migration, a small percentage decrease from 2000. The destinations of population flow in this period continued to be the southeastern coastal provinces. Among the 30 largest migration flows, only one went to central China, to Chongqing—the main interior port city on the Yangtze River. Chongqing was experiencing rapid economic growth

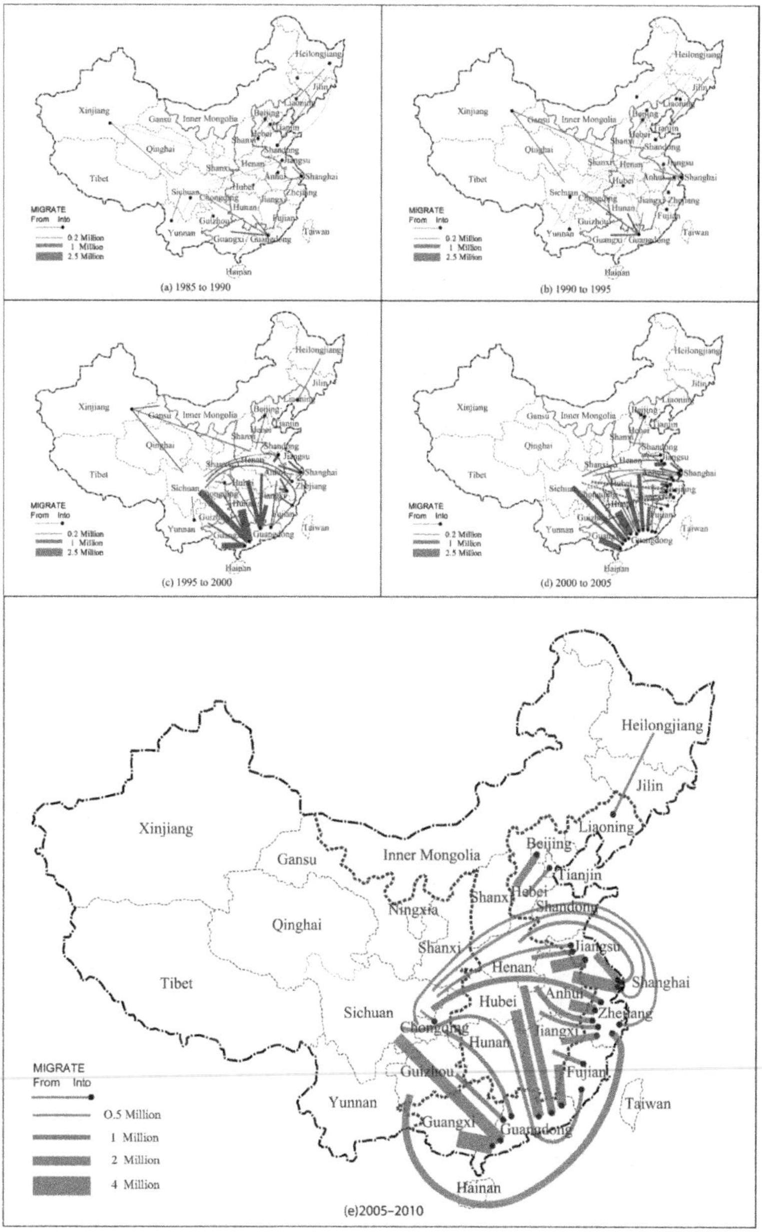

Source: Drawn by Li Zhang from 1990 census data.

Figure 6.4 Thirty largest inter-provincial migration flows 1985–2010 as a result of completion of the Three Gorges Dam and greatly improved navigation on the Yangtze River. Chongqing became an independent provincial level municipality in 1997, separate from Sichuan province, though there is a strong connection between Chongqing and Sichuan. Most of the rest of the population flows in 2000 went to the eastern region, including 26 to Guangdong, Fujian, Zhejiang, Shanghai and Jiangsu.

Our 20-year analysis of inter-provincial migration flows shows that the scale of inter-provincial migration has grown continuously. Destination areas have become more concentrated over time. Origin areas were initially concentrated, but have recently become more scattered. Most absolute and percentage emigration is now from central China. Inter-provincial migration mainly occurs within the southern provinces.

Population Flows Within Provinces

Large as the population flows from one region to another region or from one province to another province have been, migration *within* provinces in China is even larger. The sixth census reported that in 2010 the population migrating within provinces reached 135 million: 61.1 percent of China's total migrating population.

Further deconstructing the composition of migration originating within provinces, between 2000 and 2010 population flows *within* counties (including county-level cities and urban districts) accounted for about the same proportion as the flow *across* counties (including cities and districts). Migration within counties, across counties and going to a destination in a different province each account for approximately a third of total migration originating within provinces.

Between 2000 and 2010, the destinations of population flows across counties (including county-level cities and urban districts) were mainly to provincial capital cities and economically developed cities. Recently there has also been substantial migration to county seats. Population flows within counties (including county-level cities) between 2000 and 2010 were mainly to county seats and cities proper.

Population flows also occurred among rural towns and townships. Xie et al. (2013), using 2010 census data, concluded that in 2010 the migrant population in towns and townships was approximately 105.39 million—an increase of 33.53 million from 2000.

In addition to rural residents living in a village or the countryside flowing into towns proper or moving from one village to another, the most common model we found in our fieldwork was "living in villages and working in towns"—changing the place of employment without changing the place of residence. People living in villages and working in towns are not included as members of the migrating population data in the census.

Effects of Population Flows

Population flows have both positive and negative effects on origin and destination areas. These effects differ based on the region, size of the administrative unit, time period, and many other factors.

Some scholars, particularly in the past, have argued that the effects of globalization on developing countries are negative because transnational capital makes those nations dependent on the global system and developed countries (Armstrong and McGee, 1985; Friedmann, 1986; Massey, 1995). Most scholars today acknowledge these problems, but argue that the net impacts of globalization for developing countries are positive—or they can be depending upon government policy.

The most important impact of globalization is economic. The influx of large numbers of migrants from rural areas where the local economies provide only subsistence farm work or very low wage work provides abundant cheap labor to economically developing areas as members of the rural labor force shift to work in factories, assembly plants, construction, low-skilled service jobs and other unskilled work in cities. This has helped to alleviate urban labor shortages. Relatively low wages have made China competitive in the world economy and accelerated the agglomeration of FDI and enterprises in the eastern region. Migration is a principal reason for China's unprecedented economic success. While China has a disturbingly high Gini coefficient the new wealth has lifted half a billion of its poorest citizens from abject poverty in the space of 30 years, an accomplishment unique in human history.

Despite the urban–rural divide and continuing inequality, China's economic success has also economically benefitted migrants and their household members who remain behind. Migrants generally earn much more than they could earn if they stayed at their official residence address. While migrants' living conditions are often harsh and their standard of living lower than residents with local hukou, they are frequently better off in many respects than they were in the places they migrated from. Even low wageworkers in China are able to remit money to left-behind children, parents, and wives and save money (Figure 6.5).

Migration also causes financial, administrative, and crime problems for destination cities. Large numbers of migrants create financial strain and aggravate management pressure in destination areas. Local administrations need many more personnel to cope with the service demands of new migrants. For example, in 2010 two million of the 4.5 million resident population of

Source: Photo by Li Zhang.

Figure 6.5 Left-behind women doing part-time work in Mingcheng town, Gaoming district, Foshan city

Jiaxing city in Zhejiang province, near Shanghai, were migrants. Jiaxing city had to hire 5,000 additional city employees to manage and service the migrant population. Since most migrants are low wage workers, their direct tax contribution to local financial resources is often less than what services cost. There is no good way to calculate their indirect contribution, and we did not attempt to include it. If migrants' indirect contributions in the form of purchases of goods and services and additional corporate taxes paid as a result of overall increase of the local economy were included, their contribution to local economies would come closer to equaling and in some cases would likely exceed the amount they cost local governments.

As discussed in detail in Chapter 2 on hukou, while migrants were denied education, health, social service, pension, housing, and other social welfare benefits equal to residents with local hukou in the past, in many cities and towns—particularly small cities and towns—they now have benefits similar to or equivalent to residents with permanent residence status, and the gap is closing.

Most researchers agree with the World Bank and Development Reform Commission of China's State Council that hukou and social insurance systems in China that are managed by local governments have restricted population mobility. Our field research and other recent empirical studies suggest that hukou and other institutional obstacles are no longer sufficient to explain the current state of population mobility in China. We conclude that labor market segmentation and market forces—not hukou regulations per se—are the primary drivers of migration. While we generally agree with mainstream proposals for hukou reform and applaud the DRC and World Bank for their thoughtful analysis, we emphasize that China's goal of creating a harmonious society without urban–rural duality needs careful attention to economic and social policy at every level. Eliminating formal hukou restrictions alone will not reduce the dual system for a long time.

Studies have found that migrants commit a disproportionate percentage of crimes and are also disproportionately crime victims, so a large increase in migrants puts pressure on local administrations to expand their police forces. A study by Zhihua Zhu, inspector of the Public Security Bureau of Zhejiang province, Changkang, Zhou, the associate head of the youth crimes research society of Zhejiang province, and Yonggang Sun, their colleague, found that crimes committed by the migrants in the Yangtze River Delta account for approximately 60 percent of total crime cases, and those in townships account for over 80 percent (Zhu et al., 2009). Renmin University professor Yumin Ye surveyed more than 30 cities, including Beijing, Shanghai, Hangzhou, Tianjin, Chengdu, Qingdao, Shenzhen, and Dongguan, examining the ratio of crimes committed by the floating population to all crimes reported in urban criminal cases. Most ratios range between 68 and 88 percent. They were lower in a few small cities. In Chengdu, members of the floating population committed 70 percent of the crimes, and also comprised 70 percent of the victims (Ye and LeGates, 2013). Most crimes are minor, such as petty theft, rather than serious crimes that involve physical injury. Thefts tend to spike just before the New Year holiday, presumably because migrants feel pressed for money to travel home and for gifts for family members to save face.

The population flows from origin areas also have both positive and negative effects. Generally the origin areas have a large population base, a comparatively low urbanization level, and an undeveloped economy. While migrants may be contributing to farm work, working in other low-wage, low-skilled jobs, looking after children, and doing household chores, they are essentially "surplus rural labor" in Arthur O. Lewis' terms (Lewis, 1954). The outflow of population alleviates employment pressure in the origin areas. Migrant workers remittances can promote the development of their rural hometowns (Kleinwechter, 2012). Studies show that most remittance money is spent on physical improvements to houses and greater consumption rather than investment in productive enterprises (Démurger, 2011; Kleinwechter, 2012). Still, more money flowing into poor rural areas stimulates the local economy and has multiplier effects. Thus the migrating population has improved local living standards and contributes to the alleviation of rural poverty in many parts of China.

The massive outflow of rural labor also causes social problems in the origin areas. Perhaps the most severe are the impact on so-called left-behind children and left-behind elders (Biao, 2007; Chang et al., 2011; Mu and van de Walle, 2011; Ye and Lu, 2011; Hu, 2012). While it is hard to quantify economically, the absence of many working-age adults from their families creates more work for seniors and deprives children of the presence of their parents for much of their formative years.

NEW TRENDS AND THEORETICAL FRAMEWORK

New Trends in Population Flows

Since 2010 additional census data on population flows has become available. For the most part the trends described above are continuing.

The total number of Chinese migrants who stayed in places other than their home townships for half a year reached 245 million in 2013—an increase of 16 million over 2011 (NPFPC, 2012, 2014). The number of rural migrants reached 166.10 million—an increase of 7.47 million over 2011 (MHRSS, 2011, 2013). If rural migrants who worked in towns and live in villages are included, the total number of rural migrant workers was 269 million in 2013 (MHRSS, 2013).

Most forecasts project that migration in China will continue to increase. For example, the United Nations predicts that another 300 million Chinese will migrate from rural to urban areas by 2050 (United Nations, 2014). Our view, based both on our macro-level structural analysis of recent data and field research on the individual choices driving migrants' behavior, is that the total number will be lower than projections by the United Nations, World Bank and the State Council's Development Research Commission.

Population flows are the outcome of the spontaneous choices of hundreds of millions of families pursuing their best interests, as they perceive them, under China's existing institutional framework and conditions. This intrinsic economic rationality has greatly contributed to the overall economic development of regions and the nation. However, it also produces negative social effects, such as left-behind children, left-behind elders, left-behind wives, empty nesters, marital separation, vacant or nearly vacant hollow core villages in origin areas, and overcrowding, congestion, and urban crime in destination cities (Figure 6.6). Chinese policy documents often use a medical metaphor, referring to China's current urbanization pattern as "unhealthy" and policy statements, including China's 2014 National New-style Urbanization Plan, state a policy goal of moving towards "healthy" urbanization.

Theoretical Framework

Based on our literature review, observations, interviews and surveys of a stratified random sample of Chinese directly experiencing the complex forces at play as globalization impacts modern China described in Chapters 1 and 5, we conclude that western theory contributes to understanding why people migrate, but does not adequately address the unique conditions in China where members of a household unit decide location preferences of household members.

British–German geographer Ernst-George Ravenstein (1834–1913) published two classic articles with the same title in 1885 and 1889, "The Laws of Population Migration," which are among the most influential in the field of population migration and posit seven laws of population migration (Ravenstein, 1885, 1889).

University of Chicago demographer Donald Bogue, a former president of the Population Association of America (PAA) and the founder of PAA's journal *Demography*, based his classic study of the mechanism of population migration on Ravenstein's laws (Bogue and Hagood, 1953). This study argued that the cause of population flows and immigrants' relocation in market economies that permit the free flow of population is determined by peoples' individual desires to improve their living conditions. People leave their places of origin because of unfavorable local economic and social conditions and move to destinations with actual or perceived better conditions to improve their livelihood. The two factors—conditions in their origin location and conditions in their destination jointly determine individuals' migration choices (Bogue and Hagood, 1953).

In the 1960s, building on Ravenstein and Bogue's theories, University of Georgia demographer Everett S. Lee (1966) argued that both source and destination regions exert both push and pull forces. Lee added a third set of factors that mainly include distance, physical barriers, language and culture differences and the value judgment of migrants of these factors.

The above theoretical studies on population migration mechanisms have been enormously influential and the considerations they raise are relevant to China. However, they are dated and were not based on (indeed did not

Note: The left is a rural discarded house in Ju county, Shandong province in 2013.The right is a rural luxury five storey house, owned by one household, without occupants in Quzhou city, Zhejiang province in 2014.

Source: Photo by Li Zhang.

Figure 6.6 Rural discarded house and luxury five storey house even consider) conditions in China. China is a special case and the classic models only partly explain migration dynamics in China. Two factors in contemporary China exert particularly powerful influences on migration: the hukou system and the Chinese tradition of household rather than individual decision-making.

Chinese scholars such as Tsinghua University professor Qiang Li (2003) argue that China's push–pull migration model is significantly different from other countries, because of the obstacles posed by the hukou system.

Ulrich Kleinwechter, a research scholar at the International Institute for Applied Systems Analysis has developed a series of models of China's migration processes that describe different positive and negative impacts of migration on origin and destination areas theoretically (Kleinwechter, 2012). Kleinwechter has incorporated the effects of hukou and household decision-making into his models. Kleinwechter argues that Chinese individuals' decisions to migrate are strongly influenced by three main things: work, life, and preparation/arrival considerations. Their expectation is that work will be better at the destination—that the earnings of one or more household members who migrate will be sufficiently higher to justify the move from the point of view of the household and that living conditions at the destination will be at least acceptable in the short term. Kleinwechter's diagrams illustrate both positive and negative impacts on both areas where migration originates and its destination. Some of the effects are easy-to-identify first order effects, such as migration providing cheap labor to destination areas (positive) or draining the labor force necessary to continue farming in rural areas (negative). But many of the effects are derivative and more complex. For example farm laborers' income in origin areas should rise as the supply of able-bodied farm workers decreases because of the law of supply and demand.

Before they migrate, migrants conduct a job search to identify a specific job or a destination with many job opportunities. They often do an additional job search on arrival at a potential destination. The decision whether or not to migrate and where to go is affected by migrants' calculations about how difficult leaving their residence will be and how complicated logistics will be where they arrive as well as the perceived advantages of being in a new location. The former may include considerations such as how their departure will affect other members of their household (wives, husbands, parents and/or children) who need care, how farmland to which they have use rights may be used to generate food and income without their labor, how health, education, welfare, pension and other entitlements where they live will be affected and what benefits, if any, they can expect where they go.

On arrival migrants face logistical questions that affect migrants everywhere—where to live, how to get to work, prospects of being caught and the consequences if they work illegally, how to cover expenses until they are paid. They also face other questions unique to China such as how complex registering with the local security bureau will be, whether local authorities are likely to destroy informal settlements that provide them inexpensive housing close to jobs, and whether or not accompanying children will be allowed to attend local schools even if they are not legally supposed to. Finally potential migrants assess what life in the destination will be like: their access to public services, housing, and security and what prospects are for mobility—moving from a less good initial job to a better one or climbing a career ladder from working on a production line in a factory to a clerical job, to low levels of management and perhaps on up the hierarchy of a business and eventually starting their own business in the city or back home.

Kleinwechter's analysis contributes important theoretical insights about migrants' decisions to migrate, but empirical evidence is necessary to understand variations and the way in which recent changes are affecting these decisions.

Based on two years of observation in Dongguan and other cities in the Pearl River Delta, Chinese–American journalist Leslie Chang found that "factory girls" who had migrated from rural areas to work in manufacturing and assembly work frequently changed jobs and were often upwardly mobile—quickly moving from the lowest paid jobs in factories with the worst working conditions to better jobs at higher wages (Chang, 2009). Almost none wanted to return home to their place of origin.

Our analysis of recent macro-level data, field observations, interviews and surveys provides empirical evidence for a nuanced understanding. In order to understand how actual and potential migrants and those who stayed behind made their decisions, particularly important are our surveys conducted in villages and towns in Huaiyuan county in Anhui province, Haimen city in Jiangsu province, and emigration from rural areas and urban streets in Gaoming district in Guangdong and Shanghai described in Chapter 1. One important purpose of this research was to find out more about characteristics of the migrant population, their source and destination areas, and the reasons why some family members chose to migrate.

The following sections describe our findings regarding the factors influencing population flows and new trends based both on macro-level structural analysis and survey research on individual and household choices.

FACTORS RELATED TO THE ORIGIN REGIONS

Employment Elasticity Coefficients

At the macro-level we relied on longitudinal analysis of employment elasticity coefficients as a useful measure of the relationship between increases in employment and increases in GDP. An employment elasticity coefficient is the ratio of an increase of employment to the corresponding increase in GDP, that is, the percentage points that employment increases for every percentage point GDP increases. A higher coefficient indicates a stronger ability to accommodate the labor force, and a lower coefficient indicates a weaker ability. At times and locations where the coefficients are high migration is likely to occur because the economy can absorb labor. In China's increasingly connected information network potential migrants learn where jobs are abundant and wages are comparatively high.

Changing employment elasticity coefficients in Guangdong, Zhejiang, and Jiangsu provinces provide important insights about China's changing economy and employment. From 1995 to 2005, the coefficients rose, but began to decline after 2005. This suggests that the pattern of employment increase generated by unit GDP growth that has existed in provinces with high population inflows is weakening. The result reflects the weakening ability of these provinces to create jobs (Figure 6.7).

High Living Costs in Migrant Destinations

Housing costs account for a significant proportion of migrants living costs and add greatly to their difficulty in settling in cities. Most migrants are renters; so comparing rents in regions where migration originates and ends is one indicator of how housing costs deter migration.

Reliable longitudinal rent data in China is not available. Indices of the price of existing or newly constructed housing provide a rough proxy. The best index of Chinese housing prices is produced jointly by the Peking University—Lincoln Institute for Urban Development and Land Policy Research Center (LC) and the Tsinghua University Hang Lung Real Estate Research Center (HLRERC) based on the methodology developed by American economists Karl Case and Robert Schiller for the Case-Schiller index—the leading US residential real estate price index. The LC and HLRERC publish a Quality-Controlled Housing Price Index (CQCHPI) with longitudinal data on housing prices in the downtown area of eight cities: Beijing, Shanghai, Tianjin, Shenzhen, Chengdu, Dalian, Wuhan and Xi'an. The data available as this book went to press show changes in new housing prices for Beijing, Shanghai, Tianjin and Shenzhen from

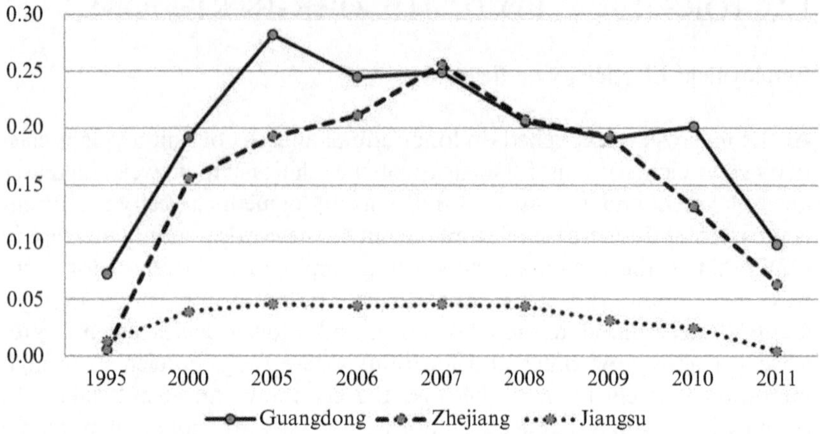

Source: Compiled by Li Zhang from the *Guangdong Statistical Yearbook 2012*, *Zhejiang Statistical Yearbook 2012* and *Jiangsu Statistical Yearbook 2012*.

Figure 6.7 Employment elasticity indices in three labor-gaining provinces, 1995 to 2011

the first quarter of 2009 through the third quarter of 2014. The average annual housing price increase in the downtown area of these four cities was 17.78 percent during this five-year and nine-month period.

The LC-HLRER housing price data gives some indication of the enormous magnitude of housing price increases in urban China, but since most migrants are renters and housing markets are segmented, an even better way to understand urban rental housing prices and their impacts on migrant behavior is by asking migrants themselves about the rental housing prices they pay, their ability to afford rental or owned housing, and how housing prices impact their decisions about whether or not to migrate initially and then whether to stay in the urban area, move to a different urban area or reverse migrate (Chen et al., 2011).

In our interviews we found that very low-income migrants often choose substandard and crowded very low cost housing in villages, buildings that will be torn down at construction sites, crowded company dormitory housing where a dozen or more may share the same room, or poorly constructed new migrant housing in peri-urban areas in order to use savings and earnings for other necessities and for remittances to their families. Following are findings from our field research that help in understanding the relationship between housing costs and migration.

The major destinations for China's migrant population are concentrated in Jiangsu, Zhejiang, and Guangdong provinces, and China's four provincial-level cities. Migrants to these areas are generally in large metropolises within these provinces, where living costs are relatively high. For example, in Shanghai, Beijing, Shenzhen, Xiamen, and Guangzhou the average housing price in May 2015 exceeded US\$3,000/m^2, and was as high as to US\$5,776/m^2 in Beijing (City House, 2015). The average housing price in capital cities of the major source regions of the migrant population (Henan, Hubei, Jiangxi and Anhui provinces) is below US\$1,500/m^2 (City House, 2015). Moreover, the homes of most migrant workers in the provinces where most migration originates are located in the countryside, where housing costs are far below the average for the entire city-region. Our research group found that housing prices in rural towns in Hubei, Anhui, and Henan provinces were generally between US\$300 and US\$500/m^2 or even lower. National Population and Family Planning Committee data show that the average rent for migrants with rural hukou living and working in cities was 237 RMB/month/person in 2011, but it varied in different cities, towns and provinces (NPFPC, 2012: 40). The monthly rent for a 50m^2 one-bedroom apartment in Shanghai in 2011 was generally above 1,000 RMB, but rent for the same type of apartment in capital cities of the provinces with high population outflow rates was no more than 500 RMB in the same year. The rent is much lower in other cities and county seats of those provinces. Rental houses in suburban villages and towns near large cities is often an even cheaper housing option, but many of these units are substandard—physically deteriorated, lacking indoor plumbing, and with shared kitchens. Many migrant workers (and their families, if present) are economically forced to live in these settlements, frequently in crowded conditions with several related or unrelated people per room. One 100m^2 apartment can be divided into 10 or more tiny rooms to rent. This congests elevators, breaks plumbing, creates noise at night and creates many other problems. Respondents to our surveys and people living in housing like this that we interviewed made it clear that they were unhappy with their housing situation.

Over 60 percent of the respondents to our 2014 survey of 109 migrant workers in Gaoming district, Foshan city, responded to a multiple choice question asking them to identify the biggest obstacle(s) to settling in Foshan urban area in the future said that housing is a primary factor.

First Generation Migrant Workers and Reverse Migration

The first great wave of rural Chinese migration to cities occurred in the 1980s. The majority of these early migrants were young—generally in their 20s. Thus, the present age of the earliest wave of migrant workers is now

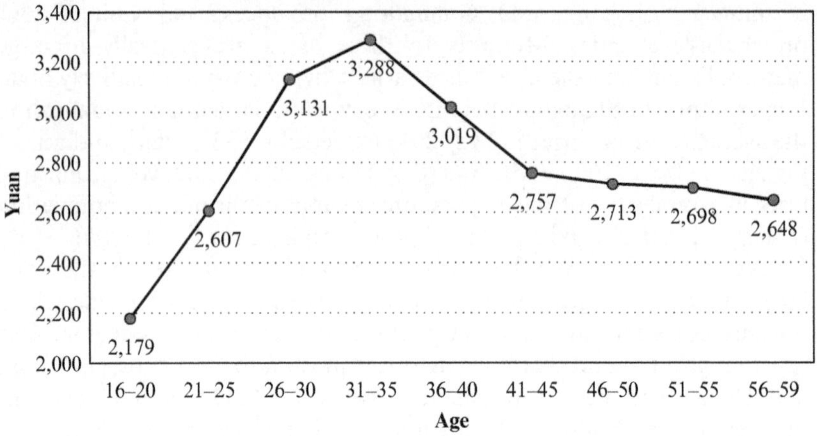

Source: NPFPC (2013).

Figure 6.8 Salary of rural migrant workers in different age groups, 2012 (RMB)

between 50 and 60 years old. Many first generation migrants had only a primary school education or less and have had little or no additional education or training, so they are poorly prepared for jobs that require even modest education.

More than 80 percent of China's migrant population works in manufacturing, (35.2 percent) wholesale and retail industries (18.8 percent), hotel and catering industries (10.6 percent), social services (8.7 percent), and construction (7.5 percent) (PRC-NPFPC, 2013). These industries are labor-intensive, and employers favor young and middle-aged workers. Construction is physically demanding and employers prefer young, able-bodied males for this work. Figure 6.8 shows that the wages of migrant workers increase with age until they turn 35 (probably because of their growing work experience). However, beyond the age of 35 their wages drop (probably because of their decreasing work efficiency). Only 16.9 percent of migrant workers older than 50 have received non-agricultural skills training—the smallest proportion of any age group (PRC-NPFPC, 2013). This combination of age disadvantages and low skills makes it increasingly difficult for upper-middle-aged migrant workers to retain their work or find new employment if they lose a current job. The employment competitiveness of this group of migrant workers further declines as age increases. Therefore, quite a few older migrant workers choose to exit the urban labor market after reaching middle age. This reduces the supply of low-end urban laborers. Many members of this cohort return to their hometowns to farm contracted land, work in local factories, help with household chores, look after children or elderly parents, work as both part-time farmer and worker, or retire altogether.

FACTORS RELATED TO ORIGIN REGIONS

Increasing Employment Opportunities in the Interior

Since migrants weigh the pros and cons of living in different regions, conditions in origin regions have a large impact on reverse migrations as well as initial migration. Conditions in origin regions are generally improving.

From 2008 to 2012 GDP in provinces with large population outflows (Henan, Jiangxi, Anhui, Sichuan, Hunan, and Hubei) experienced annual GDP increases much higher than the national average (Figure 6.9). The high rate of economic growth was primarily a result of the rapid development of industries in central and western China. In addition to their abundant low-skilled labor, heavy investment in transportation and other infrastructure and national level subsidies as a result of the "Develop the West" and "Central China Rising" campaigns made these provinces increasingly competitive. Many labor-intensive industries that were once concentrated in eastern China have moved to the central and eastern regions. A number of

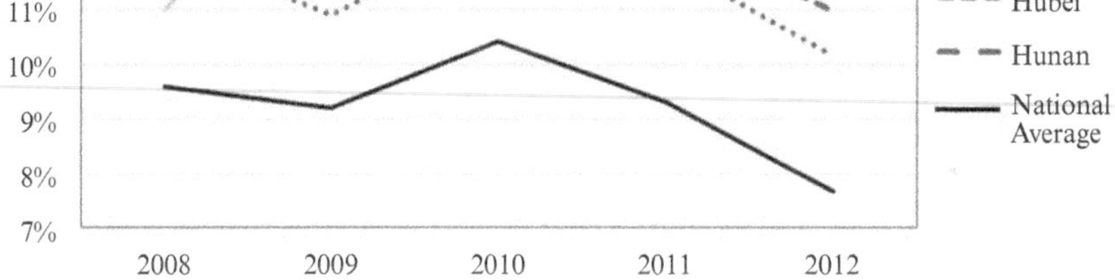

Source: *China Statistical Yearbook* (NBSC-csy, 2013).

Figure 6.9 GDP increases, selected provinces with high emigration from 2008 to 2012

high-tech enterprises have also moved to inland regions because of the relatively low land and labor costs, increasingly better educated local workforce, improving infrastructure, improved quality of life, government subsidies and other advantages and many more are planning to move. A combination of favorable economic factors and governmental policies have enabled the regions of population outflow to generate more employment opportunities. Prospects are good that these trends will continue.

China's Shrinking Surplus Rural Labor Supply

Difficulties in recruiting low-skilled labor, not only in eastern China, but also in high-labor-demand areas of central and western China in recent years suggest that the surplus rural labor force is changing from the status of an unlimited supply to a limited supply and that problems regarding demand and supply are emerging (Chan, 2009a).

According to China's Sixth Census in 2010, there were 990 million members of China's working-age population within the age bracket of 15 to 64 (NBSC-census, 2012). The United Nations has calculated that China's working-age population will peak in 2015 at 1.015 billion and then decline annually to around 986 million in 2030 (United Nations, 2012). According to the sixth census, the average age of the people now migrating to cities is 31 (NBSC-census, 2012). This is eight years older than it was in 1982 when the average age of migrants was 23 (Duan et al., 2008). As earlier migrants age, and new migrants are significantly older, the number of able-bodied young workers is shrinking. Based on the Tongji research team's surveys, most available rural young and middle-aged members of the labor force have already migrated to cities as migrant workers, given current conditions in China's agricultural sector. Unless agricultural efficiency is improved, the future supply of surplus rural labor will be limited, but if farming becomes much more efficient this will continue to release surplus rural labor. Agricultural modernization that increases lot sizes, uses high yield scientific farming methods, and employs modern technology could release many more rural agricultural laborers.

As described in Chapter 8 on towns, villages, and rural urbanization, hollow core villages are very common in Chinese rural areas where many people have emigrated (Liu et al., 2010). In these villages many houses are abandoned and the remaining population consists mostly of the elderly, left-behind children, and wives. The population structure in many parts of China's rural areas is changing into an inverted pyramid structure—top-heavy with elderly people and with a narrowing base. In our Haimen city survey, over 30 percent of the permanent residents of the villages surveyed were over 65 years old.

Emerging Advantages of Rural Hukou

Under China's existing urban–rural dual system, rural hukou is directly linked to a number of benefits including rights to receive a contract to use arable land, residential homestead land for a house and related buildings, a share of rural agricultural cooperative dividends (including proceeds if the land is requisitioned) and more permissive family planning policies.

This interest pattern is well established. Even the central government's newly introduced unified hukou system that removes the difference in registration between agricultural and non-agricultural hukou (PRC, 2014) will not change the reality. In the past decades and still today, China's social welfare system is based on the hukou types. Some scholars feel that after urban and rural hukou are unified into a single registration system without discrimination against rural people, social injustice will eventually disappear. While this may be true in the very long run, our research suggests that even when all hukou distinctions are completely abolished it will take a long time for migrant workers to be fully integrated into urban society and for barriers to migration to disappear entirely.

On the other hand, rural residents' land rights interests can be valuable in several ways. While arable land is owned by rural collectives, farmers enjoy long-term contracted use rights to specific parcels that they can farm or rent. Typically these contracts remain unchanged for 30 years, and may be renewed indefinitely so long as the individual has not left the rural collective unit. Generally, as long as a migrant worker whose hukou has not changed after relocation fulfills his obligations according to the land contract agreement, his contract rights will be legally protected. In addition to obtaining food for their own household, land for a house, and income from farming, rural hukou may bring other benefits if the land is rented, developed, or requisitioned. Depending on the location and quality of land, these rights can be quite valuable.

Many villages develop collectively owned residential or commercial land for factories, housing, rural tourism, or other income-generating uses. Residents may receive cash from the profits of the collective business (similar to a stock dividend) or be able to enjoy a collectively owned asset such as a village hall.

Residents of rural villages engulfed by cities so that they are urban villages (*chengzhongcun*) (literally "village in city") often become rentiers (people living from rents)—able to live very well just on rental income.

Residents of strategically valuable land who bargain successfully may receive generous compensation when their land is requisitioned. For example an investigation in Shanghai found that in one *chengzhongcun* each household had 6.7 rooms to rent and the average rental income was

2,798 RMB/month: one-third of the household's total income per month. The average room size of each tenant in the housing rented was only 4.7m^2—a quarter of the average living room size of Shanghainese (Wang et al., 2012).

According to surveys by China's National Population and Family Planning Committee, about 60 percent of the migrant population with rural hukou say they are unwilling to exchange their rural hukou status for non-agricultural hukou (NPFPC, 2013). Among the 40 percent who said they would be willing, 35 percent said they are reluctant to abandon their right to contracted land. Thirty-four percent of those unwilling say they would choose to keep their rural hukou due to their wish to retain their land (ibid).

These findings contrast with the prevailing opinion of most scholars that hukou is the major barrier which has made it difficult for rural people to become permanent fully fledged urban citizens with urban hukou. While this may have been true in the past, it is no longer the case today.

DOMESTIC FACTORS DRIVING POPULATION FLOWS IN THE NEW ERA

Formal Migration: Market-oriented Economic Factors Surpass Social Factors

In addition to the macro-level structural forces discussed in Chapter 5 on globalization and urbanization, changing domestic conditions are affecting population flows in China. Population mobility across China has been rising over the years, and institutionalized controls of formal migration where a change of hukou status occurs are also changing. Marriage-related migration accounted for 28 percent of all formal migration in 1987. This ratio dropped to 5 percent in 2010. The proportion of formal migration for business reasons increased from 9 percent to 45 percent (Table 6.4).

Taking up business, job transfers, and official employment and enrollment are classified as economic reasons, and schooling, marriage-related migration, accompanying family members, looking for relatives and friends, relocation, and retirement are classified as social reasons. The main reasons for migration in the 1980s were for social reasons (64 percent). After 1990, economic reasons gradually replaced social reasons. The proportion of migration attributed to economic reasons rose to 49 percent in 2010, while the proportion for social reasons decreased to 44 percent, so currently economic reasons are the most important mechanism motivating formal migration.

Table 6.4 Main reasons for migration 1987, 1990, 2000, and 2010

		1987	1990	2000	2010
Total		100%	100%	100%	100%
Business		9%	25%	30%	45%
Job transfers		13%	12%	4%	4%
Official employment by government and state-owned companies and the enrollment in colleges or universities		6%	6%	3%	–
Study		8%	12%	12%	12%
Marriage		28%	14%	12%	5%
Accompanying family members		16%	10%	13%	14%
Looking for relatives and friends		10%	10%	5%	4%
Relocation		–	–	15%	9%
Retirement		2%	2%	–	–
Others		8%	9%	6%	7%
Total		100	100%	100%	100%
Economic reasons	Administrative factors	19%	18%	7%	4%
	Market factors	9%	25%	31%	45%
Social reasons		64%	48%	56%	44%
Other		8%	9%	6%	7%

Note: Figures rounded to nearest 1%.

Source: Census data in 1990, 2000, 2010; 1% Sample Census data in 1987. Compiled by Li Zhang.

If the economic reasons for migrating are further divided into market factors (taking up business) and administrative factors (job transfers and official employment and enrollment), then administrative factors in the 1980s accounted for 19 percent and market factors accounted for only 9 percent. By the 1990, the administrative factors weakened slightly, but market factors rose to 25 percent. After 2000, administrative factors decreased to 4 percent and market factors increased to 31 percent. In 2010, market factors continued to increase to 45 percent, exceeding that of social factors and becoming the primary reason for migration (Table 6.4).

Family Considerations Surpass Individual Economic Rationality

While income disparities and consumption differences between urban regions and rural areas drive migration, decisions about migration in

China are strongly influenced by family considerations (Zhu, 2003b, 2007). Thus, we propose that micro-level analysis should shift from analysis of each individual "economic man" to household units—the "economic family" (Zhao and Chen, 2013). Chinese households seek to maximize total family income and the total assets of the family and decisions about which individual household members should perform which economic and non-economic role where are usually made by the family unit.

Our surveys and interviews with rural migrant workers confirm that able-bodied male and some female labor force participants working in urban areas earn much more income than in rural areas. Less able-bodied men and women left behind in rural areas can farm on land the household has use rights to, take care of the elderly and children, and may find jobs in nearby towns, which help reduce housing expenses men would have to pay in urban areas if they were accompanied by their wives and children. The pressure to purchase property in a city does not exist if migrant workers do not intend to settle in the city permanently. This is usually the most efficient family labor allocation arrangement and the most economical pattern of family consumption. However, members of the household have to endure the negative aspects of living separately.

Our survey of Gaoming district, Foshan city, found that 68 percent of migrant workers surveyed migrated alone. More than half (54 percent) said they would choose to return home eventually. The main factors influencing their decision to return home were caring for the elderly (51.8 percent), followed by housing prices in the city (43.5 percent).

The phenomenon involving a large number of people leaving their hometown has disrupted traditional household structures and the entire composition of villages in rural areas including: the separation of husbands and wives when the husband migrates and the wife remains or husband and wife migrate to different places (Chang et al., 2011), left-behind children when both their father and mother migrate (Hu, 2012), left-behind elderly (Chang et al., 2011), and other strains on families. As the young labor force in rural areas goes out to work, the traditional mode of young adults caring for their elders is on the verge of collapse. Data from the Ministry of Civil Affairs shows that in 2012 over 50 percent of the population in urban and rural areas of China were empty nesters. About 50 million elderly people have been left behind in rural areas without even one immediate family member to look after them—more than 40 percent of the rural elderly population (China News Web, 2013). One recent study concluded that elderly household members in need of support is a main reason migrant workers return to their hometowns in rural areas and counties and decreases the probability that migrant workers will stay in cities by 7.3 percent (Li and Long, 2009). The Confucian cultural norm of while parents are still living at home children should not move far away still plays a role in China, but it is weakening as many households are compelled by economics to make choices that they would not otherwise make.

Li and Long's study (2009) also found that the probability of married migrant workers choosing "Be more willing to go home," "Do not know," and "Be more willing to return to the county towns or small towns in their old homes in the long run" are 10 percent, 3.4 percent, and 0.5 percent higher than for unmarried migrant workers. The probability of married migrant workers choosing "Be willing to give up contracted lands to become urban residents" is 14 percent lower than unmarried migrant workers.

Our research group's interviews in Huaiyuan county are consistent with the findings reported above. The most common stated goal of the population migrating to work in a city is to save money for housing and other consumption when they go back home in the future so they can take care of the elderly parents or children and pursue a higher quality of life. The willingness of migrant workers to stay in cities is reduced because of their considerations for the elderly as well as their whole family.

The Impact of Education, Information, and Young People's Values on Migration

The impact of globalization and urbanization has penetrated China's vast rural areas because of modern media and information technology as well as face-to-face interactions between rural residents and city dwellers. Large numbers of rural youth born in the 1980s and 1990s—well informed about life in China's cities through media and information flowing from friends and family members who have migrated—aspire to live in cities and no longer want to do farm work. Their level of education is much higher than the level attained by migrant workers born in the 1950s, 1960s and 1970s. Comparison of data from the Fifth and Sixth Censuses shows that in 2010, the education level of the rural population aged 20 to 39 years was much higher than the education level of the same age cohort in 2000 (NBSC-census, 2002; NBSC-census, 2012). The younger the age, the higher the level of education received. More than a quarter of all youth aged 20 to 24 years now have high school degrees or above—double the percentage in 2000. Post-secondary education in two and four-year college courses and other forms of education and training is also growing very rapidly in China (Bradsher, 2013). China is investing more than 3.8 percent of its GDP—$355 billion in 2013—in human capital every year (NBSC-csy, 2014). Education spending by local, provincial, and national governments more than quintupled between 2001 and 2011 and the number of college degrees awarded grew from under two million to nearly eight million between 2000 and 2010 (ibid). *The New York Times* summarizes: "Just as the United States helped build a white-collar middle class in the late 1940s and early 1950s by using the G.I. Bill to help educate millions of World War II veterans, the Chinese government is using large subsidies to educate tens of millions of young people as they move from farms to cities" (ibid).

Chuanjiang Liu (2010), a professor at Wuhan University has studied the difference between first generation migrant workers (born before 1980) and the second generation migrant workers (born after 1980), based on a sample of 1,100 migrant workers in Wuhan city. Liu concludes that second generation urban migrant workers have different characteristics than first generation migrants. The former have less agricultural ability, but better education, stronger personal values, better adaptability, value urban life more and have stronger intentions to live long term in cities.

Both migrant workers born before 1980 and after 1980 migrate to cities for an urban job with a better income than that in rural areas. The first generation usually considered this a temporary move, did not see much connection between the move and their personal development, and aspired to return to their places of origin and resume the lifestyle to which they were accustomed. In contrast, most second generation migrant workers want to change their lives and consider migrating into cities the best path towards a new and better life (Figure 6.10). In the eyes of the first generation of migrant workers, migrating to work was similar to traditional farmers taking sideline jobs, but would last for a longer time and the work places could be further away (Yuan et al., 2009). For the current generation of young people it is a leap to the beginning of a new way of life.

Our field interviews confirmed that the new generation of young people in rural areas prefers to live and work in cities. They go to the city not merely to earn more money or because there is not sufficient agricultural land or non-agricultural employment opportunities in rural areas. Aware of the excitement and many recreational, cultural, economic, marital and other opportunities available in cities they yearn to experience city life and grow personally from the urban environment.

Based on our review of the macro-level data and information from our fieldwork, we predict that for at least the next twenty years China's urbanization process will continue to be boosted by high social mobility and an abundant human resource base. Young people will continue to migrate from rural areas and increasing agricultural productivity will create new human capital resources for cities.

Note: The woman in the top left is an illegal street peddler in a suburb of Shuyang county in Jiangsu province. The young men in the top right and bottom left are migrant labors at the Shanghai Hongqiao train station. The old women in the bottom right are from rural areas cutting trees on a street in Shuyang county.

Source: Photo by Li Zhang.

Figure 6.10 Flowing population in cities and towns, May 2015

The Quality of Public Services and Migration Decisions

The urban–rural dual system in China leads to obvious differences between urban and rural public services such as public transportation, water, electricity and other infrastructure, basic education, medical care, and pensions. Studies show that migration has both negative effects and positive effects on the education of the left-behind children, but the negative effects dominate (Ye, 2011; Hu, 2012). Remittances to the rural family can improve the living conditions of the family (Hu, 2012), but the lack of family care during children's growing stages may be harmful. When making migration decisions, children's education and access to other public services have become increasingly important. Our survey respondents reported that "getting better education resources" has become an important consideration, even the most important consideration in some cases, for parents migrating to urban areas.

In our survey of Gaoming district of Foshan city, 28 percent of the residents chose "children's education" as the primary factor that would determine their decision to migrate. Among them, respondents with rural hukou were more concerned with their children's education, than respondents with urban hukou. Thirty-two percent of them gave education as their primary reason for their location preference, higher than people with urban hukou.

At its current development stage, cities in China still need a large number of migrants to work in low-end and low-paid industries, assembly work, and in other low-paying jobs. The low-skilled and low-paid nature of the industries determines the low cost and low quality of the living environment for these workers and contributes to the formation of migrant population communities on the outskirts of cities and urban villages within cities (*chengzhongcun*). The migrant population with low incomes living in these communities is an indispensable force for city development in the short term. Therefore, attention should be paid to the improvement of municipal facilities and public services for these communities (Gransow, 2012). The urbanization process can be smoother and the quality of life of migrants improved if this part of the population is integrated into the urban society.

Traditional Culture, Nostalgia, and Reverse Population Flows

Many first generation migrant workers spent their childhood and adolescence entirely in the countryside. They did not leave the village to make a living until their early adulthood. They were socialized in rural areas, and they defined their world with rural areas as the reference. The strong sense of belonging to what urban sociologists and anthropologists term "folk" or "gemeinschaft" societies (Redfield, 1954; Tönnies, [1887]2002) where residents know everyone in a small community and are bound together by shared culture and kinship ties, and relationships are informal is totally different from urban "gesellschaft" city life without familiar folk culture, most people are strangers, and interactions transient and based on formal legal relationships (Simmel, [1903]1950; Wirth 1938; Tönnies, [1887]2002). Many migrants never fully acculturate or feel comfortable in the strange environment in the cities to which they migrate.

Questions we asked rural residents in our surveys in Huaiyuan county in Anhui province about their opinion of the ideal place to live found that with increasing age the percentage of rural respondents who said they want to live in rural areas tended to increase and the number of respondents who said they want to live in cities decreases. The proportion of respondents aged 40 to 50 years old, 50 to 60 years old, and over 60 years old who said they are willing to live in rural areas were 33.78 percent, 39.47 percent, and 46.67 percent, respectively. This result reflects the attachment to rural life among the first generation migrant workers. Thus, we found that attachment to rural life greatly affects the settlement choice of elderly migrant workers.

Another recent study found that the proportion of the migrant workers born before 1980 who are willing to return to their hometown is 8 percent higher than that of migrant workers born after 1980 (Li and Long, 2009). This is consistent with studies of migrants in other countries. A classic study of European, Puerto Rican and African-American migrants to New York City by Nathan Glazer and Daniel Patrick Moynihan found that while they often had nostalgia and positive images of life in their rural communities of origin (or in the case of African-Americans to the rural southern United States), they tended to forget the negative aspects and downplay the disadvantages of rural life (Glazer and Moynihan, 1970). When faced with an actual decision to move back to their countries of origin and the realities of what they would lose and gain by reverse migration, migration appears much less attractive and many fewer East European Jews, Puerto Ricans, Italians, Irish and Blacks from the rural south of the US actually move back than say they intend to. While both survey research on what elderly people say about where they would like to live and data on actual reverse migration is useful, the latter are more valid measures than the former.

Recent research shows that a substantial number of Chinese migrant workers say they intend to return to their hometown (Kleinwechter, 2012), where the possibility of adapting to life is higher (Hu et al., 2011). Many migrant workers who have accumulated work experience and savings in a city prefer self-employment after returning to the hometowns. Their entrepreneurship may not only provide employment for themselves, but may create new jobs, which can promote rural development and reduce wealth disparities between urban and rural areas (Démurger, 2011; Kleinwechter, 2012).

According to our observations, the gap between urban and rural public services in some regions is shrinking as national policy has already begun to tilt toward the rural areas and pay attention to rural facilities construction. Increased numbers of rural people who migrated to cities are returning to the countryside and towns where they came from and this trend is likely to accelerate in the future.

SUMMARY

The large-scale movement of population greatly impacts both origin and destination regions. Population flows contribute to providing a labor force to the destinations and promote the development of local economies. However, the arrival of large numbers of migrants greatly challenges local governance, finance, administration, and infrastructure.

Population flows relieve the employment burden on the source regions in two ways—through remittances from migrants back to the source region and through increasing wages for the remaining labor force that does not migrate due to the laws of supply and demand. As fewer prime workers compete for jobs in regions that are exporting labor, wages for remaining prime workers are bid up. And as there are not enough prime workers, jobs become available to workers who might not otherwise be employed, thus alleviating poverty.

Population flows in China continue to change. The migrant population is more likely now to choose to return to their hometown (not necessarily rural areas) because of more industrial investment in regions where migration originates, high housing prices in destinations, and aging of the earliest waves of migrant workers, making them less able to compete with younger workers and more likely to reverse migrate. The economies of some source regions are developing more rapidly than before, which creates more job opportunities. By contrast, rural areas still lack a young labor force. As the benefits of rural hukou improve, some young workers are remaining and some migrant workers are choosing to return to their hometowns.

In terms of why formal sector migrants chose to migrate, economic factors now outweigh social factors. Economic considerations are usually based on the welfare of an entire household rather than individuals' self-interest. The decisions of new generation migrant workers about where to live goes beyond considerations of individual economic rationality. Other factors, such as improving public service quality in rural areas and Chinese traditional Confucian culture affect rural residents' decision-making about which family members, if any, should migrate and where. The decisions made by tens of millions of households in the context of globalization and institutional constraints shape the overall landscape of China's social mobility. Compared with other developed countries, the distinguishing feature of China's social mobility is the current scale of the rural population flows to cities, which is increasingly driven by household choices and pursuit of individual values.

China's newly published National New-style Urbanization Plan (2014) specifies the policy orientations of "cultivating large city clusters in central and west China, enhancing the radial effect of key cities, and accelerating the development of small and medium-sized cities." Recent "Instructions of the State Council on Furthering Reform of the Hukou System" (PRC-MSC, 2014) loosen the policy on change of hukou status for migrants: "fully lifting the constraints on hukou relocation in official towns and small cities," "gradually lifting the constraints on hukou relocation in medium-sized cities," and "strictly controlling the population scale of large metropolitan regions." Owing to the rapid economic and social development in central and west China, national policy has shifted towards promoting urbanization and development there. If this policy succeeds, key cities in central and western China will become larger, wealthier and more powerful. As medium and small-sized cities and towns (particularly county seats) implement social governance reforms and relax constraints on changing from rural to urban hukou, their populations are likely to grow more rapidly than in the past and their share of all urbanization in China stands to be enlarged.

The major source regions of China's migrant population have been supplying surplus labor to cities for more than three decades. We believe that now they can and should increasingly take responsibility for promoting labor-intensive industries that conform to the local population structure and contribute to improvement in employment so that more and more members of the rural population can get local non-agricultural jobs. Conditions for healthy urbanization can be consolidated through reconfiguration of job opportunities in space.

Given China's current development trends, policymakers need to pay attention to both migration source and destination regions. Population flows, both as decisions based on household consideration and the personal values of migrants, and driven by institutional factors, deserve attention. Population flows are displaying new dynamics. Changes are occurring in relation to the driving forces in regions where migration originates and destination regions. Recently many new policies for social governance and hukou reform addressing the urban–rural dual system have been implemented and it is likely more will follow the State Council's 2014 call for further hukou reform (PRC-MSC, 2014). As shown by our studies, diverse factors are affecting decision-making of the population that makes up these flows. Hukou reform alone is insufficient to shape the spatial reconfiguration of China's population and migration.

Hopefully, the kind of careful empirical research we have been doing and discuss in this book will help policymakers develop approaches to respond to highly variable factors affecting population flows in China as it becomes ever more integrated into the global economy, central and western China develop and urbanize, and the economy of eastern China becomes even more advanced.

NOTES

1. The floating population who moved from one district to another district (39.91 million people in 2010) are not included except noted.
2. In addition to census and population and sampling surveys that we analyze in this chapter, China's former Population and Family Planning Commission (NPFPC)—one of the predecessors to the current National Health and Family Planning Commission created in March 2013—organized data integration and conducted research on population flows for the population of childbearing age each year. The NPFPC has published an official and annual *Report on China's Migrant Population Development* since 2010.
3. Chongqing city became an independent municipality directly under the central government in 1997, so the matrix is 30*29 in 1990 and 1995, and 31*30 in 2000.

7. China's evolving city system and large city clusters

While China is a very large country—with a land area about the size of the United States—it contains about one-fifth of the world's population. Much of Qinghai province, the Tibet and Xinjiang Autonomous Regions, and other parts of China's land area are sparsely inhabited or empty desert, mountain, or grassland. Accordingly, for millennia China's population has been concentrated in central and eastern China—particularly the Pearl River Delta including Hong Kong, the Yangtze River Delta with Shanghai as its core, and the Beijing–Tianjin corridor. At different times since the Tang dynasty capital cities of important Chinese dynasties were very large: notably Chang 'An (Xian), Kai-Feng, Hangzhou, Nanjing, and Beijing. But they were centers of political and military authority not much integrated with small and medium-sized cities, towns, and villages near them or larger systems of cities in China (Friedmann, 2005). China's very large cities and the relationships among them have emerged only in the last three decades.

THE EMERGENCE OF LARGE CITY CLUSTERS

The New International Division of Labor, the Global Spread of Economic Activities and Urbanization in Developing Countries

Vast changes have occurred in the global economic landscape since the beginning of the twentieth century. The theory of comparative advantage originally proposed by the influential classical political economist David Ricardo (1772–1823) is still helpful today. Ricardo argued that countries should concentrate their economic development in industries where they are most internationally competitive, relying on trade for raw materials and goods they do not possess or which can be produced more cheaply elsewhere (Ricardo, [1817]2005). This implies a high degree of international division of labor. China's recent development history is generally consistent with this line of theory.

This traditional pattern, in which products are manufactured in one country that has a comparative advantage and then traded among countries, has undergone continuing transformation. In addition to the continuous expansion of international trade, conditions for the appearance of the New International Division of Labor (hereafter, NIDL) have matured for a number of reasons:

- First, a large surplus labor force is generated in the transformation from traditional agricultural society to modern society in developing countries. This is an important reason for the low price of labor in developing countries. If the labor is mobilized this gives developing countries a competitive advantage in producing products that require low-skilled labor;
- Second, modern management makes possible the spatial separation of the non-technical part of industrial production from the technical part of industrial production;
- Third, the development of cheap and rapid international transport and communication facilitates the organization of international production (Frobel and Heinricha, 1980).

Scholarly writings about the New International Division of Labor (NIDL) first began to appear in the 1950s and have been evolving continuously since then. NIDL is characterized by intra-product specialization dominated by global production networks, which are in turn driven by Multi-National Corporations (hereafter, MNCs).

MNCs develop complex global supply chains. For example, the production chain of Apple Incorporated's iPhone components is distributed worldwide, with components manufactured by enterprises in the United States, Germany, Japan, Korea, China, and elsewhere shipped to China for assembly, and finished iPhones in turn are shipped worldwide.

Information on the cost of materials and labor in products produced by MNCs is essential for their strategic planning and for rivals to develop competing products. Many analysts seek to provide this information. Andrew Rassweiler, the senior director of materials and cost benchmarking at a private firm name IHS Technology provides estimates of the cost of materials and labor for different high-tech products. According to Rassweiler (2009) the cost of materials in the global production chain, for an iPhone 3Gs in 2009 was US$172.46, and the assembly cost only US$6.50—less than 4 percent of the total cost of production. Rassweiler estimated the assembly cost based on the cost of materials. His method is disputed. It is very difficult to apply given that material costs are a business secret and acquiring the true transaction data is often impossible, particularly when aggressive batch purchases by a powerful MNC like Apple Inc. can make their transaction prices low. However, China's manufacturing industry, exemplified by the giant Taiwanese-based MNC, Foxconn Incorporated, is at the lowest end of the global value chain. The massive labor force liberated from rural areas of China is being utilized to keep production costs as low as possible and maximize profit on iPhones, other consumer electronic items, and virtually every imaginable product. China's economic and social development and its urbanization are fueled by an enormous supply of labor producing products for the global marketplace.

National and regional space is restructured when NIDL impacts countries' economies. Wallerstein (2011) linked the world system to the international division of labor in which different countries and regions play roles as cores, peripheries and semi-peripheries.

As global cities have emerged in China, many local cities have expanded and improved, because of NIDL. According to China's National New Style Urbanization Plan (PRC, 2014), in urban areas between 2000 and 2012 the percentage of residents with tap water in their homes increased from 63.9 percent to 97.2 percent; the percentage of residents with fuel gas increased from 44.6 percent to 93.2 percent; road length per capita increased from $14.4m^2$ to $32.9m^2$; per capita housing area increased from $6.1m^2$ to $20.3m^2$; availability of wastewater treatment increased from 34.3 percent to 87.3 percent. Despite these impressive gains China's rapid development and large increase in city sizes has created many issues: air and water pollution, traffic congestion, real estate bubbles, chaotic peri-urban areas, and spatial inequality.

The World City Network

Technology has profoundly affected geographical distance. The world has become a global village owing to convenient air, marine, railway, and highway transportation as described in Chapter 5. Data in Figure 7.1 show that from 1980 to 2011, the volume of containers in 20 major ports around the world increased by 15 times and the number of aviation passengers increased by 5.7 times. The rapid development of the Internet and digital communications technology has made it possible for individuals to communicate everywhere in the world and for organizations to communicate vast quantities of information instantaneously.

Not only is the world becoming smaller, but world connections are becoming closer. Spanish sociologist/urban planner/communications professor Manuel Castells, describes the global process of urbanization in the early twenty-first century as characterized by the formation of a new

Ranking	1980 Port	1980 Throughput	1990 Port	1990 Throughput	2000 Port	2000 Throughput	2011 Port	2011 Throughput
1	New York New Jersey	1.95	Singarpore	5.2	**Hongkong**	**18**	**Shanghai**	**32**
2	Rotterdam	1.9	**Hongkong**	**5.1**	Singarpore	17	Singarpore	29.9
3	**Hongkong**	**1.5**	Rotterdam	3.7	Busan	7.5	**Hongkong**	**24**
4	**Kaohsiung**	**1**	**Kaohsiung**	**3.5**	**Kaohsiung**	**7.4**	**Shenzhen**	**23**
5	Singarpore	0.92	Kobe	2.6	Rotterdam	6.3	Busan	16.2
6	Hamburg	0.78	Los Angeles	2.6	Shanghai	5.6	**Zhoushan**	**15**
7	Oakland	0.78	Busan	2.4	Los Angeles	4.9	**Guangzhou**	**14**
8	Seattle	0.78	Hamburg	2	Long Beach	4.6	**Qingdao**	**13**
9	Kobe	0.73	New York New Jersey	1.9	Hamburg	4.3	Dubai	13
10	Antwerp	0.72	**Keelung**	**1.8**	Antwerp	4.1	Rotterdam	11.9
11	Yokohama	0.72	Yokohama	1.7	Shenzhen	4	**Tianjin**	**12**
12	Bremen	0.7	Long beach	1.6	Port Klang	3.2	Port Klang	9.76
13	Baltimore	0.66	Tokyo	1.6	Dubai	3.1	**Kaohsiung**	**9.6**
14	**Keelung**	**0.7**	Antwerp	1.6	New York New Jersey	3.1	Hamburg	9.02
15	Busan	0.63	Felix Stowdong	1.4	Tokyo	2.9	Antwerp	8.66
16	Tokyo	0.63	San Juan	1.4	Felix Stowdong	2.9	Los Angeles	7.94
17	Los Angeles	0.62	Bremen	1.2	Bremen	2.8	Paz	7.5
18	Chittagong	0.56	Seattle	1.2	Gioia Tauro	2.7	**Amoy**	**6.5**
19	Long beach	0.55	Oakland	1.1	Tanjung Pera Paz	2.5	**Dalian**	**6.4**
20	Melbourne	0.51	Manila	1	Yokohama	2.3	Long Beach	6.06
	Felix		**Shanghai**		**Ningbo**			
	San Juan		**Shenzhen**		**Guangzhou**			
	Manila		Port Klang		**Qingdao**			
			Dubai		**Tianjin**			
			Gioia Tauro		**Amoy**			
			Tanjung Pera Paz		**Dalian**			

Ports ranked below top 20 next period

Ports ranked below top 20

→ Chinese ports

Source: *Containerization International Yearbook*s 1980, 1990, 2000, and 2011. Compiled by Lijuan Wang.

Figure 7.1 Top 20 world container ports, 1980 to 2011 (million TEU) spatial architecture made up of global networks connecting major metropolitan regions and their areas of influence (Castells, 2010).

Columbia University Sociology Professor Saskia Sassen argues that global cities house both the corporations generating globalization and advanced producer services in finance such as lending, underwriting, economic analysis, and insurance; professional services such as law and accounting; and creative work such as design and advertising services that enable corporations to operate at a huge scale throughout the world (Sassen, 2001). Advanced producer services are characterized by firms selling specialized knowledge products to other firms. This service provision entails very high value added products that empower global corporations to operate and develop their worldwide businesses. Sassen coined the term global city to refer to cities whose economies depend on provision of worldwide services. Global cities are both the market for these high value added services and the site where they are produced. Sassen concluded that these advanced producer services are highly concentrated in New York, London, and a few other top global cities.

Peter Taylor, an economic geographer based at the University of Northumbria, England, leads one of the most sophisticated efforts to analyze world and global cities: the Globalization and World Cities Research Network (GaWC). Taylor and his GaWC colleagues do research and write extensively about the world city network. Taylor's book, *World Cities Network* (Taylor and DeRudder, 2015) takes the position that the world city network consists of many city nodes—not just a few top command and control centers like London and New York—connected by transportation and communication networks. It is useful to conceptualize the emerging Chinese city system this way. Population and industrial concentration into LCCs is making LCCs the drivers of urbanization.

Different tiered cities in the world city network have become the nodes connected to all cities in the world. Population and industry has been concentrating in these nodes and areas influenced by them.

The US cities with the densest urban population in 2014 were New York, Boston, and Washington in the east, cites around the five Great Lakes in the north, and Los Angeles in the west. In Europe the most densely populated regions are the London and Paris metropolitan regions. In Japan the densest regions are along the Pacific Ocean.

Worldwide between 1990 and 2014, urban population growth has principally occurred in the developing countries in Asia and Africa, particularly China (United Nations, 2015). The United Nations projects that the proportion of megacities and megalopolises (with a population larger than 10 million) will continue to increase.

Large City Clusters as Key Containers for Urbanization

Because China has such a large population, its contribution to total world population growth is very large, even though the population growth of many smaller developing countries is faster. For millennia China's population has been distributed unevenly and during the last thirty years migration has accentuated the imbalance. Population clusters in the great river deltas, where there is fertile arable land, and areas that are accessible. The annual average growth rate of the urban population in a number of large city-regions has exceeded 5 percent. These densely agglomerated city-regions are developing into Large City Clusters (hereafter LCCs) or megalopolises.

Most of the world's industry is concentrated in LCCs and more than half of the world's wealth is concentrated in 1.5 percent of the global land area (World Bank, 2009). The combined population of North America, the European Union, and Japan is less than 1 billion people, one-seventh of the total people in the world, but more than 75 percent of the world's wealth is concentrated in these three regions (ibid). In Japan, 73.6 percent of GDP and 68.7 percent of the country's population are concentrated in Japan's three major megalopolises. Tokyo, with less than 4 percent of Japan's land area, has one-quarter of Japans population (World Bank, 2009: preface). In the United States, 243 million people live in urban areas, on only 3 percent of the national total area (US Census Bureau, 2015). In addition analyzing their population and wealth a number of scholars have attempted to calculate the contribution these dynamic and productive LCCs and megalopolises make to innovation (Florida, Gulden and Melander 2007).

In China the concentration of population, industry, and wealth in a small part of the country's total land area is similar to the global pattern described above. In 2012, the total GDP of China's three megalopolises—the Yangtze River Delta megalopolis, Pearl River Delta megalopolis, and Jing-Jin-Ji (Beijing, Tianjin and Hubei) megalopolis—was 19 trillion RMB (over US$3.06 trillion)—higher than the GDP of the UK, Italy, France, Russia, or India, According to our calculations, more than 36 percent of China's GDP is created on 3.6 percent of its land area.

Global urban regions have emerged and play an increasingly important role in the global economy (Han, 2015). Advances in communications and transportation technology and improvement of infrastructure connecting global urban regions have strengthened the global city network. As populations and industries continue to be concentrated in global node cities and their surrounding regions, the urbanization process of these areas is accelerating. China is at the epicenter of these changes.

The word metropolis and the more precise term metropolitan area are also used to describe urbanized regions with one or more central cities and surrounding cities, towns, and counties that are closely related to it such as the New York, London and Melbourne MAs (Metropolitan Area).

The United Nations defines metropolitan regions to include both the contiguous territory inhabited at urban levels of residential density and additional surrounding areas of lower settlement density that are under the direct influence of the city—for example, through established transport networks, road linkages or commuting patterns (United Nations, 2014). The precise criteria the United States has used in different censuses emphasizes employment and commute sheds to define standard metropolitan statistical areas. In the same vein Professor Yixing Zhou, a Peking University professor emeritus, advocates a standard metropolitan statistical area in China for LCCs (Zhou and Shi, 1995).

In some developed areas, a number of MAs are becoming connected by expressways and railways to shape one urban region. The Population Division of the United Nations uses the term "Urban Agglomeration" (UA) to describe areas like this (UNPD, 2014). UAs are similar to MAs, but products of a higher stage of urbanization. There are other terms describing what are essentially urban agglomerations including: megacity region (Hall, 2009), interlocking metropolitan region (Zhou and Shi, 1995), extended metropolitan region (Ginsburg, 1991).

As globalization and modernization continue, regional infrastructure, especially highways, expressways, airports, and conventional and high speed railways are closely linking areas within and between urban agglomerations and information technology is making it much easier for people to communicate. As a result, cities within a region and in different regions are in a much better position to interact with each other. For example, a city with 450,000 people, located 70km from a metropolis with two million people can have a close relationship with the metropolis that was impossible as recently as 30 years ago. Information can flow between the two cities instantaneously and people and cargo can shuttle between the cities in one hour, conveniently and at a much lower cost than in the past.

The above discussion of the variety of terms and concepts used to describe large, populous regions with one or more cities and surrounding urban areas reflects both the diversity of such areas and the ongoing scholarly debate about how to categorize and name them. Many of the terms used by demographers, urban scholars, and census bureaus could be used for analysis of current conditions in China. For the balance of this chapter we will use the term large city cluster (LCC) to refer to functionally related groups of cities and their surrounding urbanized areas.

FORMATION, CLASSIFICATION, AND FUNCTIONS OF LARGE CITY CLUSTERS IN CHINA

Formation of Large City Clusters in China

The formation of LCCs in China is closely connected with market-oriented reform and the introduction of a series of economic policies described in earlier chapters of this book involving the rural Household Contract Responsibility System (HCRS), agricultural product circulation, Town and Village Enterprises (TVEs), hukou, the taxation system, administrative divisions, decentralization, and particularly creation of experimental economic zones. These reforms unleashed economic forces that have led to China's remarkable development and urbanization in the last thirty years. They led to an enormous expansion of the Yangtze River Delta and Pearl River Delta mega regions and the formation of the Jing-Jin-Ji mega region. Less recognized, these reforms significantly promoted the development of small and medium-sized cities and towns discussed in Chapter 8 and different spatial structures and interactions among clusters of cities and their surrounding urbanized areas discussed in this chapter. Influenced by the progress of globalization and the NIDL, a number of LCCs in China are maturing and others are taking form.

In China during the 1990s a number of important studies about the forces that led to the creation of LCCs were published.

One group of studies describes how industrialization, commercialization of agriculture, market development, the development of township and private enterprises and foreign investments drove development of the Pearl River Delta and Yangtze River Delta megalopolises (Xu and Zhou, 1994; Ning et al., 1998; Gu and Zhang, 2000; Xu et al., 2000). A second group of studies focuses on how industrial policy, decentralization, household registration policy, and zoning policy reform promoted the development of LCCs (Xu and Zhou, 1994). A third group of studies focused on historical environments and geographic location as prerequisites for the development of LCCs (Yan et al., 1997; Xue et al., 2000). After 2000, discussion of driving forces behind the creation of LCCs ceased to be popular. Following is a review of Chinese scholarship on the formation process of LCCs. Urban population statistics in the following section are from the Population Division of the United Nations.

1978–1990: Cities primarily in the Yangtze River Delta and north of the Yangtze

At the very beginning of China's reform and opening up, the development of Chinese cities was still restrained by the planned economy. The growth of the economy and the population was under the control of the national government. Hukou restricted the growth of the urban population (Chapter 2). The urbanization level in China was only 19.4 percent in 1980. Only Shanghai and Beijing were megacities, with urban populations larger than 5 million, and only 17 cities had an urban population larger than 1 million at that time. Most of these were the capital cities of provinces. These large cities were principally in eastern China, along the lower reaches of the Yangtze River, the Yangtze River Delta, northeastern China and north of the Yangtze River. The large cities that have grown in south China since reform and opening were just beginning to develop.

Between 1980 and 1990 market-oriented reform measures promoted the development of cities and towns as described in Chapters 4 and 5. Initially reform was mainly implemented in rural areas, Special Economic Zones, and coastal port cities. Institutional reform in cities such as substituting taxes for submission of profits to the central government and compensable transfer of use rights in state-owned land did not begin until the middle and late 1980s. During the latter part of the 1980s city populations began to grow very rapidly, with an annual average growth of 1 percent to 5 percent. By 1990 the number of large cities had increased to 34, but the number of megacities remained unchanged. The Yangtze River Delta megalopolis continued to increase, and other LCCs began to take shape in the Pearl River Delta and the center of Liaoning province.

1990–2000: Administrative division adjustment and the rapid growth of cities

At the beginning of the 1990s, market-oriented reforms in China were further strengthened. The system of commercial use rights transfer of state-owned land in cities and towns was implemented on a larger scale, which promoted the expansion of urban industrial space, helped attract investment, and accelerated industrialization. Major reform of state-owned enterprises begun in 1997 continued removing obstacles to economic reform and invigorating state-owned enterprises. Re-employment of laid-off workers occurred at the time. China's housing system was changed from a welfare allocation system to a market-oriented system, activating the urban real estate market and substantially increasing the value of urban land. Hukou reform and the reforms of administrative divisions, such as "converting counties to cities" and "city–county consolidation," were implemented simultaneously—increasing the number and size of cities initially on paper, but in due course in reality.

These reforms propelled the development of cities in the 1990s, and the urban population continued to grow rapidly. A large number of small cities grew into medium-sized cities, and several medium-sized cities grew into large cities. Beijing and Shanghai became super-megacities in this period, with urban populations over 10 million. By the end of the 1990s five additional cities—Guangzhou, Shenzhen, Tianjin, Wuhan, and Chongqing, had also become megacities with populations exceeding 5 million (Figure 7.2).

Benefiting from reform of administrative division adjustments and other changes, China's urban population grew more rapidly in the 1990s than in the 1980s. The city cluster phenomenon became more apparent and speeded up. The major regions of city growth were in the Yangtze and Pearl River Deltas, the Shandong peninsula, Wuhan and its surrounding region, the Liaoning peninsula, Jing-Jin-Ji corridor and the west coast of the Taiwan Straits.

2000–2010: Globalization and the continued growth of Chinese cities

After 2000, changes in administrative divisions gradually stabilized, and cities maintained growth momentum. In this period, the entry of China into the World Trade Organization (WTO) and the influence of housing reform and development, state-owned enterprise reform, growth of the private sector, and hukou reform spurred the continual rapid growth of China's urban population. The number of super-megacities, megacities, and large and medium-sized cities continuously increased, the distribution of cities became denser, and LCCs and megalopolises appeared in each region. The Yangtze River Delta megalopolis, The Shandong peninsula LCC, and the Chengdu–Chongqing LCC were notable and the growth rates of cities in the Yangtze River Delta megalopolis were particularly impressive.

2010–2015: Megalopolises and LCCs continue to take shape

Cities of all sizes and levels have been growing rapidly since 2010. Tianjin has reached the status of a super-megacity and Harbin a megacity. The nature of China's megacities and the way in which cities in large city clusters relate to each other has become clearer.

At the time this book went to press in spring, 2015 there were six super-megacities with populations larger than 10 million and nine megacities with populations between 5 and 10 million in China. The number of small and medium-sized cities and the spatial connections between many small and medium-sized cities, urbanized peri-urban areas, and central cities has become closer everywhere in China. In addition to the denser distribution of cities in east China, LCCs in central China with Wuhan, Zhengzhou, and Changsha as the central cities are taking shape. In western China the Chengdu–Chongqing LCC is experiencing rapid growth.

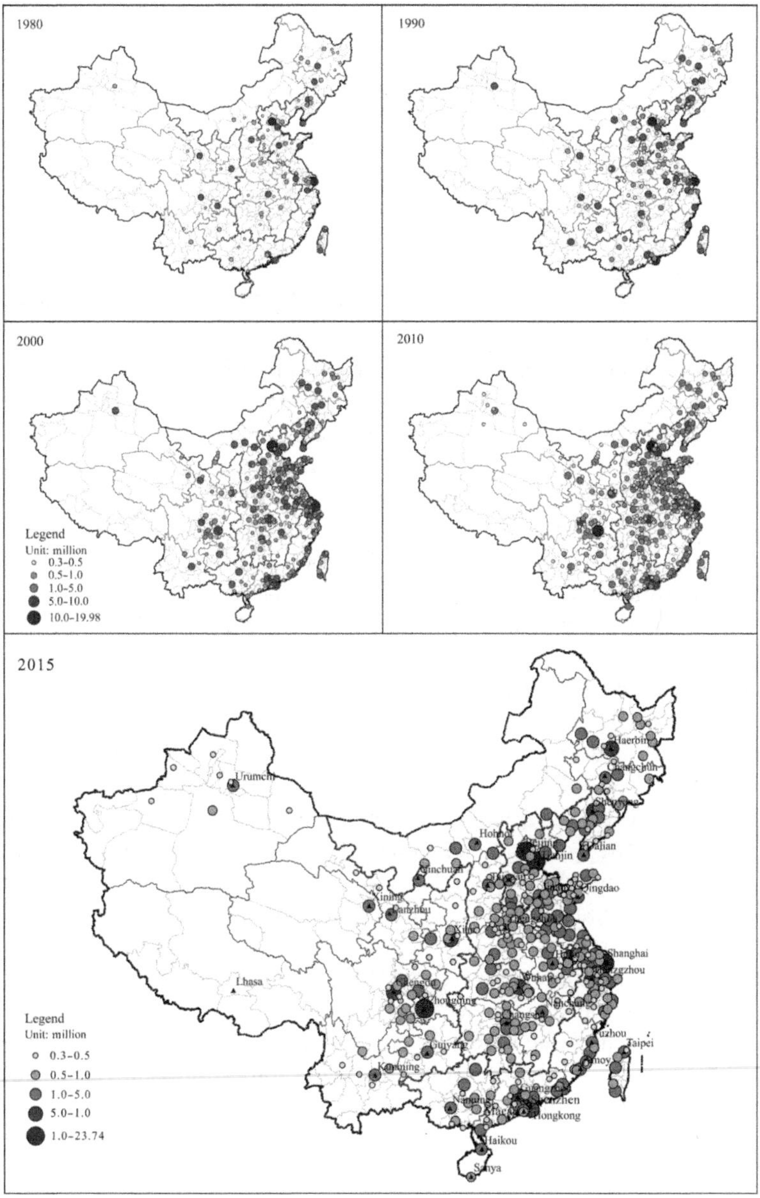

Source: UN (2015). Compiled and drawn by Lijuan Wang.

Figure 7.2 Chinese cities with 30,000+ population by city size class, 1980 to 2015

From 1980 to 2015, the growth of cities of all sizes in China presents two key features.

First, generally the smaller the city, the more rapidly it grew. Most small and medium-sized cities are now experiencing annual average growth rates above 5 percent. In contrast, megacities and super-megacities are growing at a slower rate than the small and medium-sized cities, but they are still growing and, because of their enormous population bases, continue to account for a large part of China's overall urban population growth.

Second, cities in regions with a denser concentration of cities are generally growing more rapidly than cities in regions with a less dense concentration of cities.

Large city clusters have been emerging at different rates in different parts of China. Recently LCCs have been growing at the fastest rate in dense regions with many cities such as the Yangtze and Pearl River Delta megalopolises, central and south of Liaoning province, and the Shandong peninsula. LCCs in central Henan and the central Shaanxi plain have been growing at a moderately fast rate. LCCs have emerged more slowly in low-density regions where cities are distributed sparsely, such as Xinjiang, Yunnan, Inner Mongolia, and Guangxi provinces, though recently the tempo of LCC formation even in these areas has increased (Figure 7.3).

Defining Large City Clusters in China

China's urbanization model is different from the model in Europe and North America. In Europe and North America at the time Jean Gottmann (1961) coined the term, megalopolises had grown and were continuing to grow due to the expansion of cities. The growth pattern was characterized by spreading outward. Urbanization involved the spread of housing, industry and urban culture to rural areas. Now much of the continued expansion of cities in North America and Europe is lower density/higher amenity suburban housing, technology-related industry that does not involve manufacturing, services, and local-serving retail.

China's urbanization model is also different from the model elsewhere in Asia. University of British Columbia geography professor Terry McGee (1991b) argues that there is a new, distinctly Asian, form of urbanization that is neither rural nor urban he calls a desakota—very dense, formerly rural areas that mix agriculture and small and medium-sized industry. McGee invented the word desakota based on his research in Indonesia and elsewhere in Southeast Asia (McGee, 1991b). The term combines the Bahasi Indonesian words for village (desa) and city (kota) to describe a unique type of place that blends features of both villages and cities. Since the 1970s, the transfer of industries from developed countries to

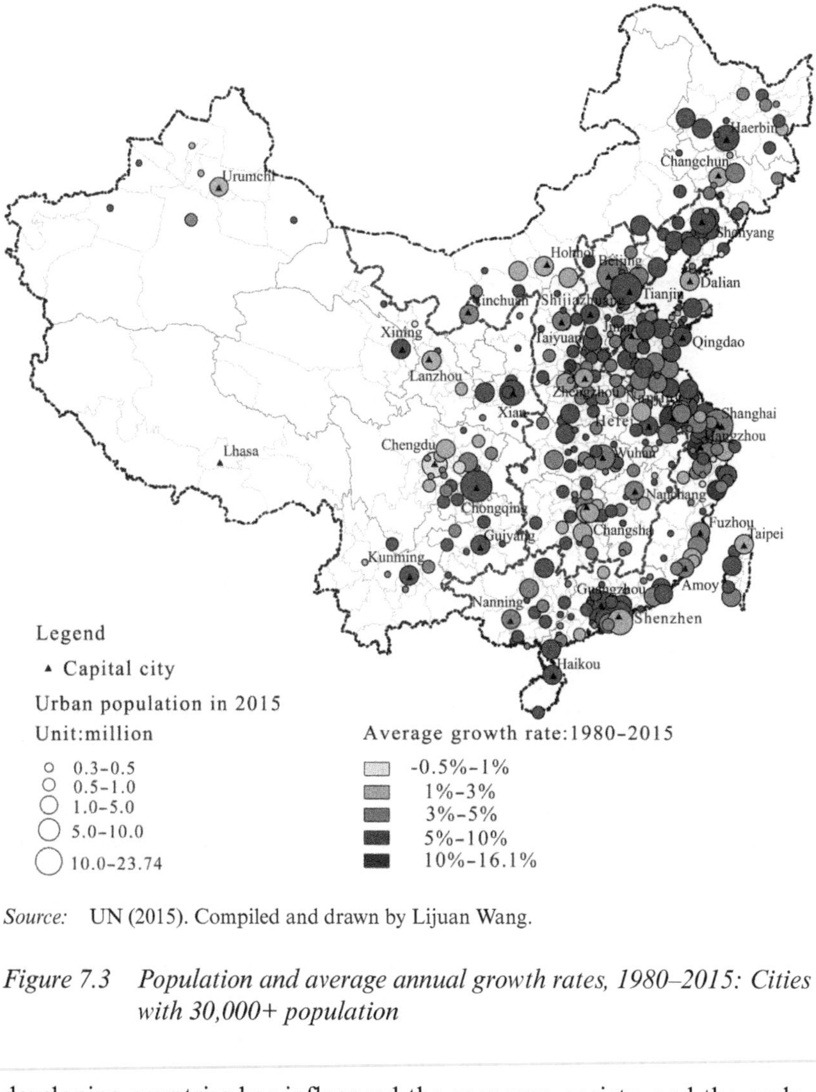

Source: UN (2015). Compiled and drawn by Lijuan Wang.

Figure 7.3 Population and average annual growth rates, 1980–2015: Cities with 30,000+ population

developing countries has influenced the economy, society, and the evolution of the spatial organization of the areas surrounding cities, especially megacities. Mixed urban and rural landscapes, as well as mixed agricultural and non-agricultural activities, have emerged. Professor McGee calls the combination of core cities, peri-urban areas and desakotas along transportation corridors connecting metropolises mega-urban regions. According to McGee desakotas are typically unplanned or poorly planned and take a variety of forms. Professor Zhou Yixing, a Chinese geographer at Peking

University, calls such areas in China Metropolis Interlocking Regions (Zhou, 1995a).

In China areas resembling Indonesian desakotas have arisen not only as urban centers have expanded, but even more often as industrializing villages become more like towns and cities with substantial small and medium-sized industries. This especially happened in the Yangtze River Delta and Pearl River Delta. Anthropologist and consultant Gregory Guldin describes the processes he observed in southern China as former villages became mixtures of agriculture and industry as deagriculturalization, townization, and urbanization came in place (Guldin, 1996).

Research and Scholarly Debates on Chinese LCCs

Because the widespread emergence of LCCs is a recent phenomenon, still taking shape, and represents a new stage of urban development, the definition of LCCs in China is currently hotly debated. Chinese scholars disagree about the definition and the number of LCCs in China (Zhou, 1991; Yao and Chen, 2006; Fang, 2009; Ni, 2008; Ning and Zhang, 2012; Zhang, X., 2014).

Professor Shimou Yao from the Nanjing Institute of Geography and Limnology of the Chinese Academy of Science and his colleagues researched LCCs in China for the first time and presented their findings in *Large City Clusters in China* (Yao and Chen, 2006). Yao divided LCCs into three types: (1) six super LCCs in the Yangtze River Delta, Pearl River Delta, Jing-Jin-Ji, Shandong peninsula, central and south of Liaoning, and the Sichuan Basin, (2) medium-sized LCCs in the central Shaanxi plain, the central plains in Henan and surrounding regions, Changsha–Zhuzhou–Xiangtan, Fujian, Wuhan, and Harbin–Daqing–Qiqihaer, and (3) small regional LCC groups.

Based on a literature review and meta-analysis, in 2009 Chuanglin Fang, a geography professor at the China Academy of Sciences, defined 23 LCCs in China, located in all of the provinces in China, except Tibet (Fang, 2009). The sizes of the 23 LCCs as defined by Professor Fang are significantly different from each other, and some barely qualify by standards other scholars use to define LCCs.

Professor Yuemin Ning, a geographer at East China Normal University, defined 13 LCCs based on his analysis of both space and scale factors, using 2000 population census data (Ning and Zhang, 2012). Professor Ning's core idea was to consider the metropolitan region as the unit of analysis. The standard he used was: (1) that the population of a central city should exceed 2 million or that two or more cities have a population larger than

1 million and (2) urbanized regions are closely connected with the central cities and other cities exist.

Shanghai University of Finance and Economics professor Xueliang Zhang identified 24 LCCs on the basis of indicators in China's National Major Function-oriented Zoning Plan, the urban population, and the number of metropolises (Zhang, X., 2014).

The definition of LCCs provided by Professor Yueming Ning, based on 2000 census data, is the most consistent with international classifications of LCCs. However, his definition is based on the metropolitan region as the unit of analysis. It is quite restricted and does not include some LCCs such as Kunming, Yinchuan, and Urumqi proposed by other scholars.

China's National New Style National Urbanization Plan defines 21 key urbanized regions in China as of 2014, but it does not specifically call them LCCs and does not distinctly indicate their location and boundaries either in words or maps.

LCCs: a clarification and update

In order to provide a clear definition of LCCs in China and our own conclusions about the number of LCCs and where they are located, we developed our own methodology, building on Professor Ning's pioneering work, and analyzed the most recent data available. Our methodology is as follows:

1. Municipalities directly under the central government, provincial capitals, and sub-provincial cities with a population of more than 1 million are defined as the central cities of LCCs;
2. Prefecture-level cities within 100km from the edge of the built-up area of the central cities and prefecture-level cities within 50km from the prefecture-level city are classified as part of the LCC;
3. Cities in an LCC that have traditionally been closely connected with each other and share a sense of regional identity are included;
4. In addition to the above conditions, all the population that is closely connected by highway or express railroads is included in the urban population of the LCC;
5. Regions of integrated development and generally recognized LCCs have been clarified based on clearly defined national strategies, such as official definitions of the Yangtze River Delta megalopolis, Pearl River Delta megalopolis, and the Jing-Jin-Ji megalopolis are also included.

Based on this methodology we identified 26 LCCs in China as of spring, 2015. We categorized the 26 LCCs into three types: (1) megalopolises,

(2) pre-megalopolises, and (3) ordinary LCCs. We define these LCC types as follows:

1. Megalopolis
   We define a megalopolis as a region in which the total population is larger than 30 million. (This is the population scale of the northeast coast of the US in 1950 which Jean Gottmann defined as megalopolis.); per capita GDP is more than US$7,920 (49,104 RMB) which is the middle-income line according to Woo (2012) which we discussed in Chapter 9; the urbanization level exceeds 53 percent which was the world urbanization level in 2012; there are two or more megacities (with a population larger than 5 million) and more than five large cities (with a population of more than 1 million); and there is some level of integration between urban and rural development for the region. According to this definition there are three megalopolises in China as of 2015: the Yangtze River Delta megalopolis, Pearl River Delta megalopolis, and the Jing-Jin-Ji megalopolis in the Beijing–Tianjin–Hebei region.
2. Pre-megalopolis
   We define a pre-megalopolis as a region where LCCs have the potential to grow into a megalopolis. The total population of a pre-megalopolis must be larger than 20 million; per capita GDP exceeds US$6,336 ($7,920, which is the income threshold we used to define a megalopolis *80 percent) (40,000 RMB) or the total GDP is over 20 billion RMB; the level of urbanization exceeds 42 percent (80 percent of the world level in 2012); there is one megacity with a population larger than 5 million, two cities with populations larger than 2 million or three cities with populations larger than 1 million, and five or more cities with populations larger than 500,000; and development of the urban and rural areas is integrated to some extent. Based on this definition we identified seven pre-megalopolises in China as of 2015 in Chengdu–Chongqing, central and south of Liaoning, the central plains (Henan), Shandong peninsula, west coast of the Taiwan Straits, Wuhan and surroundings, and the Changsha–Zhuzhou–Xiangtan pre-megalopolis.
3. Ordinary LCCs
   We define the remaining 16 LCCs as ordinary LCCs as of 2015.

Unless otherwise specified, LCC refers to any of these 26 LCC types: megalopolises, pre-megalopolises, and ordinary LCCs (Figure 7.4).

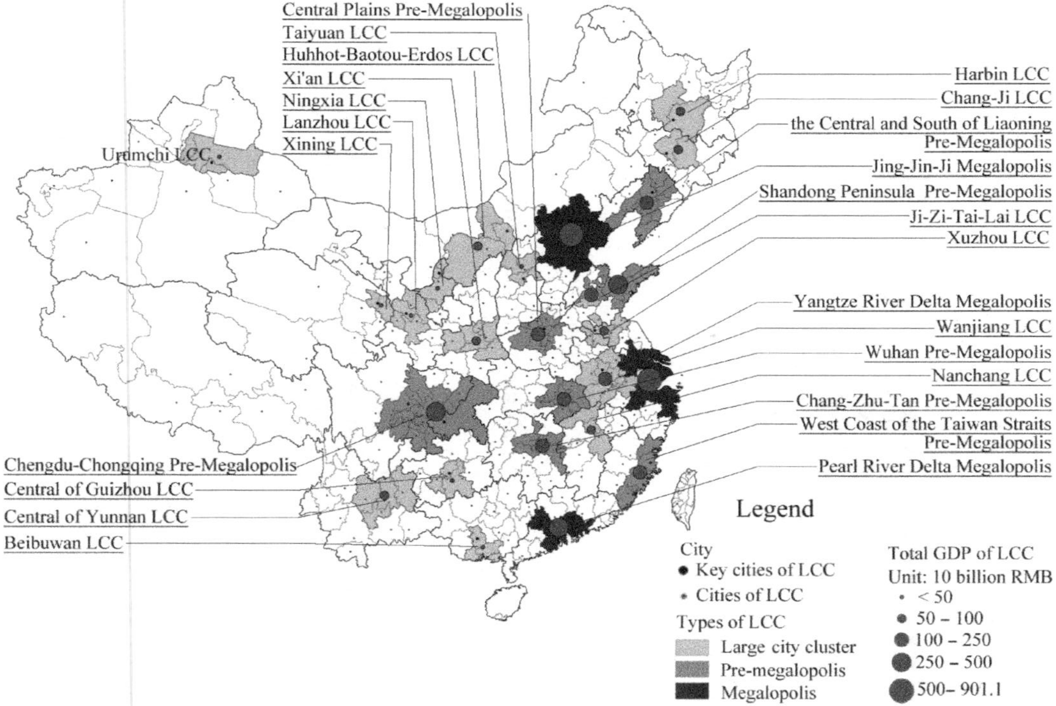

Source: NBSC-csy (2013). Compiled and drawn by Lijuan Wang.

Figure 7.4 Distribution of LCCs

THE ROLE OF LARGE CITY CLUSTERS IN CHINA

Leading Role at the National Level

China's 26 LCCs play a key role in the urbanization process in China. The total area of the three megalopolises—the Yangtze and Pearl River Delta and Jing-Jin-Ji megalopolises—is 347.4 thousand km^2 on only 3.6 percent of China's national land area. In 2012, the total population of these three megalopolises was 253 million—18.7 percent of China's population. Their total GDP was 18.99 trillion RMB (US$3 trillion), accounting for 36.6 percent of China's national GDP (NBSC-csy, 2013).

If the seven pre-megalopolises are included, the total area of China's ten existing and seven emerging megalopolises is 624.3 thousand km^2; 6.5 percent of China's national land area. Their population is 557 million accounting for 41.1 percent of China's national population and their GDP is US$5.44 trillion (33.73 trillion RMB), accounting for 64.9 percent of China's national GDP (NBSC-csy, 2013).

The total area of all 26 LCCs is 1.926 million km^2, accounting for 20.1 percent of the national land area, their population is 784 million, accounting for 57.9 percent of the national population, and their GDP is 43.22 trillion RMB, accounting for 83.2 percent of China's GDP (NBSC-csy, 2013). LCCs have become the backbone of the economic development and urbanization of China.

The economic output of China's cities is essentially consistent with the spatial distribution pattern of the national economy. The economy in east China is most developed; the economy of central and western China less developed. The Yangtze River Delta megalopolis has the most developed economy with a GDP of US$1.45 trillion (9.01 trillion RMB), accounting for 17.4 percent of the national GDP in a total area of just 109.9 thousand km^2—less than 1 percent of China's land area. The Yangtze River Delta megalopolis is followed by the Pearl River Delta megalopolis and Jing-Jin-Ji megalopolis, accounting for 10.0 percent and 9.2 percent of China's GDP respectively. Figure 7.5 shows that the eastern coastal area has the highest economic density, especially the Yangtze and Pearl River Delta megalopolises.

While generally China's population and GDP match, there are some exceptions—particularly in regions that are rich in coal or other natural resources. Generally, the central and eastern regions have higher population density than the western region. The Yangtze River Delta megalopolis has the largest population (109 million) and the Xining LCC has the smallest population (3.7 million).

The Pearl River Delta megalopolis has the highest population density

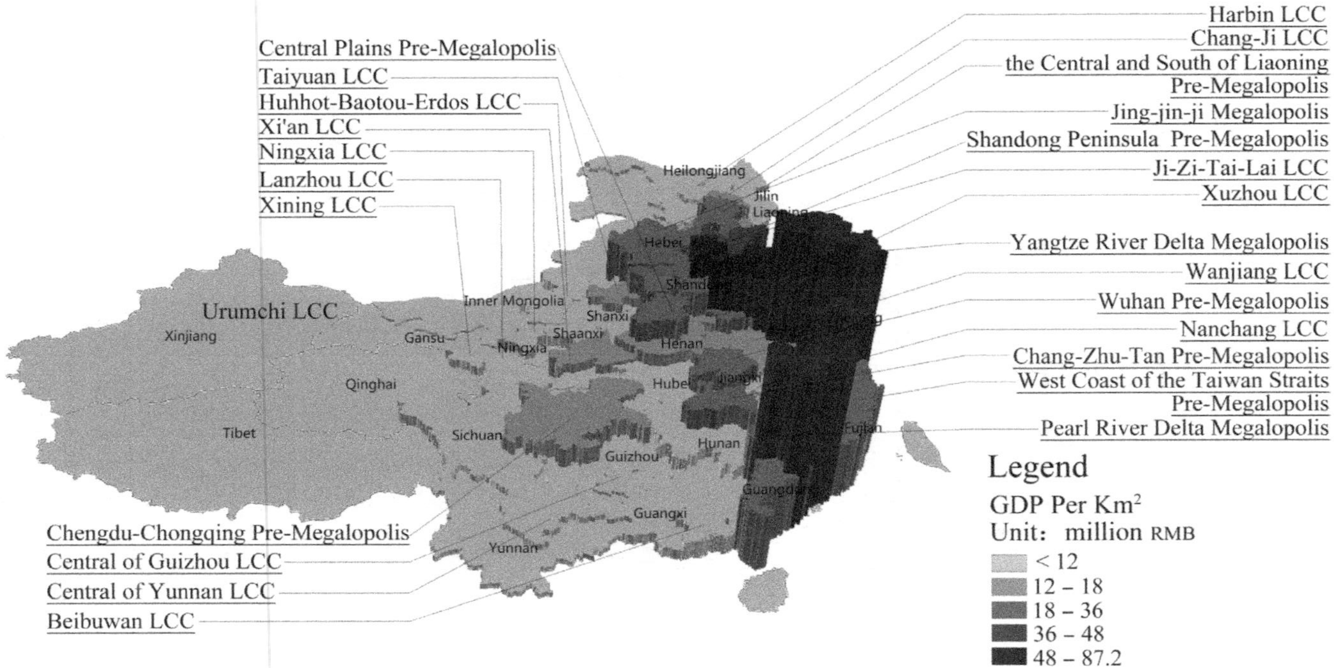

Source: NBSC-csy (2013). Compiled and drawn by Chuyang Lin.

Figure 7.5 GDP per area in large city clusters and provinces, 2012

(1,037 persons/km^2). The north slope of Tianshan Mountain LCC has the lowest population density (only 61 persons/km^2).

The Hohhot–Baotou–Erdos LCC has the highest per capita GDP: 120,000 RMB per capita. This is because of the region's abundant coal resources and mining activity. The Hohhot–Baotou–Erdos LCC is followed by Pearl River and Yangtze River Delta megalopolises, with per capita GDP of 84,100 RMB/person and 82,500 RMB/person, respectively. The Lanzhou LCC has the lowest per capita GDP: only 23,600 RMB/person.

The Role of LCCs at the Regional Level

LCCs are engines not only of China's national economy, but also of regional economies. Accordingly we developed a methodology to analyze the role of LCCs in the regional economies where they are located and estimated their impacts. We measured the role of LCCs at the regional level using two concentration indices—one with the ratio of LCC GDP to the GDP of the province in which the LCC is located and a second with the ratio of the LCC population to the total population of the region in which it is located. A high score on either of the two indices indicates that LCCs play an important role in the regional economy, and vice versa.

For all LCCs that are entirely within a single province we used the province where a LCC is located as the regional unit to measure the LCC concentration index. In the three cases where LCCs cross provinces—the Yangtze River Delta megalopolis in Jiangsu, Zhejiang and Shanghai; the Jing-Jin-Ji megalopolis in Beijing, Tianjin and Hebei; and the Cheng-Yu megalopolis in Sichuan and Chongqing we combined data on the provinces. We calculated separate indices for 2000, 2010 and 2012.

Concentration of Economic Activity in LCCs

Figure 7.6 illustrates the extent to which GDP was concentrated within each of the 26 LCCs in 2000 and in 2010. The horizontal axis is set to show the total volume of LCC GDP relative to its regional total GDP in 2010. The point where the horizontal and longitudinal axes cross is set at 70 percent which is an estimate of the total GDP produced by all LCCs to China's total national GDP. The data in Figure 7.6 must be interpreted with caution because the total GDP provided by individual subregions is larger than the total reported for all regions. This is because some prefectural-level administrative divisions include revenue they count as generated within the division which actually occurs in other parts of China in order to claim as large a GDP contribution as possible. China's

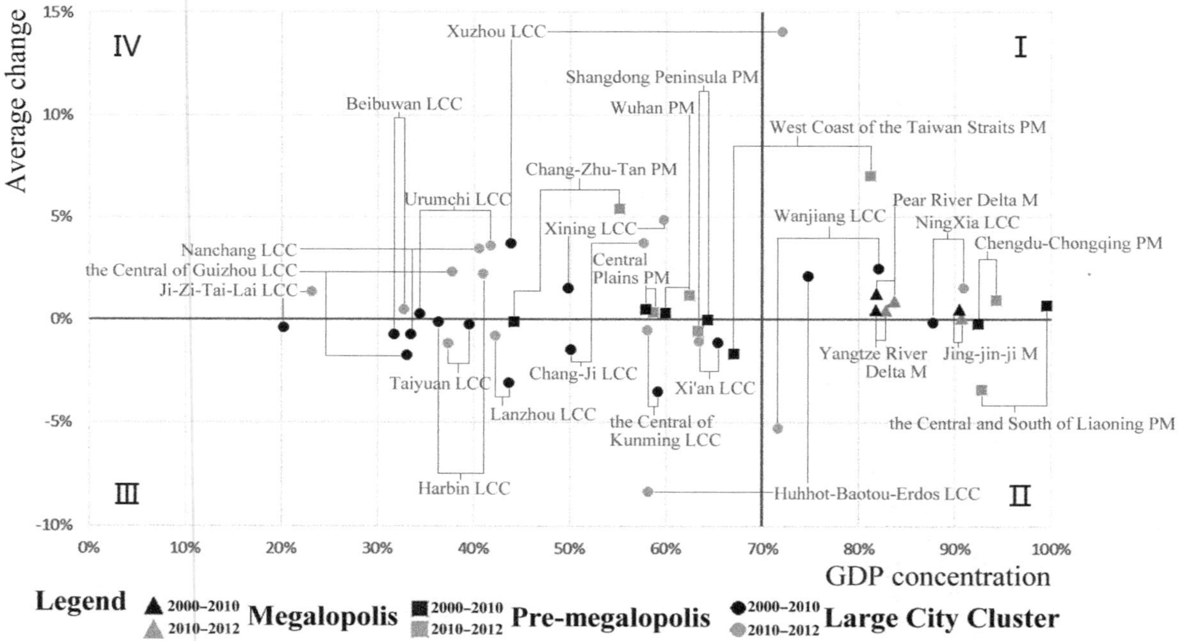

Note: Not corrected for inflation.

Source: NBSC-csy (2001, 2011, 2013). Compiled and drawn by Chuyang Lin.

Figure 7.6 GDP Concentration index of LCCs to the province where they are located, 2010 and change between 2000 and 2010 and 2010 and 2012 provincial and national statistic bureaus adjust data supplied by regions and provinces to avoid double counting, so the national total is lower than the sum of the data supplied by lower levels of government.

Four quadrants are numbered with Roman numerals clockwise beginning with quadrant I in the top right. Megalopolises are represented by triangles, pre-megalopolises by squares, and ordinary LCCs by circles. The percentage of total provincial GDP generated within the LCC is displayed on the horizontal axis. The further to the right the LCC is, the greater the degree to which GDP is concentrated within the LCC.

There is a large variation in the range to which LCCs concentrate the economic activity in their provinces from a low of 20 percent to a high of 100 percent. The vertical axis shows how much GDP concentration increased or decreased annually between 2000 and 2010. There were significant changes in the degree to which economic activity was concentrated in LCCs between 2000 and 2010. The range of change extended from a high of a little more than + 25 percent (Xuzhou LCC) to a low of a little more than −10 percent (Liaoning LCC).

The five LCCs in quadrant I have a high degree of concentration (above 80 percent), and the degree of concentration increased between 2000 and 2010 (they are above the line). However the increase was not very great. For example, the square located slightly above the horizontal axis at the extreme right in quadrant I represents the central and south of Liaoning pre-megalopolis which shows that nearly 100 percent of Liaoning province's economic activity was generated within this LCC. This is largely due to administrative divisions within Liaoning province claiming GDP generated elsewhere which was then deducted at the provincial level.

Quadrant I contains the Yangtze and Pearl River Delta megalopolises, Jing-Jin-Ji megalopolis, central and south of Liaoning pre-megalopolis, and the Hohhot–Baotou–Erdos (Inner Mongolia) and Wanjiang (around the Yangtze River within Anhui province) ordinary LCCs.

Quadrant II contains only two LCCs: the Chengdu–Chongqing pre-megalopolis and the Ningxia ordinary LCC. Both had a high degree of concentration (close to 90 percent). The degree of concentration in these two LCCs decreased between 2000 and 2010, but only very slightly.

Quadrant III contains LCCs with degrees of concentration between 20 percent and 83 percent. The percentage of provincial GDP LCCs in this quadrant generated decreased between 2000 and 2010. Quadrant III includes three pre-megalopolises—the Changsha–Zhuzhou–Xiangtan, Shandong peninsula, and west coast of Taiwan Straits LCCs—and 10 ordinary LCCs.

Quadrant IV contains LCCs with economic concentration similar to quadrant III. The LCCs in this quadrant had weak economic concentration bases, but increased significantly between 2000 and 2010. The central plains and Wuhan pre-megalopolises and three ordinary LCCs fall in quadrant IV.

In order to understand recent changes in LCC economic concentration we analyzed changes in GDP concentration in LCCs between 2010 and 2012 and constructed a data graphic with four quadrants. The data is described by gray legends in Figure 7.6. Following are the most significant findings.

Between 2000 and 2012, the west coast of the Taiwan Straits Pre-megalopolis, the Ningxia LCC and the Chengdu–Chongqing LCC moved from quadrant II (high, but declining) to the first quadrant (high and increasing). This suggests that economic development is beginning to be concentrated in the LCCs in these three populous relatively underdeveloped areas. More significant changes have occurred in the third and fourth quadrants. The number of LCCs in the third quadrant decreased from 13 to 6. Except for the Wanjiang LCC (Anhui), Hohhot–Baotou–Erdos LCC (Inner Mongolia), Taiyuan LCC (Shanxi), and Shandong peninsula LCC (Shandong) and Lanzhou LCC where concentration decreased, the degree of concentration of the remaining LCCs has changed from low concentration to strong concentration. In summary Figure 7.6 shows that the economic concentration of LCCs is increasing. In 2012, the GDP of the 26 LCCs accounted for 83.4 percent of China's total GDP (as reported by the national government adjusting for double counting by lower levels of government), 2.6 percent more than in 2010 and 11.3 percent more than in 2000. LCCs have become the major form of economic space in China.

Population Concentration

Figure 7.7 shows the concentration LCC *population* in 2000 and 2010 for each of the three types of LCC. The horizontal axis is set to show the total population of all 26 LCCs relative to the total population of their regions. The distribution of LCCs in the four quadrants is significantly different from the pattern of GDP concentration shown in Figure 7.6. This is an effective way to show differences in per capita GDP and economic efficiency.

Quadrant I shows that population is quite concentrated in all three of China's existing megalopolises—the Yangtze and Pearl River Delta megalopolises and Jing-Jin-Ji megalopolis and two of the China's seven pre-megalopolises: the west coast of the Taiwan Straits and central and south of Liaoning pre-megalopolises. By 2010 a substantial amount of China's population in the most developed provinces was concentrated in mature LCCs (megalopolises or pre-megalopolises).

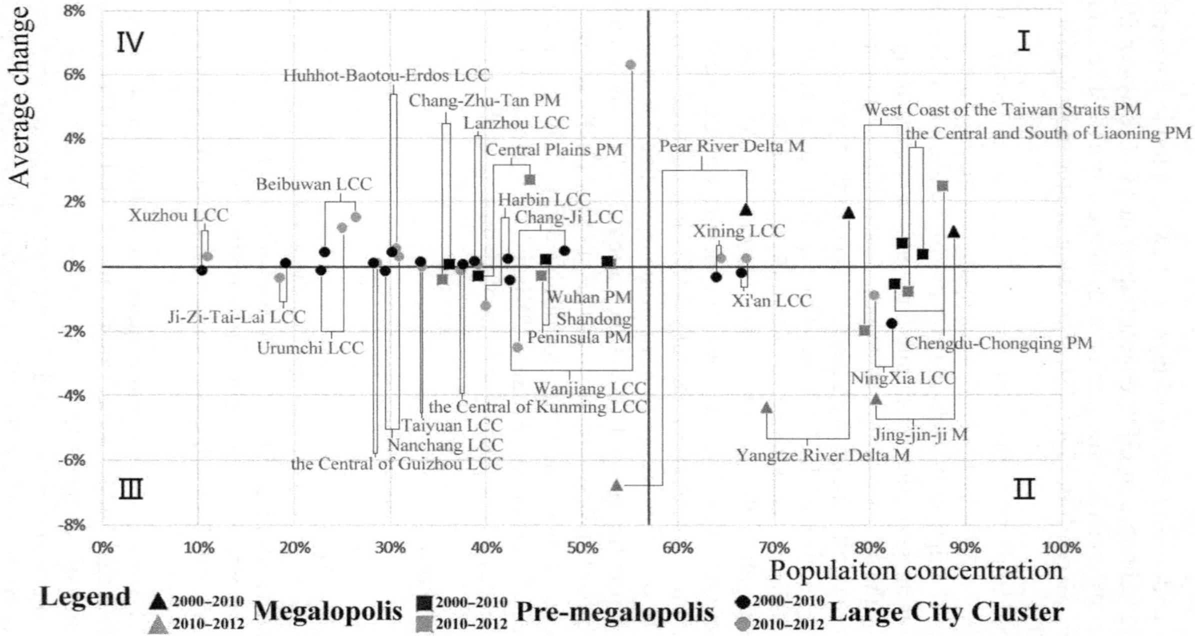

Source: NBSC-csy (2001, 2011, 2013). Compiled and drawn by Chuyang Lin.

Figure 7.7 Population concentration index of LCCs to province where they are located in 2010 and change between 2000–2010 and 2010–2012

Quadrant II shows the emergence of LCCs in central and western China. It includes the Chengdu–Chongqing pre-megalopolis and the Ningxia, Xi'an, and Xining LCCs which are all located in central and western China. More than 60 percent of the population in the provinces where these LCCs are located is concentrated within the LCCs. The concentration has decreased slightly since 2000.

Quadrant III contains only five LCCs: the central plains pre-megalopolis and the Wanjiang, Nanchang, Urumqi, and Xuzhou general LCCs. The population concentration in these LCCs is significantly lower than LCCs in quadrant I and quadrant II. Recently the concentration has decreased slightly.

Quadrant IV contains near half of China's LCCs (12 of the 26). These LCCs have a relatively lower degree of concentration—from a low of 10 percent in the Jinan–Zibo–Tai'an–Laiwu LCC (Shandong) to a little more than 50 percent in the Wuhan pre-megalopolis. Population concentration increased modestly between 2000 and 2010. This suggests that the Wuhan, Chang-Zhu-Tan, Shandong peninsula pre-megalopolises and the nine general LCCs in quadrant IV have considerable development potential.

We also constructed a data graphic between 2010 and 2012. The population concentration of LCCs changed significantly between 2010 and 2012. The Yangtze and Pearl River Delta megalopolises, and the Jing-Jin-Ji megalopolis, west coast of the Taiwan Straits pre-megalopolis, and central and south of Liaoning pre-megalopolis, which used to have a strong degree of concentration, all fall into the second and third quadrants and their population became less concentrated between 2010 and 2012. The trend of population concentration has been reversed, and the population has begun to concentrate in surrounding areas or some of the population has been lost. For example, the Pearl River Delta megalopolis shifted to the third quadrant, and the degree of population concentration decreased. This was caused by the world financial crisis in 2008 and substantial regional industrial restructuring, significantly affecting labor-intensive industry and the large number of migrants who returned home between 2010 and 2012.

The Xining and Xi'an LCCs, which are located in underdeveloped areas, moved into the fourth quadrant and exhibit a high degree of population concentration. The degree of population concentration in the Chengdu–Chongqing pre-megalopolis is increasing substantially.

The third and fourth quadrants have undergone significant changes as well. The five LCCs that fell in the fourth quadrant before 2010 are now located in the fourth quadrant with a reversed trend of population concentration. The Changchun–Jilin pre-megalopolis, Harbin LCC, Shandong peninsula pre-megalopolis, Jinan–Zibo–Tai'an–Laiwu LCC, Changsha–Zhuzhou–Xiangtan pre-megalopolis and Kunming LCC, all fall into the third quadrant where the population concentration became weaker due to population loss. Except for the Kunming LCC, the remaining LCCs used to be key areas in the planned economic period. These LCCs are facing enormous transformation pressure because of globalization and deepened market economic reforms. While the population concentration of LCCs in underdeveloped areas has been increasing since 2010, the population concentration of the LCCs with a high degree of population concentration has stopped to a certain degree.

In summary, population concentration in the three types of LCCs shows significant disparities not only among LCCs but also between LCCs and non-LCC regions. Overall, the population concentration index for all LCCs was little changed from 2000–2010. It increased only from 54.78 percent to 58.43 percent. In contrast the overall population concentration index decreased from 58.43 percent to 57.87 percent between 2010 and 2012, suggesting that population concentration in LCCs overall may slow or decline in the future. Population concentration varied considerably among LCCs. Between 2010 and 2012 population diffusion began to occur in LCCs with the highest degree of population concentration. The population concentration capacity of the LCCs that had strong industrial bases in the planned economy period has been decreasing dramatically. Decrease in the population concentration index in underdeveloped areas has been weakening and the proportion of population in non-LCC regions in these areas has been increasing, showing that the social role of the non-LCC regions is still important even if their economic role is not dominant.

LARGE CITY CLUSTERS, MEGALOPOLISES, AND THE SPACE OF FLOWS

The Space of Flows

Spanish-born US-based sociologist/urban planning/communications professor Manuel Castells, has advanced the world/global cities debate in his monumental studies of the impact of information technology on cities and society (Castells, 1996, 1997, 1998, 2001). Among his most significant contributions are the ideas of the "informational city" as a distinct type of city, the "network society" as a descriptor of the way in which contemporary society is organized, and the importance of "the space of flows"—the electronic, computerized network of telecommunications through which much of the new global economy's work is conducted in contrast to the "the space of places": that is, the physical world of neighborhoods and local business nodes within metropolitan regions. Castells argues that in cities which are high in the world city hierarchy, flows are as important, or more important than the static economic and social activities that take place in the space of places. It is the two-way movement of people, capital, ideas, and cargo from Hong Kong to south China and beyond that really defines Hong Kong: not Hong Kong's domestic economy. Flows of capital and information into and out of the Pudong area of Shanghai define Shanghai's role in the world economy as much as or more than the flow of cargo into and out of Shanghai's port.

Castells agrees with other world and global city theorists that the organization of society in the information age involves economic centralization and that technology, media, and institutionalized authority are organized in global networks. Hong Kong and Shanghai are among such important centralized places and others are emerging among Chinese cities. But in addition to these dominant cities, Castells argues that the world economy is increasingly composed of trans-territorial networks.

Borrowing from Castells, UK economic geographers Jonathan Beaverstock, Richard Smith, and Peter Taylor (2000) call for greater attention to inter-city networks—which they say are based on flows, linkages, connections and relations among cities globally.

University of Northumbria geography professor Peter Taylor, the founder and director of the Global and World Cities Network (GaWC), argues that firms benefit from two kinds of externalities—(1) externalities within cities where firms can take advantage of being close to other firms, and (2) network/connectivity externalities between cities whereby firms can take advantage of connections with firms in other cities (Taylor, 2015). Based on extensive empirical study of interconnections among major firms throughout the world Taylor has chosen to revert to the term "world city" invented by Patrick Geddes (1915) and popularized by Peter Hall (2009) rather than Saskia Sassen's (2001) term "global city" to describe the most important nodes in the world city network (ibid). He argues that Sassen placed undue emphasis on the importance of a few global cities. While Taylor acknowledges that a global hierarchy of cities exists and that New York and London (NYLON) are at the top of the hierarchy, he emphasizes connections among many world cities rather than dominance of a few cities at the top of the hierarchy.

Important questions are what is the emerging Chinese hierarchy of world cities and how do Chinese cities function as parts of a network of cities both within China and worldwide? Following Castells, Taylor, and other contributors to global and world city theory many Chinese scholars are exploring the space of flows and Chinese cities relationship to the flow of spaces and the world city network by many methods.

Zilai Tang, a professor at Tongji University's Department of Urban

Planning, and his students have explored the network of cities in the Yangtze River Delta by analyzing production service firms to describe the hierarchy between the network of cities, Shanghai, and the world (Tang and Zhao, 2010).

Miaoxi Zhao, an associate professor at South China University of Technology, Zilai Tang's former PhD candidate, and his colleagues have analyzed the air-flight network, production service firms network and city network in China (Zhao and Liu, 2012). The empirical findings and theory Tang and Zhao have developed is well known in China and is influencing scholarship and public policy.

The following sections explore the role of LCCs in China and their relationship with urban spatial structure from the perspectives of population flows, logistics flows, capital flows, and business flows.

Population flows

One of the most important connections among cities and city-regions is flows of population: both of short-term business visits and longer-term migrant flows. Given China's size, the vast floating population, and the rapid improvement of transportation, this is particularly important for China. Short, medium- and long-distance population flows are achieved through highway, railroad, ship and aircraft transportation.

Air passenger flows

The 40 Chinese airports with the largest passenger throughput in 2012 were all located in LCCs (Figure 7.8). The airports with the largest passenger throughput were the Beijing airport and Pudong and Hongqiao airports in Shanghai where the passenger throughput reached 81.93 million and 78.66 million, respectively in 2012 (Civil Aviation Administration of China, 2013). These airports only ranked behind the airports in Tokyo (Narita and Haneda), London (Heathrow and Gatwick), and Atlanta. The volume of passengers flowing into and out of the Beijing and Shanghai airports were followed by airport passenger flows into and out of Guangzhou, Chengdu, Shenzhen, Kunming, Xi'an, and Chongqing, all of which had passenger throughput of more than 20 million passengers in 2012. The passenger throughput of Guangzhou, Chengdu, and Shenzhen ranked 18th, 46th, and 48th in the world, respectively.

As a contribution to understanding China's space of flows and city network, we sorted the 2012 air passenger volume data of major Chinese airport route segments and plotted a spatial network diagram of the 40 largest flows. Figure 7.8 shows that the Beijing–Shanghai route segment had the largest passenger volume, followed by the Shanghai–Shenzhen, Beijing–Shenzhen, Beijing–Guangzhou and Beijing–Chongqing segments.

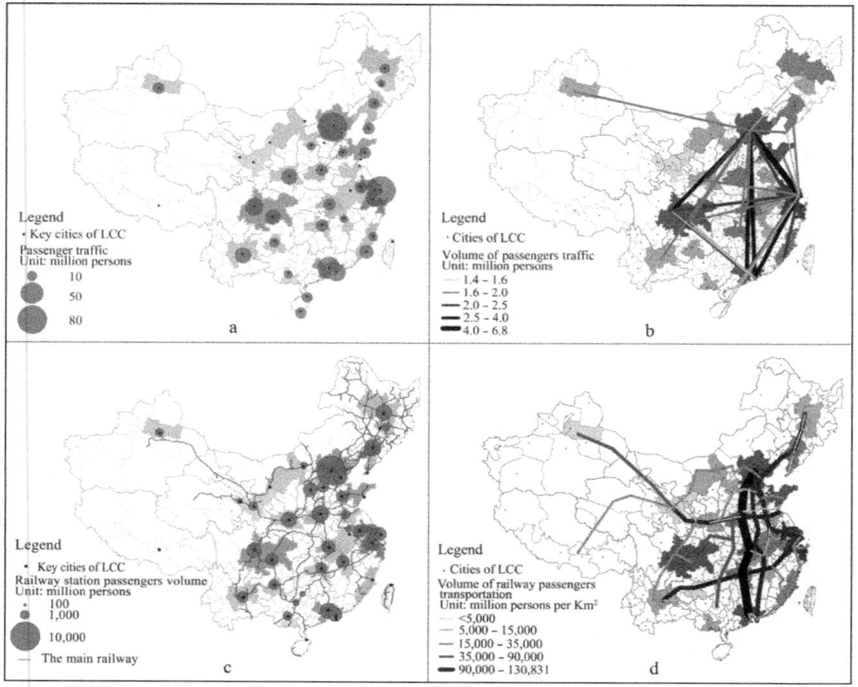

Note: (a) passenger traffic of main airports, 2012; (b) top 40 air passengers flows among China's airports, 2012; (c) passenger traffic/passenger volume of main train stations, 2013; (d) passenger flows among main railway routes, 2013.

Source: NBSC-csy (2013); Civil Aviation Administration of China (2013); Ministry of Transport of China (PRC-MTC, 2014). Compiled and drawn by Lijuan Wang.

Figure 7.8 Chinese passengers traffic and flows by air and trains

Segments with large passenger volume mainly connect other cities to Shanghai, Beijing, Shenzhen (Guangzhou) and Chengdu. They include segments from Shenyang, Dalian, Qingdao, and Xiamen to Shanghai, and from Urumqi, Kunming, and Harbin to Beijing. The aviation trunk network constitutes the core area in the shape of a quadrilateral formed by Beijing, Shanghai, Shenzhen/Guangzhou and Chengdu. The three major airport gateways to the world—officially designated by aviation authorities—are Beijing, Shanghai, and Guangzhou.

Railway passenger flows

In addition to aviation flows, railway passenger flows strengthen connections among cities in different parts of China. Constrained by topographic conditions and limited railway lines, the backbone railway network is formed by several main railway systems as shown in Figure 7.8.

For historical reasons, railways in China are quite dense in the north and less dense in the south. Connections among cities in the south depend on more diversified modes of transportation. Railway passenger flows have increased since August 1, 2008 when the first high speed railway in China—the Beijing–Tianjin high speed railway—began operation. China invested heavily in high speed rail construction as part of their 2008 economic stimulus package in response to the global financial crisis. By the end of 2014, China's high speed railway network had reached 17,000km, by far the largest high speed railway network in the world.

In order to better understand the contribution of China's rail network to China's city network and the space of flows we analyzed rail passenger volumes in 2012. Figure 7.8 shows that among the major railway lines in China, the largest passenger volumes were on the Beijing–Guangzhou, Beijing–Shanghai, Beijing–Shenzhen, Shanghai–Kunming, Lianyungang–Lanzhou and Beijing–Harbin railway lines.

In south China, the major railway lines are the Beijing–Shenzhen railway, Shanghai–Kunming railway, and Jiaozuo–Liuzhou railway. Passenger flows among cities in the north are primarily shaped by railway passenger flows. Most of the major railway stations with large volumes of passenger traffic are located in north China (Figures 7.9 and 7.10).

Highway system

China has built an impressive system of highways permitting population to flow by car, and shuttles and cargo to flow by truck. By the end of 2013, China had 104,400km (64,871 miles) of advanced modern highways, more than 30 percent of the highway mileage in the US, and China's highway density was 1.08km per 100km^2. In the NNSUP, the national highway system is planned to cover all cities by 2020.

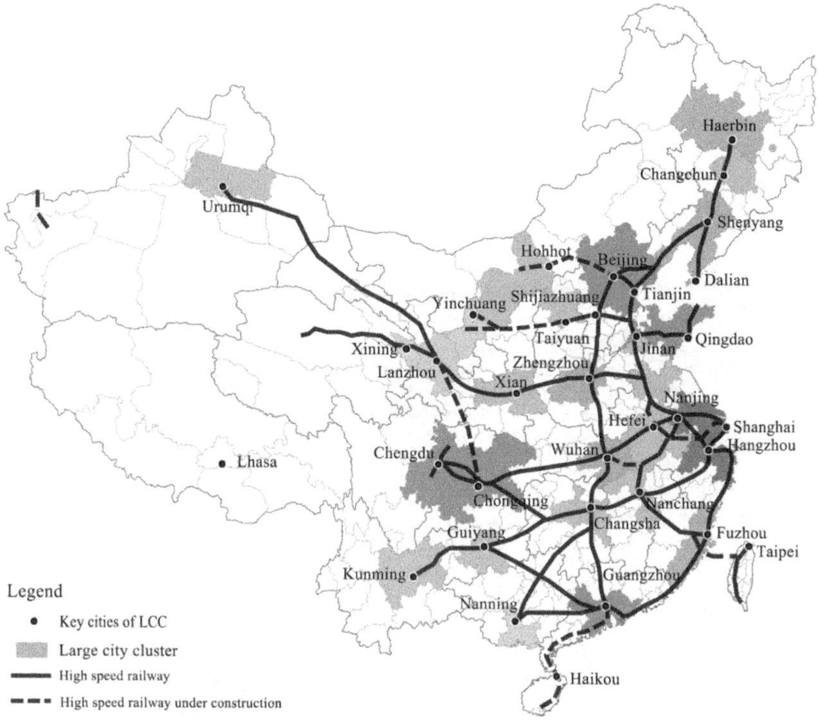

Source: Compiled by Lijuan Wang.

Figure 7.9 China's high speed railway network, 2015

Cargo flows

Cargo flows of raw materials, parts, finished cargo, and other commodities destined both for domestic consumption and export have significantly supported regional economic development and urbanization. Most cargo arrives in China by air, rail, truck, and ship from locations where they are produced and flow to destinations in China where they are consumed domestically and assembled into products for domestic and foreign markets. Most cargo exported from China flows by sea or air.

Air cargo flows

Because air transport is more expensive than shipping goods by truck or boat, an analysis of the volume of air cargo flows by plane helps clarify the spatial structure of high value commodities. Among the 40 largest aviation cargo flows in China's major cities, the pattern is similar to aviation

Source: Photo by Li Zhang.

Figure 7.10 High speed trains in China, 2015

passenger flows. The traffic flow primarily occurs within the quadrilateral enclosed by Beijing, Shanghai, Chengdu, and Guangzhou–Shenzhen. Only Kunming, Xiamen, Urumqi, and Dalian are outside the quadrilateral (Figure 7.11(a)). The flows of cargo by plane closely follow the pattern of population air traffic flows.

Rail cargo flows

Railway freight shipments between provinces illustrate the structure of interregional economic connections. Coal is the most important bulk cargo, and is primarily transported by railway. This has had an important influence on China's rail system and considerably affects interregional traffic flows of cargo by railway today. The main coal distribution centers are located in Inner Mongolia, Shanxi and North Shaanxi provinces. We constructed a 31 × 31 matrix of the flow of rail cargo among provinces in 2012 excluding the traffic flow of coal. Figure 7.11(b) shows the 40 largest railway cargo flows. It shows that the flow of cargo other than coal in China by railway principally occurs between neighboring provinces and is concentrated in the northeast and north provinces and central plains (Henan province and surrounding regions). It also shows flows radiating from Guangdong and Guangxi.

Using the same method for train passengers flows, we draw the map to show the cargo flows in the main railway routes. Figure 7.11(c) shows that while railway freight and passenger transportation routes in China are generally related, some differences also exist. The former is mainly in the north and the latter distributed mainly in the east. Freight transportation routes shape the obvious horizontal and vertical gridding, which connects the three great regions closely. Except for the northeast, the railway freight network is not yet fully developed.

Shipping flows

In addition to flows of cargo by air, railway, and highway, domestic and long-distance flows also includes movement by water. Construction of the Three Gorges Dam and economic development in Nanjing, Wuhan and Chongqing since 2005 has made the Yangtze River waterway the largest inland shipping channel in the world for eight consecutive years (China News Web, 2014b). In 2013, the flow of cargo on the Yangtze River waterway reached 1.92 billion tons and ranked first in the world for international cargo flow. With completion of the Yangshan Port, Shanghai has grown to be the largest port in the world with 31.50 million standard containers (twenty-foot equivalents, TEUs) per year. Shenzhen port is the fourth and Ningbo-Zhoushan port, Guangzhou and Qingdao ports are the sixth, seventh and eighth, respectively.

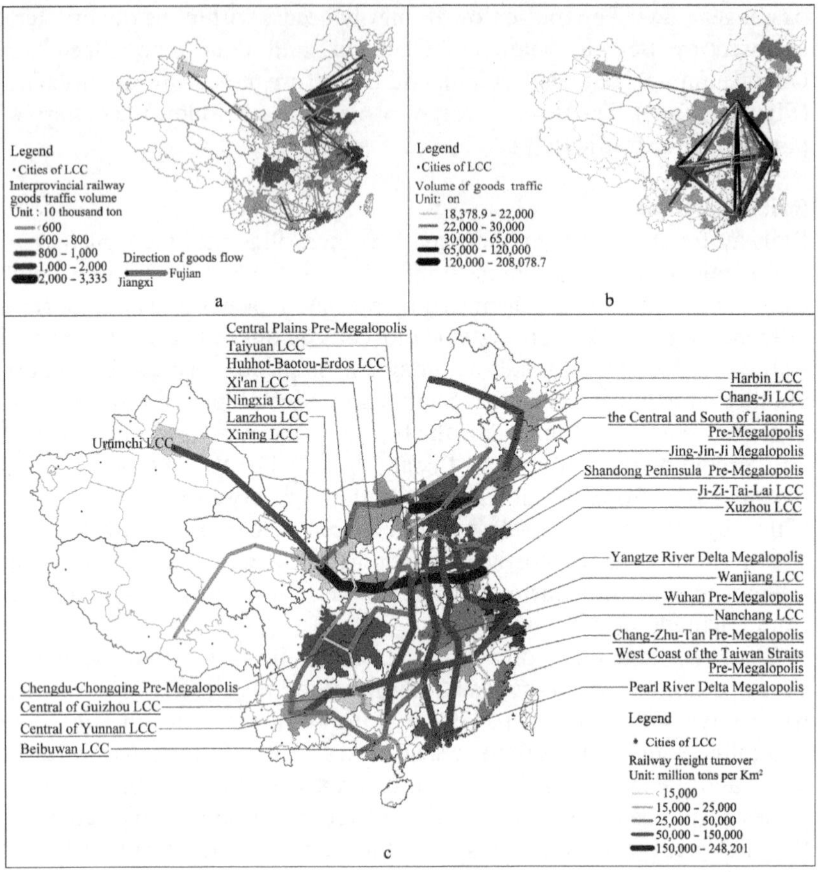

Note: (a) Interprovincial railroad goods traffic volume flows 2012; (b) Top 40 flows of goods traffic by air, 2013; (c) Railway freight turnover (except coal) on China's main railway routes, 2013.

Source: (a) NBSC-csye (2013); (b) Civil Aviation Administration of China (2013); (c) Ministry of Transport of China (PRC-MTC, 2014). Compiled and drawn by Lijuan Wang.

Figure 7.11 Chinese cargo traffic and flows by air and rail

Capital flows

Castells, Sassen, Taylor, and other scholars writing about global and world cities, information technology, and the global economy emphasize the importance of flows of capital. In the last thirty years China has become well connected to the global economy and large volumes of capital flows into and out of Shanghai, Beijing, and other Chinese centers of finance to

Hong Kong, Singapore, New York, London and elsewhere. Capital flows within China have increased exponentially and are a major driver of development and urbanization.

Capital flows between regions are one of the best indicators for measuring interregional connections. Although data on the exact volumes of capital flows are not available, information on bank deposits and loans in China's large cities are. We used city deposit and loan elasticity indices to estimate flows of capital into and out of Chinese cities.

Figure 7.12 shows total deposits in prefecture-level cities and above. The two super-megacities Beijing and Shanghai have the largest quantity of deposits, followed by Shenzhen, Guangzhou, Hangzhou, Nanjing, Chengdu, Chongqing, and Tianjin. Most deposits are concentrated in the

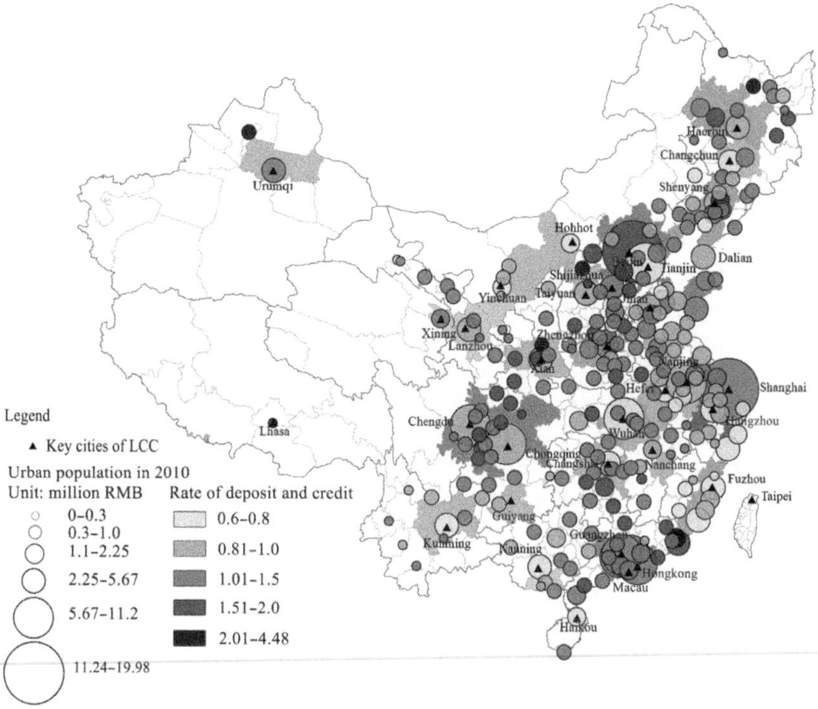

Note: Elasticity index = (ratio of deposits to loans in prefecture-level cities)/(ratio of national deposits to national loans).

Source: NBSC-csy (2013), compiled and drawn by Lijuan Wang.

Figure 7.12 Elasticity indices for bank deposits in prefecture-level cities, 2012

Yangtze River Delta megalopolis, followed by other of the largest LCCs in China—the Jing-Jin-Ji, Shandong peninsula, central plain and Chengdu–Chongqing pre-megalopolises.

A city's deposit and loan elasticity index is a good summary indicator of capital flows and calculating and comparing these indices provides a good general picture of capital movement in China's space of flows. We used the formula $E_i = (D_i / C_i) / (D_n / C_n)$ to calculate the deposit and income elasticity of prefectural-level cities and above where E_i is the deposit loan elasticity index of city i; D_i is the total deposits of city i; C_i is the total loans of city i; D_n is the total national deposits; and C_n is the total national loans.

When the elasticity index (E_i) is greater than 1.0, the city's capital is not being completely used locally. Some flows out in the form of loans. This will occur when China's central bank imposes a ceiling on the local loan volume or a city lacks local investment projects sufficient to absorb local deposits, or when local people are rich enough that there is excess capital to be invested wherever the likelihood of profit is highest. If the elasticity index (E_i) is smaller than 1.0, the city lacks an accumulation of private capital and must receive loans from banks and other financial institutions, but drawing on capital from elsewhere to promote local economic development. Figure 7.12 shows that cities where the elasticity index (E_i) is greater than 1.0 include Beijing, Shanghai, Guangzhou, Shenzhen, and most of the second- and third-class cities—most of which are less developed compared with the key cities.

Generally a city's economic status explains its capital status and vice versa. The location of a city can also help explain its capital status. The elasticity index (E_i) of the four megacities is greater than 1.0 because of the high level of local economic development and high income of the residents. The reason why the elasticity indices (E_i) of the second- and third-class cities in western China are greater than 1.0 is either because of quota controls or because local construction projects cannot absorb local bank deposits. The cities where E_i is smaller than 1.0 are primarily capital cities, megacities, super-megacities, and southeast coastal cities, that use outside sources for local loans. This finding indicates that these cities are attracting regional capital for local development, and is consistent with the national policy for central cities and development of LCCs. From another perspective, while such capital flows have the positive effect of promoting the development of key cities, they simultaneously squeeze development opportunities for the second- and third-class cities and even towns, which may increase interregional differences.

Business flows

Economic relationships among cities are the result of interregional, national, and global flows of people, cargo, and capital. The interregional distribution of business reflects the economic relationships among cities in a region (Tang and Zhao, 2010). For example, if an enterprise is headquartered in Shanghai with a division in Hangzhou, the relationship between the two cities will likely be strengthened. Peter Taylor and others use proxies such as the number of offices of major international corporations as indicators of connectivity in the world city network (Taylor, 2015), and the same logic applies at lower levels such as nation states (such as China), and regions within countries.

Miaoxi Zhao, an associate professor at South China University of Science and Technology, has analyzed 2009 data on 203,263 enterprises, which have headquarters and divisions in cities at different levels (prefecture-level cities and prefectures). In order to shed further light on inter-regional business connectivity among Chinese cities, we reanalyzed professor Zhao's data. The data form a 330 × 330 matrix, and the business flow between any two cities is the business flow of the enterprises that have headquarters and divisions in two or more cities. It is impossible to visualize all the flows in a matrix this large, so we selected the 40 largest flows to draw Figure 7.13(a): a simplified diagram of the most important intercity connectivity in China. The highest flows occur between Beijing, Shanghai, Guangzhou, and Shenzhen. These flows are followed by the flows between Chengdu, Nanjing, and Hangzhou. This is consistent with research on the distribution of producer services branches by Zhao and Liu (2012).

In addition to analyzing connectivity among cities we were interested in connectivity among LCCs based on enterprises which are located just within LCCs. To better understand LCC connectivity we merged prefecture-level cities and prefectures in LCCs to form a 26 × 26 matrix with LCCs as the unit of analysis. Figure 7.13(a) shows 40 largest flows among the enterprises in the LCCs. Figure 7.13(c) is significantly different from Figure 7.11(b). Business flows among LCCs form a network that changes from the strong triangle formed by Beijing, Guangzhou/Shenzhen, and Shanghai in the case of all large cities into a network formed by six dominant LCCs, namely, the Jing-Jin-Ji megalopolis, Yangtze River Delta megalopolis, Chengdu–Chongqing pre-megalopolis, Pearl River Delta megalopolis, Shandong peninsula pre-megalopolis, and central and south of Liaoning pre-megalopolis. This network provides fundamental support for the urbanization of China. It may be regarded as the spatial skeleton for the regional economic and population concentration of China.

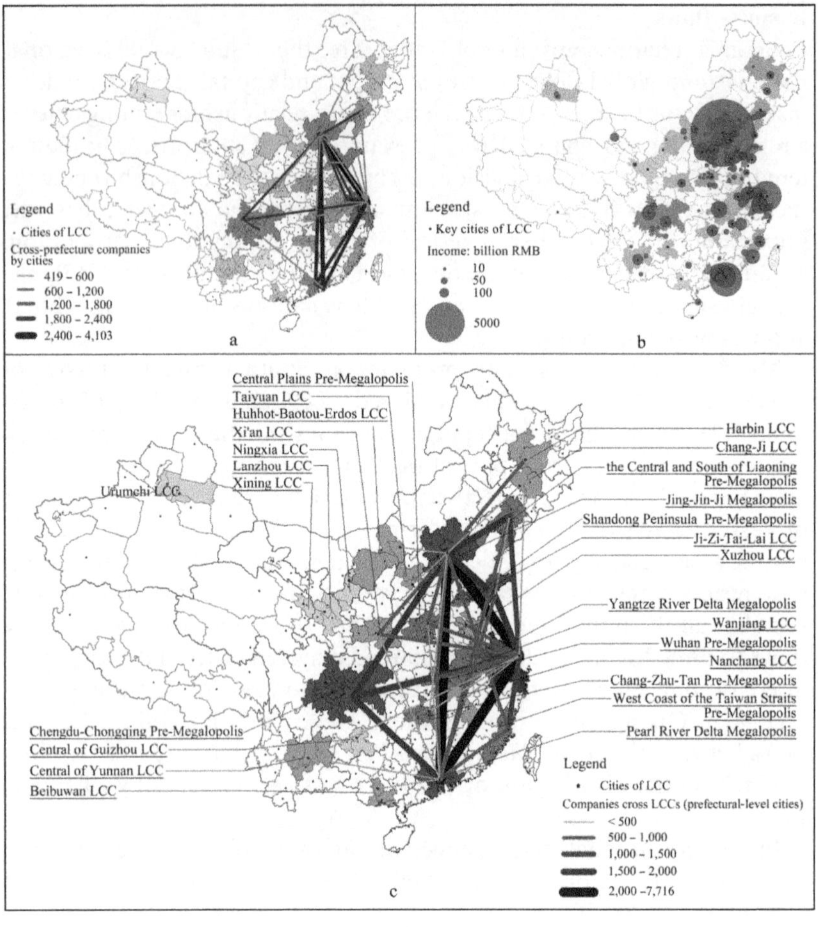

Note: (a) Inter-city company connectivity; (b) business income of Fortune 500 companies, 2014; (c) inter-LCC company connectivity.

Source: Fortunechina Web, 2014, based on Fortune. 2014. *Global 500 2014* http://fortune.com/global500/. Electronic database of all companies of China in 2009. Original data was compiled by Prof Miaoxi Zhao at South China University of Technology (2014). Maps and data graphics compiled and drawn by Chuyang Lin.

Figure 7.13 Inter-city and inter-LCCs connectivity and global connectivity

China's Macro Spatial Network

A number of Chinese experts have summarized macro spatial development in China that helps put many different pieces of information about changes in policy regarding China's macro spatial network into helpful general analytic categories.

Kai Wang, Deputy Director of the Chinese Academy of Urban Planning, Design and Research has classified changes of urban spatial structure since the founding of New China into four categories: (a) inland city layout based on the 156 industrial projects supported by the Soviet Union (1953–1963), (b) inland third-line construction far away from the cities preparing for war (1964–1977), (c) policy-driven development of coastal cities during reform and opening up (1978–1999), (d) and spatial diversification strategy oriented toward coordinated development since 2000 (Wang, 2006).

Xiaojiang Li (2012), head of the Chinese Academy of Urban Planning, Design and Research, has proposed that China's national spatial strategy has evolved from an equilibrium strategy to a non-equilibrium strategy and from the establishment of special economic zones and opening up of coastal cities at the beginning of reform and opening up to the establishment of national districts and four spatial strategies (east, west, central, northeast) described in Chapter 4 on regional policies and regional urbanization.

Four core national LCCs have taken shape, namely, the Yangtze River Delta megalopolis, Pearl River Delta megalopolis, Jing-Jin-Ji megalopolis, and Chengdu–Chongqing pre-megalopolis. Mr. Li reviewed the national spatial strategy evolution process and tentatively proposed the idea of a diamond structure made by the four national LCCs mentioned above.

A diamond-shaped structure describing the four core LCCs is consistent with our analysis, but we conclude that the Chengdu–Chongqing pre-megalopolis has not yet achieved a level of significance comparable to the other three megalopolises in east China, so the diamond is unbalanced. The Chengdu–Chongqing pre-megalopolis may become China's fourth largest megalopolis, but as this book went to press in spring, 2015 it still had a long way to go.

Forecasting the rise of new megalopolises in the future is an interesting challenge. The analysis of our study shows that four LCCs have formed in the Bohai Sea Region: (1) Jing-Jin corridors, (2) Central and south Liaoning pre-megalopolis, (3) the Shandong peninsula pre-megalopolis, and (4) the Jinan–Zibo–Tai'an–Laiwu LCC. Li (2012) argued that two additional areas may become megalopolises in the future—the Wuhan pre-megalopolis in central China and the Urumqi LCC in northwest China. It is likely to take a while for these pre-megalopolises to become full megalopolises, because they remain in the initial stage of resource concentration and still lack the economic scale or population to qualify as megalopolises. Although the central cities of the Wuhan pre-megalopolis and Urumqi LCC are reasonably well developed, their hinterlands lack strong support from the LCCs. The economic scale of these LCCs is far smaller than the central and south of Liaoning and Shandong peninsula pre-megalopolises and even smaller than of the central plains pre-megalopolis.

The distribution of international companies in China is of particular interest in understanding China's relationship to the world city network. In order to understand the spatial distribution of international companies in China, we examined the headquarters or core branches of the top 500 companies in the world that had operations in China in 2014. We used the Forbes 500 list of top corporations. If the company's headquarters was in China we used the headquarter's location. If the headquarters of the company was not in China, we used the core branch of the company in China: that is the largest branch and de facto Chinese headquarters of the company. Table 7.1 shows that the three megalopolises had nearly half of the headquarters or core branches of these top 500 enterprises (49.2 percent). Among these megalopolises, the Jing-Jin-Ji megalopolis ranks first, followed by the Yangtze River Delta and then the Pearl River Delta megalopolises. The revenue and profits of the enterprises with headquarters or core branches in the three megalopolises accounts for more than 70 percent of both total revenue and profits of multinational corporate operations in China. One hundred and nine of the Fortune 500 companies with headquarters or core branches in China are located in the Jing-Jin-Ji megalopolis. Together they account for 58.7 percent of the total profits of all Fortune 500 companies in China.

Only 13.4 percent of the headquarters or core branch offices are in the seven pre-metropolises. Among these pre-megalopolises, the Chengdu–Chongqing pre-megalopolis has 16 enterprises, the Shandong peninsula pre-megalopolis 13, and the Wuhan pre-megalopolis 10. The total revenue and profits of the enterprises in the seven pre-megalopolises are only 7.2 percent and 5.0 percent of countrywide totals, respectively. In addition to the three megalopolises, the Shandong peninsula and central plains pre-megalopolises have moderate densities of Fortune 500 enterprise headquarters and core branches. The rest are scattered in other areas.

To conclude, the regional spatial pattern of LCCs in China is a diamond-like multipoint macro spatial network. The three megalopolises in east China still play the leading role in China's economy. The three pre-megalopolises in central and south of Liaoning, Shandong peninsula and Chengdu–Chongqing are the important development poles with potential to grow to be megalopolises in the near future. The next four pre-megalopolises, in the central plains, Wuhan, Changsha–Zhuzhou–Xiangtan, and the west coast of the Taiwan Straits come next and are also important for China's regional growth, but need more time to mature into megalopolises.

Table 7.1 Distribution of headquarters and core branches of Fortune 500 companies in China, 2014

	Companies		Business income		Profit	
	Number	Proportion	(billion RMB)	Proportion	(billion RMB)	Proportion
Three Megalopolises	246	49.2%	20,546	71.1%	1,879	75.6%
Jing-Jin-Ji megalopolis	109	21.8%	14,650	50.7%	1,460	58.7%
Yangtze River Delta megalopolis	88	17.6%	3,686	12.8%	222	8.9%
Pearl River Delta megalopolis	49	9.8%	2,210	7.6%	197	7.9%
Seven Pre-Megalopolises	67	13.4%	2,087	7.2%	124	5.0%
Chengdu–Chongqing LCC	16	3.2%	474	1.6%	27	1.1%
The Central and South of Liaoning LCC	4	0.8%	168	0.6%	1	0.0%
Central Plains LCC	7	1.4%	130	0.4%	7	0.3%
Shandong Peninsula LCC	13	2.6%	412	1.4%	17	0.7%
The West Cost of Taiwan Straits LCC	9	1.8%	394	1.4%	49	2.0%
Wuhan LCC	10	2.0%	309	1.1%	16	0.7%
Changsha–Zhuzhou–Xiangtan LCC	8	1.6%	201	0.7%	6	0.3%
16 LCCs in other areas	187	37.4%	6,268	21.7%	484	19.5%
Fortune 500 Top Companies	500	100.0%	28,901	100.0%	2,487	100.0%

Source: Fortune Web (2014), Global 500 2014, retrieved on September 16, 2015 from http://fortune.com/global500.

CONCLUSION: THE RISE OF LARGE CITY CLUSTERS AND GLOBAL MEGALOPOLISES IN CHINA

In their important article titled "World-City Network: A New Metageography?," written in 2000, Jonathan Beaverstock, Richard Smith and Peter Taylor questioned the territorialist "metageography" of mainstream social science which conceives the world in terms of bordered, state-defined containers of political-economic life. Instead they sought to define a new metageography that encompasses the inter-relationships of cities and global metropolitan regions throughout the world based largely on connectivity of firms within the cities.

Building on its rapid economic growth, China is entering a new stage when economic and urbanization quality rather than simply quality will be key issues. The World Bank's 2008 *World Development Report* summarized the following three aspects of China's recent sustained and rapid economic growth: (1) urbanization has increased the spatial density of GDP and population. Thus, the layout of China's infrastructure is more efficient; (2) the construction of highways, railways, and aviation facilities have shortened temporal and spatial distances in China; and (3) China's opening up policy has reduced trade barriers between China and other countries (World Bank, 2009). In this environment, LCCs have prospered. In China's National New Style Urbanization Plan, LCCs are mentioned 50 times, which shows the importance attached by the national government to the development of LCCs. The NNSUP explicitly proposes the following measures related to LCCs:

> taking LCCs as the main form to promote the coordinated development of large-, medium- and small-sized cities and small towns; making efforts to settle 100 million people who have left the agricultural work and other resident population; optimizing the pattern of urbanization and forming the "two horizontals and three verticals" urbanization strategy by 2020; increasing the economic and population concentration capacity of LCCs and improving the integration level and international competitiveness of LCCs in East China; making the LCCs in Central and Western China important new growth poles to promote balanced regional development; optimizing and strengthening LCCs in East China; facilitating the development of the LCCs in inland China. (PRC, 2014)

Although promoting and improving LCCs have become parts of China's national strategy, the concept of LCCs has not been defined yet in official documents. The NNSUP does not provide a definition of LCCs or define the number and spatial scope of LCCs. It only cited the schematic diagram of urbanization policy in a document titled "National Major Function-Oriented Zoning" issued by National Development and Reform Commission (PRC-NDRC, 2011) to illustrate the national urbanization strategy. The National Major Function-oriented Zoning policy proposed the concept of "main urbanized areas" but does not provide a definition of LCCs.

This chapter has reviewed the background and origin of the concept of LCCs, describes previous scholarship and competing definitions of LCCs, and presented our own analysis of the formation and evolution process of LCCs and what and where they currently are. Based on the realities and the intention of national strategy regarding LCCs in China, we proposed criteria for classifying LCCs, and based on them have identified 26 LCCs.

Among the 26 LCCs, we define three as megalopolises and seven as pre-megalopolises. The rest are ordinary LCCs. This classification lays a foundation for discussing LCCs and formulating relevant policies appropriate to the different types.

The data in this chapter show that most of China's GDP is generated within LCCs and that these LCCs concentrate much of China's population on a small percentage of China's land. They play an irreplaceable role in China's national urbanization process. The GDP generated within the Yangtze River Delta megalopolis reached 9.78 trillion RMB in 2013 (Central Government Web, 2014)—higher than the GDP of Korea, Spain, or Australia (NBSC, 2014).

In this chapter, we have confirmed the vital function of LCCs and megalopolises in China's national concentration of its economy and population. At the national level, LCCs have become the engine of national economic growth and the major site of national urbanization. At the regional level, the effect of the economic concentration of LCCs has emerged, and some LCCs with a mature economy have evolved into megalopolises. The three megalopolises have evolved from the polarized development stage to a diffused and moderately stable stage, where they now play leading roles in regional economic development and urbanization in China. In particular, the Yangtze River Delta megalopolis has shifted toward the west along the Yangtze River and gradually merged with Wanjiang LCC in Anhui province. Inland LCCs have also developed rapidly.

Between 2000 and 2010 the economic concentration of LCCs divided: about the same number are increasing as decreasing. While there are exceptions, generally the greater the concentration the more rapid the rate of economic increase. In contrast, the population in most LCCs is increasing. As with GDP concentration, the greater the degree of concentration the faster the rate of population increase. However, the increases have been very small (under 5 percent in ten years) except in China's biggest super megaregions. After 2010 the most recent data shows changes in these patterns, but it is too early to tell whether these are simply a short-term response to the global economic crisis and economic restructuring.

In addition to economic and population concentration in LCCs, study of the connections among different LCCs is important. From the perspective of the space of flows, this chapter discusses flows of population, cargo, capital, and business among large cities and among LCCs. The study demonstrates that LCCs play a crucial role in the regional spatial network in China, which is a diamond-shaped multipoint pattern composed of three megalopolises and seven pre-megalopolises. This system is the backbone of the socio-economic development of China.

The research in this chapter shows that LCCs are a major focus of economic growth and the principal site of urbanization in China. In the transition phase from quantity-oriented growth to quality-oriented development, LCCs and non-LCC areas will play their respective roles. The former is the engine of the economic growth of China; the latter an important contributor to economic growth and economic diversity and equity. Although their economic functions are important, urbanization quality issues in LCCs such as social equity, community resilience, environmental quality, mobility, and livability should be considered as well. The healthy and coordinated development of LCCs and non-LCC areas is essential for promoting integrated regional development and building a harmonious society.

8. Towns and rural urbanization

City and countryside in China are not antagonistic but organically blended, containing an integral network of towns (Zhèn) between cities and countries. Towns are neither cities nor counties but a unique settlement type halfway between a city and a county.

The noted Chinese sociologist Xiaotong Fei, whose PhD supervisor was anthropologist Bronislaw Malinowski, considered rural towns a distinct social entity, at a higher level than a rural community—a community mainly composed of a working population not engaged in pure agricultural work (Fei, [1984]2004). Fei considered towns different from rural communities in terms of geography, population, economics, and the environment, but intimately related to the surrounding countryside. Other Chinese scholars agree with Fei that Chinese society is neither urban nor rural, but best conceived as a structure made up of cities, towns, and villages (Gong, 2005).

The American anthropologist, William Skinner in his exhaustive study of Chinese urbanization in late imperial China pointed out that China has had an urban–rural continuum and market towns have played an important role in rural areas for centuries (Skinner, 1977: 259).

In the early twentieth century, American historian and sociologist Josiah Galpin combined the words rural and urban into a new word he called rurban to describe the nature of the American Midwestern rural society, where, in his words, "the vast countryside is dotted with towns, which are situated in the intersection of the county and the city, and blends the development of land, civilization, culture and urban and rural residents, instead of separating the urban and rural areas" (Galpin, 1918: 64). This is very similar to Xiaotong Fei's description of towns in rural China. The concept of rurban or rurbanism was later extended to developing countries, such as India (Richard, 1970) and Indonesia (McGee, 1991).

Towns are an important, but often overlooked, component in modern China's urban system. The development of towns is closely related to modern China's socio-economic system and urbanization. The transformation of China's economy and urbanization from state controlled to market oriented after China's reform and opening up policy started with towns. Bottom-up urbanization is important.

TOWNS AND CHINA'S URBANIZATION

As described in Chapter 4 on regional policies and regional urbanization and Chapter 5 on globalization and China's urbanization, cities have been central to the rapid urbanization of China. Impressive population growth has occurred in small, medium, large and megacities. But a description of China's urbanization that considers only cities would tell only part of the story.

Towns' Contribution to China's Urbanization

At the same time that China was promoting development in cities they were promoting development of official towns and township seats in rural areas to facilitate the management and services of rural areas. The reforms that occurred in the early period of reform and opening up unleashed a wave of bottom-up urbanization in towns throughout China. Over time towns have taken on more and more urban characteristics. Towns in China can be as large as cities in Western countries with populations exceeding 100,000 residents in selected regions, such as southern Jiangsu and northern Zhejiang provinces and the Pearl River Delta.

Towns in China consist of county capitals—the seats of county government, other official towns, and townships. County capitals are usually larger and more economically developed than other official towns. An official town and a township are at the same administrative level. However, official towns generally have more urban characteristics than townships. Townships seats are usually small. They do not reach the standard of an official town, but serve as service centers in rural areas. In China's urban system, townships and towns are lower levels of county-level cities or urban districts. They have some of the public services of a municipality, but they are most closely related to rural areas as described in Chapter 3 on China's administrative divisions (Figure 8.1).

In the United States, towns rarely have a population of over 10,000 people. Their legal status and functions vary from state to state. Ordinarily counties provide services in towns. In rural areas of the US towns' economic functions are closely related to agriculture, but in suburbs they mainly house the commuting urban workforce. Many US towns have retail and service firms that serve the local population and some have manufacturing, research and development, or non-local service functions that serve a larger region. The lowest levels of government in the United States are cities and counties, not towns. Since most towns are in the unincorporated area of counties, they are usually governed by the counties where they are located which plan, regulate land use, provide

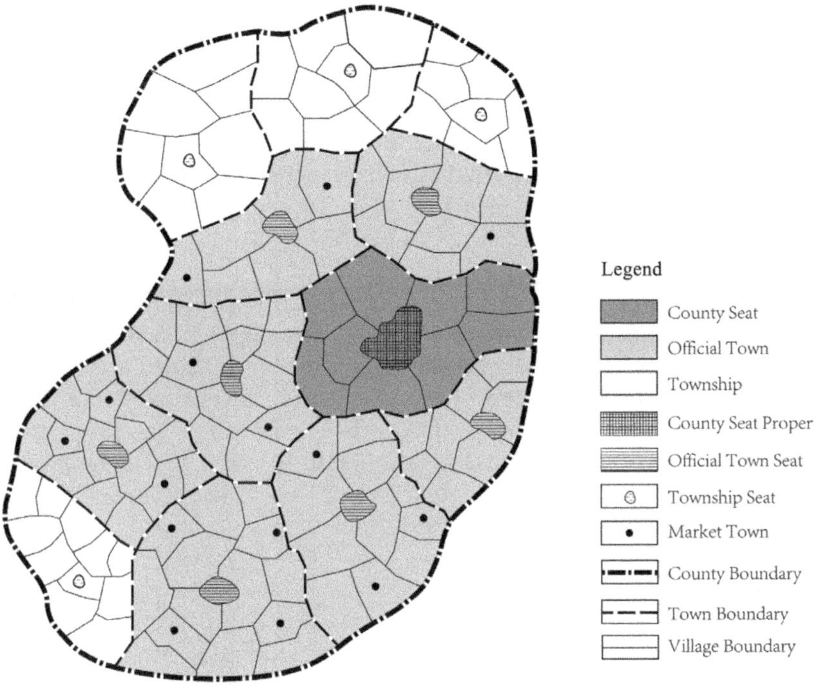

Source: Drawn by Liijuan Wang.

Figure 8.1 Administrative divisions of a hypothetical Chinese county, 2015

police and fire protection, maintain roads and other public infrastructure, and provide social services.

It is important to understand the difference between town regions and towns in China. After regionalization reform in the 1980s towns have become administrative divisions that usually administer a large rural region surrounding the town seat as described in Chapter 3. This chapter provides population statistics on both town seats and town regions. The former refers to the total population of permanent residents in the administrative division of an official town—the town proper; the latter to permanent residents of the town region.

China had 19,683 official towns in 2011. The average population in a town seat was 12,500 and the average population in a town region was 44,000 (NBSC-cts, 2012).

In rural and urban censuses for the purposes of calculating China's urbanization rate, official town seats are categorized as urban, and their residents are included in the urban population. Townships and rural regions of official towns are categorized as rural and their residents are categorized as rural population by the sixth census standard. The definitions of urban areas and urban population have been changed many times, as Chapter 6 described. Since the beginning of 1980s China's urban population and the urbanization ratio have increased rapidly and the rural population has declined since 1991. The population of town seats has increased both in absolute terms and as a proportion of the total urban population.

The growth of town seats' population contributes significantly to the growth of China's urbanized population. The population in town seats increased from 61 million in 1982 to 266 million in 2010, a growth of 205 million. The proportion of the population in town seats (classified as urban) to the nationwide total urban population increased from 29.6 percent in 1982 to 39.7 percent in 2010. In other words, the growth of town seats' population has contributed 47 percent of the increase of China's urbanization ratio since 1982 (Table 8.1).

Research on Towns in China

There are a large and increasing number of studies of towns in China, particularly since 1981 when the well-known Chinese anthropologist and sociologist Xaiotong Fei received the Huxley Medal from the Royal Anthropological Institute in London for his research on the countryside in China. Professor Fei's book *Peasant Life in China* is a pioneering work that has been influential in China and the West. In 1984 Fei published an article titled "Small Towns, Big Matters" (in Fei [1984]2004), based on his many field investigations in rural areas, that stimulated a further nationwide wave of research on towns.

Table 8.1 Change in China's total, urban, and town population, 1982–2010

	1982	1990	2000	2010
Total Population: millions	1,004	1,131	1,243	1,333
Urban Population: millions	206	296	459	670
Rural Population: millions	798	834	784	663
Urbanization Ratio	20.6%	26.2%	36.9%	50.3%
Town Seat Population: millions	61	85	166	266
Town Seat Population to Urban Population	29.6%	28.7%	36.2%	39.7%

Source: NBSC-census (1984, 1992, 2002, 2012).

While many scholars agree with Fei's opinion that towns are the key to Chinese urbanization, some researchers argue that because towns generally have low economic efficiency, low industry levels, and weak competitiveness they should not be a priority. This dispute continues today (Zhou and Yu, 1988; Chen, 1996; Niu, 2000; Zheng and Chen, 2000; Zhao, 2001; Shi, 2002; Zhao et al., 2002; Meng, 2005; Wang, X., 2010a; Li et al., 2014). Feng (2001) pointed out that research on towns in China before 2001 mostly concentrated on economic development, planning and construction, and on township and village enterprises. Xu and Zhang (2004) reviewed the literature and found that since the 1990s most studies of towns have focused on industrial agglomeration, location, spatial structure and the path dependence of small town developments. Li et al. (2006) reviewed research on small town environmental issues published in the 1990s and concluded that environmental problems in towns are major factors restricting the sustainable development of towns. However, Du et al. (2014) showed that the development pattern of towns does not necessarily lead to environmental pollution. Some scholars have summarized the overall course of the development of towns in China after the establishment of the PRC and reform and opening up (Wu and Cai, 2009; Wang and Zhao, 2009). These studies show that small town development in China has evolved over time. It appears that the development of towns requires an incubation period (Li et al., 2014).

We did a literature search of the China National Knowledge Infrastructure (CNKI) database using the key words "towns (zhen)" and "townships (xiang)" to identify the number of articles in China Social Science Citation Index (CSSCI) indexed journals on different topics related to towns and townships over time. According to our analysis of the published literature, the study of towns in China has had several stages. It reached a peak in the late 1980s to the early twenty-first century and declined afterwards. Only 68 CSSCI papers on towns were published in 2013; a quarter as many as were published in 1994.

While considerable research on towns has been conducted, there are limitations to the published literature. Most are concerned with towns' economies—generally advocating greater attention to the economic role of towns (Zhao and Sun, 1996; Jin and Qiao, 2004; Yang and Liao, 2010). Fewer studies have focused on social issues (Chen, 2000; Zhang and Liu, 2008), or on environmental issues in towns (Ning et al., 2002; Ye, 2006). Before 2010 several scholars investigated institutional innovation in towns (Wang, 2003; Chen and Liu, 2004), but few papers on institutional innovation in towns have been published since 2010. Much more attention has been given to towns in developed eastern areas of China (Peng, 2003; Geng and Chao, 2009) than to the central and western regions of China (Huang and Lin, 2001; Zhang, 2012). Finally, what studies exist are often case studies or discussion of topics at a single point in time. Systematic research on the development of Chinese towns is still scarce.

Significance of Towns

In order to understand Chinese urbanization it is important to understand the role of towns. As an important part of China's urban system and as the basic unit of urbanization, towns are important in constructing China's urban space network and in coordinating and balancing the development of cities and towns (Zhang, 2012). Towns are known in China as the "tails of cities and heads of villages." They are the main carriers of rural economic development, and their economies lie at the juncture of urban and rural economies. Developing towns is a significant approach for attracting the surplus agricultural labor force from the countryside, integrating them into the modern economy, and promoting domestic demand. It is essential for the interaction between city and countryside and for cities to effectively play a leading role in regional economic and social development. In 2014, China's National New-type Urbanization Plan (2014–2020) emphasized their importance as follows:

> The service function of towns should be enhanced. . .the capacity of economic and population agglomeration in small and medium-sized cities and towns should be strengthened. . .the development of some key towns should be emphasized, and the coordinated development of large, medium and small cities and towns should be improved. . .in accordance with the requirement of quantity control, quality improvement, land conservation, and embodiment of local characteristics. . .the promotion of towns should be in line with the dispersing of over-concentrated functions in large cities proper, the development of industries with certain characteristics, and serving "agriculture, countryside and farmers."

The development of towns has lagged behind cities except in a few of the eastern coastal areas of Guangdong, Jiangsu, Zhejiang, and Fujian. As described in Chapter 2, hukou reform in towns and other policies promoting them did not affect towns' growth as much as expected. As a result, despite the population growth and economic development in towns described in Chapter 6 on large-scale population flows, many rural residents continued to migrate out of rural areas to cities, rather than towns in central and western China. This has been a main cause of the great regional difference of urbanization in China (Zhang and Han, 2009; Zhang, 2010). However, towns are continuing to grow and now account for more than a third of China's urban population. Towns have a significant influence on national economic and social development and the entire urbanization process.

While statistical yearbooks are the best source of data on towns in China, they are not adequate. While we use statistical yearbooks as our main data source, we have supplemented their data with data we obtained in our field investigations, from unpublished local sources, survey research, observation, and interviews. Our goal is to present an analysis of the spatial distribution, policy evolution, industrial development, population agglomeration, factors restricting development, and advantages and development trends in towns in order to provide a comprehensive understanding of the role of towns in Chinese urbanization.

CHARACTERISTICS OF TOWNS

Number and Spatial Distribution of Towns and Townships

There were 33,981 official towns and townships in China in 2010. The total number has declined consistently from 57,012 in 1982: a 40 percent decrease. The number of official towns increased continuously from 1982 to 2000 and then has decreased slightly. There were 2,660 official towns in 1982 and 19,410 in 2010. In 2010 there were 669 official towns per province on average (Table 8.2). The average population of the town seat of official towns increased from 7,000 in 1990 to 13,700 in 2010.

The number of towns per square km is densest in the four super municipalities directly under the central government—Shanghai, Beijing, Tianjin, and Chongqing: 12.3 to 25.5 towns per thousand km^2. In contrast towns in Xinjiang, Tibet, and Inner Mongolia are the sparsest in China, with only 0.6 to 0.8 towns and townships per thousand km^2. In general, the distribution of official towns and townships in the eastern and central regions is much denser than that of the western region (Figure 8.2).

Table 8.2 Official towns and townships, 1982–2010

	Total	Towns	Townships	Average population in town seats (thousand)
1982	57,012	2,660	54,352	23.0
1990	56,481	12,084	44,397	7.0
2000	43,511	20,312	23,199	8.2
2010	33,981	19,410	14,571	13.7

Source: NBSC-census (1984, 1992, 2002, 2012).

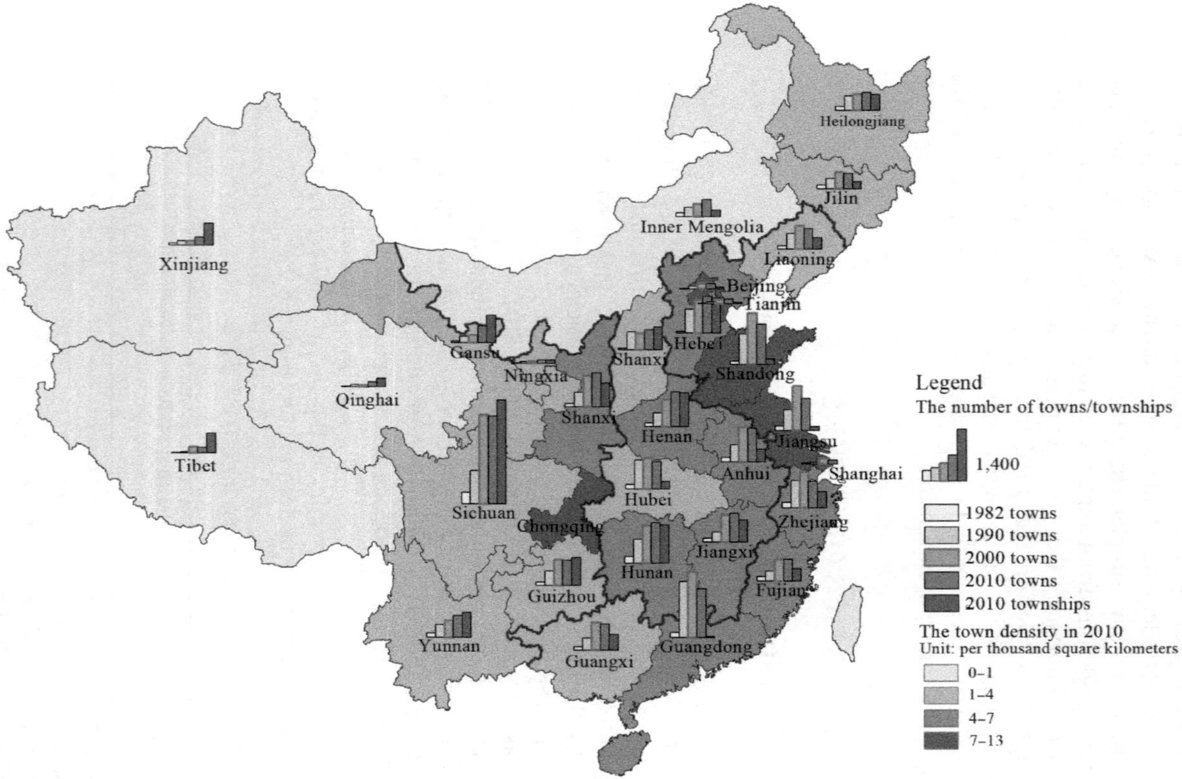

Source: NBSC-census (1984, 1992, 2002, 2012). Compiled and drawn by Lijuan Wang.

Figure 8.2 Distribution of rural towns and townships in China

Evolution Process

Before 1978: Towns' limited impact on urbanization

During the planned economy period after the founding of the PRC, the central, provincial, and local governments had a generally positive attitude toward the development of towns (Zou, 2003). Under the planned economy, the allocation of national resources mainly occurred between different cities or within cities, such as making decisions about non-agricultural hukou quotas and the location of state-owned enterprises. Thus, most rural towns were only involved in resource allocation decisions to a limited extent. Many town government officials did not have non-agricultural hukou. The development of towns did not create great pressure on China's national welfare distribution system. Thus, in this early period higher-level governments supported small town policy.

Although small town development was not formally restricted, towns developed quite slowly during the planned economy period and had little effect on China's overall urbanization level (Ma and Lin, 1993). Table 8.3 shows that the share of the population of official towns to the total rural population in 1978 was roughly the same as it had been in 1954. Bing Zou (2003), head of the Shenzhen Planning Association, has provided a comprehensive account of how the state monopoly on the purchase and allocation of agricultural products and the hukou system ran counter to market mechanisms (Zou, 2003). Zhou describes how these institutional arrangements restricted the free flow of rural economic factors and thus limited development of towns during the planned economy period.

From 1978 to 2000: Birth of the market economy and reforms affecting the urbanization of towns

China's urbanization took off after reform and opening up began in 1978 and particularly after 1984. The establishment of the Household Contract Responsibility System (HCRS) in rural areas, the abolition of state monopoly policy for the purchase and allocation of agricultural products, clarification of the tax sharing system to encourage all enterprises—including SOEs—to operate efficiently and institutional reforms of township and village enterprises brought prosperity to many towns in the 1980s and 1990s.

In the early 1980s, the HCRS released surplus rural labor, and made it imperative to create new job opportunities for former agricultural workers. However, cities continued to follow the planned economy system, and the number of new employees hired by state-owned enterprises was very limited and with many restrictions. If an individual farmer succeeded in being registered as a permanent urban resident by being recruited by a state-owned enterprise, he/she would enjoy benefits of other urban resident at only a small marginal cost to the overall system. But if this happened on a large scale, it would create costs the public sector and the central government could not afford when China was such a poor country. As a result, farmers who found work in state-owned enterprises in cities in the 1980s were only granted the status of "temporary" or "contract" workers as described in Chapter 2. They were members of the floating population. Farmers rarely transferred completely from agricultural hukou to non-agricultural hukou. During this period, the labor force released from rural areas increased, but the cities were unable to absorb them. Thus, rural towns naturally became the best available choice for these people. They were close to rural areas and provided a lifestyle partially similar to that in the city. Rural towns became a bridge and a buffer zone between cities and villages.

As the national government perceived that institutional innovation and reform experiments in rural towns did not have a significant negative effect on cities, they promoted further reform in rural towns. For example, hukou reform of "self-care rations" allowing people with rural hukou to migrate to rural towns if they were able to obtain their own food from family members or other sources was implemented in rural towns in the early 1980s, blurring the traditional line between non-agricultural hukou (with commodity grain supply) and agricultural hukou (without commodity grain supply). The rise of township and village enterprises (TVEs) broke through the traditional socialist public ownership economy and the rural land system.

The central government took notice of the vigor of small town development and introduced new policies to support their development. From 1982 to 1986, the central government allocated 110 million RMB to support village and town planning. By the end of 1986, more than 90 percent of China's approximately 33,000 towns and townships were involved in at least preliminary development planning (CSUS and MHUDP, 2009, in Wang and Zhao, 2009).

Urbanization policies in China in the 1980s made towns significant locations for new urban population. Under the strict constraint of the hukou system, towns, as buffering zones between urban and rural areas, played an important role in urbanization. Xueyi Lu, a noted Chinese sociologist, has estimated that rural population transferring to towns accounted for 94 percent of the total new urban population between 1978 and 1993 as China's urbanization level increased from 17.92 percent to 28.14 percent if natural growth is deducted from total population growth of towns during this period (Lu, 1997: 192).

The reform of China's land use system, active rural markets, and the development of township and village enterprises provided further opportunities for the development of towns. Experiments in the 1980s which were eventually extended nationwide eliminated the system of a state monopoly for the purchase and allocation of agricultural products. As a result, agricultural products and other commodities produced in rural areas and towns were allowed to circulate freely according to market supply and demand. This stimulated a great deal of activity in rural market towns, as the service and market centers in rural areas. Market trading in towns became active again. With the growth of industrialization and urbanization, China's urban consumption capacity grew, creating increasing demand for all kinds of commodities. State-owned enterprises (SOEs) in the 1980s were generally static because of failure to reform, resulting in their failure to meet increasing market demand. Township and village enterprises, although they started from a low base, thrived in the environment where products were in short supply and the growth of a market economy had stimulated vast market demand that city-based SOEs were unable to meet (Figure 8.3). In the early 1990s, the number of towns and their respective populations continued to increase. The proportion of urbanized population in towns to those in towns and cities increased from 28.7 percent in 1990 to 36.2 percent in 2000.

After 2000: Globalization and differentiation in the development of towns

China joined the World Trade Organization (WTO) in 2001. As a result, it became easier for China's manufactured products to enter global markets. However, most towns failed to transform themselves and upgrade their industry quickly enough to compete effectively in the new economy. The early industrial structures of low value added and high pollution industry, as well as the relatively low ability of management, made adapting to rapidly changing market conditions difficult for small town enterprises. Many failed, others adapted and grew, and new enterprises suited to the new economic reality emerged. The economies of towns became more differentiated during this development period. For example, Honghe town in Jiaxing city of Zhejiang province, a specialized town that produced woolen sweaters, enjoyed higher production and trading volume of woolen sweaters than the neighboring towns in the 1990s. However, the town's sweaters became low-end products by the beginning of the twenty-first century. Honghe town had not devoted sufficient attention to research and development or the logistics and building of a trading platform to compete in China's increasingly sophisticated domestic market or internationally. As a result, another town—Puyuan town, which had lagged behind grew rapidly and surpassed Honghe town as a center of sweater production.

Some towns adapted to the changed market environment and smoothly accomplished industrial transformation and upgrading. They quickly

Note: Most of the buildings are vacant. A few are used to produce shoes.

Source: Photos by Li Zhang, March, 2013.

Figure 8.3 A closed state-owned ginning factory in Yuelai town, Haimen city, Jiangsu province

Note: This town center looks like a downtown of a large city. The market administrative office for international woolen sweaters trade is located in the building on the left.

Source: Photo by Li Zhang, March, 2012.

Figure 8.4 Town center plaza, Puyuan town, Jiaxing city, Zhejaing province

integrated into the tide of globalization by fully taking advantage of a large number of small and medium-sized enterprises, small enterprise scale, flexible production systems, and diversified risk (Figure 8.4). For example, Xinqiao town in Jiangyin city in Jiangsu province, is one of the world's largest textile industry bases. It had a total area of 19.3km^2, a population of about 60,000, and GDP of 11.149 billion RMB in 2012 (Xinqiao Web, 2014).

Some towns developed very large global industries. For example, the largest national trading market for home textile products is located in Sanxing town in Haimen city of Jiangsu province (Tongji University Research Team, 2013).

With the advance of globalization, China's economy developed rapidly, and people's living standards improved greatly. As a result, domestic demand for commodities continued to increase, and towns that were able to adapt and produce products that were in demand continued to thrive with the expanding international market and growing domestic demand. This helps explain why from 2000 to 2010, the proportion of towns' population in China's total urban population increased from 36.2 percent to 39.70 percent.

With China's economy integrating into the global economy, the central government realized that the development of towns also had some inherent disadvantages, and therefore, could not be relied upon as the primary key level of government for China's urbanization. In order to compete globally, China needed large cities, megacities and large city clusters (LCCs) to serve as the engines of growth. Accordingly, the country's attitude toward the development of towns changed from categorical "positive development of towns" to more selective "focusing on the development of certain key towns" (PRC, 2014).

Township and Villages Enterprises

After reform and opening, communes and brigades—the two levels of structure in rural areas in Mao's era—were replaced by townships and towns as had previously existed. Commune and brigade enterprises located in the townships, towns, and villages were converted to town and village enterprises (TVEs) or disbanded.

Township and village enterprises (TVEs) are a special phenomenon in China. They are small-scale enterprises located in towns, townships, or villages. Most of the capital for TVEs comes from rural collective capital or farmer's individual savings. The term TVE is associated with rural enterprises that have existed from the early 1980s.

Between 1958 and 1978 rural China was organized into a series of rural people's communes consisting of production brigades (Shengchan-dadui) which in turn consisted of production teams organized to farm collectively owned arable land as a work unit. Private enterprises in communes were forbidden. Only communes or brigades could organize and run enterprises at the village, town, and township level: so-called commune and brigade-run enterprises. While many TVEs failed during the 1990s, some adapted and survived. The National TVE Law, promulgated in 1997 is still in effect and the national government collects and publishes information on TVEs each year. TVE property rights have been clarified and most of the remaining TVEs today have been transformed into modern business enterprises.

Evolution of Rural Economic Entities

Before 1978: Commune and brigade-run enterprises

While China's reform and opening up is often associated with the special economic zones created in eastern coastal China in the early 1980s, described in Chapter 4 on regional policies and regional urbanization and Chapter 5 on globalization and China's urbanization, reform began in rural areas with the Household Contract Responsibility System (HCRS) in agriculture and TVEs as successors to commune and brigade-led enterprises about the same time. Hence, TVEs had a significant impact on China's urbanization after reform and opening up.

During the Mao era people's communes were the main organizational unit in rural areas. They were economic and administrative entities collectively owned by the working masses. A pattern of three-level ownership by commune, production brigade, and production teams was developed. The economic function of people's communes and the administrative function of townships were unified. People's communes were abolished in 1984 and replaced by the governmental organization of towns and townships. Commune and brigade enterprises evolved into town and village enterprises.

In the planned economy period before reform and opening up, only people's communes and production brigades were allowed to run enterprises. Hence the name "commune and brigade-run enterprises." Commune and brigade-run enterprises were strictly limited by the "three locals" policy requiring them to use only local materials, local processing, and local selling. Industry was divided into activities closely related to agricultural and sideline products processing, manufacturing, and handcrafts. Industries unrelated to agriculture were forbidden. At this stage, the state-planned economic system prohibited individual farmers, families, or groups of peasant households from running enterprises. Given the way in which their role was defined and the many restrictions placed upon them, commune and brigade-operated enterprises developed very slowly. While they met some local needs and made some contribution to local agriculture, they did not generate products for national or international distribution. As only members of a commune or brigade could work in them, they did not attract migrants. They had virtually no impact on urbanization.

1978–1990: Employment pressure and more diverse economic organization

With the implementation of the HCRS in the late 1970s, a large amount of rural labor was released from farm work. As they left their land, the surplus famers needed new jobs. However, state-owned enterprises (SOEs) in cities and towns could not absorb a large amount of new labor.

Under Mao, China pursued an industrialization strategy of giving priority to heavy industry. State-owned enterprises supplied products related to this strategy. While production of iron, steel, cement, agricultural machinery and other basic commodities increased dramatically, SOEs during the Mao era produced few consumer goods. China's whole society experienced shortages and it was difficult to meet people's rising demands. Under the dual pressure of imbalance between the supply and the demand of labor and products, the state gradually relaxed the restrictions on the development of commune and brigade-operated enterprises by encouraging additional economic activities such as household planting and livestock raising, building construction, manufacturing, transportation, and a variety of services in rural areas. The state even allocated half of the construction funds for investment in people's communes to support new businesses in poor communes, offered low interest loans to commune's enterprises, and reduced taxes or gave tax exemptions to encourage additional local rural economic activity (Zou, 2003).

In Guangdong province, TVEs had the comparative advantage of cheap labor and land near Hong Kong and Macao, and ready access to firms with capital familiar with exporting goods. TVEs in this area responded to the outside market beginning in the early 1980s. As a result, a distinct outward-looking economy characteristic of TVEs near Hong Kong and Macao was developed in the 1980s through the "three plus one trading mix" and "putting both ends of the production process on the world market" (Zou, 2003). The three parts of the trading mix were (1) manufacturing from materials provided by an outside source, (2) manufacturing based on samples, and (3) assembling parts supplied by clients. TVEs often sold products to pay back loans or equipment provided by clients. "Putting both ends of the production process on the world market" meant that raw materials are from other countries, such as Hong Kong, Macao, and Taiwan and the finished products are exported and the client must be a foreign enterprise.

Fully fledged reform began on a massive scale in 1984. China's rural political and administrative structure and economic system was transformed. This was the first year when towns, villages, households, and groups of peasant households were allowed to run enterprises. The "three locals" restriction was loosened, greatly expanding the source of raw materials and market scope of township enterprises. Restrictions on permitted types of industry were eased, and the development of non-agricultural industries was allowed. Rural administration changed from communes back to townships and towns with administrative villages within them. Commune and brigade enterprises were restructured and renamed TVEs. Non-agricultural hukou for migrants who could provide their own food supply was allowed. The sudden transformation of the social, political, and economic regulatory environment in 1984 gave rise to a vigorous new rural economy and began to make a significant impact on urbanization, especially in coastal provinces.

Deng Xiaoping, chief architect of China's reform and opening up, described TVEs as "a suddenly rising force." The number of TVEs increased from 1.65 million in 1984 to 12.23 million in 1985 (MAC, 2003). In 1987, the total output value of TVEs reached 467.5 billion RMB, exceeding the value of China's total agricultural output (Lu, 1997: 189). This astonishingly rapid increase in rural enterprise helps explain the rapid population growth in towns that started in the mid-1980s.

1990–2000: Reform of township enterprises' property rights and gradual improvement of laws and regulations

The rapid rise of TVEs experienced a period of turmoil after 1989 when the rapid increase in the number of new TVEs came to an end and many TVEs failed. After Deng's southern tour China accelerated market reforms and embarked on its own brand of market socialism. TVEs, often restructured into larger small and medium-sized enterprises (SMEs) rebounded. The nature of TVEs, how sustainable the initial form of TVEs were, and the reasons why they declined in the early 1990s are debated.

An obvious explanation is that China's exports suffered after 1989. TVEs were suddenly unable to sell what they produced. Since they were small and lacked government backing many could not withstand even a short period of weak sales. Few were able to restructure to produce goods for the domestic market or otherwise adapt to China's changed position in the global economy. A provocative book titled *Capitalism with Chinese Characteristics* (Huang, 2008) by M.I.T. economics professor Yasheng Huang (Huang, 2008) offers an alternative explanation. Huang attributes the early success of TVEs to the fact that they were almost all truly private enterprises built from the grassroots without oppressive government bureaucratic oversight. Huang attributes their decline after Tiananmen mainly to new anti-capitalist regulations that stifled them, not to economic sanctions. Other explanations for the decline of TVEs after 1989 are based on locational disadvantages, ambiguous property rights, mismanagement, and corruption.

TVEs, because they were located in villages with populations unfamiliar with urban consumption preferences and away from urban markets where consumer demand was highest, were often unable to keep up with shifting tastes and market demand and had an inherent location disadvantage. Many were unable to adapt to changing market conditions and fierce competition and became bankrupt.

Initially TVEs' property rights were not clear. The legal borderlines between collective capital, private capital and state capital were ambiguous. Their inability to demonstrate clear ownership to land and other assets and uncertainty about who was responsible for what, made it difficult for them to obtain financing and pay debts. Ambiguous property rights also created abuses, both by TVE leaders and local governments. Some leaders of TVEs with shared ownership treated the TVEs as their own property and in some cases were convicted of crimes and sent to prison. Some local governments that were used to strict socialist ideology used public tools to shut down TVEs or put TVE leaders who were acting lawfully and in the interests of the TVE in prison.

Deng's "southern tour" took place in 1992 at a time of intense uncertainty about China's future. Deng was 88 and had no significant official leadership role. The tour occurred only weeks after the disintegration of the Soviet Union and many feared that if China continued market-oriented reforms it could fall apart. Because of post-Tiananmen international sanctions, China's relationship to the global economy was in question. Property rights ambiguity, administrative abuses, and corruption in TVEs were apparent. In a series of talks in Guangzhou, Shenzhen, Zhuhai and Shanghai, Deng criticized opponents of reform and opening up and called on the Chinese people to continue with even bolder movement towards market socialism. Deng's southern tour is widely credited with moving China back onto the course he had originally charted in 1978. It helped reverse anti-TVE policies and set the groundwork for the further increase and maturation of China's market socialist economy that has since occurred.

Rural Collective Ownership Enterprise Regulations were implemented in 1990, and China's Township Enterprise Law was formally promulgated in 1997. With a shift back towards reform and opening, relaxation of international sanctions, and more experience and clearer laws and regulations, TVEs again underwent rapid development, with some spectacularly successful enterprises continuously emerging. By the early 1990s, there were 23 million TVEs in China (Lu, 1997: 191). Eighty percent were located in natural villages, 19 percent in administrative villages and township seats, and 1 percent in county capital towns and their surrounding areas.

Property rights reform involving TVEs in the late 1990s involved more than 90 percent of the TVEs (MAC, 2009). This helped build the foundation for surviving TVEs, but for many TVEs property rights reform came too late.

After 2000: Growing competition and difficult development

China's admission to membership in the World Trade Organization in 2001 forced TVEs to face even fiercer market competition. TVEs were unable to absorb all the surplus labor in many regions. In regions where many TVEs had failed, the remaining ones were generally small scale and ill equipped to compete as part of the global economy. In regions where most TVEs survived and adapted to the new economic order, economic conditions were much better and the demand for labor higher. Therefore, the rural population continued to migrate out of areas where the rural economy was weakest—in central and western China and poorly performing areas of eastern China—into economically productive areas of Guangdong,

Jiangsu, Zhejiang and other economically strong provinces in eastern China. This helps explain the migration patterns discussed in detail in Chapter 4 on regional policies and regional urbanization and Chapter 6 on large-scale population flows.

Some migrant workers went back to their hometowns to start businesses after experiencing city life and accumulating work experience, slowly forming a new driving force for the new round of development of enterprises in towns and villages.

Capital, technology, and management experience brought by migrant workers who returned home promoted development of new township enterprises. A total of 5,600 TVE industry clusters were formed by 2008 (NBSC-cts, 2010).

After 2000 TVE's competitiveness declined compared with their position in the 1980s and 1990s. The small industry scale, low level of technology, and weak development foundation left many TVEs unable to cope with the global competition. Since most were thinly capitalized, even a slight fluctuation in exchange rates or global demand for the product they produced could result in business failure. The small scale and scattered layout of TVEs restricted industrial upgrading and structural adjustment. Therefore, TVEs faced huge transformation pressure. Many have been shut down, leaving a large number of vacant plants. The ones that survived and grew stronger were mainly specialized producers located in villages and towns that gave them a competitive advantage in the local economy or enterprises with easy access to global markets. Rural enterprises in industry clusters with comparative advantages did particularly well (Figure 8.5).

TVEs' contribution to China's urbanization

The total output value of China's TVEs increased nearly one hundredfold from 51.4 billion RMB in 1978 to 46.47 trillion RMB in 2010. TVEs contribute one-third of China's GDP (MAC, 2010). Between 1978 and 2010, the number of TVE employees increased from 28.27 million to 158.93 million: more than half of all urban employees. They contribute more than one-third of jobs in rural areas. In 2010, rural residents had an average income of 2,471 RMB from TVEs (MAC, 2011).

In 2010, most TVEs were secondary and tertiary industries. The output value of the secondary industry accounted for more than 80 percent of the total output value of the three types of industry in rural China. The output value of rural tertiary industry was small, but tertiary industry employed more than 80 percent of all employees in rural industry, and it contributed 50 percent of non-farming employment (Figure 8.6).

The spatial distribution of employees in TVEs is closely correlated with regional urbanization rates. Guangdong, Zhejiang, Jiangsu, and

Source: Li Zhang, March, 2013.

Figure 8.5 Traditional industry in rural Haimen city, Jiangsu province

Note: Tertiary industry excludes privately or individually owned businesses.

Figure 8.6 Town and village enterprises (TVEs): Percentage of enterprises, employees, and gross product by industry sector, 2011

Shandong provinces have the largest number of TVEs. They also have the highest urbanization rates of all provinces in China (Figure 8.7).

Population Concentration

Town seats in China perform an important function as centers of population concentration. Increasingly households living in the countryside and villages are concentrated there.

Rural urbanization

The vigorous development of TVEs has promoted the concentration of rural population in towns and promoted large-scale immigration, especially in the Yangtze River and the Pearl River Deltas. Immigrants have contributed to the growth of tax revenue in these areas and have upgraded the physical development level of towns (Li and An, 2010). From 1982 to 1990, population growth in towns contributed more than 90 percent of China's urban population growth (Lu, 1997: 192). Between 2000 and 2010, town population growth contributed 47 percent of China's urban population growth (NBSC-census, 2002, 2012) as rural populations move to township seats and town seats, giving birth to the phrase "rural urbanization with Chinese characteristics."

Before the 1980s, a township was a clearly delineated unit for administration of a rural region, whereas an official town was a service center for

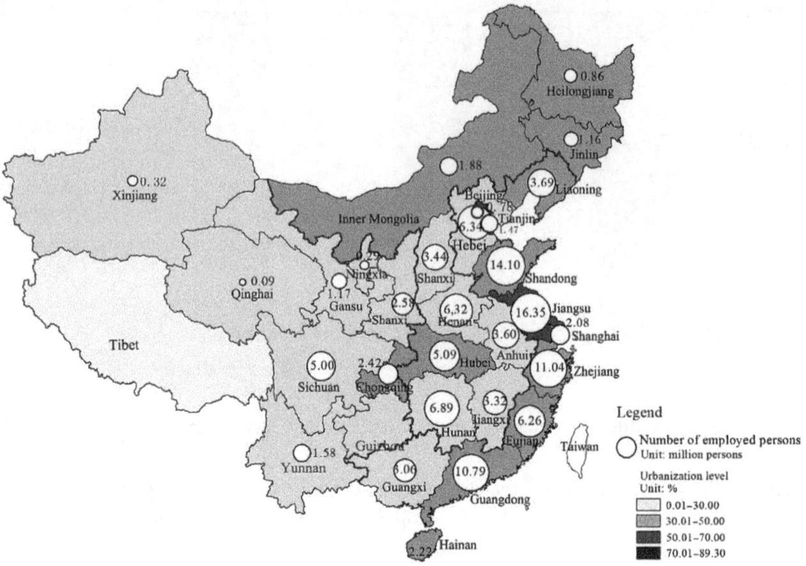

Source: Data from MAC (2012). Drawn by Lijuan Wang.

Figure 8.7 Number of persons employed in TVEs at different urbanization levels

a rural region which did not have clear boundaries. With the reform of administrative divisions in the 1980s described in Chapter 3, towns gradually evolved into a comprehensive hybrid administrative unit serving both urban and rural areas. The "town population" generally refers to the population living at the seat of an official town, including the seat of a county town. As a result, "rural urbanization" refers to population concentration in town or township seats as the result of industrialization in rural areas. Accordingly, the proportion of a town or township seat's population to the total town or township population is a good measure of China's rural urbanization rate. Table 8.3 shows that China's rural urbanization rate was relatively stable before 1978 at 6 percent to 8 percent. After reform and opening up, the rural urbanization rate increased to 12.47 percent in 1990. It increased dramatically after 2000, with an annual growth of more than 1 percent. In 2010, the rural urbanization rate reached 28.66 percent.

The increase in the rural urbanization rate was accompanied by a change in the average size of towns. In 1982, the population of China's 2,664 official towns was 61.06 million: 22,900 residents per town on average. Over 80 percent of the official towns in 1982—2,133—were county towns.

Table 8.3 Population and urbanization rate in rural areas in different years

Year	Total rural population (including town population) (millions)	Town seat population (millions)	Urbanization rate in rural areas	Average size of the town seat
1954	545	35	6.39%	–
1959	568	46	8.02%	–
1963	599	41	6.87%	–
1971	752	44	5.91%	–
1978	843	53	6.30%	2.45
1982	859	61	7.11%	2.29
1990	919	115	12.47%	0.96
2000	950	166	17.49%	0.84
2010	929	266	28.66%	1.37

Notes:

1. According to Zhigang Zhou (1993), in 1990 29.75 million residents of towns proper were registered as rural population. The data in this table includes those people.
2. Table 8.3 reports only people living in town seats—not the population of large settlements (over 3,000 people) distributed in rural areas of some towns. This is the data which towns report to higher levels of government. Town population data should include the population of these rural population centers and Table 8.4 does include this population. This difference in reporting explains why the average town population in Table 8.4 is larger than in Table 8.3.

Source: Data before 1978 were obtained from Shengzu Gu (1994). Data for 1982–2010 were obtained from censuses. The average population data in town seats were calculated by the author.

After the peak time of designating official towns in the 1980s, towns gradually evolved into regional administrative units. In 1990, there were 11,999 official towns nationwide, with a population of 114.67 million in the town seats (excluding the rural areas within their administrative jurisdiction). The average town seat population had declined to 9,557 people—less than half the 1982 average—reflecting the designation of large numbers of towns in the 1980s.

The number of official towns continued to increase and the average size of all towns continued to decline in the 1990s. In 2000, China had 19,692 official towns, with population in town seats of 166.14 million. The average population of town seats had declined to 8,437 people. The number of official towns stopped increasing in the first decade of the twenty-first century. In 2011, China had 19,683 official towns, with the population of town seats of 247 million. As designation of new official towns had stopped and the population of official towns designated before 2000 increased, the average size of town seats increased to 12,525 in 2011. The average size of county towns in 2011 was 44,800, more than four times as large as the average population of other towns: 9,718 people.

Spatial difference of town seat population concentrations

Table 8.4 presents data on the number of county towns and general towns and the average population of their town seats in each of China's regions between 2009 and 2011.

The average population of general town seats in eastern and central China was about the same in 2011 (approximately 54,000 people), but it was lower in the western region (31,610 people). There was a slight increase in the population of town seats in central and western China between 2009 and 2011, but a slight decrease in eastern China. This is mainly because of urban sprawl in some developed counties and county-level cities where the built-up area has extended beyond the boundaries of county seats.

The average population of county town seats was much larger than general town seats. In eastern and central China the 2011 average population of county town seats was approximately 54,000 compared with average population of general town seats of 12,364 and 7,596. In western China the average population of county seats was lower: 31,610 and the average population of general town seats about 7,600. The average population in general towns increased by 21 percent between 2009 and 2011. In western China it increased by 36 percent in these two years.

Over the past 30 years, population concentration in towns has been one of the characteristic aspects of China's urbanization. Between 1990 and 2000 the number of official towns increased by 8,228 and town population increased by 81 million—accounting for 50 percent of China's total urban population increase (NBSC-census, 1992, 2002).

Between 2000 and 2010 the number of official towns decreased by 702, but this was because many individual towns were merged, rather than a real decrease in the number of towns. The population of towns increased by 100 million between 2000 and 2010—accounting for 47 percent of China's total urban population increase (NBSC-census, 2002, 2012).

Population growth in towns in different provinces varies. Between 2000 and 2010 town populations increased by more than 10 million in both Hebei and Hunan provinces and by more than five million in each of six other provinces—Jiangsu, Shandong, Anhui, Jiangxi, Hunan and Sichuan provinces. Town population accounted for more than 50 percent of the urban population growth in 17 of China's 31 provincial-level divisions (Table 8.5).

Hunan and Hebei provinces were the two provinces in which the growth

Table 8.4 Number and average population of county towns and general towns by region, 2011

	Number of official towns				Average population of town seats			
	County towns in 2009	County towns in 2011	General towns in 2009	General towns in 2011	County town seats in 2009	County town seats in 2011	General town seats in 2009	General town seats in 2011
Eastern region	435	434	6,856	6,810	56,460	54,308	10,925	12,364
Central region	494	493	5,857	6,036	52,146	53,834	6,720	7,596
Western region	652	646	5,028	5,264	29,785	31,610	5,543	7,565
Nationwide	1,581	1,573	19,322	17,741	44,111	44,838	8,011	9,718

Source: NBSC, *China Township Statistics* (NBSC-cts, 2010, 2012); NBSC, *China Statistical Yearbook* (NBSC-csy, 2010, 2012).

Table 8.5 Urban and town population increase by province, 2000–2010

	Population increase between 2000 and 2010			Increase ratio between 2000 and 2010		
	Urban population (million)	Town population (million)	Town population increase to Urban population increase	Urban population	Town population	Difference
	A	B	C=B/A	D	E	F=E−D
Nationwide	211.23	100.11	47%	46%	60%	14%
East region	110.49	35.04	32%	47%	44%	−3%
Beijing	6.34	0.27	4%	60%	26%	−34%
Tianjin	3.19	−0.36	−11%	45%	−20%	−65%
Hebei	14.02	11.13	79%	80%	184%	104%
Liaoning	4.22	0.65	15%	18%	15%	−4%
Shanghai	6.07	1.15	19%	42%	64%	23%
Jiangsu	16.51	5.28	32%	53%	44%	−9%
Zhejaing	11.19	3.91	35%	50%	42%	−8%
Fujian	6.76	2.03	30%	47%	31%	−16%
Shandong	13.29	7.01	53%	39%	57%	19%
Guangdong	21.6	−0.53	−2%	46%	−3%	−49%
Guangxi	6.07	3.91	64%	49%	64%	15%
Hainan	1.23	0.59	48%	40%	42%	2%
Central region	61.85	41.11	66%	43%	77%	34%
Shanxi	5.73	3.52	61%	50%	83%	33%
Inner Mongolia	3.76	1.42	38%	38%	33%	−5%
Jilin	1.34	0.39	29%	10%	10%	0%
Heilongjiang	2.65	1.26	47%	14%	21%	7%

Anhui	9.81	6.06	62%	62%	83%	20%
Jiangxi	8.31	6.33	76%	74%	112%	37%
Henan	14.83	10.31	69%	69%	136%	67%
Hubei	4.36	3.01	69%	18%	40%	22%
Hunan	11.06	8.81	80%	64%	128%	64%
West region	38.9	23.94	62%	50%	73%	23%
Chongqing	5.2	3.12	60%	51%	89%	37%
Sichuan	10.03	6.33	63%	45%	63%	18%
Guizhou	3.29	2.12	64%	39%	52%	13%
Yunnan	6.06	4.38	72%	61%	83%	22%
Tibet	0.17	0.12	68%	33%	41%	8%
Shaanxi	5.69	3.76	66%	50%	84%	34%
Gansu	3.17	1.85	58%	53%	89%	36%
Qinghai	0.96	0.59	61%	62%	105%	44%
Ningxia	1.24	0.38	31%	70%	66%	−4%
Xinjiang	3.09	1.29	42%	49%	65%	15%

Source: NBSC-census (2002, 2012); NBSC-csy (2001, 2011).

of town population contributed the most to total urban population growth: 80 percent and 79 percent respectively.

Between 2000 and 2010 the town population in Tianjin municipality and Guangdong province both shrank. The ratio of town population growth to total urban population growth in these province-level administrative divisions was lower than any other province. The reason for the negative growth in Guangdong province is because at the beginning of reform and opening up Guandong's rural economy attracted too many immigrants, resulting in towns experiencing management pressure. In recent years, towns have gradually been merged and included into city management, and the implementation of "administrative reform of towns changing to urban streets" has led to a decrease in the average population size of the remaining towns. The decreasing population share of towns in Jiangsu province, Zhejiang province, and Tianjin municipality is also largely due to administrative reform rather than actual population shrinkage.

Table 8.5 shows that the population growth of town seats in central and western China contributed 66 percent and 62 percent, respectively, to China's total urban population growth between 2000 and 2010, but that town seats in the eastern region contributed only 32 percent. In the eastern provinces, including Beijing, Tianjin, Liaoning, Jiangsu, Zhejiang, Shandong, Fujian, and Guangdong provinces, town population growth was slower than general urban population growth. In the central and western provinces, except for Inner Mongolia and Ningxia, town population growth was faster than the general urban population growth. The population of town seats in the central and western areas grew rapidly, whereas town population growth in the eastern region appeared to slow down, though this is somewhat deceptive as most of the apparent slowdown is because of changes in administrative boundaries rather than real change.

Our field research supports the above findings. In 55 towns we surveyed in Hubei province, the average annual growth rate of town seats population was 8.6 percent from 2003 to 2009. Township population generally increased, and only four towns experienced a decline in the population of town seats. Our interviews found that because of the low average level of salaries and short commuting time between villages and towns proper, most local rural residents working in towns still kept their land, maintaining the lifestyle of "half-employee and half-peasant." The ratio of part-time workers in a town seat was as high as 80 percent, which confirms a pattern that may be called "semi-urbanization."

Market towns in the countryside

Market towns are another type of functional node in rural areas, distinct from town seats. This settlement type is distinguished by a smaller size, more rural nature, and the general absence of industry. Research by Qizai Zhang, a professor in the Chinese Academy of Social Science found that market towns in the early 1990s had only 398 people on average (Zhang, 1997: 203).

The average population of market towns increased from 2,100 in 2000 to 2,400 people in 2006 (Wang and Zhao, 2009). Although the population growth of township seats is increasing, township seats are still far smaller and less developed than town seats and seldom have the nature and quality of true urban places.

THE PREDICAMENT OF TOWN DEVELOPMENT

The central government has always implemented policies to support the development of towns as part of the process of China's urbanization. TVEs succeeded in increasing the flow of rural population into towns in some regions. However, towns in remote rural areas have inherent disadvantages compared with cities. These may include a low level of infrastructure, backward industrial structure, lack of development funds, a low level of administrative management skills and remoteness from markets. Traditional cultural values often make their residents resistant to change. As a matter of national policy China faces the dilemma of choosing between promoting more broadly based development that will help residents of rural areas and improve social equity and development focused on the most advanced and efficient locations where development will add the most to the overall national economy. This dilemma is not unique to China. All countries—developing and developed face it to some extent.

Low-level Construction and Poor Infrastructure

Many towns were transformed from townships, so they grew from small-scale places. Most towns suffered from backward infrastructure because of the lack of development history and accumulation of capital. Although a series of related policies and regulations from the state attached great importance to the development of towns, only a few of these policies were fully implemented. Most towns received limited funds and investments from higher levels of government. Authorities at the provincial level have only paid attention to a few key towns. Although population concentration and economic growth can promote the development of towns, a local development approach that improves the competitive advantage of a locality through urban expansion can also play a critical role (Han, 2010). This approach increases the efficiency of land use in towns (Liang et al., 2002).

However, most town governments do not have enough money to pay for high quality infrastructure to keep pace with fast land expansion.

Our survey of Hubei province in 2010 showed that most of the 55 towns lacked adequate own source revenue for infrastructure and industrial development and received only a small amount of funds and little policy support from higher-level governmental departments. Some towns surveyed in the research that did succeed in industrial development were unable to provide adequate services and amenities young people value such as movie theaters, shopping malls, and public gardens to the surrounding villages because of the lack of funds and economic inefficiency of scale. Some town services collapsed under the pressure to meet the demands of new industry and simultaneous pressure to extend services to surrounding villages. To some extent, county towns gradually took responsibility for health, education, and other basic public services originally borne by villages and towns. Still, our study shows that residents of 47 of the 55 towns we investigated in 2010 were dissatisfied with their public service (Tongji University Research Team, 2010).

Continuing Problems Facing Town and Township Industry

Although China's economy has surpassed Japan to become the world's second-largest economy, China's per capita GDP remains low—US$6,560 in 2013—ranked 93 in the world (World Bank, 2014a). Most large and medium-sized cities and metropolitan areas are still accumulating resources and developing and nurturing towns is still financially difficult for them. After 2000 the wave of rural industrialization in the 1980s and1990s was weakened by fierce competition brought by globalization and tougher environment regulations. The world financial crisis that began in 2008 has made development of industry more difficult in many towns (Figure 8.8).

Pressures on Different Types of Industries

In terms of industry type, apart from traditional agriculture, development of towns is mainly supported by low-end manufacturing, commerce, trade, and tourism. From the perspective of tax revenue, manufacturing is one of the main drivers of development and construction in towns and a principle source of tax revenue from towns. Industry clusters in towns in the Pearl River Delta of Guangdong, south Jiangsu and north Zhejiang provinces have formed and helped these regions prosper. However township industry clusters have not yet formed in towns in most inland provinces. No well-developed private economic groups exist in most parts of inland China, preventing the development of manufacturing.

Note: The high chimney is a source of polluted air, waste water from this factory pollutes the adjacent river, and the street is covered by coal dust from passing coal freight.

Source: Photo by Li Zhang, March, 2013.

Figure 8.8 Zhengzhang dying factory, Yuelai town, Haimen city, Jiangsu province

For thousands of years commerce and trade in towns in China has been dominated by sale of agricultural products, production and retailing of simple household goods for local markets, small-scale manufacturing, and simple services that only have an economic impact on the surrounding areas. Although a number of regional commodity distributing centers in towns have been developed, and the larger ones are successful, the level of commerce and trade in towns remains generally low. Small-town business is primarily by small enterprises and family businesses. The low level of trade limits extension of industrial chains. Commerce and trade in towns contributes little to local finances and overall economic growth because of tax exemptions and tax cuts given to small businesses.

Tourism has become an emerging commercial activity in towns in recent years. However, the development of tourism requires a specific resource advantage such as attractive scenery or historic sites and a complete industrial chain including tourism planning and promotion, and creating transportation, hotels, restaurants and other services for tourists. It takes time for a fledgling tourist business to attract enough tourists to become profitable. Therefore, a large capital investment is often needed to develop tourism, particularly in the initial period of development.

Our research on Hubei province shows that tourism is regarded as a leading industry in many towns. Some cases of successful town tourist development exist, but they are few and have not formed a trend. Because of their low level of development, most of the towns have been unable to form a sustainable tourism industry sector except in notable tourist areas such as Guilin, Xian, Chengdu, Jiuzhaigou, areas near national parks, and the peri-urban areas of big cities like Shanghai and Beijing which can provide overnight escapes for urban residents. For example, Zhejiang province has two advantages to develop rural tourism industry: the first is its beautiful mountain and water scenery resources; the second is its location near Shanghai. Even so, rural tourism in southern Zhejiang has not developed very well as of spring, 2015.

Since reform and opening up, particularly rapid development of towns as well as cities has occurred in three megaregions: the Pearl River Delta, Jiangsu province, and north Zhejiang province. The development patterns in these megaregions differ. In the Pearl River Delta development has been promoted by investment from Hong Kong, Macau, Taiwan, and other countries such as Singapore, Korea, Japan and the United States. In Jiangsu, villages and towns have developed manufacturing industry, and in north Zhejiang private capital resulted in the rapid development of towns in the eastern coastal developed area near Shanghai. However, with few exceptions, even in developed towns, the industry level is not very advanced: usually low-end manufacturing, processing, and assembly of industrial products.

With the deepening of a new round of the international division of labor, other developing countries have followed China's development pattern. Vietnam, Myanmar, Indonesia, Malaysia, India and other countries in Asia have labor resources with lower cost and higher availability than those of China. Labor costs are even lower in places like Bangladesh and Africa. As a result, low-end manufacturing industry is transferring transnationally to these areas. Many well-known multinational companies, such as Hewlett Packard and Nike, have begun to cut their costs by moving plants to Vietnam, Thailand, Malaysia, and Myanmar. Vietnam passed China for the first time in 2010 as Nike's largest original equipment manufacturer (OEM) producing 37 percent of Nike's shoe products, compared with 34 percent produced by China (Caixin Web, 2011).

If the towns in China's central and western regions continue to pursue low-end industries, they will face fiercer competition and greater risk during their development than low-end industries in eastern China have faced in the past thirty years. The industrial structure and social structure in China are confronted with pressure from overall transformation of the global economy. Industry in small and scattered villages and towns, even those in eastern developed areas, face restructuring or even collapse. Many developed towns, such as those in the Pearl River Delta, are badly in need of social transformation to solve the daunting problems that accumulated during recent fast development, such as migrant workers' social welfare equalization and regeneration of urban villages. Therefore, simply copying the path of rural industrialization in developed areas of China in the recent past is not feasible for less developed areas in the twenty-first century. Local conditions must be considered and local resources utilized in the search for a suitable path of socio-economic development.

Low Fiscal Revenue and Inadequate Funds for Facility Construction

China's hierarchical fiscal and taxation system has not solved construction funding and industrial development issues for towns. China's current fiscal and taxation system within provincial regions is not standardized. Official towns and townships are defined by law as a primary level of governmental administration, but their fiscal status is not guaranteed.

Some provinces practice contract systems of "financial responsibility" in funding towns. Other provinces designate the county government to control the finances of townships and official towns. In this way, towns at the bottom of China's "inverted pyramid" of public finance are usually badly underfunded, as illustrated in Chapter 3, Figure 3.3, showing China's administrative hierarchy and fiscal resources systems and Figure 3.4 showing the changing share of central and local government revenue and percentage local government revenue increase. Most towns' revenue is not enough to support reasonable quality public services (Tongji University Research Team, 2014, 2015).

According to our Tongji team's research in many towns in the three major regions in China, infrastructure construction in towns is still dominated by government investment, but the funds are raised mainly through non-institutional channels, such as lobbying (pao), relying (kao), and asking (yao). Lobbying means small town officials often visit upper level governments—which control capital distribution, often at the provincial level, to argue for investment in their towns. Relying means towns are not able to get investment to improve town services and economic development themselves and must rely on other levels of government to provide the services. Asking means small town officials request investment from upper level government.

After 2001, counties began to pay salaries of teachers in rural areas, which reduced pressure on township and town finances. While this was a help, it did not free up enough local own source revenue to make much of a difference in towns and townships' ability to invest in new industry.

Some provinces have experimented with intergovernmental transfer payments or revenue sharing to towns and townships and, in the case of Chengdu, to villages. In Hubei province in 2010, for example, many local governments implemented a system of excess tax restitution. If the tax collected in a township or town exceeds the pre-determined township tax base, a fixed proportion is supposed to be returned to the township or town, just as agricultural products that exceed state-mandated quotas are returned to individual households in the HCRS. However, when the system was implemented, usually either the restitution base was set too high or the proportion of restitution was set too low. In Yuelai town of Haimen city, Jiangsu province, for example, we found that the taxation of the town reached 79.43 million RMB in 2012, but 49.14 million RMB—more than 62 percent of the total tax revenue—was transferred to the national taxation office. The balance—30.29 million RMB was partly shared with higher-level government. The remaining revenue is needed to maintain existing (inadequate) services, leaving Yuelai town essentially no discretionary funding to use to promote new industrial development, construct infrastructure or improve public services unless they cut existing services even further (Yuelai Town Bureau of Finance, 2012).

Town government can sell developable construction land for housing to earn revenue, but land quotas are too low to provide enough revenue and there is not enough effective demand for housing and prices that will generate significant local revenue.

Chengdu, a pilot region for coordinated urban/rural development, has implemented a program providing block grants to villages (Ye and LeGates, 2013). In 2009 the Chengdu municipal government selected some villages as "social services and public administration to the countryside project pilot villages." The municipal government gave each of the selected villages at least 200,000 RMB (US$32,258) for public services and social management projects. The funds could only be used for specified village public service and social management projects in seven categories: sports, education, health, employment and social security, rural infrastructure and environmental construction, agricultural production services, and social management. The villagers were free to decide how to spend the 200,000 RMB among permitted uses. The pilot program was successful and in 2010 Chengdu expended the program to all villages. In 2011, Chengdu's social services and public administration to the countryside project funds were increased to 250,000 RMB (US$40, 323 per village). By the end of 2011 Chengdu had invested a total of more than 2.2 billion RMB (US$355 million) and supported nearly 20,000 village-level public services and social management projects that villagers themselves felt they most needed. This was not enough money to promote village industry, but it did give villages a new flexible source of money to meet immediate needs. The program also greatly increased villages' active participation in local decision-making.

As towns have such difficulty obtaining construction funds, what construction towns do fund is often at low-standards: poorly designed, ugly, polluting, rapidly deteriorating industrial facilities without amenities. This contributes to poor livability in towns and in turn makes it difficult for them to attract workers, creating a vicious cycle. Lack of public services for the urban workforce contributes to the problem. In our interviews in Hubei province, we found that many factories in towns have difficulty recruiting workers because of the poor quality of their development and low-quality public services. In our surveys and interviews we found that the new generation of rural workers is seeking better quality urban life rather than only higher income. As a result, a large proportion of the local workforce in rural areas of central and western China and undeveloped regions of eastern China continues to migrate from rural areas and towns and villages that can only afford to support low-quality industry and are unable to afford public services to wealthier cities competing for labor where wages are higher and the quality of factories, services, and the built and natural environments are better. This leaves local enterprises in less competitive regions suffering worker shortages, and they have to turn to migrant workers from rural areas of China with even less public services and poorer living conditions.

Towns' Deficient Administrative Management Authority and Capacity

Given the poor support from higher levels of government, the development of towns increasingly depends on attracting investment from non-governmental sources and real estate development. Under China's administrative hierarchy system, the lower the level of a government administrative division in the hierarchy, the weaker its ability to attract investment from higher levels of government (which in turn makes it difficult to attract private domestic investment or FDI). Investments towns make using their own source of revenue or what revenue they do get from other sources that succeed and might become key engines for towns' development are often taken over by cities and county towns.

In terms of real estate development, most of the land located in towns is rural collective land, which can be used for development and construction only after being transformed into state-owned land after it is requisitioned with the permission of the local Land Use Plan, which is approved by the central office of the PRC Ministry of Land and Resources in Beijing or one of its local branches. The transformation of farmland into urban development land is controlled by quotas administered by the Ministry of Land and Resources. After the allocation of quotas from the central office of the Ministry of Land and Resources in Beijing to provinces, provincial capital cities, prefecture-level cities, counties and county-level cities, most towns—which are the lowest administrative level of government—receive little or no part of annual quotas permitting them to convert agricultural land to developable construction land. Without legal construction land, expansion of industries in towns is restricted and new industries cannot be started, as no construction land is available, unless land is used illegally. This creates conditions for illegal development, corruption, and false reporting from lower levels of government to higher levels of government by towns that are desperate for construction land.

Towns are also in an inferior position when executing administrative powers. Despite their small scale, towns have to manage and coordinate all aspects of development just as cities do. However, the reality we found in surveys and interviews in provinces we studied is that towns have neither independent financial power nor enforcement power. Such institutions as planning control and land administration, taxation, environmental protection, and major utility services in most towns are under the administration of the higher-level agencies seated in cities or counties. This contributes to the poor management of urban planning, facilities construction, and administrative coordination in towns and further limits their ability to develop. The problem of poor town planning, coordination, and management is not only because of the low level of administrative and managerial skills at the town level, but also because town officials face complicated coordination problems and lack the authority to solve them.

Many Pilot Policies, Little Follow Through

Currently, the development of towns is mainly supported by the national government and provincial governments through the method of designating "key towns" and implementing "pilot projects." Many provinces have implemented so called "hundred towns and thousand villages demonstration projects." As a result, the infrastructure and the appearance of the listed towns and villages have been improved and some practical problems related to people's livelihood have been more or less solved. However, according to our surveys in Hubei province in 2010, the Haimen region in 2013, the Gaoming region in 2014, and the Quzhou region in 2015, the construction funds of the listed villages and towns in the demonstration projects are mainly from the investment and project support from the corresponding provincial or municipal departments and rarely from market or industry development.

Although pilot rural village projects are widely distributed, tasks are easier to achieve because of their small size than in larger places. Many pilot projects have focused on new rural village construction, which makes the renovated villages superior to other villages and even some town seats. Often provinces "cherry pick" demonstration towns and villages best positioned to succeed. They direct little support to backward towns.

Some newly constructed villages have very high living standards and are attractive places to live and work. New towns in peri-urban Chengdu are a notable example. Chengdu has pursued a policy of concentrating rural housing from individual plots and very small settlements into human-scale villages that retain attractive features of the vernacular landscape (Figure 8.9).

The Chengdu plain is an unusually fertile area that has supported tens of thousands of very small settlements called linpans for millennia (Abramson and Qi, 2011). Eighty percent of Chengdu's peasant farmers—4.44 million people—live in 140,000 linpans (CIPD, 2010). Most linpans consist of houses that are isolated from each other or in small clusters of two to five households. About 7 percent of Chengdu's linpan population lives in 10,000 linpans with populations of ten or more households (a little over 100 people) characterized by two- and three-story houses, most with adjoining walls, buffered by trees or bamboo and surrounded by agricultural land. Chengdu's strategy is to concentrate much of the linpan population into denser, larger new villages, returning village and some household homestead land to arable land. Some linpans are being preserved either as very small inhabited settlements or as nature preserves without people.

The new villages are larger and denser than linpans, but still human scale and retaining some of the most attractive features of linpans. Between 2003 and 2012 Chengdu constructed 1,613 new-style rural and urban communities with 1.42 million rural residents (CCURDC, 2012). By 2030 Chengdu plans to incorporate the 135,000 linpans that are not being preserved into 1,700 additional new villages with around 1.7 million residents (CMG, 2008). The new villages are being planned and constructed with features of the linpan style, including de facto greenbelts of trees and agricultural land surrounding them. These settlements will be about ten times as large as most of the larger existing linpans. Most will house 350–400 households (about 1,000 people)—a much lower density and more human scale than

Source: Photo by Richard LeGates, 2012.

Figure 8.9 Better environment of new villages in Chengdu

much new development at the fringe of existing cities and in new towns and cities elsewhere in China.

While other areas of China can learn from Chengdu and the new villages in the Chengdu plain, Chengdu has some distinct advantages that make the type of development they are pursuing particularly appropriate there, but which are not present elsewhere in China.

The Chengdu plain is fertile and well-watered, which makes it possible for farmers to earn a good living from agriculture. As the main city in southwestern China, rich in scenic and historic sites, Chengdu itself is rapidly modernizing—providing jobs for the surplus rural labor force and a market for high quality produce and other village products, and also for agritourism. Towns in poorer parts of China with fewer resources cannot replicate the Chengdu model.

Land policy, social security, and family planning in towns compared with villages often do not encourage rural residents to settle in them permanently; as towns provide more employment opportunities and relatively good basic education, some rural people choose to live in villages but to work in town seats as "half-town-resident and half-rural-peasant."

Chinas current "key town policy" has not promoted broad based positive fiscal balance and industrial development in towns. This pilot policy is difficult to apply given different local conditions, and pilot projects have had little impact as demonstrations. The most important and urgent consideration should be to find real roles in rural urbanization for the key towns that can be replicated elsewhere.

FINDINGS AND POLICY IMPLICATIONS FOR SMALL TOWN DEVELOPMENT

The Importance of Basic Public Services to Town and Village Residents

Towns are the centers of China's rural economy and society and bases supporting agricultural activities. Towns provide basic public services for rural residents in towns and townships, including education, healthcare, family planning, pension, commerce, and finance. The elements of towns, rural areas, agriculture, and farmers are closely intertwined. Based on the experience of the eastern region, much research has shown that industrialization is the main driving force in the development of towns. However, our research in Hubei, Anhui, Zhejiang and Jiangsu found that the development of towns depends not only on industrialization but also on the internal demands of rural residents for urban services, including housing, education, and civic amenities (Tongji University Research Team, 2010,

2012a, 2012b, 2013, 2014, 2015). In most of the towns we surveyed, industry is not well developed and often quite poor, but town seats' population is growing nonetheless. Town seats' population concentration is significantly associated with the quality of their living environment.

We asked samples of rural Hubei, Quzhou and Gaoming residents the main reason they or people like them from their area migrated in the past and what they thought would be the main reason in the future. Respondents reported that in the 1980s people mainly moved to get higher paying jobs, and in the 1990s for a combination of higher salaries, convenience of commuting to non-agricultural jobs, and children's education. In contrast they reported in the survey and also in interviews that in the future, people's moves would be based mainly on their assessment of the quality of the location's living environment, children's education, and public facilities.

To conclude, population concentration in towns is not only driven by industrialization but also by more convenient facilities, a better living environment, and higher-quality education. Policies for the future development of towns should consider these desires.

The Role of Towns in China's Agricultural Population Transfer and Overall Urbanization

In 2014, China's rural population numbered 619 million (NBSC, 2015). Considering the huge size of China's rural population, and the wide variety of conditions in different parts of rural China, the paths of future urbanization in China will inevitably be diversified.

Thirty-seven percent of the 866 rural Hubei province villagers we surveyed in 2010 said they intend to move to cities or towns in the future. Among the 320 villagers who intended to be urbanized, 39 percent said they intended to move to a county seat and 31 percent to a town. In 2015 we did similar field research in the Quzhou region of Zhejiang province. There only 9 percent of the villagers we interviewed said they intended to move to cities and 11 percent to rural towns (Tongji University Research Team, 2015). Fewer villagers in Quzhou expressed an interest in moving to urban areas, and the majority said they would prefer to move to a town rather than a city.

This field research permits an informed estimate of how many rural residents may choose to move to cities in the future. Averaging our various surveys from different parts of China, the mean percentage of rural people who said they intended to move is about 30 percent. Considering the huge population base in inland China, 186 million additional rural people in China may be planning to migrate, about 100 million of whom say they intend to move to towns. If the population without urban hukou already living in cities and towns who say they are willing to transfer permanently is considered, the rural population potentially willing to move would be even higher.

The scale and mechanization of agriculture in China still lags far behind developed countries. China's National Statistics Bureau has calculated the average number of working days per mu it took to produce each of China's three main crops (wheat, corn, and rice) in 2008 in China and in the United States (NBSC, 2009, 2014). A mu is a very small parcel of land: about one-sixth of an acre. The overall average for all three crops was 6.17 days of work per mu—over 12 times as many days as the 0.5 days required in the United States on average. It took more than 19 times as many working days per mu to raise tobacco in 2013 as it did in the United States and almost 100 times as much to produce silkworm cocoons (ibid).

Among the towns we surveyed, per capita cultivated land averaged only about 1 mu. In the 55 towns we surveyed in Hubei province, only 10 towns had some reasonably large-scale cultivation. In these towns, every household was responsible for approximately 20 mus of farmland. Labor productivity in rural areas of China has large room for improvement.

In 2014, there were 242 million members of the rural workforce (NBSC-csy, 2014). Based on this data, a conservative estimate is that, if agricultural labor productivity is doubled, 121 million members of the labor force could be released from rural areas. Assuming that a household ordinarily consists of a husband, wife and one child, the number of people moving from rural areas could be as high as 200 million people.

Low labor productivity means that there is great potential for the future transformation of rural society and this could be a strong driving force for China's urbanization.

People in the countryside are aging. How and where the 200 plus million current rural residents likely or potentially planning to migrate in the next decades will settle are key issues for China's new style urbanization. Towns, as well as cities, will play an important role in new urbanization. Reverse migration and the special appeal of hometowns are important elements for urban planning (Figure 8.10).

Reverse Migration and the Special Appeal of Hometowns

Migrants are pushed by increasing living cost in urban areas and pulled by the attraction of rural relationships and love of country living (Li and Yin, 2012). Compared with cities, towns are closer to the countryside and usually enjoy a better ecological environment and land resources than cities and metropolitan areas. Compared with villages, most towns are closer to

Source: Photo by Li Zhang, November, 2013.

Figure 8.10 Fishing village, Qingdao city, Shandong province cities and enjoy better public services and social welfare. With proper planning, towns become true town-country magnets offering the best of city and countryside as Ebenezer Howard imagined more than a century ago (Howard, [1898], 2010). They attract not only nearby rural residents, but also rural and urban migrants from other parts of China.

As described in Chapter 5, in recent years cities, especially larger cities, have been faced with increasing housing prices and living costs. In megacities, such as Shanghai, Beijing and Shenzhen, housing prices even in the outer suburbs are often above 10,000 RMB/m^2, and individual units may cost over one million RMB, which very few migrant workers can afford.

Aside from housing prices, basic living costs and children's education expenses are much higher in cities than in towns. As a result many migrants choose to spend money they make in cities back in their hometowns to support family members, build or improve homesteads, buy or rehabilitate houses or for other forms of consumption rather than purchasing housing or making other investments in the cities where they work. Because they have much more purchasing power in their hometowns, returning home at some point is attractive to many migrants. This is true not only when they retire, but also if they need to return to look after family members, or feel they have acquired enough savings or learned skills they think will make it possible to start businesses in their hometowns.

Migrant workers are mostly young at the time they first migrate. The majority of all migrant workers are between 20 and 40 years old. These workers usually are the support for their families, paying most or all of the cost of children's education and care for parents and other elderly household members. Many are the main source of new capital investment and savings for their households.

Migrants who migrate in their teens or twenties remain connected with traditional rural society and people from their communities of origin through social networks of migrant workers. Migrants often settle in enclaves populated by migrants from their place of origin within cities. Most can afford to return home for the New Year festival and other important family occasions such as weddings and funerals. In other words, migrants—even migrants who have been away from their villages of origin for a long time—remain rooted in rural areas.

There is a growing body of literature on reverse migration of migrant workers in China (Cheng et al., 2011). According to 2011 Ministry of Agriculture data, about 1.23 million migrant workers returned to their hometown, not only for holidays but to resettle permanently, in 2011 (MAC, 2012). The Ministry of Agriculture projects that this number will grow in the future.

Studies show that members of the labor force who return home and remain in the labor force are likely to be engaged in non-agricultural work (Demurger and Hui, 2010). They are more likely than local residents to make investments that help improve agricultural productivity (Zhao, 2002) and promote the diversified economic development of their hometowns (Murphy, 1999).

Generally, migrant workers who were born in the 1960s and 1970s say they are more motivated to eventually return home than those born in the 1980s and later (Yuan et al., 2009). While most empirical studies of reverse migration report that a substantial number of migrants eventually return to their hometowns and even more say they intend to, the samples, methodology, time the research was conducted and the findings vary.

Research on migrant workers in two populous provinces, Anhui and Sichuan provinces, by the Rural Economy Research Center of the Ministry of Agriculture found that in 1999 28.5 percent of the migrant labor force eventually went back to their hometowns (Bai and Song, 2002).

According to a 2006 survey of 100 counties in China by the State Council Development Research Center (DRC), 18.4 percent of migrant workers went back to their hometowns (Han, 2009).

A 2012 study by Xun Li, a professor at Sun Yat-sen University, and his colleagues found that 37.5 percent of migrant workers in a sample from Guangdong province returned to their hometowns.

According to a survey on migrant workers in Beijing in 2007, 33 percent of migrant workers said they were willing to return to their hometowns (Li and Long, 2009).

According to research conducted by the Labor and Social Security Bureau in Guizhou province (2011) 70 percent of migrant workers who returned home because of the global financial crisis said they would choose to stay home in the future if that were a viable option and 89 percent of these respondents said they expected to do non-agricultural work.

Recent research has consistently found that younger migrants are much less interested in returning to their hometowns than older migrants. According to the survey by the Tongji University Research Team in the Haimen region of Jiangsu province in 2013, 46 percent of migrant laborers born before 1983 said they are willing to return to the countryside to live when they are old, but no young migrants, born after 1983, said they would like to return (Chen and Zhang, 2014). The investigation in Foshan in 2014 found that 66 percent of the migrant laborers, born before 1984 prefer to settle down in their hometowns—county capitals, general towns, or villages, but that the proportion of migrant laborers, born between 1984 to 1994, who said they would prefer to settle down in their hometowns decreased to 44 percent (Tongji University Research Team, 2014).

In contrast to these studies which found few young people expressing an interest in returning to the countryside, Jing and Ma found that as many as one-third of migrants from the "post 1980s" and "post 1990s" generations would be willing to return home (Jing and Ma, 2012).

Studies have shown that only a few migrants who return to rural areas are willing to do farm work as their only income source after returning home. This suggests that if possible they will go to towns and work in the manufacturing or service industries, including sideline industries or settle in villages where commute time to these types of jobs in the village or a nearby town is short enough to make it possible for them to live in the countryside and work in a city or town where they can find non-agricultural work.

Towns as Transition Zones between Urban and Rural Areas and Suitable Places for Farmers to Engage in Sideline Businesses

The bi-directional connection between urban regions and rural areas makes towns an irreplaceable part of the urbanization process. Unlike villages, the distinctive features of towns are that they share some attractive characteristics of cities such as public services, municipal facilities, and sometimes a modern atmosphere. And unlike cities, towns have attractive features of the countryside. They are transitional zones between urban and rural areas. With better finances, public services and living environments, living conditions in towns could become similar to or superior to those of cities, but so far the development of towns in general has fallen behind that of cities.

Spatially, seats of most towns are small. Except for the sparsely populated province of Qinghai and the autonomous regions of Xinjiang, Tibet, and Inner Mongolia, the administrative region of towns in most provinces and autonomous regions is between 100 to 400 square kilometers, with a radius of around 5 to 10 kilometers—a 20-minute ride by an electric bicycle, which is a popular form of transportation in China's countryside with a speed between 20 and 30 kilometers per hour. In the era of motorization, commuting distance need not lead to conflicts between life and workplace. Shuttling between towns and the countryside is convenient. Therefore, towns not only provide public services for the surrounding countryside but also favorable conditions for the rural labor force to seek jobs.

Recent research has found strong connections between residents living in the countryside and towns. According to a 1999 survey of 13 towns in Shanghai by a Tongji University team, 58.4 percent of workers in TVEs engaged in both agricultural and industrial production and 60.7 percent of the employees in town seats had rural registered permanent residence

(Zou, 2003). A 2010 study conducted by another Tongji University team found that 80 percent of workers in town enterprises in Hubei province were also engaged in farm work part-time.

Li and Yin's (2012) study of the Yunfu region of Guangdong province and our investigation in the Bengbu region of Anhui province, Haimen region of Jiangsu province, Foshan region of Guangdong province, Jiading region in Shanghai, and the Quzhou region in Zhejiang also found that participation of the rural labor force in sideline businesses is a common phenomenon (Tongji University Research Team, 2012a, 2012b, 2013, 2014, 2015).

Towns are the transition zones between cities and countryside during the process of Chinese urbanization, places for the rural population to experience urbanized life, and reservoirs for the rural surplus labor force to transfer to cities. At the same time, the fundamental function of towns in China continues to be as administrative and commercial centers of rural areas. These characteristics determine the irreplaceable position and role of towns in China's future urbanization.

Assuring the Development of Towns by Further Institutional Reform

The sound development of towns requires favorable institutional support (Tian and Chang, 2003; Zhao, 2001). Practice has shown that giving towns more administrative authority during appropriate stages of their development can promote rapid economic and social development and unleash local development potential, so exploring institutional innovation is necessary.

Healthy towns that develop economically and attract new residents should be an important component of China's overall urbanization strategy. Over time the largest and most successful towns may evolve into small cities, as is already happening in Zhejiang province in some pilot towns where industrial development has been particularly successful. In 2010 the Zhejiang provincial government indicated that 27 pilot official towns were authorized with administrative power at the county level and targeted to be developed into small cities (Zhejian Provincial Government, 2010).

The sound development of towns requires support from government policies and cooperation by higher levels of government. Towns face greater risks of being affected by external disturbance than larger and more diversified urban areas, because of their limited population and economic scale. In China towns need higher levels of government to support them by policies such as sharing quotas to convert agricultural land to construction land and reducing the high proportion of tax revenue handed up to higher levels of governments or returning more funding for facilities construction and other needs. The sound development of towns needs a series of policies and institutional assurances, including institutional innovation, exploitation of new paths suitable for the development of selected towns, improvement of their planning and management capacity, and reform of town fiscal and taxation systems in order to ensure adequate funds for public infrastructure and facilities, housing and protection of the environment as well as direct investment in industry. Renewing traditional ideas, towns should be guided by a series of regulations and policies to fully play their roles in China's urbanization process, including reducing the pressure of urbanization in major population inflows to megacities. The development of towns should adapt to local conditions. Different paths of development should be explored under different geographical, resource, economic, social, and cultural conditions of different kinds of towns. It may be difficult for underdeveloped towns in the central and western regions in the current global economy to implement rural industrialization development models that worked well in in the coastal areas of China in the past (Zhang, 2011; Shi, 2013). In short, diversified development paths for towns should be explored based on consideration of actual local area conditions.

CONCLUSION: SMALL TOWN, GRAND STRATEGY

Despite the disadvantages of having low social welfare benefits, less good education (or at least the perception that it is less good), less modern cultural attractions, high commuting costs to reach downtowns or markets, and boredom experienced by young people, towns still have many advantages over cities, including proximity to nature, good quality of living, traditions for the elderly, use rights in arable land and homesteads, lower housing costs, the possibility of fair or even windfall profits if land is requisitioned, and improving public services. However, town development lags behind development of cities and metropolitan areas because of social, economic, and institutional issues, discussed in this chapter. Nevertheless, small town development is still a major strategy for Chinese urbanization.

In the current economic environment in China, attention should be paid to both cities and city clusters, and counties and towns should be included in analyses of clustering to promote sound urbanization. If towns are guided well by systematic and innovative policies, it should be possible for them to absorb between one-third and a half of the 263 migrant workers likely to return to their home towns (PRC-MHRSS, 2013). Government should develop appropriate policy to help them settle in a combination of county capitals, general towns, townships, villages and rural areas within towns' administrative regions, and provide them stable lives, jobs, and opportunities to start businesses. This could dramatically lessen the pressure on traffic congestion, air pollution, and inefficient public facilities that are particularly acute in China's large and megacities.

Social problems, such as the hollowing out of rural villages, rural population aging, and poor quality of children's education, can be solved or relieved by a successful towns policy. From the perspective of the current age structure of migrant workers, the "post 1960s" and "post 1970s" generations have stronger affection for their hometowns than the "post 1980s" and "post 1990s" generations. Studies discussed above suggest many of them are willing to return home.

In addition to considering the healthy urbanization of about 200 million migrant workers, as many as 200 million additional potential surplus laborers in rural areas should also be considered. Among the 200 million surplus laborers in rural areas, some are redundant because of their low productivity. However, many of these potential migrants are teenagers who will enter the labor market as they grow up. This segment of the young population tends to transfer to developed regions and cities where they can take advantage of modern amenities. Therefore, if most towns keep the current service level and living environment, attracting the future generation to come back after they leave their homes will be difficult.

China's urbanization development is now in a phase of medium-term acceleration. Most cities (especially those in the central and western regions) are not in a position to offer much support for the development of townships, towns, and counties because they are still accumulating land, capital, and a workforce.

Towns in less developed areas of China cannot uncritically copy the successful development pattern of towns in the coastal areas in the past. Towns cannot become the main location of future urbanization (Zhang, 2012; Lu and Han, 2013; Zhang and Zhao, 2014), but they should certainly be made a part of sound urbanization. The double pressure of two "200 millions"—200 million surplus rural laborers who might be incorporated into the modern workforce and 200 million migrants who may reverse migrate back to their hometowns will make implementation of "new style urbanization" difficult. Only by understanding a whole "grand strategy" for towns joining efforts of governments, enterprises, citizens, and policymakers, and by responding to current global and domestic trends can China best manage population flows and industry restructuring in its ongoing urbanization process.

9. Double dual transformation: understanding urbanization with Chinese characteristics

Considering its enormous scale and impact, China's urbanization in the last three decades is an economic and social event of global significance as well as a monumental change for China's own citizens. As China moves into the rank of developed and urbanized countries in the next twenty to thirty years its economic and social transformation will have an even more profound impact not only on the Chinese people, but the entire world.

Before reform and opening up, China's nationwide urbanization level increased by less than 8 percent from about 10 percent in 1949 to just under 18 percent in 1978 (NBSC-csy, 1984). During what we term the transition period after reform and opening up, it has increased by more than 37 percent to about 55 percent today (NBSC, 2015b). The transition period was remarkably different from Mao's age. China is still at the stage of economic development Walt Whitman Rostow terms the "drive to maturity" (Rostow, 1956) and at the mid to late stage of accelerating urbanization according to the Davis and Northam S-shaped urbanization curves discussed in Chapter 1 (Davis, 1965; Northam, 1979). While we believe that China's future urbanization will be slower than World Bank, UN and other experts predict, it is likely that China's urbanization level will reach 75 percent within 30 years and China will be at the flat top of the S curve—essentially urbanized.

China has a large population and huge economic power. The low starting point of development combined with great regional disparities in development conditions require development to proceed in very diverse ways. Thus, China can serve as an example of development for a wide range of other developing countries. Like China in its early stage of reform and opening up, many countries in Asia, Africa, the Indian subcontinent, and Latin America have underdeveloped economies, dense populations, limited resources and weak economic and political foundations. Under the influence of globalization and deepening of the division of labor, these countries are seeking paths of economic and social development best suited to their conditions. Virtually all are now challenged by pressure from accelerating urbanization. A good understanding of China's development path—its experiments and setbacks as well as its remarkable achievements—is important not only for China itself, but also for other developing countries.

An understanding of China's urbanization should be grounded in theory and informed by empirical research. In this spirit, this chapter begins by reviewing theory that is particularly helpful in understanding China's urbanization: dual development theory developed by Arthur O. Lewis (Lewis, 1954), Simon Kuznets' theory of the relationship between development and income inequality (Kuznets, 1955), the middle-income trap proposed by Indirmet Gill, Homi Kharas and other World Bank experts (Gill et al., 2007), the demographic dividend (Bloom, Canning, and Sevilla, 2003), Maslow's hierarchy of needs (Maslow, 1943), and the relationship between economic development and urbanization proposed by Harvard economics professor and former World Bank vice president Hollis Chenery and University of Miami International Studies professor Moise Syrquin (Chenery and Syrquin, 1975).

Building on these theories, we construct a theoretical framework for explaining urbanization with Chinese characteristics we term the double dual transition model. The double dual transition model fits a market-driven economy running in parallel with the state-controlled economy, and simultaneously improving the quality of cities in parallel with the massive increase in the quantity of all the physical components of cities and regions that will inevitably occur as China continues to develop and urbanize. While the double dual transition model helps explain the "urbanization path with Chinese characteristics" it is highly relevant to the many developing countries that are striving to produce more livable, humane, equitable, and sustainable cities using the mix of governmental and market approaches best suited to them. Compared with the divided, unstable, and often violent conditions wrecking many developing countries in the Middle East, Africa, and some Central and South American countries, China has ensured social stability and basic living standards while experiencing urbanization at the largest scale in human history much more rapidly than the developed countries during their periods of rapid urbanization.

THEORY

Dual Economic Theory and the Lewis Turning Point

In 1954, Arthur O. Lewis, a Nobel Prize winning economist at the University of Manchester, proposed a dual structure model of economic development, which divides the economies of developing countries into two sectors—a traditional agriculture sector and a modern industrial sector (Lewis, 1954). Although Lewis' dual economic theory has drawn criticism from other economists (Jorgenson, 1961; Fei and Ranis, 1964; Todaro, 1969) as reviewed below, it is widely accepted as a classical framework to analyze urbanization in developing countries.

Lewis' model attributes modernization to economic structure transformation as societies move from backward traditional agricultural societies to modern industrial societies. The model emphasizes the vast surplus rural labor force in developing countries that is not really needed to do the work necessary in agriculture. The marginal productivity of the surplus agricultural labor force is almost zero. This leads to low income in the agricultural sector. In contrast, Lewis argued, the industrial sector in developing countries represents advanced productive forces. The marginal productivity of the industrial labor force is higher than agriculture, as are wage levels, which induces the agricultural labor force to continuously flow from rural to urban areas. Lewis argues that the transition will continue until the surplus rural labor is entirely absorbed by cities and rural salaries equal urban salaries. This is the first turning point. In addition to the first Lewis turning point, Lewis identified a second turning point related to productivity (Lewis, 1968). As the productivity of the traditional low-efficiency agricultural sector rises as the rural labor force is transferred to the higher-efficiency industrial sector the marginal productivity of the modern sector of the economy will gradually decrease. As a result, the difference in productivity between the two sectors will decrease. Eventually, the productivity of the traditional agricultural sector and modern sector will converge and the dual economic structure will disappear. At this second turning point, a developing country like China becomes a developed country.

Lewis' model is based on a distinct meaning of urbanization: First, the model unifies the agricultural sector and cities, and it takes the city as the starting point for economic development. According to Lewis, capital and new ideas are not distributed evenly throughout an economy. Economic development is a process of the ongoing expansion of the modern urban industrial sector. The main source of economic development is urban industrial profit, which leads to capital accumulation. New employment opportunities are created by the ongoing expansion of employment in the two different economies and depend, according to Lewis' theory, upon reconfiguration of manpower resource between urban and rural areas brought about by urbanization. Agriculture can be modernized by capital and ideas from the modern urban economic sector. Lewis envisages agricultural and industrial convergence as a result of capital equipment, advanced technology and a modern organization of the agricultural system.

Lewis' "dual economy model" has had a great impact on the formulation of many developing countries' economic policies, including policy in China. The model is the theoretical basis of many population and urbanization studies—especially studies of rural population migration. It was remarkably prescient in describing the rural–urban migration that has occurred in China we describe in Chapter 6.

Although the Lewis' model produced a paradigm shift in thinking about development and has had a powerful influence on the formulation of developing countries' policies and urbanization studies, his hypotheses do not precisely match conditions in many developing countries, including China and in the half century since his classic article appeared scholars have made important theoretical additions to it (Jorgenson, 1961; Fei and Ranis, 1964; Todaro, 1969). While under a strict application of the Lewis theory this should not occur, in China we found simultaneous labor shortages in eastern China and surplus rural labor in central and western China. The Lewis model assumes that a higher rate of capital accumulation will lead to a higher economic growth rate in the modern sector and more rapid job creation, but some Chinese firms are re-investing profits in precision instruments and labor saving technology rather than expanding production under existing conditions. Thus a higher rate of capital accumulation will not necessarily increase employment and may lower the employment rate for low-skilled workers. This is beginning to occur in the most developed parts of China. Advanced economic activities such as finance and research and development and high value added manufacturing relying on information technology and robotics might produce smaller and more skilled labor forces in the most advanced parts of China. China's National New Style Urbanization Plan anticipates that this will occur and considers it is desirable in some parts of eastern China.

When will China Reach the Lewis Turning Point?

Evidence about how close China is to achieving the Lewis turning points is contradictory and scholars disagree about when China will reach the turning points, or whether it already has reached one or both, at least in some areas.

Professor Fang Cai from the Chinese Academy of Social Sciences, an expert on population, labor, and employment in China has concluded that China is now close to the first Lewis turning point (Cai, 2010, 2011a, 2011b). There are a number of indicators that back up his analysis. Recently there has been a severe shortage of ordinary workers in coastal regions and some inland provinces. This phenomenon can only be partially explained by changes in people's concepts about working and consumption. Now that the majority of Chinese have sufficient income to meet basic necessities more and more people—particularly young people in urban areas—are using their discretionary income for self-satisfaction. They spend discretionary income on better living and working conditions, consumer goods such as electronic products, travel, and leisure. For example, even a young migrant worker who is able to earn only US$500 per month can own an expensive iPhone in China. Young people often spend all their earnings without saving. This is very different from that of old generations of migrants from rural areas.

Other evidence suggests that overall China is still quite a way from the Lewis turning point. Overall the income gap between urban and rural China is still large. China's 2013 average per capita disposable income in urban areas was 26,955 RMB—over three times the average per capita disposable income in rural areas of 8,896 RMB. Salaries of ordinary urban laborers are still relatively high compared with incomes of agricultural laborers, and they are increasing, so more rural workers will continue to be attracted into the urban areas. China's *de jure* urbanization level—the population with non-agricultural hukou—is still low and the income from agricultural activities is also still low.

Despite the ongoing controversy concerning the coming of Lewis' turning points, it is clear that China's supply–demand relationship for rural labor has changed. Consistent with our emphasis on how large and diverse China is and the need to examine issues at multiple levels, both our macro-level structural analysis and fieldwork on individual behavior suggests that the question of when China will reach the Lewis turning point has no single answer. There will be many Lewis turning points in different parts of China at different times. Some developed areas of China that are as large as other countries may have already reached the second Lewis turning point or are close to it. Other large poor and undeveloped regions remain far from the first turning point. As described in Chapter 4 on regional policies and regional urbanization and Chapter 6 on large-scale population flows, much of China's agriculture is still small scale and backward. Agriculture modernization can still release a large number of workers. The permanent settlement choice of new generation young people will be mostly in cities.

A declining birth rate and the rise of ordinary laborers' salaries are two marks of the coming of Lewis' turning point (Cai, 2007). In China, the birth rate has declined from 18.25 percent in 1978 to 12.08 percent in 2013, and the natural growth rate also declined from 12.00 percent to 4.92 percent (NBSC-csy, 2014). The decrease in China's birth rate leads directly to the slowing down of the growth of the rural surplus labor force and the transition from the stage of unlimited to a limited supply of labor. Variations in the salary of ordinary laborers indicate that the equilibrium of the supply and demand of China's rural labor force has been disrupted. According to the official national survey at fixed observation points in rural areas from 2003 to 2006, the monthly salary of peasant workers increased from 781 RMB to 953 RMB (US$126 to US$154), with an annual average increase of 7.37 percent (Zhao, 2007: 23). Nationally, the annual average increase in peasant salaries from 2006 to 2013 was 24.82 percent and in 2013, the national average salary of peasant workers was 2,609 RMB (US$421) (China News Web, 2014a). The accelerating growth of salaries (including rural salaries) reflects China's growing economic dominance, but also changes in supply–demand relationships in labor markets throughout China.

Simon Kuznets and the Kuznets Curve

Simon Smith Kuznets, a Nobel Prize winning Belarusian-American economist, statistician, demographer, and economic historian, argues that as countries develop income distribution will eventually become more equal (Kuznets, 1955). Kuznets concluded that income distribution takes the form of an inverted u-shaped curve as countries develop; that after the income gap between rich and poor reaches a peak level, it will narrow (the Kuznets curve). As the income gap narrows, income distribution within a country will become more equitable. If the salaries of ordinary laborers in both the industrial and agricultural sectors rise after reaching the Lewis turning point, then if Kuznets is right, a country's income distribution should become correspondingly more equitable. Both theories are fundamentally important to China.

As much of China's surplus rural labor force has been absorbed into the urban labor force and China has moved from a poor underdeveloped country to a middle level of development, income inequality as measured by the national Gini coefficient has risen rapidly. In our opinion a Gini coefficient or any other simple measure of inequality for a country as large and diverse as China gives a partial and distorted picture of income inequality. The most extreme examples of inequality in China occur as a result of initial public offerings (IPOs) or other extreme increases in the value of stock that is highly concentrated in the hands of a few company founders and investors. This involves ownership of assets, rather than income. Failure to consider long tails in distributions is an error in statistical interpretation and the tails of asset (and sometime income) distributions can be very large in the most dynamic sectors. A Gini coefficient does not consider consumption or reinvestment of wealth. Wealthy individuals in China may consume much more than ordinary Chinese, but most of their wealth is reinvested and further builds the national economy. Per capita income is not a very good indicator of quality of life. Shelter, food, and other life necessities are much less expensive in less developed rural areas. Many households with rural hukou live on homestead land on self-built housing they can maintain themselves, so shelter costs are often minimal. They supplement food from household plots, so food costs are very low. And clothing and other necessities are inexpensive. Despite the limitation of Gini coefficients as a measure of inequality it is clear that there are large income and wealth disparities in some regions in China and they are growing. Reducing disparities—not only between urban and rural China but also among provinces and regions is a national priority.

Does Kuznets' theory work for China's market socialist economy? Is his sixty-year-old theory valid in today's global high-tech economy? Professor Fang Cai at the Chinese Social Science Institute points out that given the continuing government role in managing the economy, income equality in China is strongly affected by national policies (Cai, 2011b). Recent scholarship suggests that income inequality is continuing to increase in the most developed countries as a tiny percentage of the wealthiest individuals have both disproportionately high incomes and control a disproportionate share of national wealth (Stiglitz, 2015).

The Demographic Dividend

Princeton University demographer Frank W. Notestein (1945) divided demographic transition as societies develop into three stages of: (1) high birth and death rates and low growth, (2) high birth rates, low death rates and high growth, and (2) low birth rates, low death rates and low growth. In early demographic studies, the focus of concern was fertility, birth and death rates, and total population, with no attempt to relate demographic transition to economic development (Cai, 2011b). As the developed countries and the emerging industrialized countries have experienced simultaneous demographic transition and economic growth, demographers have developed a greater awareness of the aging society during demographic transition and the adverse impact this may have on economic growth. At an early stage of demographic transition, the high proportion of productive (working-age) population will result in economic growth over the normal level. David Bloom, a professor of economics and demography at Harvard's T.H. Chan School of Public Health and his colleagues term this the demographic dividend (Bloom, Canning and Sevilla, 2003). Chinese demographer Xueyuan Tian, a research fellow at the Chinese Academy of Social Science, has defined the period with a high proportion of working-age population and low social dependency ratio as the "golden age" when the maximum benefits of labor force and population age structure can be realized (Tian, 2014). China's long-term high speed economic growth can be attributed in part to the demographic dividend. As shown in Table 9.1, the proportion of China's working-age population increased by 15.07 percent from 59.46 percent in 1982 to 74.53 percent in 2010. During this same period the social dependency ratio (the number of people aged less than 15 and more than 64 to the number of working-age people between 15 and 64) dropped by 34.01 percent from 68.19 percent to 34.18 percent. Wang et al. (2004) estimate that every one percent decline in China's social dependency ratio contributes 0.115 percent to economic growth. If Wang's estimate is accurate, the 34.0 percent decline in China's dependency ratio between 1982 and 2010 contributed an average of 3.91 percent to annual economic growth as measured by per capita GDP. During this period, the average annual increase in China's per capita GDP was around 9.14 percent. Accordingly the demographic dividend may have contributed more than 42 percent to the growth of China's per capita GDP from the early stages of reform and opening up to the present. But this pattern will not continue.

China's demographic dividend peaked between 2011 and 2014 and is now decreasing. The proportion of working-age population has begun to decline slightly—by 1.14 percent over the course of these four years. As a result, China's social dependency ratio increased by 2.07 percent during these four years. So far the impact of the decrease has been slight. Based on the above assumptions, this reversal contributed a 0.238 percent decrease to China's per capita GDP during this period. But the cumulative impacts of China's shrinking demographic dividend are likely to be substantial over time.

As life expectancy increases and the full impact of China's one child policy is felt, the proportion of elderly population (over 65) to China's total population is increasing significantly. As shown in Table 9.1 between 1982 and 2013 the proportion increased every year, from 4.91 percent of the population in 1982 to 9.67 percent in 2013. The United Nations defines an aging society to be any society in which 7 percent or more of the population is 65 or older or 10 percent of the population is 60 or older. By this standard China is an aging society. The decline of birth rates and the social dependency ratio combined with the increase in salaries is further evidence that the era of the demographic dividend in China is approaching a turning point.

Maslow's Hierarchy of Needs

In addition to the healthy physical development of cities, responding to human needs at ever higher levels is important. Once provision of

Table 9.1 China's population structure in 1982 to 2014 (unit: million)

Year	1982	1990	1995	2000	2005	2010	2011	2012	2013	2014
Total Population A	1,003	1,131	1,189	1,266	1,282	1,340	1,347	1,354	1,361	1,368
Age B 15–64	597	755	792	888	915	998	1,003	1,004	1,006	1,004
C 0–14	358	313	318	290	251	222	222	223	223	226
D 65–100	49	62	80	88	116	119	123	127	132	138
Proportion of working-age population B/A	59.46%	66.77%	66.57%	70.15%	71.38%	74.53%	74.43%	74.15%	73.92%	73.39%
Dependency ratio (C+D)/B	68.19%	49.77%	50.22%	42.56%	40.10%	34.18%	34.35%	34.86%	35.28%	36.25%
Proportion of aged population D/A	4.91%	5.55%	6.70%	6.96%	9.07%	8.87%	9.12%	9.39%	9.67%	10.09%
Proportion of young population C/B	59.93%	41.47%	40.16%	32.64%	27.39%	22.28%	22.10%	22.20%	22.20%	22.51%
Ratio of aged population to young population D/C	13.78%	20.03%	25.05%	30.40%	46.41%	53.42%	55.44%	57.05%	58.94%	61.06%

Source: NBSC-census (1984, 1992, 2002, 2012); NBSC-csy (2014); NBSC (2015).

adequate food, shelter, and clothing is assured it is important to meet other human needs—particularly related to health.

Maslow's hierarchy of needs developed by American psychologist Abraham Maslow depicts human needs as endless, in which more demands follow after possessing basic life necessities (Maslow, 1943). Maslow's hierarchy holds true for the current urbanization process in China. Once basic survival demands have been satisfied, newly transitioned urban dwellers express higher-level demands: for better housing quality, more and better resting and recreational space, clean air and water, social justice, more material goods of all kinds, and equal opportunity and freedom to achieve individual aspirations. The satisfaction of those demands step by step is an inevitable historical process in China's urbanization, and fulfillment of higher order demands a key measure of the success of the double dual track transition in China's urbanization.

The Middle-Income Trap

The World Bank classifies the world's economies based on estimates of gross national income (GNI) per capita. As of 2013 they defined low-income economies as those with a GNI per capita of US$1,045 or less, middle-income economies as those with a GNI per capita of more than US$1,045 but less than US$12,746, and high-income economies as those with a GNI per capita of US$12,746 or more. The World Bank further divides the line between lower-middle-income and upper-middle-income economies at a GNI per capita of US$4,125.

Because GNI and GDP in China so far are very similar, GDP is a reasonable proxy for GNI. China's GDP per capita was US$1,124 in 2002 so by the World Bank definition China reached middle-income status more than a decade ago (World Bank Web, 2014). In 2010 China's per capita GDP reached US$4,375 qualifying it as an upper-middle-income economy (United Nations, 2015). China is projected to enter the high-income category in 2023 if its annual GDP continues to increase by an average of 7 percent. In 2013 based on the World Bank's classification criteria, there were 57 high-income countries, 98 middle-income, and only 31 low-income countries in the world (World Bank, 2015).

While classifying countries into categories based on the level of their economic development is helpful and the middle-income trap is very relevant for China, we are skeptical about the validity of per capita income as a measure of a country's citizens well-being and do not agree with the World Bank's categories. The standard for defining middle-income countries should take into account the purchasing power of each currency.

Conversion of national currency figures using their exchange rate in relation to the US dollar is not a valid measure of how well off the country's residents really are. Food, shelter, and other basic living costs in rural China are very low in US dollar terms. Low incomes by international standards can provide a good basic lifestyle in China. In 2013 based on the World Bank's classification criteria with the conversion by purchasing power, there were 103 high-income countries, 115 middle-income, and only 10 low-income countries in the world, which is clearly inaccurate. Measuring countries' rankings using purchasing power parity (PPP) is more accurate.

An important World Bank report titled *An East Asian Renaissance: Ideas for Economic Growth* (2006, in Gill et al., 2007) by a team led by the World Bank's chief economist for East Asia and the Pacific, Homi Kharas and economic adviser, Indermit Gill introduced the important concept of a "Middle-Income Trap" in which countries become stuck after they reach a middle level of development and started a lively debate about why the middle-income trap occurs and how countries can avoid it.

Looking at the growth trajectories of countries that had moved from poor and undeveloped to a middle level of development, Kharas and Gill found that once developing countries reached what Rostow calls the stage of economic take off their economies often grew rapidly to a point, but then dramatically slowed or stopped. They remained "trapped" in middle-income status. Only the most developed countries in North America and Europe and Japan and Korea in Asia have succeeded in breaking out of the middle-income trap to move into the top rank of world economies. Kharas and Gill attribute the period of rapid growth to the initial comparative advantage countries with abundant cheap labor and low land costs have in attracting low value added industry and assembly work and to the growth they can quickly achieve by importing existing technology. But as their pool of surplus labor shrinks, labor costs rise, urban land becomes more expensive and they exhaust the easy productivity gains affordable technology achieves, the initial development model stops working. To move higher up the ranks of the world economy they must make very large-scale investments in expensive cutting edge technology and educate or import highly skilled workers—which is expensive. Immanuel Ibrahim Wallerstein, an American sociologist and world systems theorist argues that the world system is divided into *core*, *semi-peripheral* and *peripheral* regions (2011). It is very difficult for a peripheral country to shift to the semi-periphery and it is also difficult for a semi-peripheral country to shift into the core countries category.

Soon after China achieved middle-income status by World Bank standards in 2002 scholars began to debate how it might escape from the middle-income trap. The debate has intensified now that China has crossed the dividing line into upper-middle-income status.

Fang Cai has linked the middle-income trap and the Lewis turning point. He argues that China must improve income distribution (Cai, 2008) and change the traditional development style to a new sustainable growth policy (Cai, 2012).

Shijin Liu, the associate president of the State Council's Development Research Center (DRC) and his colleagues analyzed more than thirty countries with populations of more than ten million and concluded that it is less likely that China will remain stuck in the middle-income trap than countries in Latin America (Liu et al., 2012). Liu feels that China's real challenge is accumulated structural conflicts, financial risk, and the difficulty of moving from an economy which is merely efficient in performing routine tasks to one that is able to continually innovate (Liu et al., 2012).

Bingwen Zheng, Professor and President of the Latin America Laboratory in the Chinese Social Science Institute, emphasizes the importance of China's moving from the present stage in which it has successfully achieved efficiency in many areas to making original innovations and describes ten traps Chinese government should face in the near future besides the middle-income trap. The other nine traps are also related to economic increase. They consist of an economic structure transformation trap, regional inequality trap (in Latin American countries), social welfare trap, over- and under-urbanization trap, housing bubble trap, aging population trap, finance crisis trap, US currency exchange rate trap, being conceited trap, and a populism trap.

Wing-Thye Woo, a Malaysian-American professor of economics at the University of California, Davis, has developed a "catch up index (CUI)" defining high-, middle- and low-income countries by the ratio of the average per capita income level of the country to the average per capita income level of the United States (Woo, 2012). Woo's CUI is expressed as a percent. He set the CUI for middle income at 20 percent, and the CUI for high income at 55 percent of US per capita income, which is much stricter than the World Bank standard.

We conducted our own research on the middle-income trap, reducing the two thresholds to 15 percent and 40 percent, respectively. In our analysis we define a low-income country as a country with a CUI under 15 percent, a middle-income country as one with a CUI between 15 percent and 40 percent, and a high-income country as a country with a CUI above 40 percent. By this definition, the thresholds of per capita GNI (PPP) defining a middle-income country were between US$7,920 and US$21,120 in 2013. By this standard of the 228 world economies, in 2013 68 fell into the high-income category, 66 in the middle-income category and 94 were low-income countries, based on the US Central Intelligence Agency data (CIA, 2014). China's per capita GDP (PPP) in 2013 was US$9,800 dollars, which would place it at the lower bound of the middle-income category, rather than in upper bounds based on the United Nations definitions. We believe this is a more realistic description of China's current economic status.

In order to place China's situation in perspective and form a better idea of prospects that it can break out of the middle-income trap, it is helpful to understand the comparative magnitudes of change in countries at a mid-level of development in the major regions of the developing world using appropriate heuristic categories and indicators of development.

In order to better understand how fast the economies of China and other middle-income developing Asian countries are "catching up" with other large cities in Asia and Latin America we selected the largest seven middle-income countries in Asia and the seven largest in Latin America (including Mexico) and analyzed trends in their per capita GDP (PPP), CUI and the proportion of their population that was urban from 1980 to 2013 using these categories. Because most developing African countries fall into the low-income country category we did not analyze African countries.

As shown by Table 9.2, all seven countries in Latin America in 1980 were middle-income countries, but in Asia only Malaysia qualified as a middle-income country. Between 1980 and 2013 all seven countries in Latin America remained middle-income countries. The CUI of Argentina, Brazil, Peru and Venezuela declined during these 33 years, that is, the gap in economic development relative to the US expanded. Except for Chile, where the CUI grew by 17 percent, growth in the other two Latin American countries, Columbia and Mexico, was between 0 percent and 1 percent. In contrast, except for the Philippines, the CUI of the six countries in Asia increased by between 4 percent and 17 percent. The increases were highest in Thailand (10 percent), Malaysia (14 percent), and especially China (17 percent). The economies of the larger Asian countries are catching up much faster than Latin America and China is developing the fastest.

Table 9.2 also sheds light on the relationship between middle-income status, catching up, and urbanization. The urbanization level of the Latin American countries was much higher than of the Asian countries in 1980: 72 percent on average compared with 27 percent. The average urbanization level of the seven Latin American countries has increased by 12 percent from 72 percent in 1980 to 84 percent in 2014. All are now at or close to the level of full urbanization with urbanization rates between 76 percent (Columbia) and 92 percent (Argentina). Although the starting point of the urbanization level of Asian countries was lower in 1980, the 22 percent increase was nearly double the increase in the Latin American

Table 9.2 Economic and urbanization increases, selected large Latin American and Asian countries, 1980 to 2013

		GDP per capita (PPP)		Catch Up Index			Proportion of Urban Population		
		1980	2013	1980	2013	Change	1980	2014	Change
Selected Latin American Large Countries	Argentina	4,868	18,600	39%	35%	−4%	83%	92%	9%
	Brazil	3,653	12,100	29%	23%	−6%	66%	85%	19%
	Chile	2,331	19,100	19%	36%	17%	81%	89%	8%
	Columbia	2,552	11,100	20%	21%	1%	62%	76%	14%
	Mexico	3,787	15,600	30%	30%	0%	66%	79%	13%
	Peru	2,931	11,100	23%	21%	−2%	65%	78%	13%
	Venezuela	5,577	13,600	44%	26%	−18%	79%	87%	8%
	Average	3,671	14,457	29%	27%	−2%	72%	84%	12%
Selected Asian Large Countries	India	425	4,000	3%	8%	5%	23%	32.4%	9%
	Indonesia	662	5,200	5%	10%	5%	22%	53%	31%
	Malaysia	2,445	17,500	19%	33%	14%	42%	74%	32%
	Philippines	1,356	4700	11%	9%	−2%	38%	45%	7%
	Thailand	1,075	9900	9%	19%	10%	27%	49%	22%
	Vietnam	561#	4,000	4%	8%	4%	19%	33%	14%
	China	253	9,800	2%	19%	17%	19%	54%	35%
	Average	968	7,871	8%	15%	8%	27%	49%	22%

United States	12,598	52,800	100%	100%	0%	74%	81%	7%
Upper-Middle-Income Countries*	1,359	10,790	11%	20%	9%	34%	63%	29%
High-Income (non-OECD) Countries*	9,595##	29,900	76%	57%	−19%	72%	80%	8%
World*	2,797	12,221	22%	23%	1%	39%	54%	15%

Note:
* Data is for 2012 and from World Bank (2014a).
\# Data is for 1985.
\## Data is for1989.

Source: US Central Intelligence Agency *Factbook* (2014).

countries: from 27 percent in 1980 to 49 percent in 2014. The Philippines and India had relatively low urbanization rate increases (7 percent and 9 percent respectively). Increases in the urbanization rates of the other large Asian countries were much higher. China's increase—35 percent—was the highest, but the increases in Indonesia (31 percent) and Malaysia (32 percent) were not far behind.

We draw a number of important lessons from the above findings. First, China has avoided over-urbanization—a level of urban development above the ability of the urban economic sector to absorb surplus rural labor. This has had a significant positive impact on the quality of life of China's citizens. China does not have the large urban slums that can be found in large cities in Latin American, African and South and Southeastern Asian countries at a middle level of development. This is a direct result of over-urbanization in these countries.

Second, China may be uniquely positioned to break out of the middle-income trap. It is an outlier on nearly every dimension measuring economic progress. It has succeeded in rapid innovation and structural transformation to a greater degree than any other country. If, as World Bank economists Homi Kharis and Indermit Gill propose and Cui Wing-Thye Woo, Fang Cai, Liu Shijin, Bingwen Zheng, and others agree, innovation and the ability to continually transform the economy are key to breaking out of the middle-income trap, China appears better positioned than other less nimble economies. China's new central government is working hard to increase domestic demand. The Chinese government intends to stimulate consumption and economic growth by promoting urbanization. The new Chinese leadership recognizes the importance of a skilled labor force and "creative destruction" in which older industries must innovate to survive. It has invested heavily in education and human resource development at every level. China's new-style National Urbanization Plan envisions that the best developed parts of eastern China will evolve to rely mainly on high-tech, automated, advanced industries with highly skilled workforces, research and development, and other innovative activities (PRC, 2014).

Third, that many countries—but particularly China—face what we call a "middle-income urbanization trap." The quality of urban life does not keep pace with economic development.

The Middle-Income Urbanization Trap

China's dual economy, urban–rural income gap, high Gini coefficient, unequal social services for urban migrants, and poor physical quality of much of China's built environment described in previous chapters, are all indicators of China's middle urbanization trap rather than middle-income trap. The logic of this dilemma is similar to the logic Homi Kharas and Indirmit Gill used in defining the middle-income trap. In early stages of development as China's wealth increased like other rapidly developing countries they could afford to build new infrastructure, factories, and housing. But to keep labor costs low and remain competitive internationally much of what was built was low quality and there was little attention to the natural environment or the quality of urban life. The challenge for the next phase of China's urbanization is similar. Will China continue to produce a low cost built environment that is not harmonious with the natural environment consistent with a level of economic development trapped in the middle-income range or can it break out and produce a high quality built environment in an environmentally friendly landscape comparable to the most advanced countries?

Not a single country has developed into a high-income country with a low urbanization quality. Achieving healthy urbanization and livable, humane cities are essential if China is to escape both the middle-income trap and the middle urbanization trap (Figure 9.1).

Source: Photo by Li Zhang.

Figure 9.1 Polluted environment in suburb of Ningbo city, Zhejiang province

As pointed out by Hao and Zhao (2013), urbanization is the consequence of economic and social development, rather than the tool to promote economic growth. That is what is meant by the endogeneity of the middle-income trap (Hao and Zhao, 2013). The urbanization level is an index; simply striving to achieve a higher urbanization rate should not be the goal of governmental policy. Long-term neglect of environmental impacts, the growing income gap, and propping up industries that need to be restructured may increase the urbanization rate in the short run, but not healthy and sustainable urbanization.

China's rapid urbanization level increase is closely related to the constant migration of rural population to cities as described in Chapter 6 on large-scale population flows. Like other middle-income countries developing into high-income countries, China is now facing the transition of economic structure and development mode and social development reform. How to avoid being caught in the middle-income trap and the middle urbanization trap are topics of equal importance. Since the middle-income trap has received a great deal of attention it is time to focus attention particularly on the middle urbanization trap.

ECONOMIC DEVELOPMENT AND URBANIZATION THEORY

Besides the dual economic model, demographic dividend, Kuznet's curve, and the middle-income trap, a number of economists and geographers have developed theory about the relationship between economic development and urbanization, the most notable is theory developed by Hollis Chenery, a Harvard economics professor and one-time World Bank vice president and Moshe Syrquin, a professor of International Studies at the University of Miami and extended by other economists. Following is a discussion of this body of literature.

The Relationship between Economic Development and Urbanization

The relationship between economic development and urbanization has been widely discussed by Chinese and Western scholars (Berry, 1962; Chenery and Syrquin, 1975; Zhou, 1982; Meng, 1990; Knox, 1994; Zhang and Zhao, 1998; Ma, 2002; Henderson, 2003; Quigley, 2009; Au and Henderson, 2006; Lu and Chen, 2006; Zhang, 2008; Zhao and Zhang, 2009; Chen et al., 2013; Zhang, F., 2014; Wu, 2015).

While their datasets, time periods, and methodologies differ, these studies show that most developed countries have experienced parallel urbanization characterized by economic growth and urbanization growing in tandem (Chen et al., 2013) with some dispersion around the mean—a development model first fully described by Hollis Chenery and Moise Syrquin in 1975.

Outliers furthest away from the level of urbanization that would be predicted by a regression formula are characterized as "over-urbanized" or "under-urbanized" countries. The most common policy recommendation for under-urbanized countries is to push urbanization more rapidly and for over-urbanized countries to make more balanced development in all aspects. Existing studies focus on the macro-level relationship between economic development and urbanization and summarize urbanization with a single statistic: the percentage of the population living in urban areas, that is, the *quantity* of urbanization produced by a specific level of economic development. Discussions of the relationship between the level of development and the *quality* of urbanization are seriously lacking. There is a large descriptive and anecdotal literature about bad conditions in cities in poor countries, but macro-level theorists have not focused on this relationship.

Following is a summary of the early Western scholarship, Chinese studies and theory, and recent work by Henderson, Au, and Quigley building on the Chenery–Syrquin model. In the following section we describe our own re-analysis of the Chenery–Syrquin model using the most recent available data and modifications that tailor the model to China. We conclude that China's *level of urbanization* lags its level of economic development much less than generally believed, but that the *quality* of China's urbanization is significantly lower than it should be given China's current level of economic development. In our opinion the time is ripe to shift the discussion to improving the quality of urbanization in different parts of China and in different contexts rather than how to speed up urbanization, distribute it among the great regions of China, or see it as just a driver for economic development. Livability and equity concerns can and should receive much greater consideration in China's emerging "new style" urbanization. We further develop this recommendation and provide ideas on how to implement it in the concluding chapter.

Western economists, geographers, planners, and policymakers began debating what relationship, if any, exists between urbanization and economic growth more than fifty years ago, based on indicators such as the percentage of total population living in urban areas and per capita gross domestic product (GDP).

In 1962 US geographer Brian Berry analyzed 95 countries using principal components analysis in order to see if there were statistically significant relationships between urbanization and any of 43 factors. Berry found that there were significant positive relationships between economic development, technology, population, and education and urbanization and confirmed the positive relationship between economic growth and urbanization (Berry, 1962).

Thirteen years later Hollis Chenery and Moshe Syrquin developed a celebrated model to estimate relationships between economic development and many factors, including a country's level of urbanization. Chenery and Syrquin's conclusions were based on an analysis of historical sectoral data on 101 countries through 1964 (Chenery and Syrquin, 1975). Chenery and Syrquin found a strong positive correlation between a country's level of economic development and its urbanization level. The Chenery–Syrquin model has had a powerful impact on development policy everywhere in the world, including China.

Recently Brown University economics professors Chun-Chung Au and Vernon Henderson revisited the question of how a country's urbanization level is related to its level of economic development. Au and Henderson argue that there is a best degree of urban concentration in terms of maximizing productivity growth, but no strong correlation between productivity growth and urbanization (Henderson, 2003; Au and Henderson, 2006). U.C. Berkeley public policy professor John Quigley argues that since China is less urbanized than its development level would predict, national policy should encourage it to urbanize more rapidly (Quigley, 2009).

Many Chinese scholars have explored the relationship between economic development and urbanization in China based on the Chenery–Syrquin model or analyses and models of their own using different datasets and adaptations to Chinese conditions (Zhou, 1982; Meng, 1990; Zhang and Zhao, 1998; Ma, 2002; Zhao and Zhang, 2009; Lu and Chen, 2006; Chang and Brada, 2006; Zhang, 2008; Yew, 2012; Chen et al., 2013). Following is a review of the most important studies.

Using regression analysis on 1977 data on urbanization and GDP of 137 countries, Zhou (1982) reached essentially the same conclusion that Chenery and Syrquin reached using 1964 data. Accordingly Zhou argued that China's urbanization not only lagged far behind the world's average level, but was lower than it should have been at the end of the Mao era in 1977 based on China's level of economic development at that time.

Chang and Brada (2006) offer an interesting alternative interpretation of China's early period of economic development. They argue that China was not under-urbanized before or during the early period of reform and opening. In their opinion China's urbanization lag only emerged in the late period of reform and was mainly a result of the slow pace of hukou reform.

One of the authors of this book—Min Zhao—has criticized studies of the relationship between economic development and urbanization in China on methodological grounds. In a 2008 article Zhao and his co-author, Ying Zhang, one of his master's students, criticized direct application of the Chenery–Syrquin model to China for failure to consider cumulative currency inflation and the actual population of China (Zhang and Zhao, 2003; Zhao and Zhang, 2009). They produced a set of modified formulas to adapt Chenery and Syrquin's 1975 model to China based on regression and curve fitting of 1999 data from 148 countries and Zhou et al.'s 1982 studies. The mathematical model that is the basis of their article is described and summarized below. They used GNP data as a proxy. Current dollar values were calculated by using a GDP deflator index. US$1.00 in 1964 is equivalent to US$5.72 today (Areppim, 2014).

Zhao and Zhang pointed out that the relationship between urbanization and GDP per capita is not an absolute logarithmic curve; rather the relationship falls into a normal interval. In their opinion, possible reasons why the urbanization level of a country might be higher or lower than its corresponding GDP level may be explained to some extent by the disparity in the population size of each nation and the proportion of the population in one or more megacities. After re-interpreting the constraint conditions of the Chenery–Syrquin model, Zhao and Zhang developed an equation that describes the urbanization level and industrialization level of China that provides a more accurate way of evaluating the relationship between urbanization and economic development in general and provides a much more accurate interpretation of the special case of China (Zhang and Zhao, 2003). They concluded that in 1999 the urbanization level of China was only slightly below the world norm—about what the model would predict.

To test precisely, Min Zhao and Ying Zhang (2009) then divided economic development into primary, take off, culmination and post-urban stages. The relationships between urbanization and development were quite different in the four different stages. This implies that a country may not follow the general norm in different development stages. For this book we updated their results with the latest available data. The following section describes these new findings in detail. This is important for China today as the national government has taken the position in the NNUP and elsewhere that there are identifiable laws of urbanization, that China must follow them in order to develop, and that orderly urbanization will benefit China's economy.

Revisiting the Relationship between Urbanization and Development

In order to reach our own conclusion about the relationship between urbanization and development in China today we updated Chenery and

Syrquin's model. We set N equal to 1,300 because the current population of China is approximately 1.37 billion and inflated 1964 dollar values to 2010 values. In 2010, China's per capita income was approximately US$4,430, and the urbanization rate was approximately 49.7 percent. According to the adjusted Chenery–Syrquin model, China's urbanization rate should have been approximately 60 percent. So, if the Chenery–Syrquin model accurately describes China's development situation their conclusion and the conclusion of other scholars who have re-analyzed this relationship based on the Chenery–Syrquin model would be correct—that China is under-urbanized. But considering the huge change brought about by technological advances and economic structural changes in China from 1970 to 2010, which is a very important variable in Chenery and Syrquin model, the fixed values in the Chenery–Syrquin model should be retested.

For this reason, we did a new logistic regression analysis using 2010 United Nations data on the urbanization level and per capita GDP of 191 countries (UN, 2014). Overall, our results are consistent with prior studies of the relationship between per capita GDP and urbanization. Figure 9.2 is a scatterplot with a logistic regression line that shows that the countries with higher per capita GDP generally have higher urbanization levels. As with prior studies we found quite a bit of dispersion around the regression line, showing that many countries with similar urbanization levels have per capita GDP levels higher or lower than the predicted value.

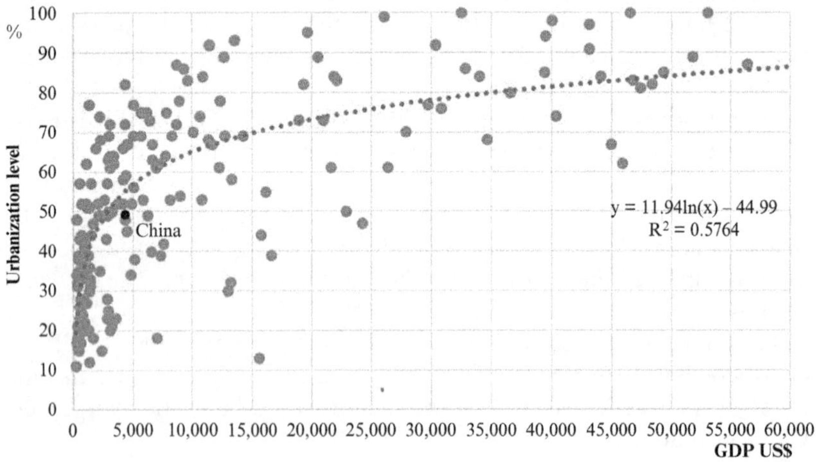

Source: UN (2014).

Figure 9.2 Relationship between urbanization level and GDP per capita of 191 countries in 2010

This is true for countries with urbanization levels in the 50 percent to 60 percent range similar to China.

The value of R^2 describes the goodness of fit ranging from 0 to 1, with higher values showing a better fit. The value of R^2 showing the relationship between the level of development and urbanization in 2012 (0.5764) is notable, but not remarkable as shown in Figure 9.2. In other words, based on an improved model sensitive to relationships during different phases of development and new data we conclude that China's current urbanization level is about right given its level of development. It is only a little lower than predicted. This is the most interesting result. China falls only a little below the regression line, suggesting that China is only slightly "under-urbanized" if at all. The policy implication is that there is no need to artificially speed up urbanization in China.

The Relationship between Development and Urbanization in China

In addition to our re-analysis of development and urbanization in the 191 country sample, we also tested the correlation between China's economic growth and urbanization in the period of 1982–2012. The goodness-of-fit (R^2) of the logarithmic curve is 0.9811—a very strong positive correlation. The relationship between the observed value and the fitted curve is generally clear, with only minor deviations in either direction during some periods. From 1982 to early 1995, the relationship between economic growth and urbanization was strong and consistent. In some years, the urbanization level increased at the same time that per capita GDP measured in US dollars dropped. However, after the mid-1990s, urbanization started to synchronize with economic growth. An obvious correlation between the two appeared. Another clearly discernible trend was that the actual value from 1995 to 1999 and after 2008 was slightly beneath the fitted curve, indicating that China's actual urbanization level was somewhat lower than predicted as represented by the curve. From 2000 to 2008, the value was above the fitted curve, which indicated that during these years the actual urbanization level was higher than the curve predicted in Figure 9.3.

While we are skeptical of deterministic models and immutable laws of urbanization, this analysis provides good evidence to support the national government's expressed faith in urbanization as a key to economic development in the NNUP. But the relationship is two-sided. Not only is urbanization important for China's continued economic development, but China's urbanization can only develop in a healthy way if economic growth levels roughly parallel urbanization. Otherwise, China will face low-quality urbanization and perhaps even excessive urbanization that has created

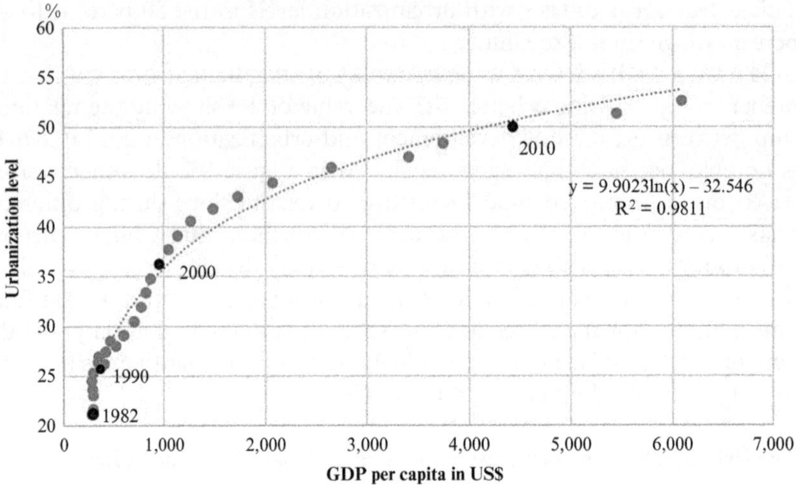

Note: GDP is based on 2012 US dollars.

Source: *China Statistical Yearbook* 2013 (NBSC-csy, 2013).

Figure 9.3 Relationship between urbanization increase and economic growth in China, 1982–2012

such enormous problems in cities like São Paulo, Brazil and Lagos, Nigeria whose urbanization level has far outstripped economic development.

While there have inevitably been problems of imbalance and misguided policies in China's unprecedented, enormous, and rapidly changing urbanization process, changes in government policy at every level have so far succeeded overall in avoiding the problems of massive slums and unemployment that characterize many of the largest cities in Latin America, Africa, and parts of Asia. We believe China should continue to promote balanced urbanization at a realistic pace and in different ways given local conditions. Although Chenery and Syrquin, Henderson and Au, Quigley, Zhou, Ma, Yew and other macro-level theorists, econometricians, and modelers have all made contributions to our understanding of the relationship between economic development and urbanization, it is very important to be sensitive to reality on the ground in different contexts and at different stages of development. In our view, China's urbanization policy should reflect regional differences and balance the goal of economic development with equity, sustainability and other goals. We return to the question of how fast China should urbanize and how a shift to quality urbanization over speed can avoid the middle-income urbanization trap in Chapter 10.

The Real Issue: Why Urbanization Quality Lags Economic Growth in China

Although different ways of measuring the relationship between the urbanization level and the economic growth level of China are valid, there are a variety of views on whether now or in the past China's urbanization level relative to its level of development has been lower than world norms and, if so, by how much. Normative opinions about how serious a problem under urbanization is also vary. The dominant point of view is that urbanization in China lags economic growth and that it should proceed more rapidly. Based on our research we reach a somewhat different conclusion. We believe that China's urbanization rate is consistent with, or only slightly below world norms in relation to its level of economic development in terms of magnitude, but China's urbanization level lags economic development in terms of quality. China now has the resources to provide much higher quality urbanization in the future and to remediate some of the damage done by low-quality urbanization inherited from the past. China's low-quality urbanization is particularly manifest in poor infrastructure in medium and small-sized cities and towns and the inability of migrants with rural hukou to receive adequate social services or settle permanently in urban areas where they work, air and water pollution, and livability standards in many communities lower than other countries at comparable levels of development provide and that China can now afford. We will return to these issues in the concluding chapter.

A DYNAMIC PERSPECTIVE: INTERPRETATION WITH PRACTICAL IMPLICATIONS

Our Theoretical Framework

China has achieved impressive economic development and urbanization progress since reform and opening up began in 1978, which has attracted worldwide attention. While many scholars have explored the characteristics of Chinese urbanization (Chapter 1), no widely accepted theory and no clear understanding of Chinese urbanization exists because of the complexity of China's reform and the rapidity of its development. Here we try to generalize the Chinese urbanization dynamic, based on our macro- and micro-level analysis and our practice and observation of Chinese development in recent decades and the experience of both developed countries and developing countries. We first review the urbanization models of developed countries and developing countries before we offer a theoretic explanation of Chinese urbanization.

In developed countries, historically in the phase of industrialization surplus rural labor migrated to cities to find work, and then settled down to become urban citizens without major obstacles. Due to the development of urban industries in those countries and the colonization of the Americas and other new lands including Australia and New Zealand before World War II, urbanization in these countries proceeded comparatively smoothly. Generally, this process in developed countries has only developed in one track, which can be called normal urbanization (Figure 9.4).

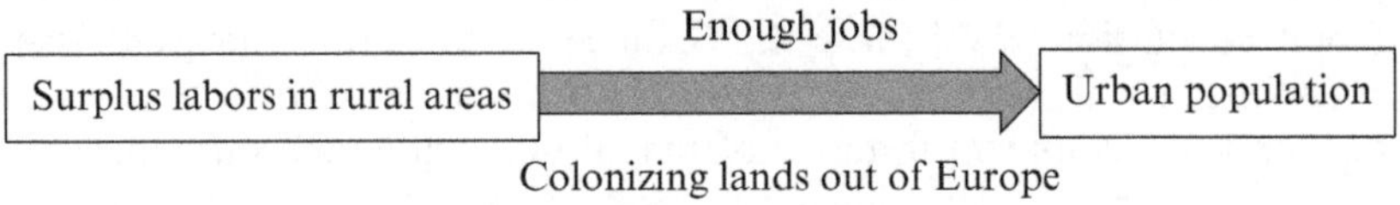

Source: Drawn by Li Zhang.

Figure 9.4 Urbanization model for developed countries

In most developing and undeveloped countries (including middle-income countries) the surplus rural workforce is also intent to migrate to find jobs and settle down in cities, but their cities are not able to supply enough jobs—even informal jobs—or even minimally adequate social welfare. Therefore, only some of the people who can work have been able to settle down well in cities. For the rest of the people it is difficult to find formal jobs, so they cannot live in well served urban areas with formal housing. Due to the traditional rural land system, which doesn't assure peasants' right to arable land properly, in many undeveloped and developing countries (except China), the people who have lost their rural land have almost no chance to return to their home villages. Then slums grow up in urban suburbs, such as those in India, Indonesia, the Philippines, Argentina, Brazil, Peru and Mexico. Generally, this process in developing countries has two tracks—normal urbanization and semi urbanization (Figure 9.5).

In addition to differences in migration, there are also differences in the mechanisms between planned economies and market economies. In planned economies government guides migration flows, urban construction and industrialization while market economies rely on capital and markets for urban construction and industrialization play little or no role in guiding migration flows.

Chinese urbanization has its own characteristics, which are different from all other developed countries, developing countries and undeveloped countries, and its economic system is also different from either traditional

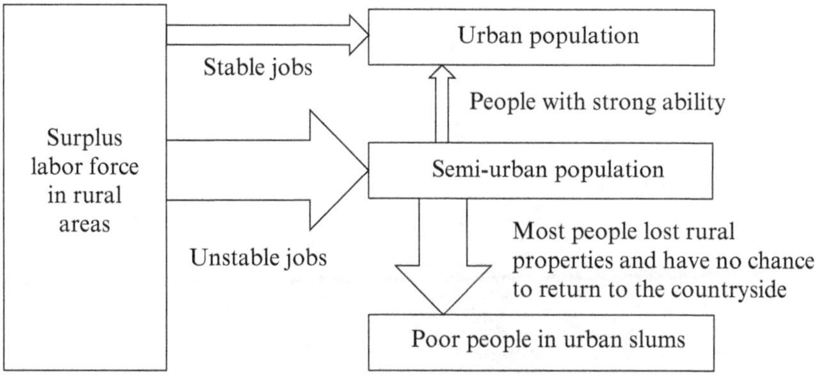

Source: Drawn by Li Zhang.

Figure 9.5 Urbanization model for developing countries except China

socialist economies or pure capitalist economies. Under the theoretic construction in our study, the Chinese urbanization process could be understood dynamically having double dual running tracks.

China's Double Dual Urbanization Tracks

It is useful to conceptualize Chinese urbanization as two sets of railroad tracks—each with two rails. The first set of tracks involves the shift from a planned to a market-oriented economy; the second a shift from emphasis on the quantity of urbanization to the quality of urbanization. The rails proceed from 1978 as the point of origin and are heading towards the future. China has proceeded further on each of the two tracks faster than any society in human history. The tracks now point in the right direction. But there is still a long distance to go before China achieves the kind of harmonious, sustainable, green, low carbon, resilient, equitable, livable urban pattern to which it aspires.

The first track moving towards a market-oriented economy has two rails, consisting of endogenous institutional reforms and responses to exogenous globalization forces.

The first rail in the track heading towards marketization of the economy involves endogenous reform. It started with rural reforms—the most fundamental of which was releasing surplus rural labor—and then hukou, finance, administrative division, economic, and land rights reform and industrial restructuring and optimization. This track has existed in China since 1978 as the Chinese economy has evolved from a planned

Source: Li Zhang.

Figure 9.6 Clean, orderly and active central pedestrian street in Harbin city, Heilongjiang province economy to its current form of a socialist market economy. The track has moved step by step to relax official control of people's migration and private business.

In our analysis migrants' urbanization involves two processes: one process in changing migration policy is expanding the normal urbanization process for people from rural areas who are permitted to fully settle down in cities and towns permanently where the urban government approves their urban residency (hukou) status; the second process is the informal urbanization process for the people from rural areas who either cannot or do not want to settle down in cities and towns permanently, where the urban government does not grant them urban hukou status. Those migrant laborers without urban hukou are sometimes referred to as the semi-urban population. In the coming years reforms well underway in each of these areas can continue to improve China's urbanization.

The second rail of the track moving toward a market-oriented economy is the globalization process as described in Chapter 5 and its influence on migration and regional disparities as described in Chapter 2. After reform and opening up, especially after China's admission to the World Trade Organization (WTO) in 2001, China became deeply engaged in global markets and, to a large extent, became "the world's factory." In the world economic system, China's economic system continues to adapt to the global context.

The second track involves the shift from an emphasis on the quantity of urbanization to the quality of urbanization. It includes a rail of endogenous structural optimization in social equity and justice and a rail of exogenous global competitive pressure. The first rail requires government to pay much more attention to social welfare reforms to cover rural and urban people equally, supply urban and rural infrastructure with the same standards, and provide urban and rural public services more uniformly. The latter is a driving force from outside to promote China's inner reforms to meet the challenges from other developing and developed countries. Generally, human beings and society are the focus of the second dual track (Figure 9.7).

Policy for each of these dual tracks has made possible the success of Chinese urbanization so far. The effective operation of the tracks has been backed by a double set of dual transitions, discussed below.

The First Dual Track Transition: Changing the Planned Economy to a More Decentralized Market-Oriented Economy

China's rapid urbanization during the past three decades is proceeding at the same time that China has been transitioning from a planned

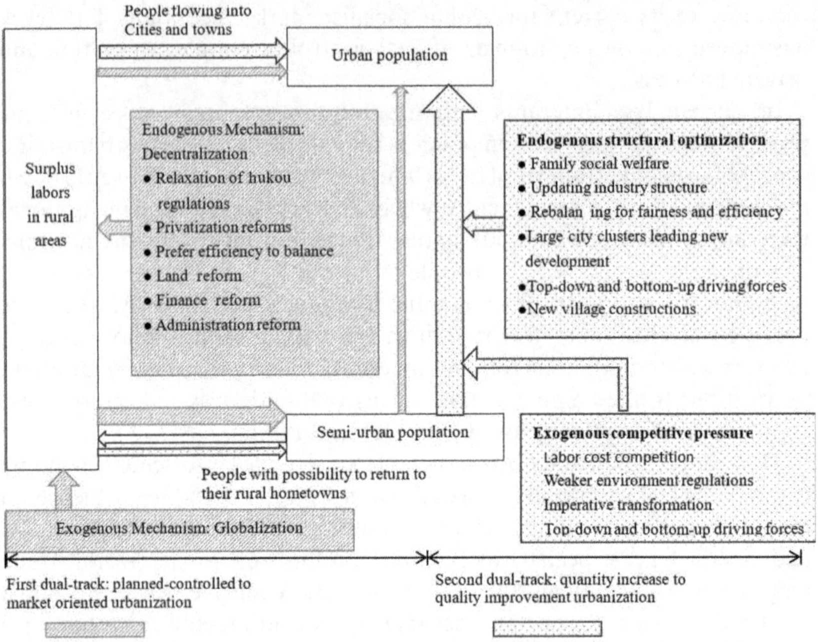

Source: Drawn by Li Zhang

Figure 9.7 Chinese urbanization model—double dual track transition

economy to a market-oriented economy. This process is being promoted both by institutional reform and China's integration into the global economy.

Before reform and opening up, China had a centralized planned economy. Rural population migration was restricted by the hukou system. Private enterprises were not allowed to exist. Urban employment opportunities were confined almost entirely to state-owned enterprises, and planned capital investments and service sector expansion provided only a limited number of new jobs in urban areas during this period. This was an important reason for very limited rural migration to cities.

After 1978 many youth who had been sent to the countryside during the Cultural Revolution returned to cities, competing for very limited job opportunities (Liu, 2009). The rural household contract responsibility system (HCRS) liberated the rural labor force. This caused a large increase in the rural surplus labor force, creating huge employment pressure on Chinese society. To adapt to this situation, many new employment patterns were established.

In the early 1980s, efforts at marketization were first made in rural towns and the countryside. Compared with cities, rural areas had a weak development foundation and hence less institutional restrictions. This was conducive for the creation of rural markets. Rural areas were burdened by too many un- and under-employed people—mainly peasants liberated from working the land. Because of a combination of historical factors, a good location, and transportation infrastructure, township enterprises in southern Jiangsu and the Pearl River Delta were the first to prosper. Their achievements were recognized first by the well-known sociologist Xiaotong Fei and later by national leader Xiaoping Deng. Soon bottom-up industrialization in rural areas came into being (Chapter 7).

Along with the marketization process, China's hukou system became more flexible. Hukou-related administrative constraints were first lifted in rural towns in 1984, and peasants were allowed a free right to settle down in rural towns if they provided their own food, rather than relying on government food rations. In 1997, newborn children were allowed to have hukou registered in the same place as either their father or mother. In 2001, the quota for the change from agricultural to non-agricultural hukou (2–5 percent every year) was canceled. By 2001 institutional constraints placed on the urbanization of China's rural population at the national level had been basically abolished. The rural population was able to migrate freely between urban areas and rural regions. However, as described in Chapter 2 it was still difficult for peasant workers to acquire urban hukou in larger cities or to enjoy equal social welfare as the urban residents. Market realities rather than legal restrictions continued to shape migration.

To facilitate marketization, national policies tended to favor efficiency over equity. Under the preferential national policy, eastern China became economically active first. Since the government gave efficiency priority, regional disparities were constantly expanding. Rural–urban development and income gaps increased. The new development landscape characterized by coexisting development stages, development levels and development space had been formed.

A series of reforms of administrative divisions described in Chapter 2 fundamentally changed responsibility and power relations between the central and local governments. The reform measures included upgrading counties into cities, merging counties, changing townships into official towns, merging townships and/or towns, and changing counties and/or county-level cities into districts. This brought about a new set of responsibility and power relations not only between the central and local governments but also between the local governments themselves.

During the marketization process, the national taxation system was also reformed. The tax sharing system was introduced in 1993. Central taxes, local taxes, and shared taxes were specified. The relationship between the central and local governments was clarified. This secured central government revenue and provided greater motivation for local economic development. Local tax revenues have been rising since 1993. The central government's revenue rose, both in absolute terms and as a percentage of total revenue (Figure 3.4). Sufficient tax sources are a good guarantee of resource allocations by the central government. Sufficient capital supply is now available for transfer payments as well as the construction of major infrastructure as described in Chapter 3.

Land system reform was also underway as the taxation system was being reformed. The core content of rural land system reform was to separate land contract rights from collective ownership through the land contract responsibility system. The urban land system reform at the end of 1980s involved separating land use rights from state ownership. Without changing the ownership of urban land, which belongs to the country by the constitution, urban land use rights could be traded. This was an important step in the marketization reform. Rural productivity was liberated and a large increase in the surplus rural labor force occurred. This helped satisfy the demand for labor during rapid industrialization and urbanization.

Market-oriented housing reform introducing commodity housing during the late 1990s was a radical change from the welfare-oriented public housing distribution system. This resulted in a surge in the commercial value of urban land. The revenue from urban land leasing had now become an important source of urban revenue that has even exceeded tax revenue in some cities.

During this process, the tide of globalization also produced a profound impact on China's urbanization. China's entry into the World Trade Organization (WTO) in 2001 marked the beginning of China's deep integration into global markets as described in Chapter 5. The influx of multinational enterprises and capital was a powerful stimulus to China's urbanization. In addition to capital, multinational enterprises also brought advanced management and technologies, which served as the seed of China's modernization from a traditional agricultural country. In response to globalization, China's enormous rural to urban migration occurred as described in Chapter 6.

The two processes—endogenous and exogenous—were the underlying forces for the unprecedented high speed urbanization of China. Migration of rural population to cities, population of small-sized cities to central cities and migration from inland provinces to coastal provinces represent the largest urbanization in the shortest time in human history. This transition is a true dual track transition, with both exogenous globalization and endogenous institutional innovation.

The Second Dual Track Transition: From the Pursuit of Quantity to the Pursuit of Quality

The transition of the mechanisms motivating urbanization from state-controlled to market-oriented was great progress. However, the market is not omnipotent and the transition from a state-controlled to a market-oriented economy is far from enough. China's rural population can migrate to cities based on market signals, but it is very difficult for them to integrate completely into an urban way of life. Currently a large proportion of the peasant workers do not actually turn into new urban residents, and do not enjoy the same social welfare as local residents. We have defined these people as China's semi-urban population. While raising the urbanization level, it is equally important to improve the quality of urbanization. The most important step in improving the quality of urbanization in China is to turn the semi-urban population into an urban population with all the rights and benefits of other residents—granting them, in the words of Chinese policy documents—full "citizenization." In the West urban planning is generally conceptualized as physical planning for matters such as land use, transportation, open space, housing, infrastructure, and environmental protection; not social planning for matters such as education, health, social security, and welfare. In free market countries economic development planning is much more limited than in China. Physical improvement of China's cities and better urban design are important parts of urban planning. But in China social planning to improve the quality of people's lives is also an explicit planning goal. Economic, physical, and social planning all occur at every administrative level.

China's semi-urban population is now living in an institutional lacuna. They have access to urban infrastructure, but do not fully enjoy the same social welfare as residents with urban hukou. China's success in industrialization is largely due to the contribution made by the semi-urban population. Their labor produces the goods that fuel China's export-oriented economy and account for China's extraordinary GDP growth. Their high mobility between rural and urban areas gives flexibility to the urban economy, since the rural population can choose to return to their hometown in case of insufficient job opportunities and economic crises. This is also one reason why China does not have extensive urban slums as in other developing countries. The further transition of the semi-urban population is the key step for China to enter a new level of urbanization. In the NNSUP released in 2014, one of the specified goals was transforming some 100 million new migrants and semi-urban people and rural people to a new urban population by 2020.

The second step in improving urbanization is agricultural policy to narrow the rural–urban income gap. China has made progress along this track. China has not experienced the emergence of extensive slums during the past decades of development. Rural household income even exceeds urban family income in Zhejiang and Jiangsu provinces and some other parts of China. However, the rural–urban income gap is expanding in some regions. The agricultural tax was canceled in 2006, and the central government invests heavily in rural cooperative medical service, old-age insurance for peasants and rural infrastructure construction. The quality of China's rural environment is improving. Peasants' social welfare has been strengthened, and peasants' living standards have been raised. Rural population in some regions has managed to increase household income by large-scale agricultural production, industrialized management and the development of tertiary industry. Many efforts to modernize agriculture in China are underway including consolidating parcels to permit larger-scale farming, greater reliance on agricultural technology, scientific farming methods, and branding and improving the marketing of agricultural products.

The third step in improving China's urbanization involves upgrading and improving China's industrial structure. The industrial development model dominated by low-end manufacturing and heavy and chemical industries with serious environmental pollution and resource depletion, is being improved. Remediation of environmental damage caused in the past and new building according to much higher (but much more costly) environmental standards is an enormous challenge for China.[1] The proportion of low value added polluting secondary industry is declining, while less environmentally damaging, higher value added tertiary industry and high-tech manufacturing is increasing. High speed railways, airplanes, automobiles and information infrastructure have become the backbones of the manufacturing industry. The new industrial system is characterized by the production of new materials, new energy, machinery and electronic products, which is less environmentally damaging as well as greatly enhancing China's global competitiveness.

The fourth step in improving China's urbanization involves achieving balanced urban–rural development. Over the past three decades, China's high speed urbanization has taken place at the cost of the interests of rural areas and the peasants. Central and western China were generally neglected with respect to development opportunities before 2000. The central government is now working to adjust regional development policy and urban–rural development policy, with more resources and capital invested in central and western China. Many national-level new districts have been approved in inland provinces.[2] China's New Village Movement has been underway in rural areas for many years, and the rural landscape is improving.

The fifth step in improving China's urbanization involves adapting to the rapidly changing situation in other developing countries. Emerging economies in South and Southeastern Asia are catching up. India, Indonesia, Myanmar, Thailand and Vietnam are gaining competitiveness with their low cost labor. China is adapting to the new situation, with greater emphasis on the development of high value added and high-tech industries as opposed to low-end labor-intensive industries. As described above, China's economy is differentiated regionally. From east to west there is generally a reduction in the level of development and some development is phased over time. Our research suggests that market forces are already driving a shift of much manufacturing and assembly industries to central and western China. Smart national, provincial, and municipal policy can speed up and rationalize this process. Shifting some of China's most labor-intensive, least sophisticated industries to less developed countries in Asia and Africa is already well underway. Accelerating this trend is another way for China to improve its economy and urbanization pattern.

A sixth way to improve China's urbanization involves improving the way in which top-down experiments interact with bottom-up reforms. China's urbanization has benefitted from national-level institutional reform and support for experiments. In parallel with China's bottom-up transition, more top-down reform experiments are underway. Since the mid and late-2000s, various provinces have been seeking financial and other support from the central government, so as to become part of the national development strategy. The provinces and the municipalities directly under the central government come up with plans and reform schemes which are then submitted for approval by the State Council. The exploration of reform in both bottom-up and top-down ways has greatly motivated local governments and provides ways for the central government to test new policy. Top-down and bottom-up reform efforts have laid a solid basis for economic upgrading and the improvement of urbanization quality (Figure 9.8).

The transition from the planned economy to a market-oriented economy is the first track in China's double dual track transition. It stimulated fast economic growth and urbanization development. The transition from the pursuit of quantity to the pursuit of quality is the second track. It is driven both by globalization pressure and by growing internal awareness. This transition is another dual track transition, with both endogenous structural reforms and exogenous competitive pressure. In this process, rural population continues to migrate to cities, and more importantly, the semi-urban population is encouraged and facilitated to transform into new urban residents.

At this phase the two dual track transition processes are occurring

Source: Photo by Li Zhang.

Figure 9.8 Prosperous development in Pudong district, Shanghai municipality

simultaneously. The second dual track transition started later and is more difficult and is a greater challenge to the capacity of the central government and local governments. But China now has both the resources and the expertise to carry it out. If China is able to set the global standard for quality urbanization, this will be a transition as profound as the change that occurred with reform and opening. It will have a profoundly positive impact on the Chinese people and will be of global significance for the environment and a model for other countries.

SUMMARY

This chapter is devoted to the topic of urbanization in China that has been discussed and hotly debated worldwide. Theories related to China's urbanization were introduced, including Lewis' turning points, Kuznets' curve, the demographic dividend, the middle-income trap and middle urbanization trap concepts, and the relationship between urbanization increase and economic increase.

We believe that after three decades of development and urbanization, China has come to the turning point in terms of population, social and economic structure. Through research on developing countries in

Latin America and South and Southeastern Asia, we have found that China is facing a greater risk of a middle urbanization trap endogenous to China's development mode than a middle-income trap in the conventional sense that faces many other countries. If the transition from the pursuit of quantity to the pursuit of quality cannot be accomplished, China's economic and social development will be greatly impacted, and may meet with the same fate as other developing countries. In spite of these challenges, recent history and our data on China's current position provide evidence that the Chinese government will be able to survive the current difficult transition stage of development and urbanization.

The dynamic double dual track transition of China's urbanization under our theoretical framework proposed in this chapter provides an in depth explanation of urbanization with Chinese characteristics. After reform and opening up, China's urbanization can be divided into the stage of the first transition (planned economy to market-oriented economy) and the stage of the second transition (pursuit of quantity to pursuit of quality). The transition from a planned economy to market-oriented economy is jointly propelled by globalization integration and internal institutional reform. The latter transition is propelled by global competitive pressure and internal structural optimization. The content of the double dual track transition is closely related to guidance of economic and social structure change and population flows in China.

NOTES

1. China's energy consumption in 2013 was equivalent to 3.75 billion tons of standard coal, which is 2.58 times that of 2000 (1.455 billion tons) and 6.57 times that of 1978 (0.571 billion tons), respectively (NBSC-csy, 2014). The total national emission of wastewater in 2012 was 68.4 billion tons and of industrial waste gas 64 trillion cubic meters, which were 1.49 times and 3.20 times that of 2003, respectively (NBSC-csy, 2013). Large amounts of wastewater emissions caused the pollution of main rivers and groundwater, threatening drinking water safety. Increased waste gas emissions have heightened the number of days of haze in Chinese cities and the incidence of pulmonary disease. Environmental pollution is most severe in east and north China. The 2015 Ambient Air Pollution Report by the World Health Organization (WHO) reported that among 91 countries investigated, China was one of the 20 countries with the worst air quality. Atmospheric particulate matter (PM) consists of microscopic solid or liquid matter suspended in the earth's atmosphere. It is generally measured by the levels of particulates of different sizes measured in micrometers. The smaller the particulate matter size the greater the risk to human health. The haze data of 1,626 cities around the world show that 17 Chinese cities were ranked among the 100 cities with the worst PM10 and 13 among the 100 cities with the worst PM2.5 levels (WHO, 2014).
2. Such as the Chongqing Liangjiang New District, Gansu Lanzhou New District, Sichuan Tianfu New District, Shaanxi Xixian New District and Guizhou Gui'an New District.

10. Conclusion

During the past three decades of China's urbanization, the transition from state-controlled to market-oriented development guided by national policy and the ongoing transition from pursuing fast growth to restructuring and improving the quality of urbanization have become increasingly mutually dependent and inseparable. The simultaneous occurrence of these two transition stages provided China with an opportunity. However, owing to the speed with which socio-economic development in China has occurred, it was impossible to complete institutional transitions such as transforming peasant workers into full citizens, or transforming China's population from a semi-urban to an urban population immediately. With the vast remaining supply of rural surplus labor that will likely continue to be released as a result of agricultural modernization, the semi-urban population will continue to exist or even expand. This will hinder the improvement of urbanization quality unless government at every level adopts appropriate policies to manage migration and improve the quality of urbanization. The transformation from a semi-urban to an urban population has two potential pathways.

The first path is to promote very fast economic development and urbanization. If the continuing flow of rural surplus labor into cities continues to fuel a very rapid increase in development this may generate enough revenue for China to absorb the semi-urban population if China invests the additional revenue to do this. This path may be quicker, but it is riskier and is likely to involve more stress for individuals and governments and less good urbanization quality.

The second path is for governments to slow down and redirect the growth of the semi-urban population so that necessary economic development to support it occurs more or less simultaneously. This will allow China to accomplish the transformation more gradually and with greater attention to the quality of urbanization. With more time to plan and experiment it will be less stressful for governments. And while it may take longer to urbanize migrants, the process is likely to be less stressful for them.

In our view either path may be appropriate in different parts of China in some circumstances. But generally pursuing the second path is superior. Pursuing high rates of urbanization to meet artificial targets should not be the goal. Rather managing urbanization to produce high quality urbanization and share the benefits of development is a better approach.

The onset of the global economic crisis in 2008 provided compelling evidence that China's economy can neither develop in isolation nor withstand continuously extreme imbalance. In 2014, China's GDP growth rate declined to approximately 7 percent from its previous double-digit growth rates. It appears that China's current economic development level and capacity are unable to sustain urbanization through the first pathway alone by simply responding to enormous rural to urban migration flows driven by a combination of private market forces and government policy. Slowing down and redirecting migration of the rural labor force required by the second pathway is in order.

Social development requires a large amount of government support. Fully urbanizing an additional rural and semi-urban migrant population of over 100 million by 2020 is a tremendous task, and large public financial resources are indispensable. If urbanization is to maintain such a high development speed, economic growth needs be maintained at a high level to provide money for income distribution and social welfare. China's current economic growth rate is already unprecedentedly high in the world's economic development history. In the context of a lingering global economic recession, maintaining stable growth of the Chinese economy is not easy and returning to the time of double-digit growth probably impossible. To obtain funds needed for improving the quality of urbanization, China needs to pursue structural optimization and environmentally friendly development to overcome the well-known middle-income trap (Gill et al., 2007) and the middle urbanization trap which we introduced in Chapter 9.

Our analysis of population flows documented the massive and continuing rural–urban migration from central and western China to developed parts of eastern China. Chapter 4 describes other flows (urban–urban, rural–rural, and urban–rural). Two particularly noteworthy recent developments are reverse migration from urban areas to rural areas and increasing flows into provincial capitals and large cities in central and western China. Good policy can take advantage of these new developments by supporting positive aspects of the flows.

Reverse migration from cities to the countryside comes from two main sources: (1) older urban migrants who can no longer compete with younger, stronger, better educated workers returning to their roots in the countryside to retire or find new work in a less competitive environment and (2) retirees who value the quality of life in the countryside. Policies to support older migrants finding new work in the countryside and sound housing from the remaining stock in hollow core villages can help individuals and their families and make effective use of existing resources. Similarly encouraging migration to the countryside in appropriate situations can relieve pressure on urban housing markets and provide a good use of existing rural housing stock.

There are now approximately 269 million urban peasant workers in China (PRC-MHRSS, 2013), the majority of whom live in cities and towns. The number of landless peasants in suburban areas has continuously increased. This enormous semi-urban population has resulted in numerous social issues (Hsing, 2012). It puts enormous pressure on governments to continue a certain level of unequal social welfare benefits for people with rural hukou. Further development and reform are both crucial.

NEW CONTEXT AND NEW CHALLENGES

The quantity and quality of urbanization are intertwined elements that affect the results of a country's rapid urbanization. The simultaneous improvement of the two requires economic strength and appropriate and timely policy. China is now at a decisive moment given its actual development situation. It faces fundamental choices of how urbanization should proceed. The national government recognizes this and is searching for the best paths forward. The information in this book can help governments at all levels develop appropriate urbanization policy.

The Rural Labor Force Supply, Urbanization Rates, and Urban Quality

Ensuring the gradual reduction of China's semi-urban population and maintaining a middle level of economic growth is crucial in realizing the second transition from an emphasis on quantity to quality. Therefore, new employment demand should remain larger than the labor force.

Data from previous censuses allow us to calculate the net increase of working population in the past and to understand China's current and likely future labor force supply situation (Table 10.1). The fastest increases in China's labor force supply occurred between 1982 and 1987 and 1995 and 2000.

Supply continued to increase between 2000 and 2010. However, the growth rate slowed dramatically. In 2005–2010, the increment was 41.18 million—21.57 million less than that in 2000–2005. Based on the age structure of the population, labor force increase between 2010 and 2015 will be about 2.72 million, only one-fifteenth of the increment between 2005 and 2010. The peak of rural labor force supply will occur

Table 10.1 Working-age population changes in 1982 to 2030 (million)

Years	Total population	Work-age population	Proportion of work-age population	Work-age population increase	Work-age population decrease	Net increase of work-age population in five years
1982	1,008.18	620.03	61.50%	–		–
1982–1987	1,072.33	706.21	65.86%	–		86.18
1985–1990	1,133.68	756.62	66.74%	–		50.41
1990–1995	1,211.21	791.60	65.36%	–		34.98
1995–2000	1,265.83	887.93	70.15%	–		96.33
2000–2005	1,307.56	950.68	72.71%	–		62.75
2005–2010	1,339.72	998.43	74.53%	–		41.18
2010–2015	1,401.59	995.28	71.01%	74.50	71.78	2.72
2015–2020	1,432.87	982.75	68.59%	70.51	83.04	−12.53
2020–2025	1,448.98	977.59	67.47%	73.85	79.01	−5.16
2025–2030	1,453.30	944.68	65.00%	80.66	113.57	−32.91

Note: Working-age population refers to the population aged from 15 to 64.

Source: Data before 2010 was compiled from *China Statistical Yearbooks*. Data from 2015 to 2030 was compiled from *World Population Prospects: The 2012 Revision* (United Nations Population Division, 2013).

around 2015. The labor force supply will continue to decline after 2015. By 2030 it will likely be about 50.6 million fewer than in 2015.

China is currently in a period with the largest pressure on the rural surplus labor force it has ever experienced. Since the growth of China's labor force has slowed down and the labor force will decline in the future, pressure on local governments to grant urban hukou and increase spending on social welfare for newly citizenized former semi-urban residents will be alleviated—though the pattern will be felt differently in different parts of China. This makes it a particularly opportune time for China to improve urbanization quality and to transform the semi-urban population to a full urban population.

A decreasing labor force and slower rural to urban migration also has implications for China's administrative divisions (discussed in Chapter 3). In 2010 China had 658 official cities—three times the number that existed in 1980. After an initial wave of designating new cities in the 1980s, policy in recent years has favored restructuring local government into fewer larger units that manage city regions. There should be little pressure to significantly increase the number of administrative units in the future, except for some developed provinces such as Zhejiang and Jiangshou provinces where pilot experiments of upgrading official towns to cities are being promoted. However, continuing restructuring will likely be beneficial. In Chapter 3 we discussed a number of modifications of administrative divisions other than creating new ones or redesignating and renaming existing ones, such as changing an administrative division's borders, its position in the administrative hierarchy, changing the location where administrative organs within an administrative division are located, and changing subordination relationships. Further changes along these lines may be in order.

Changing Demand for Unskilled Labor in Urban Industries

The demand for rural surplus labor is changing. According to an investigation by the PRC's Ministry of Human Resources and Social Security, many enterprises had recruitment difficulties in the past. China's rural surplus labor force is no longer as "unlimited surplus" as before. After industrial restructuring in China, the demand for labor among China's industries changed from a critical shortage before the financial crisis to a structural shortage today, based on China's success with economic stimulus and economic restructuring and shrinkage of new entrants to China's working-age population.

Industrial development requires self-regulation in the labor supply–demand relationship. Given a labor supply shortage and rising wages, industries with large labor demands reduce the demand for labor by downsizing, relocating factories to locations where they can acquire a sufficient labor force at a cost that allows them still to make an acceptable profit, or responding in other ways. Foxconn, the largest Original Equipment Manufacturer in the world, has planned to introduce 30,000 industrial robots to its factories to replace human workers each year (PCWorld, 2015).

China's labor force supply–demand relationship is unbalanced in structural terms. For example, the top ten occupations with the largest labor force shortages in Guangdong province during the first quarter of 2014 belonged to the manufacturing and service industries that all require a certain level of skills, whereas the supply of surplus labor is largest for occupations that only require minimal skills (Table 10.2). Demand by urban industries for low-skilled labor has decreased after industrial restructuring, whereas the demand for high-skilled labor has increased. Thus, the supply–demand situation of China's labor force has changed from surplus supply to structural shortage.

Social Harmonious Development and Urbanization Quality

A repeated goal in China's policy pronouncements is to create a harmonious society. The goal of a harmonious urban society is expressed in the

Table 10.2 Top 10 occupations with the most severe labor shortage and the most surplus labor force in Guangdong Province, first quarter of 2014

	Occupations with the severest labor shortage				Occupations with the most surplus labor		
	Occupational category	Employment gap	Ratio of job vacancies to job seekers		Occupational category	Number of surplus job seekers	Ratio of job vacancies to job seekers
1	Assembler	31,393	1.59	1	Administrative clerk	−2,204	0.67
2	Restaurant attendant	28,303	2.45	2	Typist	−1,981	0.40
3	Workman in printing and dyeing industry	3,087	2.23	3	Driver	−908	0.73
4	Shop employee	3,043	1.81	4	Accountant	−771	0.68
5	Electronic component maker	2,724	4.68	5	Purchasing agent	−702	0.78
6	Seamer	2,684	4.14	6	Cashier	−525	0.73
7	Beautician and hairdresser	2,474	2.66	7	Electrician	−484	0.78
8	Security staff	2,444	1.74	8	Warehouse keeper	−337	0.85
9	Packer	1,970	2.81	9	Storage and transport staff	−301	0.82
10	Machine operator	1,365	1.97	10	Cleaner	−255	0.64

Notes:
1. Job vacancies-to-seekers ratio = number of job vacancies/number of job seekers.
2. Employment gap = number of job vacancies − number of job seekers.

Source: Guangdong Province Human Resources and Social Security Department (2014).

National New Style Urbanization plan and many other urban planning and policy documents.

In 2013, China's urban non-agricultural employment was 528 million (NBSC-csy, 2014, Table 4-1), and 269 million peasant workers (PRC-MHRSS, 2013) accounted for 50.93 percent of the total. There were 166 million peasant workers who had left their hukou addresses in the countryside, villages, or towns to seek employment in cities.

The contradiction between the rapidly growing migrant population and urban infrastructure supply has become increasingly serious in many areas. In some cities, infrastructure is overloaded. In many small cities and towns road systems are poor, physical infrastructure such as sewage treatment facilities, and social services such as basic medical and senior facilities, leisure and public spaces are insufficient. These issues seriously lower the quality of urbanization.

Responding to an Aging Society

In 2014 10.1 percent of China's population was 65 years or older (NBSC, 2015). In 2014 15.5 percent of China's population was aged over 60, so China's age structure will become more aged in the future.

The United Nations uses the ratio of a country's aged population (65 or older) to its child population (14 or younger) as one measure of whether a society is "aged" or not. A ratio exceeding 30 percent indicates an aging society. Another ratio used by the United Nations is the proportion of aged population (65 or older) to the total population. If this ratio is beyond 10 percent, the country is defined as an aged country. The ratio of the aged population to the child population in China in 2014 was 61.0 percent and the ratio of aged population (65 or older) to total population reached 10.1 percent, so China is an aged society by either UN criterion.

Population aging will induce a series of problems, including public financial pressure, life cycle effects on individual savings behavior, insufficient capital accumulation, and a reduction of productivity. China's per capita GDP was only US$7,352 in 2014 (NBSC, 2015b), compared with the average in aging Western countries of over US$30,000 (World Bank, 2014). China's aging population pressure is likely to be much greater than in many Western countries or Asian countries with higher birth rates in the future. Some other countries are also experiencing aging populations, sometimes greater than in China—notably Japan and Korea in Asia and Italy in Europe, but their per capita GDP is much higher than China's.

Pollution and China's Development Pattern

With rapid economic development, environmental pollution has become a major problem hampering China's socio-economic development and the quality of life in Chinese cities. The development pattern in the past three decades that emphasized rapid development with little consideration of environmental consequences is no longer appropriate for contemporary China, and must be replaced by green, sustainable, low carbon development patterns in the next round of urbanization and modernization in China. Livable cities are not only important for their residents, but essential if China is to attract and retain creative class workers that are essential if it is to compete in the global economy.

China can now afford to invest in environmental remediation to improve air quality and clean up polluted rivers and lakes and enforce much tougher standards on new construction. Government ministries, universities, and consulting companies are well aware of other countries' best practices in these areas. A great deal of research and many experimental and pilot projects to improve the environment and reduce carbon emissions are occurring all over China. Given the entire development pattern of the last three decades, remediation and shifting to new practices will take time and the speed and extent of improving China's environment must vary from place to place.

A NEW POLICY ORIENTATION

In our view, the goal of urbanization is to lay the foundation for achieving China's second urbanization transition. Since China's labor force has reached its peak and there is no longer an unlimited labor supply, this reduces pressure for the rapid growth of cities. According to our forecast of the labor force trends in Table 10.1, the rapid increase in urbanization levels in China has also reached a peak and will slow down. The average annual increase in the rate of urbanization in 2015–2020 will likely be between 0.6 and 0.8 percent and in 2020–2030 it may decrease to 0.5 percent.

If China's policy orientation shifts from favoring rapid urbanization per se to balanced urbanization that emphasizes livability, China's urbanization level should be in the range of 58 to 60 percent in 2020 and 63 to 65 percent in 2030. This is lower than the 2020 target in China's NNSUP and predictions by other scholars and organizations such as the World Bank and China's State Council's Development Reform Commission (World Bank and DRC, 2014).

Healthy urban development should be the key goal in setting China's future urbanization level, rather than attempting to reach numerical targets with as high a percentage of the urban population as possible as quickly as possible. The core principle of China's National New Style Urbanization Plan (NNSUP)—which may be translated as "strengthening the urbanization of the people," should be realized.

Economic Restructuring and Regional Industrial Distribution

Economic growth is the primary driving force of urbanization. Thus, the healthy development of China's urbanization in the future requires sustained economic growth. The present is a critical moment for industrial transformation and upgrading of China's economy due to external competition from other developing countries, such as lower labor costs in Southeast Asia, and internal demands for institutional and systemic reform and innovation.

As documented in Chapter 4 on regional policies and regional urbanization, China has great regional disparities in both economic development and urbanization processes. This disparity makes possible progressive development of urbanization in China that is not possible in smaller and more homogenous countries.

Provinces with high urbanization levels such as Jiangsu, Zhejiang, and Guangdong are now devoted to developing high-tech and low-labor-demand industries. Provinces with low urbanization levels and high population densities such as Henan, Sichuan, and Hubei, are developing labor-intensive industries because they provide employment opportunities, reduce long-distance outmigration and can improve the quality of life of rural and semi-urban residents. These provinces do not have the industrial base, capital, or expertise to undertake the kind of advanced development occurring in parts of eastern China. With rising labor costs in east China, the transfer of labor-intensive industries to the western and central regions is accelerating.

Supportive policies to guide economic restructuring and the spatial transfer of industries can provide win–win situations in which different regions of China benefit based on their development level and unique circumstances. These policies include deductions or exemptions of enterprise income tax, preferential income tax treatment of employees, and the rewards for technology progress for enterprises relocating to central and western China.

Promoting LCC Development

The sustainable development of China's economy is dependent on its ability to compete internationally. China's NNSUP recognizes the importance of large city clusters (LCCs) and takes the position that they should be strengthened. In Chapter 7 we agree and argue that LCCs should be the basic unit to advance China's global competitiveness. Chapter 7 described the methodology we used to define and map large LCCs, our definition of 26 existing LCCs, and an extended analysis of differences among them.

Chapter 7 describes how LCCs in China differ in the percentage of industry and population of the province where they are located that lies within them and how rapidly their share of provincial industry and population is changing. Urbanization-related problems vary for different types of LCCs. In the upcoming period of slower urbanization, some LCCs will still be able to attract large population flows because of their sound infrastructures and abundant employment opportunities; others will develop more slowly. In some provinces the percentage of GDP generated within LCCs will increase; in others parts of the province will develop more rapidly than the LCCs. The three developed megalopolises—the Jing-Jin-Ji and Yangtze and Pearl River Delta megalopolises, should further optimize their spatial structure. Coordinating the location of development zones, logistics centers, and the location of mega-projects like airports, bridges, highway and train lines, ports, and tunnels to avoid duplication and reinforce synergies is important for these regions. The seven pre-megalopolises should reinforce their industrial bases and lead rapid development of small and medium-sized cities in the local region. The other 16 ordinary LCCs should actively play their vital roles of attracting resources and balancing the development of provincial economies.

Promoting Social Justice and Harmonious Development

Efficiency is the essence of market economies. However, justice is also a key support for sustainable socio-economic development. In the long run unbalanced and unjust social development is inefficient as well as undesirable on moral grounds.

Although China's urbanization rate reached 54.77 percent in 2014 (NBSC, 2015), nearly 70 percent of the urban population enjoy all the national social insurances the urban population receive. The remaining 30 percent (about 220 million semi-urban residents), who also work and live in the cities and towns, usually receive much more limited social welfare benefits.

In an open society, urbanization occurs because of the spontaneous social mobility of individuals given the comparative advantages of cities to the countryside in a given location based on the level of socio-economic development at the time. Although the market plays a fundamental regulatory role, individuals are the main agents of urbanization. Considering

China's special historical background and institutional environment, the transformation from peasants to urban residents is affected by institutional factors such as land tenure, hukou, and social welfare entitlements. With the deepening of reform and opening up, numerous institutional obstacles were either eliminated or reduced. Peasants' choices to migrate and reside in cities and register as urban residents is increasingly based on the choices they make about how to maximize personal and familial interests, as they perceive them, rather than either "being selected" or "being citizenized" (Hao and Zhao, 2013).

The role of the government in urbanization is essential. All levels of government should assume their responsibilities to manage urbanization during the current period of social transition. These responsibilities include overcoming institutional barriers caused by historical practices and improving institutions and public services to guarantee individuals' rights to independent choices.

The reduction and eventual elimination of welfare disparities in cities, as well as facilitating individuals' social mobility are among the most important issues facing China as it shifts from pursuit of the quantity to the quality of urbanization. To this end, all types of social welfare among vulnerable urban groups including marginal people should be strengthened. Preferential policies enjoyed by the local urban population alone, including better medical treatment, education, housing and pensions, should be extended to the entire urban population (including the semi-urban population) as quickly as financially and politically possible. The gap between different groups in the cities can be reduced, and the semi-urban population can be better integrated into urban society as the NNSUP proposes.

Discrimination against the migrant population should be eliminated. Welfare policies favorable to new urban residents should be formulated. Programs such as medical security, school attendance of their children, unemployment relief, and public housing should be based on people's real residence rather than hukou status and address. "Cities with invisible walls" should become cities without barriers. In reforming the rural land system, peasants' rights should be increased and protected so that they, too, can receive the benefits of China's progress as well as city dwellers. Currently peasants have use rights to farm, forest, and homestead land for their own use or to rent, but they can't freely sell or exchange these rights. Consideration should be given to granting them the right to trade or sell their use rights.

Urbanization policies based on local conditions

Undifferentiated urbanization policies will not work, considering the huge regional disparities in China and geographical differences in development and urbanization. Differences in regional economic development in China will persist for a long period and different urbanization rates will continue in different regions. Accordingly different goals should be set for the urbanization of various regions. Urbanization should be propelled based on specific conditions of economic growth, industrial restructuring, and varying urbanization modes.

In provinces with backward economies and low urbanization levels such as Guizhou and Yunnan, there is still great pressure from the migration of the surplus rural population. In addition to promoting development of local labor-intensive industries, trans-provincial approaches to urbanization should be fully utilized. Information channels for employment in other provinces should be established and improved, and the rural population should be encouraged and guided to take non-farming jobs. Through these approaches, the urbanization of these less developed provinces can be accelerated by transferring the rural population to other provinces with developed economies and abundant employment opportunities.

While our re-analysis of data on the relationship between development and urbanization concluded that overall China is only slightly under-urbanized if at all, provinces with low economic growth rates and high urbanization levels such as Jilin and Heilongjiang run the risk of becoming over-urbanized and face the challenges of inadequate employment and urban poverty. Further reforms should be conducted to stimulate local economic vitality and improve their urbanization progress through dynamic development.

For provinces with comparatively developed economies, but relatively low urbanization levels such as Shandong and Hubei, labor-intensive industries should be reinforced to provide sufficient employment opportunities for the progress of urbanization. New city growth poles should be identified and fostered in combination with improved public infrastructure service levels.

For provinces with developed economies and high urbanization levels such as Jiangsu, Zhejiang, and Guangdong, urbanization quality should be further improved. These provinces are well positioned to equalize urban and rural public services and improve the quality of life of semi-urban residents more quickly that other, less favored, provinces.

As for sparsely populated provinces in west China where the economy is dominated by agriculture and animal husbandry (Tibet, Xinjiang, and Qinghai), environmentally sensitive policies that respect local characteristics should be emphasized during the urbanization process. Setting the same urbanization level goals across all provinces is irrational for those western provinces.

Smart Growth and Smart Shrinkage

So-called "smart" growth is a concept included in much planning in the US and increasingly elsewhere in the world. While the term is often used loosely to apply to virtually any planning ideas proponents advocate, originally smart growth referred to a set of policies implemented by the state of Maryland to concentrate development at relatively high average densities in already built-up areas. In this meaning of the word it is a useful concept for China.

In the past three decades, Chinese cities have experienced much more rapid spatial expansion than population growth. Newly developed areas of most world cities have lower average densities than the previously developed core cities (Angel, 2012), but given China's huge population and limited arable and livable land, compact development—particularly on the urban fringe—is even more critical than elsewhere in the world. China's total urban population in 2014 was 749 million—2.47 times its urban population in 1990 (NBSC, 2015). In 2013 the area of urban construction land reached 47,109km^2—4.06 times as much as in 1990 (NBSC, 2014). It is evident that the old development pattern is not sustainable.

As the increase in China's semi-urban population slows, theoretically the demand for additional new urban construction land should also decline. In many regions, demand of land for future urban development can be satisfied by redevelopment of existing developed land. Shanghai's latest strategic urban plan calls for zero growth in urban construction land after 2020 (The Central People's Government of PRC News Web, 2014). Although implementing Shanghai's reduction plan will be difficult, this plan should be followed through. In general future urban planning should be shifted from relying on an increase in new construction land to smart expansion and internal growth. Peri-urban areas should be developed at higher average densities and empty villages and vacant houses in China's rural areas should be used in new ways. In theory, little or no net demand for expansion of rural construction land exists in these areas. As China's urbanization level increases, the total rural population will further decline and the demand for rural construction land will inevitably shrink further. Planned smart shrinkage rather than simply allowing market forces to operate makes sense in these areas (Hao and Zhao, 2013). Thus, efficiently utilizing rural space will be a challenge for future urbanization policy and physical plans in China. Based on our recent investigation of rural districts and urban consumption demands, some vacant rural houses may be used for recreational purposes, as nursing homes, or in other ways. Specific policy to guide this transformation is needed.

In conclusion, the general principles of future urban and rural development involve both "smart growth" and "smart shrinkage." Developing suburban industries is necessary for many cities. However, extensive and disorderly development that uses precious peri-urban land inefficiently should be discontinued. During the development process, both meeting the needs of industry and people's quality of life needs are essential. Planning should seek to achieve coordination and spatial integration of industries into the fabric of the city.

In the face of continuous hollowing out of rural settlements, and the abnormal expansion of some villages, new ideas should be proposed for spatial development in rural areas. "Smart shrinkage" is a necessity. Newly proposed policies include relocation and integration of villages and service facilities, homestead replacement, and new rural planning. Protecting peasants' rural collective assets is a key problem to be resolved. Smart shrinkage of rural regions should assure adequate public services remain available to the population of towns and villages even as their populations decline. Their environmental quality should be maintained even as their financial resources shrink and the population base declines.

Changing regional policy

National level regional policy since the founding of the PRC has evolved in response to domestic and international politics, stages of development, and theories of the best way to promote overall growth.

During the first decade after the founding of the PRC the national government favored large projects building basic industry in inland regions and areas in north China with coal and iron resources and rail access to the Soviet Union. After breaking with the Soviet Union, regional policy was dominated by defense considerations and investment flowed to third front areas in central and western China to build their capacity to resist if coastal cities were invaded or destroyed. With reform and opening up, policy favored coastal cities—"the East takes the lead in development" and the national government supported national economic development zones in east coast cities. Since 2000 the emphasis has been on "balanced development among the three great regions" and the national government has invested heavily to develop the west and to encourage coordinated urban–rural development.

The NNSUP suggest a variety of strategies for developing central and western China, distributing national economic development zones (NEDZs) and other strategic support more evenly among regions, focusing on key developments, promoting agglomerations and LCCs, and organizing development along great north–south and east–west transportation corridors.

Our analysis of the spatial distribution of urbanization comparing provinces and the three great regions of eastern, central, and western China in Chapter 4 from 1982 to 1990, 1990 to 2000, 2000 to 2010, and since 2010 using the Thiel index and other statistical and GIS spatial analysis documents the increase in urbanization in every province in China and the increase of inter- and intra-regional disparities in development and urbanization. For the entire period from 1982 to 2012, the urbanization levels of the coastal provinces adjacent to major command and control centers of the global economy—Guangdong province (adjacent to Hong Kong) and Jiangsu province (adjacent to Shanghai)—increased the fastest of all provinces in China. But since 2000 growth rates in eastern China have slowed and the rate of urbanization increase in central and western China has increased.

Given the great differences among different regions in China a variety of different regional development approaches are appropriate. We emphasize the importance of both policies to encourage endogenous development in villages, towns, and small cities and strengthening LCCs as China's links to advanced sectors of the global economy.

GLOBALIZATION, FOREIGN DIRECT INVESTMENT, DEVELOPMENT AND URBANIZATION

The Changing Significance of FDI

Foreign direct investment (FDI) has played an important role in China's development and urbanization, but its nature, importance, and role have changed over time. Initially most FDI came from or via Hong Kong and Macau (later also Taiwan) and played a key role in jump-starting development in National Economic Development Zones in coastal China and later all over China. We conclude that dependency theory critical of the role of FDI because it forces weak developing countries to remain suppliers of raw materials and simple manufactured and assembled goods that are dependent on developed countries for capital and more advanced products, does not describe the Chinese case. China implemented policy that permitted it to use FDI to develop its economy without becoming dependent. On the contrary, today China has caught up with or surpassed other developed countries in design and manufacturing of many advanced high value added products. China's FDI was only 2.6 percent of Gross Capital Formation in 2013. Its investments in other countries are now larger than the FDI it receives. FDI is still very important for China, because of the linkage to the outside world and knowledge transfer in high technology, finance, and other advanced sectors of the economy rather than as a funding source.

Implementing China's National New Style National Urbanization Plan

The central government's 2014 National New Style Urbanization Plan (NNSUP) is a grand plan for a new period in Chinese urbanization. The NNSUP is the first nationwide plan for urbanization in China and arguably only the second national urbanization in the world after Bhutan, which adopted a National Urbanization plan in 2002.

The NNSUP calls for 100 million additional people to settle in cities or change from semi-urban population to fully urban citizens by 2020. It sets 60 percent as the target urbanization rate measured by the de facto urban population and 45 percent as the target urbanization rate measured by the *de jure* urban population with urban hukou in 2020. It projects that the urbanization growth rate will rise by one percentage point every year. These two are the crucial development goals supported by a series of system reforms.

The most important aspect of the NNSUP lies in reform measures it proposes rather than its development goals. In China's policymaking process broad national goals articulated in policy documents such as the NNSUP are followed by more specific policies at the national level, which in turn leave provinces and local government room to implement the policies in different ways. This process is likely to occur with the NNSUP plan in the coming years. The NNSUP proposes launching reform measures in the hukou system, welfare equalization, public service promotion, and other complex systems such as China's land use rights system.

The NNSUP has a number of key assumptions and components. Our research shed light on many of them.

First, the plan takes the position that the Chinese economy has reached a key point of structural transition and industries with low technology, low value added, and high energy consumption will have to be upgraded, or go out of business. This scenario is not favorable to increasing urban employment. Although the growing service sector will create job opportunities, whether it can provide abundant employment opportunities on the scale of the manufacturing sector remains uncertain. Without a sufficient supply of jobs, the transfer of rural and semi-urban population will create policy risks.

Second, our nationwide investigation of rural regions indicates that except for a few remote mountainous and ethnic regions, nearly all the existing rural surplus labor force has now migrated, with the aged, women, and children staying behind. This raises important questions about possible sources of population for future urbanization.

The first possible source is the "left-behind" population in the countryside consisting largely of the aged, women, and children in rural regions. The urbanization process is extremely difficult for this group. Families with members living separately in two places are the result of a choice to separate mainly based on economic considerations. If the economy of a destination cannot support the urban life of a whole family, they will likely become the urban poor even if they have been transformed into full urban residents with non-agricultural hukou. Therefore, the prospect of urbanization for this population in large cities far from their places of origin is not good. Completing urbanization near the village or countryside where they now live, while working in nearby counties and towns, may be a better choice for this group. The economic and social costs may be lowest if they reside in their rural hometowns. While not ideal, this is likely to be a pattern during the next phase of China's urban transition. A combination of improved rural social welfare, better local job opportunities, and continuing remittances from family members who have migrated should make their lives much better than in the recent past.

The second population group is the new generation of youth who will enter the labor force in the near future. The increment of this part of the future labor force is easy to calculate. According to the sixth census, there were 42 million members of the rural population aged 10–14 years old in 2010. They will gradually become the adult labor force in 2015–2020. Most of them will choose to migrate to the cities for reasons we have discussed: because they are increasingly well educated, they value the higher wages they can command in cities, and the educational, cultural, and career advancement potential of a new urban lifestyle is attractive to them. Even if this population is completely urbanized, they will only contribute a small percentage to China's urbanization rate. Where will the remaining increment of over 50 million projected in the NNSUP come from? Will promoting the urbanization of 50 million more people at this point while China's economic and urbanization transition is underway be necessary? Rather than assuming all urbanization is desirable, policymakers at every level should carefully consider the pros and cons on a variety of scales.

Third, our research on the dual track model of China's urbanization indicates that both semi-urban and urban populations play important roles in the stable and rapid development of urbanization. Social systems such as China's land rights and social welfare systems that are based on the hukou system play a vital role. Although we argue that the hukou system should be reformed, it is criticized by most scholars and the Chinese leadership is committed to hukou reform as part of its national urbanization strategy, at China's present stage of development hukou remains the most critical factor that ensures social stability during rapid urbanization (Chapters 2 and 8).

Past failed hukou reform experiments at the beginning of 2000 that proved too costly and disruptive and calculations of the enormous cost of fully folding urban migrants without urban hukou into social welfare systems by Kam Wing Chan, and the DRC of the State Council and World Bank make a persuasive case that it will take time to reform hukou.

A large number of semi-urban dwellers can work and live in cities, and still maintain close relationships with their rural hometowns. These relations are very important for older peasant workers who lack even basic education and skills. While agricultural hukou is an obstacle to enjoying equal welfare in cities, it serves as a social safety net that provides basic living security in times of economic distress. As the reform of the hukou system is being promoted vigorously in China, policymakers should proceed only as rapidly as possible given conditions in different parts of China. The hukou system cannot be simply abolished, and urban–rural integration cannot realistically be implemented in every aspect all at once. Instead, the equalization of public services in urban and rural regions should be achieved progressively with specific targets for each step.

Fourth, numerous problems have appeared owing to rapid urbanization during the past three decades. Social conflicts such as economic inequality and urban–rural disparities have reached critical points. The urbanization processes of any developed country are supported by economic growth. The negative relative development of some countries in Latin America and South and Southeastern Asia described in Chapter 9 demonstrate that without strong economic growth, high urbanization rates bring urban unemployment, poverty, slums, and social instability. Once caught in the "middle urbanization trap" described in Chapter 9, it is difficult to escape. Given China's enormous population and the magnitude of migration being caught in the urbanization trap this could have catastrophic consequences.

The NNSUP will undoubtedly accelerate the healthy and rapid development of Chinese urbanization. What exact new reform measures the national government will launch to help carry out the NNSUP and how provinces and lower levels of government will respond remain to be seen. But the general direction of change is promising. The findings and suggestions in this book are consistent with the new direction.

Markets, Globalization, and the State

A historical retrospective facilitates a comprehensive understanding of the future. Looking back on China's urbanization process over the past three decades, there is a clear symbiotic relationship among markets, globalization, and the state. Unlike either developed Western countries or developing countries, China has chosen an urbanization path that is closely related to the relationship of all three. China is not following either the neo-liberal path of the capitalistic world, or the path of traditional socialist countries with centralized planned economies. China's urbanization process is pragmatic: "crossing the river by feeling the stones" with constant experiments, trial and error, and corrections. The pilot village and town reforms in the 1980s, which focused on China's rural land system and township enterprises, successfully mobilized enthusiasm for bottom-up entrepreneurship and stimulated the rapid rise of a rural market economy. At the end of the 1980s, China began permitting rural households to exchange use rights in collectively owned land, so long as it remained in agricultural use. In Chengdu and some other parts of China an extensive market for the exchange of agricultural use rights exists. Households may lease rights to their arable land for as long as thirty years. Some entire villages lease village land on behalf of the collective who receive rents, but are free to work in non-agricultural activities. Large assembled parcels of agricultural land are often leased to modern agri-businesses with the capital and expertise to engage in agricultural modernization. Since 1993 tax sharing between the national and sub-national governments has provided lower levels of government financial resources and a greater say over local expenditures.

At the middle of the 1990s, the state realized that township and village economies could not be the main participants in the global economy, and began a decisive shift to urban development and reform (Huang, 2008). Reforms of state-owned enterprises and housing were launched, which laid the foundation for China's rise in the early twenty-first century.

As China joined the WTO in 2001 and was better integrated into the global market, dramatic economic progress ensued. In order to avoid enlarging urban–rural disparities, cities were encouraged to assist rural regions. The cancellation of the agricultural tax in 2006 is an embodiment of the integrated development of urban areas and rural regions principle. In 2014, the NNSUP paid increased attention to the urbanization of the people and sustainable development of China's environment, resources, economy, and society. A series of policy adjustments has responded to different stages of China's development and facilitated simultaneous economic growth and urbanization development in China.

Towns, Villages, and Rural Urbanization

In Chapter 8 on towns, villages, and rural urbanization we describe towns as a unique settlement type halfway between a city and a county: "the tails of cities and heads of villages." County capitals, other official towns, and townships help connect cities and the countryside. China had 19,410 official towns in 2010: about an eightfold increase from 1982. While reclassifying lower-level administrative divisions accounted for much of the increase in the 1980s, towns have grown in population and real urban characteristics so that today they account for a substantial part of China's de facto population. The increase is town seats—the urbanized part of towns has contributed to 47 percent of the increase of China's urbanization ratio since 1982 (Table 8.5). Towns are centers of endogenous entrepreneurship in China. In 2010 TVEs contributed more than 46 trillion RMB to China's economy—one-third of China's GDP.

We emphasize the importance of supporting towns and TVEs. Because they are low in China's administrative hierarchy many towns do not have enough own source revenue to maintain adequate basic services. Restructuring local government finance to reward towns that have the potential to develop and demonstrate initial success could help improve China's economy and improve the balance and quality of urbanization.

Promoting China's Double Dual Track Transition

The double dual track transitions resulting from socio-economic development throughout China now underway can support healthy social and economic development if good policy is implemented for each of the four tracks. The transition from a centralized planned economy to a market-oriented economy took place earlier than the transition from a pursuit of economic growth and urbanization outcomes measured as successful only by measure of quantity to a more sensitive approach that considers the quality of urban development.

The two dual track transition processes that co-exist at present are not the only direction of China's urbanization development. In our view, the success of the next phase of China's urbanization lies in the choice of an in-between path, where national regulation and market orientation each play important roles across all development stages. Both quantity and quality should be promoted during the urbanization process.

Based on the sixth census, approximately 6–8 million rural youth are predicted to migrate to cities every year from 2014 until 2030. Owing to aging of the urban population, this migration should not cause high employment pressure if it is distributed rationally through a combination of planned policy interventions and market forces. However, such a large volume of newly increased urban population (often semi-urban at least for a transition period) poses a great challenge for the government. As proposed in the NNSUP, the urbanization of the people is the focus of China's future urbanization. The orientation towards quality promotion is a crucial policy, although not the only goal.

China's economic development situation over the past three decades indicates that economic growth provides the driving force for urbanization. However, urbanization quality is far from satisfactory considering the past emphasis on the development of industry with little regard to the quality of urban life where it is located. During China's current structural transformation and economic upgrading, how rapidly urbanization will occur in the near future is uncertain. The urbanization development over the past three decades accelerated China's economic growth, and now enormous domestic demand will be a key driver of further economic development in the future. However, policymakers should be careful not to assume that urbanization per se can drive China's future economic growth. Urbanization can exert positive effects on economic growth. However, it is important to be cautious about the cause and effect relationship. Urbanization development should not be narrowly used as a sectoral policy tool only to stimulate economic growth. Rather, urbanization itself should be people-oriented—considering livability and the quality of life that a certain level of urbanization can provide. The wishes of the public need to be respected when transforming the semi-urban population to urban residents. The system design and public goods supply should be improved step-by-step to match actual national economic and local development conditions.

The coming years will be a crucial test for China and the world. If China's economic restructuring and new style urbanization are successful they can improve the lives of 1.37 billion Chinese, and contribute a great deal to the rest of the world.

Appendix: Tongji University field research 2010–2015

Field research described in this book was conducted in five areas of eastern, central, and western China by Tongji University faculty/student teams between 2010 and 2015. All of the investigations involved a combination of survey research, interviews, observation, and review of local secondary data, including unpublished local data. Following is a description of the five field research projects. Throughout the book we have referred to this research using the location and year in which it was conducted.

FIFTY-FIVE TOWNS IN HUBEI PROVINCE, MAY 2010

A research team from Tongji University and Huazhong Science and Technology University conducted a survey and interviews in Hubei province on Hubei's urbanization strategy for the Hubei provincial government in May 2010 with assistance from the Hubei Province Department of Housing and Urban–Rural Development. This research sheds light on the rationale for the urbanization policy of one of central China's most important provinces and empirical evidence of its impact on residents.

The team conducted a survey in 55 out of a total of 741 small towns in Hubei province. The sampling ratio was 7.42 percent. A stratified random sample was drawn to capture the major differences within Hubei province. Individuals and households were sampled in towns in 28 counties and county-level cities, including key towns, ordinary towns, economically strong and weak towns, towns in plain areas and mountainous regions, towns near cities and outer suburbs, tourist towns, trading towns, and industrial towns. A total of 1,387 residents in 55 towns, 110 administrative villages, and 200 enterprises were surveyed.

SEVENTEEN TOWNS IN HUAIYUAN COUNTY, ANHUI PROVINCE, AUGUST 2013

A Tongji University team conducted field research in Huaiyuan county, Anhui province in August 2013. Anhui is a relatively poor province in central China. Huaiyuan county is of particular interest because nearly one-quarter of the county's population with local hukou have migrated and are no longer living at their official residence address. Understanding Huaiyuan county provides insight into the mechanics of migration from central China and migrants' motivations.

Huaiyuan county has one capital town and 18 general towns. In 2013 Huaiyuan county's population was 1,265,000. Nearly 300,000—almost one-quarter of the county's population—had migrated. The average per capita GDP income in Huaiyuan county in 2013 was 15,000 RMB—about US$2,419. Understanding the situation in Huaiyuan county and particularly the motivations driving such a large outmigration shed light on the role of migration in China's regional urbanization. The fieldwork in Huaiyuan county consisted of a workshop attended by leaders of township government and entrepreneurs, interviews with township residents, surveys of township residents, visits to observe enterprises and town centers, interviews with village leaders, interviews with villagers, and a survey of villagers. The team surveyed functional departments, such as the Construction Bureau of Huaiyuan county, to better understand the development situation in Huaiyuan county. The surveys were conducted in all but one of Huaiyuan county's towns. A total of 810 questionnaires were answered, 390 from township residents and 420 from villagers. Six hundred and eighty-eight of the surveys were usable; a response rate of 84.93 percent.

YUELAI AND ZHENGYU TOWNS, HAIMEN CITY, JIANGSU PROVINCE, MARCH, 2013

A Tongj team conducted field research in Yuelai and Zhengyu towns and Haimen city in Jiangsu province in March 2013. Jiangsu province is adjacent to Shanghai and borders the Yanghtze River. Haimen city is a county-level city. While Jiangsu province is one of China's most developed provinces, the majority of Haimen city's administrative area is still rural. Thus, Haimen city provides a particularly interesting setting in which to study the impact of industrialization on nearby rural areas.

The permanent resident population of Haimen city was 1.01 million and per capita GDP was 73,490 RMB (US$11,853) in 2012. The city has three urban zones and nine rural towns under its jurisdiction. Our field research was conducted in two of the towns: Yuelai town and Zhengyu town.

In Yuelai town the population with local hukou was 109,200 in 2012 and the permanent resident population was 73,000. The total area of Yuelai town is 141.44km^2, and the town has 25 administrative villages and four neighborhood committees. The population with local hukou in 2012 was 61,200 and the permanent resident population was 55,300.

The total area of Zhengyu town is 62.32km^2. Zhengyu town's total *de jure* population (with local hukou) at the time of the study was 61,257; the de facto population (living in the region) was 55,309. Zhengyu town has 17 administrative villages and two neighborhood committees.

The team interviewed representatives of departments under the jurisdiction of the town government, including environmental protection, water conservation, and finance. The team also interviewed representatives of 20 township enterprises, heads of three villages, and leaders of six production teams and conducted in-depth interviews in two production teams: the nineteenth production team of Wanzhong village and the twenty-sixth production group of Xinmin village. Twenty-two households with at least one family member at home in the Wanzhong village production team were surveyed directly and information concerning another 16 households with no one at home was provided by the leader of the production group. The same survey method was adopted for the Xinmin village production group with 16 households with someone at home and 13 with no one at home. Twenty-seven interviews were completed regarding 28 people who had migrated from Haimen city to work in Shanghai. A total of 98 questionnaires were answered by township residents of Zhengyu and Yuelai towns. The sampling ratio of township residents was 6.10 percent. For the rural residents in the two towns, 105 questionnaires were answered. The sampling ratio for rural residents was 0.94 percent. The Tongji team also interviewed leaders of the Haimen city Construction Bureau in depth.

GAOMING DISTRICT, FOSHAN CITY, GUANGDONG PROVINCE, MARCH 2014

The fourth research site was in a district within Foshan city in Guangdong province in Southeastern China conducted in March 2014. It provides a good opportunity to better understand the impact of development on urban and rural areas near rapidly developing urban areas.

Most jurisdictions of Gaoming district are rural areas. The population of Gaoming district with local hukou in 2012 was 296,800 and the permanent resident population was 423,100. Per capita GDP was 118,972 RMB.

The district has three towns with 51 administrative villages and one urban street under its jurisdiction. (A "Street" is a type of Chinese district as described in Chapter 3.)

The Gaoming district research included five parts. First was a survey of township residents in three towns. The sampling ratio of township residents was 3.29 percent. Ninety-nine questionnaires were completed. Second was a survey of rural areas in 44 out of Gaoming district's 51 administrative villages (86.27 percent). A total of 353 completed questionnaires were obtained with a sampling ratio of 2.8 percent. Over 200 villagers were also interviewed while they were answering the questionnaires. Third, employees of township enterprises in the three towns were surveyed and 109 questionnaires were obtained. Fourth, the team conducted a survey of parents of students of primary and secondary schools throughout the city. A total of 2,598 completed questionnaires were collected, with a sampling ratio of 6.18 percent.

In addition to these surveys and interviews we interviewed department heads of the three towns and the leaders of departments directly under the municipal governments in order to better understand the overall economic and social development of Gaoming district.

QUZHOU CITY AND NEARBY TOWNS AND VILLAGES, MARCH AND APRIL 2015

A Tongji research team investigated 27 towns and five urban streets in Quzhou city—a prefecture-level city in southwestern Zhejian province between March 13 and 29, 2015.

In the first week the team visited each town and street and then selected 14 towns for in-depth investigations. Team members interviewed government leaders of the town and respected people in some selected villages. Four hundred and sixty-seven questionnaires were completed in this fieldwork, covering 14 selected towns. Between April 17 and 22 an international team including professors Li Zhang, Min Zhao, Richard LeGates, Lee Inhee and Yoo Jaewoo from Busan University in South Korea, Yuka Himeno from Oita University in Japan and graduate students from Tongji, Busan and Oita Universities visited Quzhou. The team studied the relationship between villages, towns, peri-urban areas and urban development to gain a deeper understanding of Chinese urbanization by communicating with professors from other countries.

Bibliography

ENGLISH REFERENCES

Abramson, D. and Y. Qi. (2011), '"Urban–rural integration" in the earthquake zone: Sichuan's post-disaster reconstruction and the expansion of the Chengdu metropolis', *Pacific Affairs*, 84(3), 495–523.

Angel, S. (2012), *Planet of Cities*, Cambridge, MA: Lincoln Land Institute.

Areppim (2014), Currency converter, retrieved on September 18, 2015 from http://stats.areppim.com/calc/calc_usdlrxdeflator.php.

Armstrong, W. and T. McGee (1985), *Theatres of Accumulation: Studies in Asian and Latin American Urbanization*, New York: Methuen.

Au, C. and J. Henderson (2006), 'Are Chinese cities too small?', *The Review of Economic Studies*, 73(3), 549–576.

Beaverstock, J., R. Smith and P. Taylor (2000), 'World city network: A new meta-geography?', *Annals of the Association of American Geographers*, 90(1), 123–134.

Berry, B. (1962), 'Some relations of urbanization and basic patterns of economic development', in Forrest R. Pitts (ed.), *Urban Systems And Economic Development*, Eugene, OR: University of Oregon, 1–15.

Biao, X. (2007), 'How far are the left-behind left behind? A preliminary study in rural China', *Space and Place*, 13(3), 179–191.

Bloom, D., D. Canning and J. Sevilla (2003), 'The demographic dividend: A new perspective on the economic consequences of population change', *Population Matters Series*, Santa Monica, CA: Rand Corporation.

Bogue, D. and M. Hagood (1953), *Sub Regional Migration in the United States, 1935–1940. Vol. II: Differential Migration in the Corn and Cotton Belts*, Miami, OH: Scripps Foundation Studies in Population Distribution, 6, 124–127.

Bracken, G. (2012), *Aspects of Urbanization in China: Shanghai, Hong Kong, Guangzhou*, Amsterdam: Amsterdam University Press.

Bradsher, K. (2013), 'Next Made-in-China boom: College graduates', *New York Times*, January 16.

Brandt, L. and T. Rawski (eds) (2008), *China's Great Economic Transformation*, Cambridge: Cambridge University Press.

Brenner, N., R. Keil and X. Ren (2015), *The Global Cities Reader* (2nd edn), London and New York: Routledge.

Cai, F. (2007), 'Lewis turning point of Chinese economic development', in F. Cai (ed), *Report of China Population and Labor: No.8, Lewis Turning Point and its Policy Challenges*, Beijing: Social Science Literature Press, 22–36.

Cai, F. (2008), 'Chinese economy: How to break through the low middle income trap', *Journal of Graduate School of Chinese Academy of Social Sciences*, (1), 4.

Cai, F. (2010), 'Demographic transition, demographic dividend and Lewis turning point in China', *China Economic Journal*, (2), 107–119.

Cai, F. (2011a), 'Hukou system reform and unification of rural–urban social welfare', *China & World Economy*, 19(3), 33–48.

Cai, F. (2012), 'Is there a "middle-income trap"? Theories, experiences and relevance to China', *China & World Economy*, 20(1), 49–61.

Cai, Y. (2013), 'China's new demographic reality: Learning from the 2010 census', *Population and Development Review*, 39(3), 371–396.

Campanella, T. (2008), *The Concreted Dragon*, New York: Princeton Architectural Press.

Cannon, T. and A. Jenkins (1990), *The Geography of Contemporary China*, London: Routledge.

Castells, M. (1996), *The Rise of the Network Society*, Oxford: Blackwell.

Castells, M. (1997), *The Power of Identity*, Oxford: Blackwell.

Castells, M. (1998), *The End of the Millennium*, Oxford: Blackwell.

Castells, M. (2001), *The Internet Galaxy, Reflections on the Internet, Business and Society*, Oxford, Oxford University Press.

Castells, M. (2005), 'Space of flows, space of places: materials for a theory of urbanism in the information age', in Richard LeGates and Frederic Stout (eds) (2015), *The City Reader* (6th edn), London and New York: Routledge, 229–240.

Castells, M. (2010), 'Globalization, networking, urbanization: Reflections on the spatial dynamics of the information age', *Urban Studies*, 47(13), 2737–2745.

Central Committee of the Chinese Communist Party (CCP) (1982), Document 51 'Instructions on the Reform of Administrative Divisions and the Implementation of the System of Cities Leading the Counties'.

Central Intelligence Agency (2014), *The World Factbook*, retrieved on September 18, 2015 from www.cia.gov/library/publications/the-world-factbook/rankorder/2004rank.html.

Chan, K. (1992), 'Economic growth strategy and urbanization policies in China, 1949–1982', *International Journal of Urban and Regional Research*, 16(2), 275–304.

Chan, K. (1994), *Cities with Invisible Walls: Reinterpreting Urbanization in Post-1949 China*, Hong Kong and New York: Oxford University Press.

Chan, K. (1996), 'Post-Mao China: A two-class urban society in the making', *International Journal of Urban and Regional Research*, 20, 134–150.

Chan, K. (2003), 'Chinese Census 2000: New opportunities and challenges', *The China Review*, 3(2), 1–12.

Chan, K. (2007), 'Misconceptions and complexities in the study of China's cities: Definitions, statistics, and implications', *Eurasian Geography and Economics*, 48(4), 383–412.

Chan, K. (2008), 'Internal labor migration in China: Trends, geographical distribution and policies, proceedings of United Nations expert group meeting on population distribution, urbanization, internal migration and development', ESA/P/WP.206, United Nations, 93–122.

Chan, K. (2009a), 'Population, migration and the Lewis turning point in China', in F. Cai and Y. Du (eds), *The China Population and Labor Yearbook, Vol. 1: The Approaching Lewis Turning Point and Its Policy Implications*, Leiden, Netherlands: Brill, xix–xli.

Chan, K. (2009b), 'The Chinese hukou system at 50', *Eurasian Geography and Economics*, 50(2), 197–221.

Chan, K. (2010), 'Fundamentals of China's urbanization and policy', *The China Review*, 10(1), 63–94.

Chan, K. (2012), 'Crossing the 50 percent population rubicon: Can China urbanize to prosperity?', *Eurasian Geography and Economics*, 53(1), 63–86.

Chan, K. (2013), 'A roadmap for reforming China's hukou system', *China Dialogue*, October, 22.

Chan, K. and W. Buckingham (2008), 'Is China abolishing the hukou system?', *The China Quarterly*, 195, 582–606.

Chan, K. and Y. Hu (2003), 'Urbanization in China in the 1990s: New definition, different series, and revised trends', *The China Review*, 3(2), 48–71.

Chan, K. and M. Wang (2008), 'Remapping China's regional inequalities, 1990–2006. A new assessment of de facto and de jure population data', *Eurasian Geography and Economics*, 49(1), 21–56.

Chan, K. and L. Zhang (1999), 'The hukou system and rural–urban migration in China: Processes and changes', *The China Quarterly*, 160, 818–855.

Chang, G. and J. Brada (2006), 'The paradox of China's growing under-urbanization', *Economic Systems*, 30(1), 24–40.

Chang, H., X. Dong and F. MacPhail (2011), 'Labor migration and time use patterns of the left-behind children and elderly in rural China', *World Development*, 39(12), 2199–2210.

Chang, L. (2009), *Factory Girls*, New York: Spiegel & Grau.

Chang, S. (1976), 'The changing system of Chinese cities', *Annals of the Association of American Geographers*, 66(3), 398–415.

Chen, J., F. Guo and Y. Wu (2011), 'One decade of urban housing reform in China: Urban housing price dynamics and the role of migration and urbanization, 1995–2005', *Habitat International*, 35(1), 1–8.

Chen, M., W. Liu and X. Tao (2013), 'Evolution and assessment on China's urbanization 1960–2010: Under-urbanization or over-urbanization?', *Habitat International*, 38, 25–33.

Chen, W. (1996), 'An approach to the policy of urban development', *Geographical Research*, 16(3), 16–22.

Chen, Z. (2008), 'Urbanization and spatial structure evolution of urban systems in China. Institute of developing economics Japan external trade organization', 34 pages, retrieved on September 18, 2015 from www.ide.go.jp/English/Publish/Download/Vrf/pdf/439.pdf.

Chenery, H. and M. Syrquin (1975), *The Patterns of Development, 1950–1970*, London, Oxford University Press for the World Bank.

Cheng, T. (1991), 'Dialectics of control: The household registration (hukou) system in contemporary China' (PhD dissertation), New York: State University of New York at Binghamton.

Cheng, T. and M. Selden (1994), 'The origins and social consequences of China's "hukou" system', *The China Quarterly*, 139, 644–668.

Christaller, W. (1966), *Central Places in Southern Germany*, Upper Saddle River, NJ: Prentice Hall.

Containerisation International (1980, 1990, 2000, 2011), *Containerisation International Yearbook*, retrieved on May 20, 2015 from http://europe.nxtbook.com/nxteu/informa/ci_yearbook2013/index.php?startid=31#/0.

Davis, K. (1965), 'The urbanization of the human population', *Scientific American*, 213(3), 40–53.

Démurger, S. (2011), 'Return migrants: The rise of new entrepreneurs in rural China', *World Development*, 39(10), 1847–1861.

Démurger, S. and X. Hui (2010), 'Return migrants: The rise of new entrepreneurs in rural China', *World Development*, (4), 1–15.

Démurger, S., J. Sachs and W. Woo et al. (2002), 'Geography, economic policy, and regional development in China', *Asian Economic Papers*, 1(1), 146–197.

Development Reform Center of the PRC State Council and the World Bank (DRC and WB) (2013), *China 2030: Building a Modern, Harmonious, and Creative Society*, Washington, DC: World Bank.

Development Reform Center of the PRC State Council and the World Bank (DRC and WB) (2014), *Urban China*, Washington, DC: World Bank.

Development Zone Research Center of Saidi Consultant Company (DZRCSCC) (2014), Research report for China's national economic development zones in 2013.

De Vries, J. (1984), *European Urbanization, 1500–1800*, Cambridge, MA: Harvard University Press.

Dollar, D. and A. Kraay (2002), 'Growth is good for the poor', *Journal of Economic Growth*, 7(3), 195–225.

Fan, C. (1995), 'Of belts and ladders: State policy and uneven regional development in post-Mao China', *Annals of the Association of American Geographers*, 85, 421–449.

Fan, C. (2001), 'Migration and labor-market returns in urban China: Results from a recent survey in Guangzhou', *Environment and Planning A*, 33, 479–508.

Fan, C. (2005), 'Interprovincial migration, population redistribution, and regional development in China: 1990 and 2000 census comparisons', *The Professional Geographer*, 57(2), 295–311.

Fan, C. (2008), *China on the Move. Migration, the State, and the Household*, Oxon: Routledge.

Fan, C. and M. Sun (2008), 'Regional inequality in China, 1978–2006', *Eurasian Geography and Economics*, 49(1), 1–20.

Fan, C. et al. (2008), 'Creative destruction and the water town of Luzhi, China', *Tourism Management*, (4), 648–660.

Fei, H. (1939), *Peasant Life in China: A Field Study of Country Life in the Yangtze Valley*, New York: E.P. Dutton, 49.

Fei, J. and G. Ranis (1964), *Development of the Labor Surplus Economy*, Homewood, IL: Richard D. Irwin for the Economic Growth Center, Yale University.

Florida, R. (2015), *The Rise of the Creative Class—Revisited: Revised and Expanded*, New York: Basic Books.

Florida, R., T. Gulden and C. Mellander (2007), 'The rise of the mega-region', *Cambridge Journal of Regions, Economy and Society*, 1(3), 459–476.

Fortune Web (2014), 'Global 500 2014', retrieved on September 18, 2015 from http://fortune.com/global500/.

Friedmann, J. (1986), 'The world city hypothesis', *Development and Change*, 17, 69–73.

Friedmann, J. (2005), *China's Urban Transition*, Minneapolis: University of Minnesota Press.

Frobel, F. and J. Heinricha et al. (1980), *The New International Division of Labor*, Cambridge, Cambridge University Press.

Fujita, M. and D. Hu (2001), 'Regional disparity in China 1985–1994: The effects of globalization and economic liberalization', *The Annals of Regional Science*, (35), 3–37.
Fujita, M. and P. Krugman (1995), 'When is the economy monocentric?: von Thünen and Chamberlin unified', *Regional Science and Urban Economics*, 25(4), 505–528.
Galpin, C. (1918), *Rural Life*, New York: The Century Co.
Geddes, P. (1915), *Cities in Evolution: An Introduction to the Town-planning Movement and the Study of Cities*, London: Williams and Norgate, 34–35.
Geng, H. and G. Chao (2009), 'The hurdles and redevelopment countermeasures of towns in southern Jiangsu province: A case study on the plan for the development of Chengdong district in Jiangyin city', *Urban Planning Forum*, (6), 53–59.
Giles, J., A. Park, F. Cai and Y. Du (2012), 'Weathering a storm: Survey-based perspectives on employment in China in the aftermath of the global financial crisis (SSRN Scholarly Paper No. ID 2016749)', Rochester, NY: Social Science Research Network. Retrieved on September 18, 2015 from http://papers.ssrn.com/abstract=2016749.
Gill, I., H. Kharas and D. Bhattasali (2007), *An East Asian Renaissance: Ideas for Economic Growth*, Washington, DC: World Bank Publications.
Gilpin, R. (2011), *Global Political Economy: Understanding the International Economic Order*, Princeton, NJ: Princeton University Press.
Ginsburg, N. (1991), 'Extended metropolitan region in Asia: A new spatial paradigm', in N. Ginsburg, B. Koppel and T.G. McGee (eds), *The Extended Metropolis: Settlement Transition in Asia*, Honolulu: University of Hawaii Press, 27–46.
Glazer, N. and D. Moynihan (1970), *Beyond the Melting Pot: The Negroes, Puerto Ricans, Jews, Italians, and Irish of New York City*, Cambridge, MA: MIT–Harvard Joint Center for Urban Studies.
Goodman, D. (2004), 'Campaign to "open up the West": national, provincial-level and local perspectives', *The China Quarterly*, 178, 317–334.
Gottmann, J. (1961), *Megalopolis*, Cambridge, MA: MIT Press.
Gransow, B. (2012), 'Contested urbanization in China: Exploring informal spaces of migrants-in-the-city', *Harvard Asia Quarterly*, 14(1/2), 12–24.
Gregory, P. and R. Stuart (2013), *The Global Economy and Its Economic Systems*, Boston, MA: Cengage Learning.
Guldin, G. (1996), 'Desakotas and beyond: urbanization in southern China', *Ethnology*, 35(4), 265–283.
Hall, P. (2009), 'Looking backward, looking forward: The city region of the mid-21st century', *Regional Studies*, 43(6), 803–817.

Hall, P. and K. Pain (2006), *The Polycentric Metropolis: Learning From Mega-City Regions in Europe*, Oxford and New York: Earthscan.

Han, R. and L. Wang (2013), 'Challenges and opportunities facing China's urban development in the new era', *China Perspectives*, 2013(2), 15–27.

Han, S. (1998), 'Real estate development in China: A regional perspective', *Journal of Real Estate Literature*, 6, 121–133.

Han, S. (2010), 'Urban expansion in contemporary China: What can we learn from a small town?', *Land Use Policy*, 27(3), 780–787.

Han, S. (2015), 'The giant city-regions in China's new urbanization', in T. Wong, S. Han and H. Zhang (eds), *Population Mobility, Urban Planning and Management in China*, New York: Springer International Publishing, 145–169.

Han, S. and S. Wong (1994), 'The influence of Chinese reform and pre-reform policies on urban growth in the 1980s', *Urban Geography*, 15(6), 537–564.

Han, S. and S. Wong (1998), 'Revolution, space and urbanization: The ideological foundation of Chinese urban development', *Asian Profile*, 26, 91–120.

Hao, J. and M. Zhao (2013), '"The middle-income-trap" and new thinkings on China's urbanization strategy', *Urban Planning Forum*, (5), 6–13.

Henderson, J. (2003), 'The urbanization process and economic growth: The so what question', *Journal of Economic Growth*, 8(1), 47–71.

Holz, C. (2002), 'Institutional constraints on the quality of statistics in China', *China Information*, 16(1), 25–67.

Howard, E. ([1898]2010), *Tomorrow: A Peaceful Path to Real Reform*, London: Swann Sonneschein. Cambridge: Cambridge University Press.

Hsing, Y. (2012), *The Great Urban Transformation: Politics of Land and Property in China*, Oxford: Oxford University Press.

Hu, F. (2012), 'Migration, remittances, and children's high school attendance: The case of rural China'. *International Journal of Educational Development*, 32, 401–411.

Hu, F., Z. Xu and Y. Chen (2011), 'Circular migration or permanent stay? Evidence from China's rural–urban Migration', *China Economic Review*, 22, 64–74.

Huang, Y. (2005), *Selling China: Foreign Direct Investment During the Reform Era*, Cambridge: Cambridge University Press.

Huang, Y. (2008), *Capitalism with Chinese Characteristics: Entrepreneurship and the State* (Vol. 1). Cambridge: Cambridge University Press.

International Air Transport Association (2014), 'IATA annual review', retrieved on September 18, 2015 from www.iata.org/publications/Pages/annual-review.aspx.

IUSSP (International Union for the Scientific Study of Population) (1982),

'Multilingual demographic dictionary', retrieved on September 18, 2015 from http://en-ii.demopaedia.org/wiki/Main_Page.

Jing, X. and F. Ma (2012), 'The study of rural migrant workers—adaptation to urban life in the perspective of intergenerational difference', *South China Population*, 27(3), 65–72.

Jorgenson, D. (1961), 'The development of a dual economy', *The Economic Journal*, 309–334.

Kasarda, J. and E. Crenshaw (1991), 'Third world urbanization: Dimensions, theories, and determinants', *Annual Review of Sociology*, (17), 467–501.

Kentor, J. (1981), 'Structural determinants of peripheral urbanization: The effects of international dependence', *American Sociological Review*, (46), 201–211.

Kirkby, R. (1985), *Urbanization in China: Town and Country in a Developing Economy 1949–2000 AD*, New York: Columbia University Press.

Kleinwechter, U. (2012), 'Rural–urban migration in China: An analytical framework of migrants contributions to rural development', *Journal of Alternative Perspectives in the Social Sciences*, 4(4), 757–789.

Knox, P. (1994), *Urbanization: An Introduction to Urban Geography*, Upper Saddle River, NJ: Prentice Hall.

Kuznets, S. (1955), 'Economic growth and income inequality', *American Economic Review*, 49, 1–28.

Lee, E. (1966), 'A theory of migration', *Demography*, 3(1), 47–57.

Lee, J. (2000), 'Changes in the source of China's regional inequality', *China Economic Review*, 11, 232–245.

LeGates, R. and Y. Ye (2012), *Coordinating Urban and Rural Development in China*, Cheltenham, UK and Northampton, MA, USA: Edward Elgar Publishing.

Lewis, A. (1954), 'Economic development with unlimited supplies of labor', *The Manchester School of Economic and Social Studies*, 22(2), 139–191.

Lewis, W. (1968), *Reflections on Unlimited Labour*, Princeton, NJ: Woodrow Wilson School of Public and International Affairs.

Li, B. and X. An (2010), 'Migrants as a source of revenue in towns in China', *Environment and Urbanization*, 22(1), 51–66.

Li, G. (2008), 'The analysis and evaluation of the compatible relationship between industrialization and urbanization in China', *Areal Research and Development*, 27(5), 6–16.

Liang, L., J. Chang, C. Wu and K. Borchard (2002), 'A study on land system innovations in the construction of towns in China', *Chinese Geographical Science*, 12(1), 80–85.

Lin, G. (2007), 'Reproducing spaces of Chinese urbanization: New city-based and land centered urban transformation', *Urban Studies*, 44(9), 1827–1855.

Liu, Y., Y. Liu, Y. Chen and H. Long (2010), 'The process and driving forces of rural hollowing in China under rapid urbanization', *Journal of Geographical Sciences*, 20(6), 876–888.

Lora-Wainwright, A. (2012), 'Rural China in ruins: The rush to urbanize China's countryside is opening a moral battleground', *Anthropology Today*, 28, 8–13.

Lu, D. and V. Sit (2001), 'China's regional development policies: A review', in D. Lu and V. Sit (eds), *China's Regional Disparities: Issues and Policies*, Hauppage, NY: Nova Science Publishers, 19–38.

Lu, J. and C. Han (2013), 'Discussions on towns and the path of development of Chinese urbanization', *Studies on the Socialism with Chinese Characteristics*, 1, 98–104.

Lu, M. and Z. Chen (2006), 'Urbanization, urban-biased policies, and urban–rural inequality in China, 1987–2001', *The Chinese Economy*, 39, 42–63.

Ma, L. (2002), 'Urban transformation in China, 1949–2000: A review and research agenda', *Environment and Planning A*, 34(9), 1545–1569.

Ma, L. (2005), 'Urban administrative restructuring, changing scale relations and local economic development', *China Political Geography*, 24, 477–497.

Ma, L. and G. Cui (1987), 'Administrative changes and urban population in China', *Annals of the Association of American Geographers*, 77(3), 373–395.

Ma, L. and C. Lin (1993), 'Development of towns in China: A case study of Guangdong province', *Population and Development Review*, 19(3), 583–606.

Ma, L. and F. Wu (2004), *Restructuring the Chinese City: Changing Society, Economy and Space*, London: Routledge.

Mackenzie, P.W. (2002), 'Strangers in the city: The hukou and urban citizenship in China', *Journal of International Affairs*, 56(1), 305–320.

Mallee, H. (1995), 'China's household registration system under reform', *Development and Change*, 26, 1–29.

Mallee, H. (2006), 'Book review: Organizing through division and exclusion: China's hukou system, by Wang, F., 2005', *China Journal*, 55, 173–176.

Maslow, A. (1943), 'A theory of human motivation', *Psychological Review*, 50(4), 370.

Massey, D. (1995), *Spatial Divisions of Labor: Social Structures and the Geography of Production*, London: Psychology Press.

McGee, T. (1988), 'Industrial capital, labor-force formation and the urbanization process in Malaysia', *International Journal of Urban and Regional Research*, 12(3), 356–374.

McGee, T. (1991a), 'Eurocentrism in geography—the case of Asian urbanization', *Canadian Geographer*, 35(4), 332–344.

McGee, T. (1991b), 'The emergence of Desakota regions in Asia: Expanding a hypothesis', in N. Ginsburg et al. (ed.), *Extended Metropolis: Settlement Transition in Asia*, Honolulu: University of Hawaii Press, 3–26.

McGee, T., G. Lin, A. Marton, M. Wang and J. Wu (2007), *China's Urban Space: Development under Market Socialism*, London and New York: Routledge.

Miller, T. (2012), *China's Urban Billion: The Story Behind the Biggest Migration in Human History*, London: Zed Books.

Mu, R. and D. van de Walle (2011), 'Left behind to farm? Women's labor re-allocation in rural China', *Labour Economics*, 18, S83–S97.

Murphy, R. (1999), 'Return migrant entrepreneurs and economic diversification in two countries in south Jiangxi, China', *Journal of International Development*, (4), 661–672.

Myers (1997), 'Latin American cities: Internationally embedded but nationally influential', *Latin American Research Review*, 32(1), 109–123.

Northam, R. (1979), *Urban Geography* (2nd edn), New York: John Wiley & Sons.

Notestein, F. (1945), 'Population: The long view', in T. Schultz (ed.), *Food for the World*, Chicago, IL: University of Chicago Press, 36–57.

O'Brien, K. and L. Li (2006), *Rightful Resistance in Rural China*, Cambridge: Cambridge University Press.

Orfield, M. (2011), *American Metropolitics: The New Suburban Reality*, Washington, DC: Brookings Institution Press.

Pannell, C. (2002), 'China's continuing urban transition', *Environment and Planning A*, 34(9), 1571–1589.

PCWorld (2015), 'Foxconn expects robots to take over more factory work', retrieved on September 18, 2015 from www.pcworld.com/article/2890032/foxconn-expects-robots-to-take-over-more-factory-work.html.

Perkins, D. (2013), *Agricultural Development in China, 1368–1968* (2nd edn), Piscataway, NJ: Transaction Publishers (first edition published in 1984).

Quigley, J. (2009), 'Urbanization, agglomeration, and economic development', in M. Spence, P. Clarke and M. Buckley (eds), *Urbanization and Growth*, Washington, DC: World Bank, Chapter 4.

Ran, M. and B. Berry (1989), 'Underurbanization policies assessed: China, 1949–1986', *Urban* Geography, 10(2), 111–120.

Ranis, G. (2004), 'Arthur Lewis's contribution to development thinking and policy', *The Manchester School*, 72(6), 712–723.
Ravenstein, E. (1885), 'The laws of migration', *Journal of the Statistical Society of London*, 48(2), 167–235.
Ravenstein, E. (1889), 'The laws of migration', *Journal of the Royal Statistical Society*, 52(2), 241–305.
Redfield, R. (1954), *The Role of Cities in Economic Development and Cultural Change*, Chicago, IL: University of Chicago Press.
Regional Plan Association (2015), *America 2050*, retrieved on September 18, 2015 from www.america2050.org/.
Ren, X. (2013), *Urban China*, Cambridge: Polity Press.
Rassweiler, A. (2009), 'iPhone 3GS carries $178.96 BOM and manufacturing cost, iSuppli teardown reveals', *iSuppli*, June 24.
Ricardo, D. ([1817]2005), *The Works and Correspondence of David Ricardo, ed. Piero Sraffa with the Collaboration of M.H. Dobb*, Indianapolis: Liberty Fund, 11.
Richard, G. (1970), 'Rajput clans and urban settlements in northern India', in G. Richard (ed.), *Urban India: Society, Space, and Image*, Durham, NC: Duke University Program in Comparative Studies on Southern Asia, 167–185.
Rostow, W. (1956), 'The take-off into self-sustained growth', *The Economic Journal*, 25–48.
Rozman, G. (ed.) (1989), *The Modernization of China* (Chinese Translation), Shanghai: The Shanghai People Press, 184–210, 473–498.
Sassen, S. (1998), 'The impact of the new technologies and globalization on cities', *Globalization and the World of Large Cities*, Tokyo: United Nations University Press, 391–409.
Sassen, S. (2001), *The Global City* (2nd edn), New York, London, Tokyo, Princeton, NJ: Princeton University Press.
Sassen, S. (2002), *Global Networks, Linked Cities*, London and New York: Routledge.
Scott, A. and M. Storper (2014), 'The nature of cities: The scope and limits of urban theory', *International Journal of Urban and Regional Research*, 39(1), 1–15.
Shen, J. (2002), 'State-sponsored and spontaneous urbanization in the Pearl River Delta of south China, 1980–1998', *Urban Geography*, 23(7), 674–694.
Shen, J. (2005), 'Counting urban population in Chinese censuses 1953–2000: Changing definitions, problems and solutions', *Population, Space and Place*, 11(5), 381–400.
Shen, J. (2006), 'Estimating urbanization levels in Chinese provinces in 1982–2000', *International Statistical Review*, 74(1), 89–107.

Simmel, G. ([1903]1950), '"Die Grossstätde und das Geistesleben" reprinted as "The metropolis and mental life"', in Jan Lin and Christopher Mele (eds), *The Urban Sociology Reader* (2nd edn), London and New York: Routledge, 23–31.

Sit, V. (2001a), 'Regional disparities in China: Background of related theories and previous studies', in V. Sit and D. Lu (eds), *China's Regional Disparities: Issues and Policies*, Hauppage, NY: Nova Science Publishers, 1–18.

Sit, V. (2001b), 'Globalization, foreign direct investment and urbanization in developing countries', *World Bank Discussion Papers*, (415), 11–46.

Sit, V. and C. Yang (1997), 'Foreign-investment-induced exo-urbanisation in the Pearl River Delta, China', *Urban Studies*, 34(4), 647–677.

Skinner, W. (1977), *Cities and the Hierarchy of Local Systems: The City in Late Imperial China*, Stanford: Stanford University Press.

Stiglitz, J. (2015), *The Great Divide*, New York: W.W. Norton.

Taylor, P. (2015), 'The world city network', in R. LeGates and F. Stout (eds), *The City Reader* (6th edn), London and New York: Routledge, 92–102.

Taylor, P. and B. DeRudder (2015), *World City Network: A Global Urban Analysis* (2nd edn), London and New York: Routledge.

Tian, L. (2014), *Property Rights, Land Values, and Urban Development*, Cheltenham, UK and Northampton, MA, USA: Edward Elgar Publishing.

Timberlake, M. and J. Kentor (1983), 'Economic dependence, over-urbanization, and economic growth: A study of less developed countries', *The Sociological Quarterly*, 24(3), 489–507.

Todaro, M. (1969), 'A model of labor migration and urban unemployment in less developed countries', *The American Economic Review*, 138–148.

Tönnies, F. ([1887]2002), *Gemeinschaft and Gesellschaft*, reprinted as *Community and Society*, Mineola, NY: Dover.

United Nations (UN) (2012, 2014), *World Urbanization Prospects: The 2012 (2014) Revision*, online edition. New York: United Nations, retrieved on October 2, 2015 from http://esa.un.org/unpd/wup/FinalReport/WUP2014-Report.pdf.

United Nations (UN) (2015), 'UN data', retrieved on September 19, 2015 from http://data.un.org/.

United Nations Population Division (UNPD) (2013, 2014), *Urban Agglomerations 2013 (2014)*, online edition. New York: United Nations.

US Census Bureau (2015), 'State and county quick facts', retrieved on September 19, 2015 from http://quickfacts.census.gov/qfd/meta/long_LND110210.htm, January 16.

US Social Security Administration (US-SSA) (2014), 'Monthly Snapshot', September.

Wallerstein, I. (2011), *The Modern World-System I: Capitalist Agriculture and the Origins of the European World-Economy in the Sixteenth Century, with a New Prologue* (Vol. 1), Berkeley, CA: University of California Press.

Wang, F. (2004), 'Reformed migration control and new-targeted people: China's hukou system in the 2000s', *The China Quarterly*, 177, 115–132.

Wang, F. (2005), *Organizing through Division and Exclusion: China's Hukou System*, Stanford, CA: Stanford University Press, 255–268.

Wang, X. (2010), 'Questions on focus on the development of small and medium cities and towns', *China Market*, 46, 44–48.

Weber, M. and H. Gerth (1951), *The Religion of China*, New York: Free Press, 237.

Wei, Y. (2000), *Development in China: States, Globalization, and Inequality*, London: Routledge.

Wirth, L. (1938), 'Urbanism as a way of life', *American Journal of Sociology*, 1–24.

World Bank (2009), 'World development report 2009: Reshaping economic geography', retrieved on September 19, 2015 from https://openknowledge.worldbank.org/handle/10986/5991.

World Bank (2014a), 'GDP per capita, PPP (current international $)', retrieved on September 19, 2015 from http://data.worldbank.org/indicator/NY.GDP.PCAP.PP.CD/countries?display=default.

World Bank (2014b), 'World development indicators 2013, Poverty gap at $1.25 a day (PPP) (%)', retrieved on September 19, 2015 from http://data.worldbank.org/indicator/SI.POV.GAPS.

World Bank (2015), 'Life expectancy at birth, total (years)', retrieved on September 19, 2015 from http://data.worldbank.org/indicator/SP.DYN.LE00.IN/countries?page=6&display=default.

World Bank Web (2014), 'Updated income classifications', retrieved on September 19, 2015 from http://data.worldbank.org/news/2015-country-classifications.

World Health Organization (WHO) (2014), 'Ambient air pollution database', retrieved on September 19, 2015 from www.who.int/phe/health_topics/outdoorair/databases/cities/en/.

Wu, F. (1995), 'Urban processes in the face of China's transition to a socialist market economy', *Environment and Planning C*, 13, 159–177.

Wu, F. (2002), 'China's changing urban governance in the transition towards a more market-oriented economy', *Urban Studies*, 39(7), 1071–1093.

Wu, F. (ed.) (2006), *Globalization and the Chinese City*, London: Routledge.

Wu, F. (2015), *Planning for Growth: Urban and Regional Planning in China (RTPI Library Series)*, London: Routledge.

Wu, L. (2013), 'Decentralization and hukou reforms in China', *Policy and Society*, 32, 33–42.

Wu, W. and P. Gaubatz (2012), *The Chinese City*, London: Routledge.

Xu, J. and A. Yeh (2010), *Governance and Planning of Mega-city Regions: An International Comparative Perspective*, Oxford and New York: Routledge.

Yang, C. and H. Liao (2010), 'Industrial agglomeration of Hong Kong and Taiwanese manufacturing investment in China: A town-level analysis in Dongguan', *Annals of Regional Science*, 45(3): 487–517.

Yang, D. (1990), 'Patterns of China's regional development strategy', *China Quarterly*, 122, 230–257.

Yang, X. and R. Rice (1994), 'An equilibrium model endogenizing the emergence of a dual structure between urban and rural sectors', *Journal of Urban Economics*, 25, 346–368.

Ye, J. and P. Lu (2011), 'Differentiated childhoods: Impacts of rural labor migration on left-behind children in China', *The Journal of Peasant Studies*, 38(2), 355–377.

Ye, Y. and R. LeGates (2013), *Coordinating Urban and Rural Development in China: Learning from Chengdu*, Cheltenham, UK and Northampton, MA, USA: Edward Elgar Publishing.

Ye, Y., R. LeGates and B. Qin (2013), 'Coordinated urban–rural development planning in China', *Journal of the American Planning Association*, 79(2), 125–137.

Young, A. (1928), 'Increasing returns and economic progress', *The Economic Journal*, 527–542.

Zhang, F. (2014), *Chinese Urbanization and the Global Economy*, Cheltenham, UK and Northampton, MA, USA: Edward Elgar Publishing.

Zhang, L. (2004), *China's Limited Urbanization: Under Socialism and Beyond*, Hauppage, NY: Nova Science Publishers.

Zhang L. (2008), 'Conceptualizing China's urbanization under reforms', *Habitat International*, 32, 452–470.

Zhang, L. (2012), 'Small towns but grand strategies—a study on the development of small towns in provinces with net out-migration', *Urban Planning Forum*, (1), 23–32 (in Chinese).

Zhang, L. and S. Han (2009), 'Regional disparities in China's urbanization: An examination of trends 1982–2007', *International Development Planning Review*, 31(4), 355–376.

Zhang, L. and M. Zhao (2014), 'Roles of rural towns in China's rapid urbanization—case study of Hubei Province', in Wong Tai-Chee,

Sun Sheng Han and Hongmei Zhang (eds), *Population Mobility, Urban Planning and Management in China*, Berlin: Springer, Chapter 7.

Zhang, L. and X. Zhao (1998), 'Re-examining China's "urban" concept and the level of urbanization', *The China Quarterly*, 154, 330–381.

Zhao, M. and Y. Zhang (2009), 'Development and urbanization: A revisit of Chenery–Syrquin's patterns of development', *The Annals of Regional Science*, 43(4), 907–924.

Zhao, Y. (2002), 'Leaving the countryside: Rural-to-urban migration decisions in China', *American Economic Review*, (2), 281–286.

Zhou, S., J. Dai and J. Bu (2013), 'City size distributions in China 1949 to 2010 and the impacts of government policies', *Cities*, 32(SI1), 51–57.

Zhou, Y. and L. Ma (2003), 'China's urbanization levels: Reconstructing a baseline from the fifth population census', *China Quarterly*, 173, 176–196.

Zhou, Y. and F. Yu (1988), 'Discussion on the urban development policy', *City Planning Review*, 3, 33–36.

Zhu, J. (2002), 'Urban development under ambiguous property rights: A case of China's transition economy', *International Journal of Urban and Regional Research*, 26(1), 41–57.

Zhu, K. and R. Prosterman (2007), *Securing Land Rights for Chinese Farmers: A Leap Forward For Stability and Growth*, Washington, DC: Cato Institute.

Zhu, K. and R. Prosterman (2010), *Status of Farmers' Land Rights in Today's China: Findings and Preliminary Recommendations from a Seventeen-province Survey*, Seattle: Landesa.

Zhu, K., R. Prosterman, J. Riedinger, J. Ye and H. Wang (2011), *A Seventeen-Province Survey on Farmers' Land Rights*, Seattle, WA: Landesa.

Zhu, L. (2003), 'The hukou system of the People's Republic of China: A critical appraisal under international standards of internal movement and residence', *Chinese Journal of International Law*, (2), 519–565.

Zhu, Y. (1999), *New Paths to Urbanization in China: Seeking More Balanced Patterns*, Hauppage, NY: Nova Science Publishers.

Zhu, Y. (2003b), 'The floating population's household strategies and the role of migration in China's regional development and integration', *International Journal of Population Geography*, 9(6), 485–502.

Zhu, Y. (2007), 'China's floating population and their settlement intention in the cities: Beyond the hukou reform', *Habitat International*, 31(1), 65–76.

Zhu, Z., C. Zhou and Y. Sun (2009), *Efforts to Prevent Floating Population Crimes from the Start. Zhejiang S2009, and Policy Analysis of Towns*, Beijing: China Building Industry.

CHINESE REFERENCES

All China Federation of Trade Unions (ACFTU) (2011), 'Occupational disease increasing 50% every year and 90% are migrant rural laborers', retrieved on August 21, 2014 from www.eeo.com.cn/2011/1216/218105.shtml.

Bai, N. and H. Song (2002), *Research on Chinese Rural Migrant Labor Reflux*, Beijing: Chinese Financial and Economic Publishing House.

Cai, F. (2011b), *Beyond the Demographic Dividend*, Beijing: Social Sciences Academic Press.

Caixin Web (2011), 'Vietnam, replacing China, becomes the largest manufacturing base of Nike Company', retrieved on September 19, 2015 from http://economy.caixin.com/2011-06-29/100305551.html.

Central Government Web (2014), 'In 2013, of the total GDP of the Yangtze River Delta region reached to nearly 10,000 billion RMB, accounted for 17.2% of the whole country', retrieved on May 20, 2015 from www.gov.cn/zhuanti/2014-02/13 /content_2604103.htm.

Chen, D. (2000), 'The planning study of towns targeted at the community development', *Urban Planning Review*, (4), 44–47, 64.

Chen, M. and T. Liu (2004), 'Analysis on system obstructions to small town sustainable development and countermeasures in China', *China Population, Resources and Environment*, (1), 60–63.

Chen, M., W. Liu and X. Tao (2013), 'Evolution and assessment on China's urbanization 1960–2010: Under-urbanization or over-urbanization?', *Habitat International*, 38, 25–33.

Chen, Y. and L. Zhang (2014), 'The study on decision-making discrepancies of urbanization on account of life cycle theory—based on case studies in Haimen rural region', Symposium Proceedings of County Territory and Development under the New Urbanization Perspective.

Cheng, Y., B. Yang and M. Zhao (2011), 'Some features and trends of urbanization in central China: Thoughts based on empirical studies of towns and villages in the north Anhui province', *Urban Planning Forum*, (2), 67–76.

Chengdu Bureau of Statistics (2015), Main data on the sixth census for Chengdu metropolis (No. 2), retrieved on October 5, 2015 from www.cdstats.chengdu.gov.cn/detail.asp?ID=65616&ClassID=020705.

Chengdu Coordinated Urban Rural Development Commission (CCURDC) (2012), 'Report on coordinated urban–rural development in Chengdu', Chengdu: CCURDC.

Chengdu Institute of Planning and Design (CIPD) (2010), 'A working progress report of township and village planning in coordinated urban-rural development of Chengdu', Chengdu: CIPD.

Chengdu Municipal Government (CMG) (2008), *Programs for Rural Areas and Guidelines on the Setup of New Village Governance Mechanisms*, Chengdu: Chengdu Municipal Government.

China News Web (2013), 'About 50 million rural elders are left behind and the problems of disability and no caring are obvious', retrieved on September 19, 2015 from www.chinanews.com/gn/2013/09-20/5302461.shtml.

China News Web (2014a), 'Fast increase of Chinese migrant labors' wages', retrieved on September 19, 2015 from www.chinanews.com/gn/2014/02-20/5861652.shtml.

China News Web (2014b), 'The cargo traffic of main line of Yangtze River reaches 1.92 billion tons', retrieved on May 20, 2015 from http://finance.chinanews.com/cj/2014/01-12/5726116.shtml.

China News Web (2015), 'Chinese oversea tourists has increased 13% in 2014', retrieved on September 19, 2015 from http://finance.chinanews.com/cj/2014/01-06/5703019.shtml.

City House (2015), 'The rank of housing price in China', retrieved on September 19, 2015 from www.cityhouse.cn/default/forsalerank.html.

Civil Aviation Administration of China (2013), *Statistical Data on Civil Aviation of China*, Beijing: Civil Aviation Press.

Chinese Society for Urban Studies and Ministry of Housing and Urban–Rural Development of PRC (CSUS and MHUDP) (2009), *The Development Report of Chinese Rural Towns and Villages Construction*, Beijing: China City Press.

Cui, G. (1989), 'Review and prospect of research on China urbanization in last decade', *Research Study and Exploit*, 8(1), 1–6.

Cui, G. and R. Ma (1999), 'Urbanization from below in China: Its development and mechanisms', *ACTA Geographic Sinica*, 54(2), 12–21.

Cui, Q., Y. Wang and J. Shi (2012), 'The integration and transition of the administrative division during the change of urban–rural relationship in metropolis', *Human Geography*, 1(27), 82–86.

Dai, J. (2004), 'Province directly administrating county (city): Local administrative system's major reform and innovation', *China Reform*, (6), 69–72.

Dai, L., Y. Zheng, F. Xue and G. Li (2014), 'The characteristics and dynamics of the extended metropolitan regions in inland China: Case study of the Changzhutan', *Urban Studies*, 21(10), 4–11.

Du, W., H. He and P. Zhang (2014), 'Small towns, urban agglomerations and pollution', *Urban Problems*, (5), 97–101.

Duan, C. and Y. Sun (2006), 'Statistical standard changes for flowing population in China', *Population Research*, (4), 70–76.

Duan, C., G. Yang, F. Zhang and X. Lu (2008), 'Nine trends of China's floating population change since the reform and opening-up', *Population Research*, 32(6), 30–43.

Fan, J. and M. Tian (2003), 'Relative analysis and provincial differences of China's urbanization and non-agricultural development', *Scientia Geographica Sinica*, (6), 641–648.

Fang, C. (2009), 'Research progress and general definition about identification standards of urban agglomeration space', *Urban Planning Forum*, 4, 1–6.

Fei, X. ([1984]2004), *The Aim for Enriching the People (The report for Chinese country investigation)*, Shanghai, Shanghai People's Press.

Feng, J. (2001), 'Review on the research of the small cities and towns development in China since the 1980s', *Urban Planning Forum*, (3), 28–34, 79.

Feng, S. (2004), *Study on Motive Force of China's Rural Urbanization*, Beijing: Economic Science Press, 12–13.

Fortune China Web (2014), 'Chinese Top 500 companies on stock market', retrieved on September 19, 2015 from www.fortunechina.com/fortune500/c/2014-07/14/content_212975.htm.

Ge, Y., X. Xu and X. Yan (2003), 'A comprehensive appraisal of the level of urbanization in China', *Human Geography*, (1), 49–52.

Gong, H. (2005), 'Towns: preferences of 'the third part of society', *Urban Problems*, 2, 13–15, 25.

Gu, C. (1998), 'Analysis on China's bottom-up urbanization system', *Social Sciences in China*, (2), 60–70.

Gu, C. and M. Zhang (2000), 'The strategy research for Yangtze River Delta megalopolis', *Urban Research*, 1, 7–11.

Gu, R. and C. Gu (2006), 'Analysis of urban public policy', *Urban Planning*, (9), 48–51.

Gu, S. (1994), *Modern Population Flowing and Urbanization in China*, Wuhan, China: Wuhan University Press.

Guangdong Province Human Resources and Social Security Department (2014), 'The enterprise employment monitoring situation of the first quarter in 2014', retrieved on September 19, 2015 from www.gdhrss.gov.cn/publicfiles/business/htmlfiles/gdhrss/gzdt/201405/47363.html.

Guo, X (2010), 'From selective institution to public institution—urban hukou reform orientations', *Social Science*, (3), 65–71.

Han, J. (2009), *Strategic Research on China's Migrant Workers*, Shanghai: Shanghai Far East Publishing House.

Han, S. and S. Wong (1998), 'Revolution, space and urbanization: The ideological foundation of Chinese urban development', *Asian Profile*, 26, 91–120.

Hao, J. and M. Zhao (2013), 'The "middle-income-trap" and new thinkings on China's urbanization strategy', *Urban Planning Forum*, 5, 6–13.

He, N. (2006), 'Theoretical study on Chinese contemporary city (197902005)', Doctoral Dissertation, Fudan University.

He, Q. and J. Liu (2009), 'Analysis on the realization route and the effect of province directly administrating county (city) system', *Economic Geography*, 29(5), 741–745.

Hu, P. and Y. Yang (2014), 'Migrant workers: Institutional factors and policy making', *Journal of Sichuan Normal University (Social Sciences Edition)*, 5, 60–65.

Hu, X. (2008), 'Debates on hukou reform', *Xiao Kang*, (2), 30–32.

Huang X. and B. Lin (2001), 'On the western small town development in China', *Urban Planning Forum*, (2), 56–58, 62–80.

Jiefang Daily (2014), 'The contributions of the top 100 transnational companies reaches 20% of Shanghai's GDP', retrieved on September 19, 2015 from http://sh.sina.com.cn/news/economy/2014-08-13/0657105783.html. 2014/09/09.

Jin, R., Z. Ma, G. Xiao and Z. Gao (2014), 'Developing medium-sized cities is scientific process of China's urbanization', *Geological Survey and Research*, (2), 81–84.

Jin, Y. and Z. Qiao (2004), 'On town industrial development', *China Population, Resources and Environment*, 2004(1), 64–68.

Labor and Social Security Bureau in Guizhou Province (LSSBGP) (2011), 'Investigations on returning migrants', retrieved on May 11, 2015 from http://gz.lss.gov.cn/gzldt/72635941449105408/.

Li, J. (2004), 'The international comparison of China's urbanization level', *Urban Studies*, (3), 1–10.

Li, Q. (2003), 'An analysis of push and pull factors in the migration of rural workers in China', *Social Sciences in China*, (1), 125–137.

Li, Q. and W. Long (2009), 'Analysis of influencing factors on willingness to return hometowns among rural migrant workers', *Chinese Rural Economy*, (2), 46–54.

Li, S., P. Yan and P. Jiang (2010), 'Study on the territorial division of labor and spatial pattern of urbanization in the context of globalization', *Progress in Geography*, 29(8), 943–951.

Li, W. and Y. Chen (2001), 'Chinese population urbanization level and structure deviation', *Chinese Journal of Population Science*, (5), 10–18.

Li, X. (2012), 'The diamond structure: On the evolution of the national spatial strategy', *Urban Planning Forum*, 2, 1–8.

Li, X. and J. Yin (2012), 'Research review on the effects of regional integration on industry', *City Planning Review*, 36(5), 91–96.

Li, Y., Y. Guan and Q. Yao (2014), 'Review on the researches of "provincial tube country" system reform', *Journal of Lanzhou Commercial College*, (3), 91–97.

Li, Y., H. Ai, F. Feng and S. Dong (2006), 'Advance in research of small town environment in 1990s', *Progress in Geography*, (1), 90–101.

Liu, C. (1988), 'Mid-size cities are key policy of Chinese urbanization', *Finance and Economics*, (7), 49–52.

Liu, C. (2010), 'China's new generation of migrant workers: Characteristics, problems and countermeasures', *Population Research*, (2), 34–39, 55–56.

Liu, J. (2004), 'Analysis on the phenomenon of "administrative economy" appeared during China's transition', *Theory Frontier*, (10), 20–22.

Liu, S., T. Chen and J. Cai (2003), 'International differences of the relationship between non-agriculturalization and urbanization of China', *Acta Geographica Sinica*, 58(6), 937–946.

Liu, S., J. Zhang, Y. Hou and P. Liu (2012), '"Trap" or "high wall", the real challenge and strategy for China's economy: An analysis based on international comparison', in B. Zheng (ed.), *Middle Income Trap: Case Studies from Latin America and Caribbean*, Beijing: Modern World Press, 285–320.

Liu, X. (2009), *The History of Chinese Educated Youth Heavy Tide: 1966–1980*, Beijing: Contemporary China Press.

Liu, Z. (2000), *Chinese Tax System Evolution in 50 Years*, Beijing: Chinese Tax Press.

Lou, J. (2006), 'To improve transferring payment institution and to promote basic public service equalization', *China State Finance*, (3), 6–8.

Lu, X. (1997), *The Transition of Social Structure*, Beijing: Chinese Social Science Press.

Lu, Y. (2008), 'Does hukou still matter? The household registration system and its impact on social stratification and mobility in China', *Social Sciences in China*, (1), 149–162.

Luo, Z. (2005), 'China's administrative region division reform and mechanism', *Urban Planning Review*, 29(8), 29–35.

Ma, F. (2001), 'Research on changes of contemporary Chinese household registration system', Doctoral Thesis, Chinese Academy of Social Sciences Graduate School.

Ma, R. and F. Wu (2007), 'Reconstruction of Chinese urban space—the process of diversification and ample space', in F. Wu, R. Ma and J. Zhang (eds), *Transformation and Reconstruction—Multidimensional Perspective of China Urban Development*, Nanjing: Southeast University Press, 1–21.

MAC (Ministry of Agriculture of China) (2003), *China TVEs Statistics Materials (1978–2012)*, Beijing, China Agriculture Press.

MAC (Ministry of Agriculture of China) (2009, 2010, 2011, 2012), *China TVEs and Agro-product Processing Industry Yearbook*, Beijing, China Agriculture Press.

MacFarquhar, R. and J. Fairbank (1990), *The Cambridge History of China.14: The People's Republic, Part 1, The Emergence of Revolutionary China*, Beijing: China Social Sciences Press, 67.

Meng, X. (1990), 'China's urbanization's "two tracks into one" path', *Urban Problems*, 1, 12–15.

Meng, X. (2005), 'Strategic choice of the development of towns: Practical proof and theoretical analysis', *Population Journal*, (2), 9–15.

Nanfang Daily (2008), 'August 6, residential permit is the starting point to break the ice of hukou system', retrieved on September 19, 2015 from http://epaper.southcn.com/nfdaily/html/2008-08/06/content_6677628.htm.

National Bureau Statistics of China (NBSC-ccs) (2005), *China Compendium of Statistics 1949–2004*, Beijing: China Statistics Press.

National Population and Family Planning Committee (NPFPC) (2012, 2013, 2014), *Report on China's Migrant Population Development*, Beijing: China Population Publishing House (in Chinese).

NBSC (2001), Communiqué on major figures of the 2000 population census (No.1), Online edition, retrieved on September 19, 2015 from www.stats.gov.cn/tjsj/tjgb/rkpcgb/qgrkpcgb/200203/t20020331_30314.html.

NBSC (2009, 2014), Data compilation of the cost and benefit of agricultural products in China, Beijing: China Statistics Press.

NBSC (2015a), 'National economy is stable in 2014', retrieved on September 19, 2015 from www.stats.gov.cn/tjsj/zxfb/201501/t20150120_671037.html.

NBSC (2015b), Statistical communiqué of the People's Republic of China on the 2014 national economic and social development, retrieved on September 19, 2015 from www.stats.gov.cn/english/PressRelease/201502/t20150228_687439.html.

NBSC-census (1984, 1992, 2002, 2012), *Data of National Population Census of China in 1982, 1990, 2000, 2010*, Beijing: China Statistics Press.

NBSC-1% census (1988, 1996, 2006), *Data of 1% Sampling Censuses in China in 1987, 1995 and 2005*, Beijing: China Statistics Press.

NBSC-cpesy (2010–2014), *China Population and Employment Statistics Yearbook*, Beijing: China Statistics Press.

NBSC-cpy (2005), *Chinese Population Yearbook*, Beijing: China Statistics Press.

NBSC-csy (1984–2014), *China Statistical Yearbook*, Beijing: China Statistics Press.

NBSC-csye (2013), *China Statistical Yearbook on Environment*, Beijing: China Statistics Press.

NBSC-cts (2004, 2008, 2010, 2012, 2013), *China Township Statistics*, Beijing: China Statistics press.

NBSC-usy (1985–2013), *Urban Statistical Yearbook*, Beijing: China Statistics Press.

Ni, P. (2008), *Chinese City Competitiveness Report*, Beijing: Social Science Document Publishing House.

Ning, Y. (1998), 'New process of urbanization—dynamics and features of urbanization in China since 1990', *ACTA Geographica Sinica*, 53(5), 470–477.

Ning, Y. and F. Zhang (2012), 'On the research of large city clusters of China', *Urban Planning Forum*, (1), 48–53.

Ning, Y., Q. Shi and Z. Zha (1998), 'The formation mechanism and cross-regional planning studies of the Yangtze Delta interlocking metropolitan areas', *City Planning Review*, (1), 6–20.

Ning, Y., D. Xiang and L. Wei (2002), 'Study on the human settlement environment with three towns in the Shanghai suburban areas as the case', *Urban Planning Review*, (10), 31–35.

Niu, X. (2000), 'Restudies on the strategy of towns' development', *Planners*, (5), 96–98.

Peng, Z. (2003), 'Regional coordination of towns development in developed area—taking Duqiao, a town in Zhejiang province, as the case', *Urban Studies*, (4), 17–22.

People Daily Web (2015), 'The first time for ODI outstripping to FDI (Market Views)', retrieved on September 19, 2015 from http://paper.people.com.cn/rmrbhwb/html/2015-01/26/content_1526312.htm.

PRC (People's Republic of China) (1953), Constitution of 1953.

PRC (1958), Regulations of the People's Republic of China on hukou (Hukou Dengji Tiaoli).

PRC (1989a), China's Urban Neighborhood Committee Organization Law.

PRC (1989b), City Planning Act.

PRC (2014), NNSUP (National New Style Urbanization Plan: 2014–2020).

PRC-MHRSS (Ministry of Human Resources and Social Security) (2010, 2011, 2013), China Annual Human Resources and Social Security Development Statistics Bulletin in 2010, 2011, 2013.

PRC-MHURD (Ministry of Housing and Urban–Rural Development) (2014), Statistics of city population in 2013.

PRC-MSC (Ministry of Social Security of China) (1951), The Regulation on Urban Household Management.

PRC-MSC (1955), Directive for establishing permanent hukou system (Guanyu Jianli Jingchang Hukou Dengji Zhidu de Zhishi).

PRC-MSC (1984), The report on the adjustment of the official towns setting up standards (Guanyu Tiaozheng Jianzhizhen Biaozhun de Baogao).

PRC-MSC (1986), Report on standards for setting up cities and conditions for cities leading counties (Guanyu Tiaozheng Sheshi Biaozhun he Shi Lingdao Xian Tiaojian de Baogao).

PRC-MSC (1993a), Division of tax revenues between the central government and local governments.

PRC-MSC (1993b), Report on standards for setting up cities (Guanyu Tiaozheng Sheshi Biaozhun de Baogao).

PRC-MSC (1997), Trial measures for reform of the household management system for rural towns (Guanyu Xiaochengzhen Huji Guanli Zhidu Gaige de Shidian Fangan).

PRC-MSC (2001), Directions on reform of the household management system for rural towns (Guanyu Tuijin Xiaochengzhen Huji Guanli Zhidu Gaige de Yijian).

PRC-MSC (2004), Regulations on lowest salary.

PRC-MSC (2008), Regulations on statistical urban–rural divisions.

PRC-MSC (2014), Instructions on furthering the hukou system reform (Guanyu Jinyibu Tuijin Huji Zhidu Gaige de Yijian).

PRC-MTC (Ministry of Transport of China) (2014), *China Transport Statistical Yearbook*, Beijing: China Communications Press.

PRC-NDRC (National Development and Reform Commission) (2011), National major function-oriented zoning.

PRC-NPCO and NBSC (National Population Census Office and National Statistical Bureau of China) (2012), Tabulation of the 2010 population census of the PRC, Digital format.

PRC-NPFPC (National Population and Family Planning Commission) (2010, 2011, 2012, 2013), Report on China's migrant population development, Beijing: China Population Press.

PRC-SSL (2011), Social Insurance Law of the People's Republic of China.

Ren, J. and G. Yang (2010), 'Analysis of China's regional economic development of the differences and their cause', *Economic Geography*, 30(5), 784–789.

Shen, J. (1999), *Urbanization and Population Regulation*, Beijing: Science and Technology Press.

Shi, Y. (2002), 'The analyses on the mistakes in the rural small town development', *Urban Planning Review*, (4), 27–31.

Shi, Y. (2013), 'New-type urbanization and small town development in China', *Economic Geography*, 7, 47–52.

Sina Web (2009), '175 people getting Shanghai hukou', retrieved on September 19, 2015 from http://sh.sina.com.cn/news/2009-12-18/0220126599.html.

Tang, Z. and M. Zhao (2010), 'Economic globalization and transformation of urban system in the Yangtze River Delta region: Interlocking network and value-added hierarchy', *Urban Planning Forum*, (1), 29–34.

Tao, Z. (2007), 'Analyzing the relation orientation of the central and local government in the system of complete financial responsibility', *Journal of Harbin University*, (5), 38–42.

The Central People's Government of PRC News Web (2014), Shanghai will achieve zero growth in urban construction land after 2020, retrieved on September 19, 2015 from www.gov.cn/xinwen/2014-04/25/content_2666424.htm.

Tian, M. and C. Chang (2003), 'Towns' development and institutional innovation in China', *Urban Planning Review*, (7), 22–26.

Tian, X. (2014), *New Reform Opportunities Rooted from Demographic Transition*, Beijing, Social Science Press.

Tongji University Research Team (2010), 'Fifty five towns survey in Hubei province', Work Report.

Tongji University Research Team (2012a), 'Towns survey in Jiading suburban region in Zhejiang province', Work Report.

Tongji University Research Team (2012b), 'Towns survey in Huaiyuan region of Bengbu city in Anhui province', Work Report.

Tongji University Research Team (2013), 'Towns survey in Haimen region of Jiangsu province', Work Report.

Tongji University Research Team (2014), 'Towns and villages survey in Gaoming region of Foshan city', Work Report.

Tongji University Research Team (2015), 'Towns and villages survey in Quzhou region of Zhejiang province', Work Report.

TT News (2014), 'Average enterprise employees pension reached 2000 RMB in 2014', retrieved on October 6, 2015 from http://news.qq.com/a/20140109/000727.htm.

Wan, C. (1999), 'Review and reflections on the reform of the household registration system', *China Population Science*, (1), 32–37.

Wang, D., F. Cai and X. Zhang (2004), 'Saving and growth effects of demographic transition: The population factor in the sustainability of China's economic growth', *Population Research*, 5, 2–11.

Wang, G. and Huang, Y. (2005), 'Interprovincial migration and economic development in east China: 1995–2000', *Population Research*, 1, 19–28.

Wang, H. (2003), 'Important issues, problems and countermeasures of planning management of towns', *Planners*, (4), 54–58.

Wang, K. (2006), 'The four major changes of urban spatial structure in China in the past 50 years', *City Planning Review*, 30(12): 9–14.

Wang, L., H. Luo, K. Zhou and H. Gao (2005), 'A quantitative analysis of regional differences in urbanization levels since China's economic reform', *Northwest Population Journal*, 6, 4–7 (in Chinese).

Wang, M., X. Lin and Y. Ning (2012), 'Migrant populations, temporary residence, and urban village renovation: A survey of migrant settlements in Shanghai', *City Planning Review*, 36(7), 73–80.

Wang, M., Q. Zhao, C. Li and Y. Gao (2006), 'Analysis of differences in regional urbanization levels in China since reform and open policy', *Ludong University Journal* (National Science Edition), 22, 232–238.

Wang, S. (1988), 'A certain number of thinking groups about our country's urbanization path mode', *Population Journal*, (2), 1–6.

Wang, W. (2003), 'Changes in household registering system against the urbanization background—Shijiazhuang city as a case', *Population Research*, 27(6), 8–13.

Wang, W. and P. Zhao (2009), 'The development of China's small cities and towns in three decades of reform and opening up', *Urban Studies*, (11), 34–38.

Wang, X. (2002), 'Comparison of urbanization and economic development', *Economic and Social Systems*, (1), 23–32.

Wang, X. (2010), 'The dynamic mechanism of FDI in the urbanization of developing countries—a literature review based on foreign researches', *Journal of Yunnan University of Finance and Economics*, (6), 59–65.

Wang, Y. (2002), 'The Chinese urbanization and institutional innovation for the administrative divisions in urban areas', *City Planning Review*, 26(6), 22–25.

Wang, Y. (2004), 'Research on the counties and cities directly administrated under the provinces and the innovation of local administrative division hierarchy system in China', *Human Geography*, 19(6), 71–74.

Wang, Y., L. Hua and Y. Zhang (2010), 'Transformation and changes in China's urban and rural administrative areas—populous provinces as cases', *Urban Problems*, (12), 9–17.

Wang, Y., Y. Wang and K. Zhang (2008), 'Analysis on Chinese cities' administrative division pattern changed and influence over the past decade', *Economy Geography*, 28(2), 196–200.

Woo, W. (2012), 'Middle income trap threatening Chinese growth: Types and countermeasures', in W. Woo, M. Lu, S. Geoffrey and Z. Chen (eds), *Escaping the Middle-Income Trap*, Shanghai: Truth & Wisdom Press, 3–36.

Wu, K. and F. Cai (2009), 'The development process and basic pattern of China's towns since 1949 and its recent new situation', *Economic Geography*, (10), 1605–1611.

Wu, L. (2005), 'Studies on mechanism of contemporary Chinese urbanization', PhD Dissertation, Nanjing University, China.

Wu, L. and C. Gu (2005), 'Globalization, foreign investment and urbanization in developing countries: A case study of Jiangsu', *City Planning Review*, (7), 28–33.

Wu, Y. (2007), 'Labor shortages continue and expand', in F. Cai (ed.), *Report of China Population and Labor: No.8, Lewis Turning Point and its Policy Challenges*, Beijing: Social Science Literature Press, 63–94.

Wu, Y. and Z. Xia (1979), 'On the topic of urbanization in socialist China', *Urban Planning Forum*, 3, 13–25.

Xie, Y., C. Duan and J. Guo (2013), 'The studies on the peasant-workers within towns', *South China Population*, (3), 73–80.

Xinhua News (2014), 'Average urban pension is 24 times to average rural pension', retrieved on September 19, 2015 from http://forum.home.news.cn/detail/130606103/1.html.

Xinqiao Web (2014), retrieved on September 5, 2014 from http://xq.jiangyin.gov.cn/.

Xu, S. and X. Zhang (2004), 'Review on the research of the small cities and towns in China since the 1990s', *Urban Planning Forum*, (3), 79–83, 96.

Xu, X. and C. Zhou (1994), 'On the formation of the Pearl River Delta metropolitan area', *Urban Problems*, (3), 3–6.

Xu, Y., X. Xu and X. Yan (2000), 'Discussion on the mechanism of typical extended metropolitan regions in China', *Human Geography*, 15(2), 19–23.

Xue, D., S. Yao and H. Zhang (2000), 'Contacting on the function and optimizing on the structure in Guangzhou urban agglomeration', *Economic Geography*, 20(6), 52–60.

Xue, F. and C. Yang (1997), 'Exo-urbanization: The case of the Pearl River Delta', *Acta Geographica Sinica*, 52(3), 193–206.

Yan, X., J. Guo and Y. Hu (1997), 'A study on the dynamics of Guangzhou–Hongkong–Macau megalopolis', *Geographical Research*, 16(2), 22–29.

Yang, X. and Y. Zhang (2000), *The New Classical Economics and Inframarginal Analysis*, Beijing: People's University Press.

Yang, Z. (2014), 'Occupational disease and injury report 2013', retrieved on September 19, 2015 from www.abler.cn/upfiles/article/20140212214733_448.pdf.

Yao, S. and Z. Chen (2006), *The Urban Agglomerations of China*, Hefei: Press of University of Science and Technology of China.

Ye, Y. (2006), 'China's town development', *China Population Resources and Environment*, (4), 1–6.

Ye, Y. (2011), *New-type Urbanization Research*, Chengdu: Chengdu Bureau of Coordinated Urban–Rural Development.

Yew, C. (2012), 'Pseudo-urbanization? Competitive government behavior and urban sprawl in China', *Journal of Contemporary China*, 21(74), 281–298.

Yuan, S., B. Yu and Y. Yang (2009), 'The life course of rural workers, returning home town: Taking Gocun in Hubei province as an example', *Youth Studies*, (4), 1–11, 94.

Yue, L., H. Yan and J. Li (2011), 'The periodical features of China's regional disparity changes: An explanation based on China' s regional policies changes', *Future and Development*, (11), 94–99.

Yuelai Town Bureau of Finance (2012), 'Balance sheet on fiscal revenue', Yulai: Town Bureau of Finance.

Zhang, B. and Y. Liu (2008), 'An empirical study on the social reconstruction of small cities and towns', *Urban Problems*, (12), 53–57.

Zhang, H. (2001), 'Development zone promoting urbanization mode—case study of Yangtze Delta', *Urban Planning Forum*, 136(1), 65–70.

Zhang, L. (2009), 'Transformation of population structure and the second transition of urbanization in China', *Urban Planning Review*, (10), 35–44.

Zhang, L. (2010), 'The transition of China's urbanization since opening reform: process and trends', PhD Thesis, Tongji University.

Zhang, L. (2011), 'A discussion on the definition of urban/rural population in the Chinese urbanization process', *Urban Planning Forum*, 194(2), 77–85.

Zhang, Q. (1997), 'Urban and rural structure', in X. Lu (ed.), *The Transition of Social Structure*, Beijing, Chinese Social Science Press, 177–209.

Zhang, X. (2014), *China Regional Economic Development Report: Resources and Environment Bearing Capacity of Urban Agglomerations of China*, Beijing: People's Publishing House.

Zhang, Y. and M. Zhao (2003), 'Urbanization and economic development: Review and extension of Hollis Chenery's study', *Urban Planning Forum*, 4, 10–18.

Zhao, C. (2007), 'Analysis of the problem "China labor of migrant workers' wage income"', in F. Cai (ed.), *Report of China Population and Labor: No.8, Lewis Turning Point and its Policy Challenges*, Beijing, Social Science Literature Press, 22–36.

Zhao, H. (2001), 'Development of towns and rural surplus labor transfer', *Population Journal*, (5), 34–37, 62.

Zhao, M. and C. Chen (2013), 'Current situation, theoretical interpretation and reflections on policy agendas of urbanization in China', *Planning Review*, 12, 9–21.

Zhao, M. and Z. Liu (2012), 'Research on China's city network based on production service industry', *City Planning Review*, 9, 23–28.

Zhao, M. and B. Sun (1996), 'Rural industry location and town development in the economically developed region', *Urban Planning Review*, (5), 18–21, 60.

Zhao, M., G. Bao and L. Hou (1998), *Landuse System Reform and Rural Development*, Shanghai: Tontji University Press.

Zhao, W. (2004), 'On the historical causes of changing system of hukou free migration in China in 1958', *Journal of Historical Science*, (10), 76–80.

Zhao, X., Y. Zhou and G. Chao (2002), 'On the difficulty and practical mistakes in the small town priority strategy', *Urban Planning Review*, (10), 36–40.

Zhao, Y. (2001), 'The institutional change, small town development and urbanization in China', *Urban Planning Review*, (8), 47–57.

Zhao, Y. (2003), 'The reform of the registered permanent residence system during economic transformation', *Urban Planning Forum*, 143(1), 16–20.

Zhejiang Provincial Government (2010), 'Twenty-seven towns are pilot to county-level administrative rights', retrieved on September 19, 2015 from http://town.zjol.com.cn/system/2014/07/25/020160753.shtml.

Zheng, B. (2011), 'Middle income trap and China's path to development: In perspective of international experiences and lessons', *Chinese Journal of Population Science*, (1), 1.

Zheng, J. and G. Chen (2000), 'Comment on urbanization policy', *Planners*, (5), 90–95.

Zheng, Q. and D. Lai (2008), 'Human capital and regional disparities in urbanization in China', *Chinese Journal of Population Science*, 1, 59–66 (in Chinese).

Zhou, H. (2006), 'Capital forms, governmental policies and inter-provincial migration', *Chinese Journal of Population Science*, (1), 42–51, 95–96.

Zhou, Y. (1982), 'The discussion on the relationship between urbanization and GDP', *Population and Economics*, (1), 28–33.

Zhou, Y. (1991), *Discussion on the Strategy of City System and Regional Tilt of China*, Heilongjiang: People's Publishing House.

Zhou, Y. (1995a), *Urban Geography*, Shanghai: Commercial Press.

Zhou, Y. (1995b), 'Two errors urban system structure analysis', *Urban Planning Forum*, 2010.

Zhou, Y. and Y. Shi (1995), 'Toward establishing the concept of physical urban area in China', *Acta Geographica Sinica*, 50(4), 289–301.

Zhou, Y. and S. Tian (2006), 'Repairing the provincial urbanization level data based on the fifth census data', *Statistical Research*, (1), 62–65.

Zhou, Z. (1993), 'Discussion on the standards of city and town population statistics in the fourth national census', *Population Research*, (3), 34–40.

Zhu, P. (2006), 'Reform of household registry and transformation of local government function—taking Zhengzhou's household registry reform as an example', *Theory Journal*, 153(11), 53–56 (in Chinese).

Zhu, Q. (2012), 'Estimation on fertility level in China 2000–2010: Preliminary study based on the 2010 population census', *Chinese Journal of Population Science*, (4), 68–77, 112.

Zou, B. (2003), *Institutional Evolution and Policy Analysis on Small Towns*, Beijing: China Architecture and Building Press.

Index